SUPERPOWER DETENTE: A REAPPRAISAL

Superpower Detente: A Reappraisal

Mike Bowker and Phil Williams

The Royal Institute of International Affairs · London

SAGE Publications · London · Newbury Park · Beverly Hills · New Delhi

SAGE Publications Ltd
28 Banner Street
London EC1Y 8QE

SAGE Publications Inc
2111 West Hillcrest Drive
Newbury Park, California 91320

SAGE Publications India Pvt Ltd
32, M-Block Market
Greater Kailash – I
New Delhi 110 048

British Library Cataloguing in Publication Data

Bowker, Mike
   Superpower detente: a reappraisal.
   1. Soviet Union. Detente with United States
   2. United States. Detente with Soviet Union
   I. Title   II. Williams, Phil   III. Royal
   Institute of International Affairs
   327.47073

   ISBN 0-8039-8041-8
   ISBN 0-8039-8042-6 Pbk

Library of Congress catalog card number 88-060381

Printed in Great Britain by J.W. Arrowsmith Ltd, Bristol

Contents

Acknowledgments

One of the most daunting yet ultimately one of the most rewarding aspects of the preparation of a book of this kind is that it requires a great deal of help, encouragement and inspiration from other people. Indeed, we are greatly indebted to several organisations and a large number of individuals. We are particularly grateful to the Leverhulme Trust, who not only made it possible for us to work at Chatham House from 1984 to 1986 but also provided funding for travel and secretarial assistance.

The initial impetus for the detente project was provided by David Watt, William Wallace and Lawrence Freedman. The importance of David Watt's original inspiration was underlined by his tragic and untimely death – and we hope that this volume has at least some of the qualities that he desired. David's successor as Director of Chatham House, Admiral Sir James Eberle, was a great source of sustenance and support throughout the project and gave us more encouragement than even he realised, making our stay at Chatham House an enjoyable as well as fruitful one. The same can be said of John Roper, who supervised the project and generally cajoled and coerced us into meeting deadlines and becoming more organised than we really desired. He also read the manuscript and offered invaluable suggestions on stylistic as well as substantive points. His friendship as well as his help were deeply appreciated.

In preparing the book we held a series of study groups at Chatham House and found these a source of useful suggestions, incisive criticisms and great stimulation. Among those who attended the meetings of the study group, which was chaired by John Roper, were Lord Thomas Brimelow, Fred Halliday, Peter Boyle, Peter Shearman, Malcolm Mackintosh, Peter Nailor, Edwina Moreton, Robin Edmonds, Dave Schwartz, Joseph Frankel, David Wedgwood-Benn, Ian Davidson, Steve Kirby, Brian White, Stuart Croft and Nicholas Wheeler, as well as officials from the Foreign Office and the Ministry of Defence. The meetings were also attended by William Wallace, Pauline Wickham, Andrew Carter, David Korn, Jonathan Stern, Robert Kleiman, Mary Bone, Christopher Cviic and Sir James Eberle, all of whom were working at Chatham House during the period of the study. To all these people we owe an enormous debt of gratitude for not only saving us from errors of omission and commission, but also for enriching our understanding of superpower relations. A special thank you must go to Tom Brimelow, who was always an incisive but friendly critic and provided us with extensive written comments on the drafts.

As part of our research we visited Moscow and are particularly grateful to the Institute for World Economy and International Relations (IMEMO), and especially Oleg Bykov, for hosting our visit. Henry Trofimenko of the Institute for United States and Canada Studies was also helpful to us during this visit. During the research we travelled to the United States on several occasions and were fortunate to be able to discuss our work on detente with a large number of people. Among those who provided help and hospitality were Hannes Adomeit, Joseph Fromm, Harry Gelman, Alexander George, David Holloway, Arnold Horelick, Robbin Laird, Murray Marder, Steven Miller, Robert Nurick, Joseph Nye and Marshall Shulman. Larry Smith, then at Harvard, gave us an invaluable analysis of American domestic politics during the period of detente, and we have drawn heavily upon his ideas. Karen and Adeed Dawisha, as always, were valued friends and superb hosts. We would also like to thank Ray Garthoff for arranging a round-table discussion for us at the Brookings Institution where we were able to benefit from the helpful comments of John Steinbruner, Michael MccGwire, Richard Betts, Paul Stares and Joshua Epstein, as well as of Ray Garthoff himself.

In developing the background which made it possible to obtain maximum benefit from the research visits, we were very fortunate to have at our disposal the Library and the Press Library at Chatham House. All the staff of both libraries were unfailingly helpful in meeting what were often onerous demands for information. In particular we would like to thank John Montgomery and Lesley Pitman in the Library and Susan Boyd and Mary Wood in the Press Library all of whom responded to queries with speed and charm. Mary Bone, also of the Press Library, was a fund of knowledge which often made us envious, and we are especially grateful for her help.

A number of people were also involved in the preparation of the manuscript. Caroline Sherrington typed most of the study group papers, while Joanne Fluck and Elizabeth Schlamm of the Department of Politics, the University of Southampton, typed several versions of the final manuscript. That there were successive final versions was largely the result of the invaluable comments made by Edwina Moreton and Lawrence Freedman, both of whom read the manuscript with great care and offered many helpful and detailed suggestions for further refinement. Pauline Wickham, publications manager at Chatham House, was a constant source of encouragement and we are grateful for her help and patience. Last but not least, we are grateful to our families who endured periods of neglect while this book was being written and revised. Despite the efforts of all these people the study inevitably contains shortcomings, for which we alone bear responsibility.

1
Differing Interpretations of Detente

In 1945, the United States and the Soviet Union were allies in the struggle against Nazi Germany. By 1947 their relationship had deteriorated into one of intense cold war. If this transformation was abrupt, it was also long-lasting in its effects – Soviet–American rivalry has been the dominant feature of the international system since the late 1940s. In the late 1960s and the early 1970s, though, it appeared that this rivalry was being mitigated as the two superpowers moved towards a relationship which at the very least appeared to be less tense and acrimonious and less susceptible to the outbreak of direct confrontation. Yet by the end of the decade the hopes for detente were disappointed and the promise of cooperation was once again replaced by the predominance of competition. The deterioration in the superpower relationship, if not as dramatic or as rapid as that of the 1940s, was still very marked.

In the early 1970s the Nixon administration claimed that the era 'of confrontation' with the Soviet Union was at an end, and the 'era of negotiation' was beginning. In 1981 the Reagan administration came to office not with a commitment to negotiate with the Soviet Union but with a promise to restore American strength and prestige. The 1970s were characterised by the incoming administration as a 'decade of neglect' in which the United States, seduced and blinded by detente, and hampered by Vietnam and Watergate, had failed to provide for its own security. The reversion to a hard-line stance, however, had preceded the Reagan administration. President Ford stopped using the word 'detente' in 1976, and in January 1980 President Carter publicly acknowledged that until the Soviet invasion of Afghanistan he had failed to understand the true nature of Soviet ambitions and Soviet power. By the end of the decade both the rhetoric and policies were very different from those of the Nixon administration. The language of economic interdependence and the notion of trade as an inducement to Soviet good behaviour, for example, had given way to the language of economic warfare and the imposition of trade sanctions against Moscow.

This shift in US foreign policy was paralleled in Moscow. The Soviet press, perhaps more than any other, had been sympathetic towards Richard Nixon as he became increasingly embroiled in Watergate. Reagan, in contrast, was pilloried in Soviet commentaries. The main Soviet complaint was not that detente was unsatisfactory but that the United States had unilaterally abandoned it. Yet there were also signs that the Soviet Union – while not as disillusioned about detente as the United States – was taking an increasingly jaundiced view of the achievements of the 1970s. The benefits from trade and technology transfer had been far less than anticipated even before the reversal in the American position, while the arms control process had also produced very mixed results.

Indeed, neither superpower was pleased with the achievements of arms control in the 1970s. In 1972 the superpowers had reached an accord on the limitation of strategic armaments which was seen as the beginning of a long-term process of regulating their arms competition; in 1979 there was considerable opposition in the American Senate to the SALT Two agreement, and it was widely argued in the United States that the problem was not the arms race *per se* but the fact that it had become one-sided. The priority was no longer arms control but correcting a strategic imbalance which, it was alleged, had moved dangerously in favour of Moscow. Ironically, Moscow also had doubts about the advantages of the arms control process. The negotiations had certainly not prevented the United States and its allies from agreeing to deploy cruise and Pershing missiles in Europe – weapon systems which significantly augmented the American capacity to strike the Soviet homeland. More generally, Moscow was irritated by the American reluctance to accept the Soviet Union as an equal. In spite of agreements which seemed to acknowledge Soviet status as a superpower, Washington had not accepted that this brought any political entitlements for Moscow, preferring instead to pursue 'exclusionary diplomacy' in crucial regions such as the Middle East. If the Soviet Union was not prepared formally to abandon detente, therefore, it was only because of the lack of alternatives.

In Europe, there was a lingering attachment to detente which helped to turn the crisis in East–West relations into a crisis in Atlantic relations. Although Afghanistan killed the remaining vestiges of US–Soviet detente, Europeans seemed to assume that detente was divisible. Simply because the Soviet Union had misbehaved elsewhere and the superpower relationship had once again become very strained, was no reason why there should be a change in Europe itself. After all, the benefits of detente had been very considerable. The consolidation of the status quo, the removal of Berlin as a flashpoint, the expansion of intra-bloc trade, and the increased human contacts between East and West – and especially the two Germanies – were of immense significance. Consequently there was an attempt by West European governments to protect the improvements of the 1970s by insulating the relationship between the blocs in Europe from events in the Third World and differentiating detente in Europe from that directly between the superpowers. This became much more difficult following the crisis in Poland which led to the imposition of martial law. Even so, the deterioration in East–West relations in Europe was far less marked than at the superpower level.

In examining why Soviet–American relations changed so markedly during the 1970s, it is useful to consider briefly the debate over the origins of the cold war. This debate is instructive not only about the questions to ask but also about what approaches to avoid. The early orthodoxy on the cold war often seemed to be little more than an attempt to exonerate the United States and demonstrate the culpability of the Soviet Union. Traditionalists saw the cold war as a result of Soviet ideological ambitions and tended to emphasise the dominant position of the Soviet Union in Europe at the end of the war, which provided Stalin with an opportunity to extend Soviet control over Eastern Europe and to threaten Western Europe. In this analysis, American policy was essentially reactive. Demobilisation was accompanied by a reluctance to get involved in Europe, and it was only a series of Soviet provocations and West European entreaties which brought the United States into a geopolitical and enduring competition with the Soviet Union and persuaded it to underwrite the security of Western Europe.

Revisionists provided what was virtually a mirror image of this interpretation with a reversal of roles between villain and hero. The desire of American capitalism to obtain markets in Eastern Europe and the resentment at Soviet domination of the area were presented as the major cause of the cold war. Soviet actions were seen as defensive, and the United States was criticised for its insensitivity to the security concerns which dictated Stalin's policies. Whereas traditionalists emphasised Soviet strength, the revisionists emphasised Soviet weakness, which was dramatically underlined by the American monopoly of atomic weapons. In a sense both approaches might be described as 'purist': they see the problem as caused by characteristics inherent in the nature of either the Soviet Union or the United States.[1]

Some explanations for the decline of detente offer appraisals which are similarly one-sided in their distribution of blame. A popular view in the United States is that detente was little more than an American illusion and a Soviet trick. One of the main proponents of this interpretation is Richard Pipes, who claims that detente reflected no more than a beguiling change in Moscow's tactics. Policies of confrontation which had been favoured by Khrushchev were abandoned by his successors in favour of a more subtle low-risk strategy aimed at making gains in the Third World. At the same time, the Soviet Union was conciliatory in Europe and in its dealings with the United States. By lulling the West into a false sense of security it hoped to gain access to the Western technology which was vital in its quest for strategic superiority. President Nixon and Dr Henry Kissinger, the main architects of detente, are chastised for 'initiating a policy that posited as its ultimate objective a complete reorientation in the world outlook of the Soviet regime', and for doing so 'without familiarising themselves either with Russian history or with communist theory'.[2] Creating a new 'structure of peace' was impossible because detente was no more than a temporary expedient for Moscow. According to Pipes, the Soviet Union was not committed to a genuine improvement in Soviet–American relations, and had simply made a tactical shift in policy which could be reversed at any time it proved either convenient or necessary. It was a fundamental error for American policy-makers to think otherwise, and to interpret a 'soft' foreign policy line 'as prima facie evidence of a change in the basic political orientation of the Soviet Union'.[3] The problem was the nature of the Soviet state, which had integrated militarism, ideology and totalitarianism and become a permanent threat to the West.[4] In this assessment it is not what the Soviet Union does which is important, but rather what it is.

The implication is that detente was based on Soviet Machiavellism and American naïvety. The corollary is that the decline of detente can be attributed to a resurgence of realism in American foreign policy. The illusions that sustained superpower detente in the first half of the 1970s were gradually abandoned in face of continued Soviet expansionism, which revealed once again the relentless nature of the Soviet challenge and the fundamental incompatibility of Soviet and American interests and objectives. The puzzle, in this assessment, is not the abandonment of detente but why Washington ever adopted a policy which so woefully failed to understand the nature of the adversary.

On the other side are analyses which see the decline of detente as a result of the needs of the American economy, the requirements of the military industrial complex, and the inherent hostility towards Moscow of American capitalism. These forces and considerations, it is argued, were always present in American politics and society but were strengthened in the 1970s by the rise of the American Right. Detente, in this view, came about only because of the intra-elite divisions caused by the Vietnam war. Conversely, the decline of detente was the result of the resurgence of the ruling oligarchy which had shaped American policy towards Moscow since the early days of the cold war. The rejection of a more conciliatory approach towards Moscow reflected the resurgence of the extremely alarmist assessment of the Soviet threat first promulgated in a joint State and Defense Department study known as NSC-68 which was presented to President Truman in 1950. In the view of Alexander Yakovlev, a leading Soviet academician, a former director of the Institute of World Economy and International Relations, and currently a full member of the Gorbachev Politburo. US policy throughout the postwar period has been dominated by chauvinism and imperialism. The messianic character of this policy, however, has been obscured by American rhetoric with its emphasis on global responsibility and the altruistic nature of America's world role. In contrast, it is argued, the Soviet Union sees no alternative to peaceful relations and mutually profitable cooperation between East and West.[5]

These analyses parallel the traditionalist and revisionist assessments of cold war origins. They are both one-sided and for the most part ignore the dynamics of the interaction process between the superpowers. Indeed, they have more in common with each other than with the sophisticated and persuasive accounts of superpower relations that have appeared in the post-revisionist phase of cold war historiography. Some of the best discussions of cold war origins by analysts such as John Lewis Gaddis, Robert Jervis and Deborah Larson take account of the part played by mistakes, misperceptions, miscalculations, domestic political pressures and the like, without discounting the importance of ideology or the basic structure of the international system which emerged in the aftermath of World War II. They recognise that the power vacuum in Europe, the bipolarity of the international system and the ideological antipathies between the Soviet Union and the United States impelled them into an adversary relationship, but acknowledge that the precise way in which superpower competition developed was also influenced by more ephemeral considerations. Their predominant concern is with providing explanations rather than attributing blame.

Similarly, the present study examines the rise and fall of detente during the 1970s, not as an exercise in assigning blame or responsibility but as part of an effort to provide greater insight into the dynamics of the Soviet–American relationship. It sets out to explore the reasons why the superpowers in the early 1970s pursued policies which seemed less antagonistic than those of earlier years. It also attempts to assess the changes which were made as part of detente and to consider why the attempt to establish a *modus vivendi* was not sustained, and why the deterioration in the relationship was so marked. In short, the analysis focuses on the origins and meaning of detente, as well as the reasons for its decline. It is concerned with several sets of questions:

The first of these concerns the *origins* of detente. Why did the superpowers attempt to move towards a less tense and acrimonious relationship in the late 1960s and the early 1970s? What were the historical circumstances which precipitated new departures in Soviet and American policies? Was there simply a temporary coincidence of interests and outlook between the superpowers, or is there a logic to detente which ensures that it is a recurring, if not inescapable, feature of US–Soviet relations?

The second set of issues concerns the *substance* of detente. In what ways was the superpower relationship during detente different from that in the period which preceded it – and indeed that which followed it? More specifically, was the detente of the 1970s any different from the previous periods of relaxation between the superpowers? Did detente involve a fundamental shift in the way the superpowers defined their interests and objectives, or was it simply a change in tactics?

The third group of questions revolves around the issue of *symmetry* in the relationship. If there was a fundamental change of approach, was it mutual or unilateral? What did the two sides want and expect from detente? Were the conceptions of detente in Moscow and Washington similar, or were they divergent and ultimately incompatible?

The fourth set of questions concerns the *duration* of detente. How long did detente actually last? Did it continue throughout the 1970s or was it a short-term phenomenon which had more or less disappeared by the middle of the decade?

The fifth group of questions concerns the *demise* of detente. Was the decline of detente in the 1970s avoidable or was it inevitable given the nature of the protagonists and the inherent potential for conflict between them? Put rather differently, was it deep-rooted antipathies and incompatible interests which destroyed detente, or did the deterioration in Soviet–American relations result from misunderstanding and poor management?

A sixth set of questions relates to *domestic factors*. If there was a management problem, to what extent was it related to domestic considerations? How did domestic politics impinge on the interaction process between the two governments? To what extent did domestic pressures account for either the rise or the fall of detente?

The attempt to answer these questions forms the core of the analysis in the following pages. Detente is looked at in historical perspective rather than in isolation. The reasons for both its rise and its demise are investigated in an attempt to examine whether it was anything more than a temporary coincidence of interests based on fallacious assumptions about the possibilities for a lasting *modus vivendi* between the superpowers. There are, however, several problems in an analysis of this kind.

Difficulties of Analysis

One of the most obvious difficulties concerns the *nature and meaning of detente*. Detente can be understood as a process, a condition or a set of policies, and the word is also used to characterise a particular historical period. Nevertheless, what all usages of the term have in common is that they describe a relationship between adversaries. As Abba Eban explained it, 'Detente is not friendship. It is not alliance. It is rooted in a recognition of difference, and inspired by a premonition of disaster. The word can be applied only to an adversarial relationship. It accepts, as a reality, the fact that values and interests are in conflict, not in harmony.'[6] Furthermore, it is possible to identify both minimum and maximum concepts of detente. At a minimum, detente involves a relaxation of tension – a notion which stems from its French meaning of relaxation and releasing a trigger. The maximalist conception of detente, in contrast, involves an attempt by adversaries to regulate and moderate their relationship through the establishment of common understandings and mutually accepted norms regarding permissible behaviour. The maximalist approach builds on the minimalist idea of tension reduction but adds to this more positive attempts at cooperation.

This distinction facilitates comparison of Soviet and American understandings of detente. Did one superpower opt for a minimalist approach and the other base its policies on a maximalist conception? Alternatively, if they shared a maximalist approach, did their conceptions of legitimate behaviour coincide, or did apparent agreement hide serious divergences of understanding and intent? Perhaps most important of all, was the decline of detente simply a recognition that the prevalent conceptions in Moscow and Washington had been fundamentally incompatible more or less from the outset?

Another set of difficulties follows from this and is inherent in any attempt to adopt a *symmetrical* approach. It may be objected, for example, that treating the superpowers in a similar way obscures important differences between them and can result all too easily in a kind of moral neutrality or moral equidistance between the superpowers. This complaint, however, tends to come from those who adopt a 'purist' attitude to the US–Soviet relationship and treat it as a Manichaean struggle between the forces of light and the forces of darkness. This analysis explicitly rejects such an approach, preferring to treat the superpowers as two states concerned with managing their rivalry in ways which enable them to uphold vital interests while avoiding nuclear war. This is in no way to depreciate the differences between the superpowers. Nor is it to advocate a third way for Europe as an honest broker between Moscow and Washington: equidistance is simply not an option for Western Europe. The contention is merely that self-righteousness, whether it comes from the Soviet Union or the United States, prevents careful and critical analysis.

Another problem is the difference in access to *information* about the attitudes and objectives of the two superpowers. On the American side the problem is often too much rather than too little information. The openness and turbulence of the American system, the requirement that key decision-makers justify their policies before congressional committees, the use of inspired leaks to the press, and the appearance of 'insider' accounts of foreign policy-making in the memoirs of former officials, make the investigator's task one of sifting through an excess of information. On the Soviet side the difficulties of access are formidable. Although a good deal is known about Soviet military capabilities, the purposes of Soviet policy remain uncertain. Because of the closed nature of the Soviet political system, however, it is tempting to assume that the Soviet Union is a monolithic actor rationally pursuing policies in a way which maximises benefits and minimises costs. Such an assessment needs to be treated with considerable caution. Clearly the foreign policy debates in Moscow are very different from those in Washington in terms of both the extent and the manner of participation. Yet to assume unanimity among Soviet decision-makers is to ignore not only the fact that differing responsibilities lead to differing concerns and recommendations, but the very nature of foreign policy itself which invites differing appraisals and recommendations. The uncertainties inherent in foreign policy-making mean that on many issues there is no automatic consensus about the risks incurred or the benefits likely to accrue and the Soviet leaders will face similar problems and dilemmas to those which confront their American counterparts. Policy often consists less of maximising gains than making painful but inescapable trade-offs between different objectives. Furthermore, in spite of Soviet ideology, which may encapsulate the long-term aspirations of the state, much of foreign policy consists of short-term reactions to the initiatives of others. Differences about appropriate reactions, as well as about precisely where the sacrifices should be made when it comes to trade-offs, make some form of policy debate unavoidable – even if its scope is limited by the dominance of the Party and the closed nature of Soviet society. With the judicious use of Soviet sources, as well as of Western commentaries, and a careful examination of Soviet actions, it is possible to gain at least some insight into the debates over detente in the 1970s.

The attempt to explain the rise and fall of detente is organised thematically rather than simply chronologically and does not attempt to provide a blow-by-blow account of the superpower relationship through the 1970s. There are two main reasons for such an approach. The first is the existence of a comprehensive and massively detailed account of Soviet–American relations from Nixon to Reagan by Raymond Garthoff. This monumental study makes any attempt at emulation both impossible and unnecessary. The second reason is that a thematic approach may highlight considerations which could otherwise be lost.

This is in no way to denigrate the more straightforward historical approach or to deny the need to place detente in historical perspective. Consequently, Chapter 2 examines the nature of the cold war and highlights the tentative moves that were made towards detente prior to the development during the late 1960s and early 1970s of Soviet and American policies which more obviously gave priority to the establishment of a less tense and hostile relationship between the superpowers. In Chapter 3 the focus is on the motives and interests of the two superpowers which led them to seek a *modus vivendi* more ambitious than anything which had preceded it. The chapter looks not only at the impulses which encouraged this process but also at the conceptions of detente held by the two sides. In particular, it assesses the extent to which superpower detente reflected not a common interest based on common objectives and shared understandings, but a coincidence of interests which temporarily obscured divergences of attitude, expectations and objectives, that were ultimately to prove destructive. Raising the possibility that, from its inception, the detente of the 1970s may have contained the seeds of its own demise is not to belittle the developments of the 1970s. Indeed, as discussed in Chapter 4, there were significant changes in several aspects of Soviet–American relations, including trade, arms control and the management of security problems in both Europe and the Third World.

Having dealt with the rise of detente, the rest of the book looks at its subsequent decline. Chapter 5 focuses on the interaction of superpower policies in the Middle East war of October 1973, a development which provided the first major test for detente. Other regional conflicts, especially Angola and the Horn of Africa, in which the Soviet Union and the United States were lined up on opposing sides, also placed considerable strain on detente, and their impact is assessed in Chapter 6. Chapters 7 and 8 examine the impact on detente of domestic factors in the United States and the Soviet Union. The assumption is that to understand the Soviet–American relationship it is necessary to view it not simply as the interaction of two sets of policies but as the collision of two complex political systems, each with its own priorities and problems. The focus is on the internal debates and controversies over detente in Washington and Moscow, and an effort is made to explore the domestic difficulties encountered by policy-makers as they tried to manage and legitimise their policy towards the adversary. Consideration is also given to the way in which the domestic debates were influenced by the competition in the Third World.

Chapters 9 and 10 look at what might be termed the 'crisis of detente' at the end of the 1970s and the beginning of the 1980s. The breakdown of arms control and the Soviet invasion of Afghanistan were crucial in the disappearance of a detente that had looked vulnerable for a long time. The period of high detente symbolised by the summits of 1972 and 1973 for the superpowers (and by the Helsinki Final Act of 1975 for the Europeans) had been followed – at least at the superpower level – by a period of ambivalence and acrimony rather than by a period of consolidation. Consequently, by 1979 detente was in considerable distress, and the American debate over SALT Two and the Soviet invasion of Afghanistan marked its demise. The concluding chapter offers an overall assessment of why detente failed. It also suggests that the detente experience of the 1970s contains a number of lessons and insights which are relevant to the future of the Soviet–American relationship and the way in which it is handled.

Notes

1. For an argument along similar lines, see O.R. Holsti, 'The Study of International Politics Makes Strange Bedfellows: Theories of the Radical Right and Radical Left', *American Political Science Review*, vol. 68, no. 1 (March 1974), pp. 217–42.

2. R. Pipes, *US–Soviet Relations in the Era of Detente* (Boulder, Col.: Westview Press, 1981), p. xiv.

3. See ibid., p. 74.

4. See ibid., especially pp. 195–213.

5. A. Yakovlev, *On the Edge of an Abyss* (Moscow: Progress Publishers, 1985), pp. 5–15.

6. A. Eban, 'Reflections on Detente', *The Jerusalem Journal of International Relations*, vol. 5, no. 3 (1981), p. 1.

2
From Cold War to Detente

Cold war and detente are often contrasted in ways which suggest that they are different types of relationship rather than different emphases in a relationship which remains a mixture of cooperation and conflict. That the superpowers did not cease to be adversaries during the detente of the 1970s is hardly surprising – especially in view of the fate of detente. That the superpowers should be regarded as partners during the cold war is perhaps less obvious. Indeed, the cold war is generally seen as a period of unremitting hostility in which the superpowers came to the brink of hostilities on several occasions. Such a view is compelling. Yet the cold war was also a period of very considerable creativity in which the superpowers established a degree of order in the international system that was both more stable and more enduring than could have been anticipated in the late 1940s as they moved from the 'grand alliance' to the 'great enmity'.

This deterioration in Soviet–American relations has been dealt with very fully elsewhere, and need not be discussed at length here. There are, however, several points which can usefully be made. The first concerns the structure of the postwar international system: Moscow and Washington found themselves in what was effectively a bipolar world, with a power vacuum in the centre of Europe. Even in the best of circumstances, bipolarity makes it very difficult for the two great powers to avoid becoming adversaries. The logic of bipolarity is the logic of insecurity: actions taken by one side for its security can all too easily be construed by the other side as threatening – a phenomenon known as the 'security dilemma'. This dilemma was intensified by the uncertainty and fluidity of the postwar international order, and the very different ideas in Washington and Moscow about the future of Europe in general and Germany in particular. In these circumstances, it was hardly surprising that Washington construed ambiguous Soviet moves as unambiguously offensive in character, or that the policies adopted by the United States were viewed in a similar light in Moscow. According to Shulman, the measures that were intended by the United States to stabilise and protect Western Europe and the Eastern Mediterranean appear to have been construed in Moscow 'within the framework of its preconceptions of the inherent aggressiveness of what it defined and stereotyped as capitalist imperialism'.[1] The result was a hardening of Stalin's policies in Eastern Europe, where the countries under Moscow's control were moulded and reshaped in the Soviet image. This in turn confirmed American beliefs about Stalin's malevolence. Indeed, the policies of both states seemed to be driven by misperceptions which resulted in a series of self-fulfilling prophecies.

Their differences were intensified by ideology. Although the process of mobilising domestic support may have added to the starkness with which Soviet–American conflict was portrayed as the two erstwhile allies moved from an ambivalent and uncertain relationship into one of overt and apparently unremitting hostility, even without the instrumental use of ideological symbolism, the cold war would have had important ideological overtones. A state founded on competitive individualism and the Protestant ethic could not come to terms easily with one based on collectivism and the subordination of the individual – especially when that state appeared to combine internal repression with external acquisitiveness. Conversely, a government based upon centralised control could not readily understand or accommodate a government which was not only alien in its principles but so ethnocentric in its demands. As a result, the potential for conflict inherent in the security dilemma was given additional impetus by the different and indeed antithetical principles on which the Soviet Union and the US were founded. In view of all this the cold war may well have been unavoidable.

Cold War Conflict and Cooperation

The cold war itself was a complex and at times almost contradictory mixture of competition and restraint. On the one side, it was characterised by harsh rhetoric, intense competition in armaments, the dominance of ideological assumptions about the adversary and an obsession with the symbols of power and influence. It was inevitable that occasional confrontation was also a feature of the superpower relationship. The cold war, though, was not wholly negative. Throughout the period there were several developments which helped not only to stabilise Soviet–American competition but also to provide a degree of order in a highly competitive and disorderly international system.

One of the characteristics of the cold war was mutual denunciation of each other's system – a feature that was intensified by the competition for allegiance of the newly independent nations in the Third World. Each superpower portrayed its own political and economic system as something to be emulated and that of the adversary as something to be reviled. This is not to claim that the vitriol about the adversary was contrived. US foreign policy-makers such as President Eisenhower's Secretary of State John Foster Dulles operated on the basis of what Henry Kissinger described as an 'inherent bad faith model' of the Soviet Union.[2] This model in turn had its roots in morality and religion. For Dulles the key to Soviet communism was that it was based on 'an atheistic Godless premise' from which everything else flowed.[3] Not only did this make compromise difficult, but it also meant that conciliatory moves by Moscow were dismissed as propaganda gestures or as evidence of Soviet weakness. Although there is less direct evidence, it seems almost certain that on the Soviet side too there were important policy-makers who were equally closed in their perception of the US and equally resistant to anything which smacked of compromise with the enemy.

These images, superimposed as they were on a bipolar structure, meant that many issues were endowed with great symbolic importance and that both superpowers became over-sensitive to possible changes in the allegiance of minor states, especially where these changes were brought about by force. The result was that, on the American side at least, what could have been dismissed as minor geopolitical challenges were endowed with immense significance. The symbolism attached to West Berlin was understandable in view of the geographical position of Berlin, the Berlin Crisis of 1948 and the importance of Western Europe in US policy. The belief that commitments were interdependent, however, and that a tough stance in regions of marginal importance was necessary to deter challenges in more significant areas, lacked discrimination and treated all American interests as vital. Such an approach – with its emphasis on projecting images of strength and resolve – was in part an understandable response to the nature of the cold war. It was also a function of American domestic politics and the power of the Right. The 'loss of China' and the subsequent rise of McCarthyism had a lasting impact on American politics and policies. Successive administrations felt that more conciliatory policies towards Moscow would expose them to domestic criticism and consequently were extremely cautious in their approach to the Soviet Union. Even so, there were usually opportunities for the party in opposition to capitalise on the failure of the administration to prosecute the struggle against the communist bloc with sufficient vigour. During their bids for the Presidency, the foreign policy platforms of both Eisenhower and Kennedy were critical of the incumbent administration's failure to adopt a tougher stance towards the Soviet Union. In 1952 containment was condemned as too passive and too costly, while in 1960 the Eisenhower administration was castigated for allowing a 'missile gap' to develop. Standing up to the Soviet Union – and its allies – was 'good politics'.

US policy-makers were prisoners of their own images as well as of the symbolism that had been used to mobilise domestic support for

American cold war policies. The images themselves incorporated what one analyst has described as 'condensation symbols'.[4] These symbols are at the same time invaluable and restricting. Their crucial feature is that they 'evoke the emotion associated with the situation. They condense into one symbolic event, sign, or act patriotic pride, anxieties, remembrances of past glories or humiliations, promises of future greatness: some one of these or all of them.'[5] The very identification of the Soviet Union as a totalitarian aggressor evoked memories of the struggle against Nazi Germany and the dangers of appeasement. It also meant that policy-makers could hardly fail to respond to any moves by the Soviet Union or its allies which appeared to present a direct challenge. The symbolism became particularly powerful at the time of the Korean war and helped to transform American attitudes towards the French involvement in Indochina. From being traditional imperialists attempting to subdue a movement which was as much nationalist as communist, the French were elevated to the status of free world allies in the global struggle against communism.[6] The roots of the subsequent American involvement in Vietnam are discernible in this shift. Indeed, symbolism was to give containment a rigidity which was to culminate in the deployment of over half a million troops to Vietnam. The link between the Truman Doctrine, Kennedy's inaugural address, with its emphasis on bearing any burden in the cause of liberty, and direct American involvement in the Vietnam war was both close and direct.

It was not surprising, in this climate, that the armaments competition took on considerable importance. The 1950s was a period of both quantitative and qualitative growth in the strategic arsenals of both superpowers. The United States, having lost a monopoly of the atomic bomb, moved on to the development of the hydrogen bomb. This advantage too proved short-lived. Furthermore, there were powerful, if exaggerated, fears from the mid-50s onwards that the Soviet Union had pulled ahead of the US. Fears of the 'bomber gap' were succeeded by concerns over the 'missile gap'.[7] In fact, the Soviet Union did not deploy many first-generation ICBMs, and the missile gap never materialised. Khrushchev, however, skilfully exploited the appearance of strategic superiority to renew pressure on West Berlin. Eisenhower was forced into embarking on a major strategic modernisation programme, which was taken even further by the Kennedy administration. The result was that by October 1961 it was clear that there was a missile gap in reverse. Nevertheless, the Kennedy administration, recognising that US nuclear superiority was only temporary, also embarked upon a major programme to strengthen US conventional forces. The arms race of the 1950s was accompanied by extensive negotiations about general and comprehensive disarmament. Yet these negotiations were little more than a propaganda exercise in which both superpowers were attempting to place the onus for the lack of progress on the adversary. Proposals were made very publicly and almost invariably contained 'jokers' or clauses which the other side could not accept.[8] The aim of the game was not to achieve disarmament but to convince world opinion that the real obstacle to progress was the obduracy of the opponent. Each side presented its own position as reasonable, and castigated the adversary for not accepting the proposals as the basis for agreement. Apart from the negotiations on a nuclear test ban, which were more serious, the disarmament negotiations of the 1950s were futile. In fact, the arms race was intensified in the late 1950s.

The period from 1958 to 1962 was probably the most dangerous phase of the cold war. This was partly a result of the personality of Khrushchev and the pressures on him for a foreign policy success, but it also reflected the symbolism that was attached to both Berlin and Cuba. The Berlin Crisis in particular can be understood initially as an attempt by Khrushchev to obtain Western acceptance of the division of Germany and in its later stages as a desperate effort to maintain the viability of the East German state in the face of a massive exodus of skilled personnel – an exodus that Khrushchev's earlier pressure on West Berlin had done much to precipitate. As one commentator has observed, finding a solution to the Berlin problem was made difficult by its importance to both Germanies. 'For West Germany, Berlin was the primary symbol of Western commitment to the security of Germany and the ever elusive goal of reunification. For East Germany, Berlin was a symbol of western interference and non-recognition.'[9] The crisis culminated in the building of the Berlin Wall in August 1961 and the brief confrontation between Soviet and American forces at Checkpoint Charlie a few weeks later. Both sides could claim success in achieving their objectives. The US and its allies had maintained the integrity of West Berlin, while Khrushchev had succeeded in stemming the exodus of refugees through the city. Although the West did not accept East German sovereignty over the city, it can be argued that the crisis, and especially the building of the Wall, was to have a beneficial long-term effect on the relations between the two Germanies. At the time though, possible long-term benefits were less apparent than the immediate and obvious risks.

The Cuban Missile Crisis of 1962 was potentially even more dangerous. The reasoning behind the Soviet decision to install missiles in Cuba remains uncertain. It does seem likely, though, that Khrushchev saw the move as a 'quick fix' in the arms race. Khrushchev, who was concerned with reallocating resources from heavy industry and the military sector of the Soviet economy to light industry and the consumer sector, may have seen medium- and intermediate-range missiles in Cuba as a way of avoiding massive investment in long-range strategic forces. Some analysts have also speculated that Khrushchev saw the move as a precursor to another attempt at settling the Berlin problem, either by renewed pressure or through a major diplomatic initiative.[10] Whatever the precise motive, it seems likely that Khrushchev was playing for high stakes. At the same time, he probably calculated that the risks were manageable. The meeting with Kennedy at Vienna in 1961 may have encouraged Khrushchev to conclude that the new American President would meekly accept the installation of the missiles as a *fait accompli*.

In the event, these assumptions proved flawed. The US discovered the missiles before the installation was complete, and Kennedy – neuralgic about Cuba after the Bay of Pigs fiasco of 1961 and under strong pressure to show that he could be tough in action as well as in rhetoric – proved a more determined adversary than anticipated. By first imposing a naval blockade of Cuba and then issuing an ultimatum to the effect that if the Soviet Union did not remove the missiles voluntarily the US would do it by force, Kennedy compelled Khrushchev to back down. Although the President was in fact willing to go further in making a formal deal – rather than simply a private commitment – to dismantle US missiles in Turkey in exchange for the removal of Soviet missiles from Cuba, Khrushchev caved in before this became necessary.[11]

The Soviet gamble had failed. The crisis, though, had highlighted as never before the dangers inherent in the cold war. This was apparent in the exchange of letters between Kennedy and Khrushchev at the end of the crisis. As Khrushchev put it: 'vested with trust and great responsibility, we must not allow the situation to become aggravated and must stamp out the centers where a dangerous situation fraught with grave consequences to the cause of peace has arisen ... we should also make certain that no other dangerous conflicts which could lead to a world nuclear catastrophe, would arise.'[12] This statement contained the germ of the idea of the avoidance of crises by the superpowers, which was to become a key feature of the detente of the early 1970s. The concerns expressed by Khrushchev and shared by Kennedy were also reflected in Soviet and American behaviour in the aftermath of the crisis when there were tentative but significant moves towards a relaxation of tension.

If the Missile Crisis dramatised the dangers of the cold war, its peaceful resolution was also testimony to the skills which the superpowers had developed in the art of crisis management. In fact, this was only one of a variety of methods which had been used in an attempt to manage and regulate an adversary relationship. During the cold war, the superpowers devised techniques of management and modalities of behaviour which enabled them to contain and moderate the dangers attendant upon bipolar competition in a nuclear world. Although the changes made during the period of detente were significant, it was the cold war itself which provided the basis for a less acrimonious and more regulated competition. In one sense, detente was simply an attempt to extend and codify existing modalities of cooperation designed to ensure that a fundamentally antagonistic relationship did not degenerate into hostilities that neither side wanted.[13] Even during the cold war, superpower competition was neither unrestrained nor unregulated, and there developed what might be termed a 'cold war international order'.

There were several dimensions to this order. The first was nuclear deterrence. The superpowers recognised very quickly that a nuclear war would be qualitatively more destructive than anything which had gone before. Moreover, the tradition of non-use of nuclear weapons, which began with the Berlin Crisis of 1948 and the Korean war, was strengthened by the growth of the Soviet and American nuclear arsenals and the realisation that any hostilities involving the use of nuclear weapons would be enormously difficult to manage and control. If the concern with strategic stability – which was seen as dependent upon the mutual invulnerability of each side's strategic capabilities – only became apparent towards the end of the 1950s, it was clear even before then that both superpowers understood the horror of nuclear war and were intent on avoiding it. This was as true of policy-makers in Washington as of those in Moscow. As Richard Betts has argued, the golden age of American superiority was a myth because 'there never was a time leaders were *confident* that the US could wage nuclear war successfully'.[14]

Nevertheless, one way in which war could have occurred was through miscalculation. The dangers of this were greatest when the international situation was fluid and uncertain – as it was at the end of World War II. Subsequent actions by the superpowers helped to reduce the uncertainties and establish a degree of predictability which – the Cuban Missile Crisis notwithstanding – reduced the chances of miscalculation. The creation of the rival blocs was a crucial element in this process. Although the formation of NATO and the Warsaw Pact added a military overlay to the division of Europe, the result was increased order and predictability. The uncertainty over the future of Europe, especially Germany, had been an important contributory factor in the development of the cold war. This uncertainty was lessened by the establishment of the two alliance systems which defined the limits of permissible behaviour in Europe. Alliances and the formal commitments they embody highlight interests for which states are willing to fight, and thereby reduce the dangers of miscalculation.

If alliance commitments are sustained, at some point they may become transformed into norms. Although the language of deterrence and commitment may still be used – and is necessary as reassurance against the violation of the norm – the adversary simply accepts the situation and is content to work within the constraints it imposes. Such an outcome is all the more likely if there is some degree of reciprocity. This seems to have occurred in Europe. Although the West Europeans remained anxious about the viability of the American security guarantee, by the late 1960s the Soviet Union, whatever its long-term aspirations, seems to have accepted the American sphere of influence as a given. Efforts to drive wedges between Western Europe and the United States were not abandoned, but Moscow appeared to recognise that there were certain advantages in the maintenance of the status quo in Europe. The rival alliance systems provided a framework for containing the German problem which, if not entirely satisfactory, from Moscow's point of view was at least preferable to some of the possible alternatives.

Spheres of influence have traditionally provided a way of moderating great power conflict. The postwar division of Europe has fulfilled much the same function. Indeed, during the cold war the superpowers developed a set of tacit codes of conduct relating to spheres of influence which were of considerable significance. Although the voluntary nature of the Western alliance made it very different from the Warsaw Pact, the demarcation functions of the alliances were very similar. Furthermore, there was a gradual if grudging acceptance by the US that the Soviet sphere of influence in Eastern Europe could not be overturned by direct Western intervention. This was apparent in 1953 when the Eisenhower administration did nothing despite unrest in East Germany, and was reinforced by American inaction during the Hungarian rising of 1956. Despite the rhetoric of 'rollback' and 'liberation', Eisenhower accepted that, in practice, any serious attempt to go beyond containment would threaten vital Soviet interests and therefore result in the war that both sides remained anxious to avoid. Furthermore, during the cold war, spheres of influence were very low on the agenda for discussion between the superpowers. Verbal condemnation of Soviet behaviour in Eastern Europe was a standard propaganda theme, but there was no serious attempt to interfere more directly with what the Soviet Union actually did in the region.[15]

Mutual acceptance of spheres of influence was extended into what might be termed a 'norm of asymmetrical intervention' outside the blocs. Although the Korean war might never have occurred had spheres of influence in Asia been more clearly delineated, when the US intervened the Soviet Union adopted a hands-off attitude and declared the conflict a civil war which should not be subject to outside interference. Soviet pilots acted as volunteers and may even have engaged in combat with American forces, but this activity was not formally acknowledged by Moscow and did not therefore constitute a counter-intervention. The desire to avoid a direct clash was evident in other instances, such as the American intervention in Lebanon in 1958, and the growing involvement in Vietnam. Military intervention, by its very nature, was a statement that there were vital interests at stake even though the situation was outside the superpower spheres of influence in Eastern and Western Europe and Latin America.

The tacit codes of conduct which the superpowers developed regarding spheres of influence and asymmetrical intervention outside these spheres helped to minimise the possibility of a direct collision. Yet, these codes of conduct did not cover all contingencies and, as noted above, the cold war was characterised by occasional confrontations. Consequently, the superpowers had to supplement their tacit understandings about spheres of influence and unilateral intervention with another set of 'rules' for the conduct of crises. These political rules of engagement emerged from the Berlin Crisis of 1948, were refined during the crises over Quemoy and Matsu in the 1950s, and proved their value during the Berlin Crisis of 1961 and the Cuban Missile Crisis of 1962. If there was something fortuitous about the way they developed, their importance is difficult to exaggerate. The desire to avoid crossing the threshold between coercive bargaining tactics and overt violence provided one of the main restraints on Soviet and American behaviour during crises, while both sides came to recognise the importance of clear and effective communication as well as the need to respect each other's vital interests.[16] Indeed, in later confrontations, the balance of interests between the protagonists was probably the most important single factor in determining their relative willingness to take risks.[17] This was the case in both the Berlin Crisis of 1961 and the Cuban Missile Crisis. The United States accepted the Berlin Wall because of a recognition that it was vital to the maintenance of the Soviet position in Eastern Europe and that challenging it would threaten vital Soviet interests. Conversely, in the Missile Crisis, the Soviet decision to accede to Kennedy's demands can be understood as a recognition that the presence of missiles in Cuba was a threat to security that the US could not tolerate. In other words, the bargaining process in crises can be understood not simply as an exercise in manipulating the shared risk of war but also as an attempt to clarify the basic structure of the crisis in terms of which side has most at stake. This is not to diminish the risks inherent in situations where the bargaining takes the form of coercive actions rather than diplomatic negotiation. The potential for miscalculation, and the possibility of events getting out of control and taking on a momentum or dynamic of their own, make crisis management a hazardous, albeit inescapable, task.

Crisis management, like spheres of influence, was based on what might be termed the 'rules of prudence' in the nuclear age. To suggest that the superpowers were prudent, however, is not to imply that they abjured all risky situations. Indeed, as Snyder and Diesing have pointed out, one of the paradoxes of the nuclear age is that although the risks are greater than ever before, the threshold of provocation has been raised, thereby 'increasing the repertoire of moves open to states in a crisis to include a broad array of physical acts that in former times might have precipitated war'.[18] Naval blockade, for example, is traditionally an act of war, yet in October 1962 it was accepted as a legitimate action short of war. In other words, the potential for exploiting the fear of war has itself added a new dimension to superpower competition. Throughout the cold war the superpowers were concerned with avoiding situations which could escalate into direct confrontation or open war, but were prepared to take risks in order to protect and promote their interests.

This duality was even reflected in doctrinal changes in the Soviet Union. The Leninist doctrine of peaceful coexistence was revamped by Khrushchev at the Twentieth Party Congress in 1956 in an attempt to reconcile Marxist-Leninist ideology with the realities of the nuclear age. By abandoning the thesis that war between the Soviet Union and the leading capitalist powers was inevitable, Khrushchev was acknowledging, if only tacitly, that the superpowers had a common interest in avoiding nuclear war. Further statements through the late 1950s and the early 1960s were explicit on this point and made clear that neither side could expect to benefit from a war – an admission which was all the more important because of the Soviet belief in the superiority of the socialist system. It was also acknowledged that there were positive benefits for the Soviet Union in a relaxation of tensions, as this would strengthen the more moderate forces in American society and place those more hostile to the Soviet Union on the defensive. At the same time, Khrushchev made clear that peaceful coexistence did not mean an end to the class struggle. Indeed, the struggle would be continued and in those circumstances where there was no risk of war could even be intensified.

This dialectical approach to coexistence can be understood as an attempt to make the world safe for the superpower competition to continue.[19] Doctrinal innovation, however, was not followed immediately by a more accommodating policy. On the contrary, the six years which followed the peaceful coexistence speech of 1956 were years in which tension increased rather than subsided. The Cuban Missile Crisis, however, brought this period to an end, and in the aftermath of the crisis steps were taken to reduce tensions. These steps marked the beginnings of what might be described as a 'minimal detente'.

Tentative Moves to a Minimal Detente, 1963–8

The detente which occurred in the aftermath of the Cuban Missile Crisis was not the first time there had been a thaw in superpower relations. During the 1950s there had been two periods when East–West tensions had eased. The first, in the mid 1950s, culminated in the Geneva Summit of 1955. The second was at Camp David in 1959 during Khrushchev's visit to the US. On both occasions, however, the improvement in Soviet–American relations was superficial and ephemeral.[20] In the first thaw an East–West agreement was reached on the status of Austria, but with the Suez Crisis and the Soviet invasion of Hungary there was a reversion to the acrimonious exchanges which had characterised the Soviet–American relationship since 1947.[21] The 'Spirit of Camp David' was even less enduring and provided no more than a brief respite in what was one of the most intense phases of the cold war. On both occasions each side was concerned with displaying its peaceful intentions and portraying the adversary as the obstacle to peace. If there was a large propaganda dimension to summitry, however, it was not all for effect. Indeed, had it not been for the U-2 incident sabotaging the Paris Summit of 1960 then further progress towards East–West accommodation might well have been made.

In the aftermath of Cuba, the moves towards a relaxation of tensions were more substantial. This reflected a significant change in the prevalent imagery and symbolism. Although the superpowers still regarded each other as a threat, the Missile Crisis had dramatically revealed the dangers of nuclear war. Such a conflict had always been a theoretical possibility but had been remote from Soviet–American exchanges; the crisis of October 1962 had made it appear a distinct probability. The superpowers had developed stabilising mechanisms to assist in the management and regulation of their competition, but although these mechanisms had worked in Cuba, the episode had revealed their fragility. The need to strengthen them, therefore, appeared rather urgent.

The extent to which this analysis was shared by both superpowers is uncertain. The lessons the Soviet Union drew from the Cuban Missile Crisis may have had as much to do with the need to augment strategic capabilities in order to avoid future humiliations as with strengthening the mechanisms for crisis control. Furthermore, the change in Soviet policy may have been facilitated by the fact that Khrushchev's deputy, Kozlov, suffered a stroke. This effectively removed one of Khrushchev's major opponents and thereby gave the Chairman greater freedom, at least temporarily. Nevertheless, it is difficult to avoid the conclusion that Khrushchev's appreciation of how dangerous the situation had been was almost certainly a major factor in the post-Cuba thaw.

If the Cuban Missile Crisis provided an incentive for the superpowers to move towards detente, its aftermath was also a period of considerable opportunity in terms of American domestic politics. By compelling the Soviets to withdraw the missiles from Cuba, Kennedy had established his credentials as a hard-liner and, therefore, had an opportunity to be more accommodating and conciliatory in his approach to Moscow. His changed approach was evident in his American University Speech of 10 June 1963, in which he outlined a 'Strategy of Peace', and identified areas where the US and the Soviet Union had common interests and could therefore cooperate.[22] This is not to imply that cold war beliefs were abandoned or that the Soviet Union was no longer perceived as a threat. On the contrary, Kennedy continued to prosecute the containment policy with vigour. He also remained intent on refurbishing American military capabilities. But this was now part of an explicit two-track policy which combined continued competition and rivalry with explicit attempts to cooperate with the Soviet Union where this was advantageous.

Although such an approach is discernible under Eisenhower, it had never been fully developed, partly because Secretary of State Dulles had clung to a zero-sum view of Soviet–American relations and tended to dismiss any overtures by Moscow either as tactical moves or as signs of weakness which could be exploited. In either case a serious American response was not warranted. Furthermore, the validity of this appraisal appeared to be confirmed by Soviet behaviour: the 'missile gap' and Khrushchev's offensive against West Berlin ruled out an American policy which gave priority to reducing tensions between the superpowers. After the Missile Crisis, however, Soviet policy also became much more circumspect, thereby justifying and strengthening the more conciliatory approach pursued by Kennedy.

If Moscow was receptive to new departures, however, the initiative seems to have come primarily from the US. In his American University Speech, Kennedy not only adopted a more conciliatory tone but he also announced that the US was stopping all atmospheric nuclear tests. Khrushchev responded a few days later with a speech which not only welcomed the Kennedy initiative, but also offered a degree of reciprocity with the announcement that the production of Soviet strategic bombers would be halted. Neither of these steps was militarily significant; but politically both were of considerable importance. They were followed by the agreement on 20 June to install a direct communications link – popularly known as the 'hot line' – between the two capitals. This was both an acknowledgment of the importance of clear communication in crises and a reflection of inadequacies in the existing machinery of crisis management. What had hitherto been tacit cooperation was now becoming more explicit and more formal.

This improvement in Soviet–American relations was taken even further with the signing of the Partial Test Ban Treaty in August 1963. Although this treaty permitted underground nuclear testing, it symbolised the common interests of the superpowers in controlling the arms race and avoiding nuclear war. It was endowed with added significance because the negotiations themselves had been difficult, because it was the first substantive arms control agreement that had been reached, and because Kennedy viewed arms control as a key element in moving towards a less dangerous relationship with the Soviet Union. According to one analyst, the President saw arms control

> as a unique means to ameliorate political tensions. Military collaboration, it was reasoned, might build mutual confidence and hence lessen the explosive potential of reciprocal fears. This link between arms control and detente was a central premise of Kennedy's foreign policy and helps to distinguish it from Eisenhower's initial test ban efforts, where the anticipated political payoff – in terms of better Soviet–American relations – was much less clearly understood.[23]

As the same author points out, this did not mean that Kennedy had a benign image of the Soviet Union. On the contrary, he believed the Soviet Union would continue its efforts to advance its position wherever possible.[24] The main point, though, was that the continued conflicts of interest between the two states did not prohibit cooperation where this benefited both parties and enhanced stability. Indeed, Kennedy rejected the advice of some of his officials to make the test ban dependent on progress in finding solutions to unresolved political issues. Linkage between issues was seen as something which would inhibit rather than facilitate progress in managing the superpower competition.

The other area where there were signs of change in Soviet–American relations was trade. With the establishment of the two blocs, the Soviet Union had opted for economic autarky, while the US had pursued a policy of economic denial through export controls. Although Khrushchev in the mid-1950s had sought changes in this area, the US had been unwilling to alter a policy established in the Export Control Act of 1949 and implemented with its allies through the Coordinating Committee (COCOM) for multilateral export controls. In fact, US policy in 1962 was becoming more rather than less restrictive. The Export Control Act was extended beyond items that could be used for military purposes to cover goods with economic significance. Even so, there was a modest growth in Soviet–American trade – albeit at a rate markedly less than that between the Soviet Union and other Western countries. In 1963, however, there was a major new departure as the Soviet Union, suffering from a bad harvest, sought to buy American grain. Khrushchev also made it clear that he regarded increased trade as an indicator of good political relations. By this time, the American farming community – despite its traditional anti-communism – was anxious to follow the example of Canada in selling wheat to Moscow, while Kennedy was reluctant to block a development which held out the prospect of a further improvement in Soviet–American relations. In October 1963 he announced the sale of grain to Moscow.

Although both the Test Ban Treaty and the grain deal were symptomatic of a less tense phase in superpower relations, they were also highly controversial. The Test Ban Treaty was ratified by the Senate with only nineteen votes against. Nevertheless, this was achieved only after an extensive campaign to mobilise support for the agreement and to neutralise the opposition of those who saw any constraint on national defence efforts as a threat to security.[25] The grain deal encountered even more opposition and was criticised by Richard Nixon as 'harming the cause of freedom'.[26] Kennedy was also forced to accede to demands from shipping and labour that at least half the grain exports be transported in American vessels. Furthermore, the attempt to expand Soviet–American trade continued to encounter opposition in the Johnson administration. In 1965 a blue-ribbon panel known as the Miller Committee recommended that trade be used to influence Soviet behaviour. In what was an early version of a strategy that would eventually be known as linkage, the committee recommended that trade 'should be offered or withheld purposefully and systematically as opportunities and circumstances warrant'.[27] In the event, this proved impossible for the Johnson administration. Although the President enunciated a policy of 'peaceful engagement' with the Eastern bloc, and believed that trade was an integral part of an approach designed to give the Soviet Union and its allies a greater stake in stability, Congress refused to acquiesce. In 1966 Congress failed to approve legislation easing American restrictions on trade with the Soviet bloc, partly because of concerns about Soviet supplies to North Vietnam. At this stage continued domestic hostility towards the Soviet Union acted as a powerful brake on a further improvement in superpower relations, as did the growing American involvement in Vietnam.

This is not to denigrate the achievements of the detente which developed after the Cuban Missile Crisis. Nor is it to suggest that this detente was based exclusively on the desire to avoid nuclear war. The detente of the 1960s can also be understood as an important, albeit tentative, response by the superpowers to changes in the international system. By the mid-1960s strict or tight bipolarity had given way to a more complex system, in which the dominance of the two superpowers in military terms was accompanied by economic multipolarity and political fragmentation. The Sino–Soviet split had gradually become apparent, with important consequences for both Moscow and Washington. On the Soviet side, there was a natural desire to improve relations with one major adversary as another one began to emerge. On the American side, the split helped to weaken the perception that the US was confronting a monolithic communist movement directed by Moscow. Indeed, one of the paradoxes of the 1960s is that, while the American image of international communism was becoming increasingly differentiated, the Johnson administration's Vietnam policy was based on assumptions about the threat which dated back to the late 1940s.

The changes in the international system since the beginning of the cold war, however, were not all on the Soviet side. There had also been important developments in the Western alliance. The economic recovery of Western Europe, by encouraging greater political independence, intensified the problems and dilemmas of alliance management which confronted the United States. The relaxation of East–West tension had a similar effect as it provided the European allies with a degree of manoeuvrability that had been absent in the 1950s. France, in particular, attempted to take advantage of the opportunities that were opened up by detente, and not only opted out of NATO's integrated military structure but also began to pursue its own policy towards Eastern Europe and the Soviet Union. In one sense this was simply a reversion to the Eastern policy traditionally pursued by France and which had been evident in the period immediately following World War II. But it was also a product of a particular Gaullist vision of a Europe which was no longer divided and dominated by the two superpowers. Although de Gaulle may have simply been attempting to maximise his freedom of manoeuvre, his notion of 'detente, entente, cooperation' gave detente in Europe an independence from Washington which was to be of considerable long-term importance.

For its part, Moscow was receptive to de Gaulle's overtures partly because French policy offered opportunities to sow discord in the Western Alliance, but also because the Soviet leaders hoped that they might be able to influence Bonn through Paris. In the event, this was to become unnecessary as West Germany too began to develop a more conciliatory approach towards Eastern Europe. In the immediate aftermath of the Berlin and Cuban crises, West Germany had been not only sceptical about detente but actually hostile towards it. Gradually though there was a realisation in Bonn that the Federal Republic was in danger of becoming isolated as France, Britain and the US moved beyond cold war shibboleths towards more cooperative and less rigid policies. This fear of diplomatic isolation was reinforced by the recognition that the Berlin Wall – and its acceptance by the West – underlined the lack of realism in the West German objective of reunification.

The result was a gradual but perceptible shift in West German policy which started to bring it into line with the policies pursued by its allies. This is not to ignore the tensions which developed between Bonn and Washington, especially over the Non-Proliferation Treaty. US–West German differences over the NPT symbolised what was to be a recurring dilemma of detente for both superpowers – how to reconcile attempts to promote their common interest in avoiding war with their obligations to allies and clients. In fact, an attempt was made in the Harmel Report of 1967 to obtain a consensus within NATO on the twin goals of deterrence and detente. The allies would attempt to find a *modus vivendi* with Moscow while at the same time acknowledging the need to maintain a strong defence posture.

Although detente was being discussed formally by the NATO allies, there was still an *ad hoc* quality about its development. This was evident in the hastily arranged meeting between President Johnson and Mr Kosygin at Glassboro, New Jersey, in June 1967. The Middle East, Vietnam and a ban on anti-ballistic missiles were all discussed at this meeting, but with little immediate effect. Although the Glassboro Summit was dismissed at the time as a failure, it began the process of dialogue over strategic arms which, in 1972, was to culminate in the Anti-Ballistic Missile Treaty and the SALT One agreement on offensive arms. Furthermore, the meeting symbolised the desire of the two superpowers to avoid confrontation both in Vietnam and in the Middle East. Even more important in this connection, was the use of the hot line in an attempt by Washington and Moscow to avoid any misunderstanding during the Six Day war in the Middle East. Although this could be dismissed as little more than an exercise in crisis management, it also had explicit elements of crisis prevention, and was once again an important development on the way to the more ambitious detente of the 1970s.

The first use of the hot line came against a background in which the harsh rhetoric characteristic of the 1950s had given way to a more restrained approach, reflecting a shift in perceptions. Each side increasingly appeared to see the other as a limited adversary with whom it was possible to reach agreement on matters of mutual concern, rather than as an implacable enemy with whom there was nothing in common.[28] Moreover, both superpowers seemed anxious to avoid further crises of the kind which had arisen in the early 1960s. Such concerns were reinforced by considerations of expediency. The Soviet commitment to a more relaxed relationship with the US, for example, not only survived the fall of Khrushchev in 1964, but was strengthened by the concern of his successors to avoid policies which simply galvanised the West into concerted opposition to the Soviet Union.

Yet for Moscow – as for Washington – the new course was not without its pitfalls. There were opportunities in the relationship with France, but the policy which began to emerge from West Germany was not unreservedly welcomed in Moscow. Although there were good reasons for Moscow to encourage a more flexible approach by Bonn, lingering concerns over the viability of the Eastern bloc in a period of reduced tension acted as a brake on Soviet detente policy. Seen against this background, the Soviet intervention in Czechoslovakia in 1968 can be understood as a prerequisite for the further progress of detente. Although the immediate impact of the intervention was to increase East–West tension and to postpone the opening of talks on strategic arms control, the reassertion of Soviet control over the bloc made possible the further development of Soviet detente policy.

In other words, during the mid-1960s, domestic pressures against moving too far too fast combined with the problems of alliance management and the natural caution of both the Johnson administration and the successors of Khrushchev in ways which made it difficult to maintain the momentum of the moves towards detente initiated by Kennedy and Khrushchev. Nevertheless, the changes were not insignificant: quiet and unspectacular progress was being made at several levels. In fact, part of the reason why detente appeared to be making little progress was that the style had changed significantly from the 1950s. Summitry, which was long on atmospherics and short on substance, was replaced by a more sober and restrained, if more modest, approach in which agreements were reached on mundane matters such as consular conventions, civil aviation and cultural and scientific exchanges as well as the more important matter of the Non-Proliferation Treaty. In Lyndon Johnson's words, 'The sum of our efforts was the conclusion of more significant agreements with Moscow in the years 1963–1969 than in the thirty years after we established diplomatic relations with the Soviet regime.'[29] For the most part such agreements were unspectacular. Nevertheless, it does seem that the detente of the 1960s went beyond reducing tension and, in hindsight, can be understood as an important stage in the transition from the tacit cooperation which developed during the cold war to the more formal, extensive and explicit attempts at cooperation which characterised the maximalist detente of the 1970s. It can even be argued that many of the policies implemented by the Nixon administration had already been mapped out by its predecessor.[30]

Negotiations on strategic arms control, in particular, were as much the product of the thinking of Johnson's Secretary of

Defense, Robert McNamara, as of Nixon's National Security Adviser, Henry Kissinger. Had it not been for Czechoslovakia, the arms control negotiations would probably have been under way by the time the Nixon administration arrived in office. McNamara had recognised that Soviet technological advances – and especially the growing invulnerability of Soviet missiles – made American strategic superiority increasingly elusive. This was reflected in the principle of Mutual Assured Destruction, espoused by the Secretary of Defense from the mid 1960s onwards. Although MAD was never accepted as the basis for American targeting strategy, it nevertheless provided a conceptual basis for the attempt by the superpowers to limit strategic armaments. Yet there was no systematic and sustained attempt to provide a conceptual framework for the political dimensions of Soviet–American relations to accompany that for the strategic relationship. Consequently, there were few indications of the extent to which detente would progress in the 1970s. The detente of the 1960s developed in an *ad hoc* fashion, and it was uncertain that it would go much further. In the event, of course, it became the dominant theme of superpower relations in the early 1970s. The reasons for this are explored more fully in the next chapter.

Notes

1. M. Shulman, *Beyond the Cold War* (New Haven and London: Yale University Press, 1966), p. 16.

2. H. Kissinger, *The Necessity for Choice* (New York: Doubleday, 1962), p. 201. See also O.R. Holsti, 'Cognitive Dynamics and Images of the Enemy' in D.J. Finlay, O.R. Holsti and R.R. Fagen, *Enemies in Politics* (Chicago: Rand-McNally, 1967), pp. 25–96.

3. T. Hoopes, *The Devil and John Foster Dulles* (London: André Deutsch, 1974), p. 83.

4. M. Adelman, *Symbolic Uses of Politics* (Urbana: University of Illinois Press, 1964), p. 6.

5. Ibid., p. 6.

6. See J. Stoessinger, *Nations in Darkness* (New York: Random House, 1971), p. 66.

7. See L. Freedman, *US Intelligence and the Soviet Strategic Threat*, 2nd ed. (London: Macmillan, 1986), and A. Horelick and M. Rush, *Strategic Power and Soviet Foreign Policy* (Chicago: Chicago University Press, 1966).

8. J. Spanier and J. Nogee, *The Politics of Disarmament* (New York: Praeger, 1962).

9. R. Stevenson, 'The Meaning of Detente' (Oxford University: Ph.D dissertation), p. 137.

10. A. Ulam, *Dangerous Relations* (New York: Oxford University Press, 1983), p. 31.

11. See E. Pace, 'Rusk reveals ploy prepared by Kennedy over Cuba', *International Herald Tribune*, 29–30 Aug. 1987.

12. See 'Correspondence between Chairman Khrushchev and President Kennedy, 28 October 1962', reproduced as Appendix 8 in R. Kennedy, *Thirteen Days* (London: Pan Books, 1969), p. 176.

13. On these modalities see D. Caldwell, *American–Soviet Relations from 1947 to the Nixon–Kissinger Grand Design* (Westport, Conn.: Greenwood Press, 1981).

14. R.K. Betts, *Nuclear Blackmail and Nuclear Balance* (Washington, DC: The Brookings Institution, 1987), p. 144.

15. See R. Cohen, *International Politics: The Rules of the Game* (London: Longman, 1981), p. 56.

16. For a fuller discussion of crisis management, see P.Williams, *Crisis Management* (London: Martin Robertson, 1976).

17. For a slightly more qualified view see Betts, op. cit., especially pp. 133–44.

18. G. Snyder and P. Diesing, *Conflict Among Nations* (Princeton, NJ: Princeton University Press, 1977), p. 453.

19. See R. Tucker 'United States–Soviet Cooperation: Incentives and Obstacles' in E.P. Hoffmann and F.J. Fleron (eds), *The Conduct of Soviet Foreign Policy* (New York: Aldine, 1982), pp. 301–14 especially pp. 305–306.

20. For a fuller discussion and a somewhat different interpretation of the summits of the 1950s see R. Stevenson, *The Rise and Fall of Detente* (London: Macmillan, 1985), especially chs 3 and 4.

21. See D.W. Larson, 'Crisis prevention and the Austrian State Treaty' in *International Organization*, vol. 41, no. 1 (Winter 1987), for an incisive analysis.

22. See A. Etzioni, *The Kennedy Experiment* (New York: Institute of War and Peace Studies, Columbia University, 1967), for a discussion of the speech and subsequent moves.

23. B.J. Firestone, *The Quest for Nuclear Stability* (London: Greenwood Press, 1982), p. 59.

24. Ibid., p. 60.

25. See ibid. for a fuller discussion.

26. Quoted in D. Caldwell, op. cit., p. 63.

27. Quoted in ibid., p. 64.

28. See M. Shulman, op. cit. for a fuller analysis. Also useful on this period is S. Hoffmann, 'Detente' in J. Nye (ed.), *The Making of America's Soviet Policy* (New Haven and London: Yale University Press, 1984), especially pp. 232–6.

29. L.B. Johnson, *The Vantage Point* (New York: Popular Library, 1971), p. 476.

30. We are grateful to John Steinbruner of the Brookings Institution for this point.

3
Superpower Interests in Detente

By the late 1960s superpower relations, although much less tense than in the period prior to the Cuban Missile Crisis, seemed almost to have stagnated. The inertia of the cold war together with preoccupations elsewhere made it difficult for the superpowers to develop new policies towards each other which were coherent and well thought out. Consequently, the detente of the 1960s can be characterised as a detente without a design. Attempts to improve the relationship were inhibited by both the deepening American involvement in Vietnam through the mid-1960s and the Soviet invasion of Czechoslovakia in 1968. Paradoxically though, Vietnam and Czechoslovakia were eventually to contribute to the reappraisals of policy in Moscow and Washington which led to the maximalist detente of the 1970s. Other developments also played a part in these reappraisals, the result of which was that both superpowers became increasingly committed to policies designed to ameliorate tensions and provide a more stable relationship.

If the interests of the superpowers in improving relations coincided, there remains an important distinction between interests which are at best complementary or overlapping and interests which are genuinely shared. There was, of course, a common interest in the avoidance of nuclear war, but this had been evident throughout the cold war, and initially had resulted in the development of codes of conduct and management techniques designed to ensure only that the cold war did not get out of control. Although the Missile Crisis of 1962 led to a less sanguine assessment of the dangers associated with superpower crises, this produced only a limited detente. The additional impetus to move towards a more ambitious and far-reaching detente came from a recognition by Soviet and American policy-makers that there were other areas in which their interests coincided. Underlying these overlapping interests, however, were incompatible expectations, divergent objectives and differing conceptions of the relationship.

This becomes clear in an analysis of the considerations which prompted Moscow and Washington to embark on a more ambitious attempt than ever before to improve their relationship. In both cases, there were certain developments which provided a *permissive* environment and others which more positively *activated* the detente policies of the 1970s. Having identified these, the problems of compatibility between the Soviet and American conceptions of detente can be assessed.

Soviet Interests and Conceptions of Detente

Although the momentum of detente slowed in the mid-1960s, the period from 1966 to 1971 was one in which the Politburo apparently undertook a major reappraisal of Soviet foreign policy. The result was a Soviet commitment to detente which was seen as the most appropriate response to new opportunities, dangers and constraints. This commitment reflected the peculiar historical circumstances of the late 1960s. Yet there was both historical precedent and ideological justification for such an approach. Indeed, cooperation with the state which poses the major threat to security has been a recurring feature of foreign policy throughout much of Russian history and was evident after the 1917 revolution, despite the fact that the leaders of the Soviet Union sought to differentiate their policies from those of their predecessors. The Nazi–Soviet Pact of 1939 was very much within this tradition and showed how immediate calculations of security and self-interest could, under certain circumstances, override ideological antipathies.

If the history of both Russian and Soviet diplomacy provided ample precedent for the development of a less hostile relationship with the United States, Soviet ideology also helped to legitimise superpower detente. The dialectical approach to peaceful coexistence which had come to the fore in 1956 enabled the Soviet leadership to cope easily with a mixed relationship in which cooperation and conflict with the adversary went hand in hand. Detente was a natural extension of the strategy of peaceful coexistence, and was a means of establishing both the permanence and the limits of competition on the one hand and the importance and limits of cooperation on the other. In this sense, the ideology was permissive – and provided a ready made framework for a change in East–West relations which the leadership wanted for hard-headed practical reasons.

There was another consideration, rooted in ideology, but related to changes in the strategic balance and in the American position in the world which gave the Soviet move towards detente in the late 1960s a particular urgency. Essentially, the Soviet leadership believed that a profound shift was taking place in the correlation of forces. Although this change was favourable to Moscow, it was not without its dangers. Soviet ideology taught that the capitalist world was at its most dangerous when it believed that its power was threatened in ways which might prove irreversible. It was crucial, therefore, to avoid provoking any tensions in the superpower relationship as parity was approaching. In other words, detente was a necessary accompaniment to the strategic stalemate which was becoming apparent in the mid and late 1960s as the United States not only completed the strategic build-up initiated by Eisenhower and Kennedy but also accepted the principle of 'assured destruction' as the main criterion for its strategic force requirements. According to Garthoff, detente as conceived by the Soviet leaders was designed 'to manage the transition of the United States into a changing world, one no longer marked by American predominance but by a political parity of the Soviet Union with the United States that matched their military parity'.[1] An attempt to reduce the tensions in the superpower relationship would also help to insulate the Soviet Union from 'the dangers inherent in a situation where the United States, smarting from its Vietnam humiliation might be tempted to recoup its prestige by drastic actions elsewhere'.[2]

If the element in Soviet ideology which taught that capitalist powers were most dangerous prior to a loss of military supremacy provided a compelling motive for detente, it was reinforced by a variety of other considerations. Indeed, it seems clear that between 1966 and 1971 the Soviet leadership concluded that detente, both with the United States and with Western Europe, was a way of containing or overcoming several major problems and dilemmas which confronted Moscow in both domestic and foreign policy.

The first of these was Soviet economic needs. By the late 1960s the Soviet economy was in difficulties and the rate of economic growth was declining rapidly. Between 1950 and 1958 Soviet GNP had grown by 6.4 per cent; between 1958 and 1967 growth had fallen to 5.3 per cent; and from 1967 to 1973 it was only 3.7 per cent, with the danger of falling still further.[3] The weakness of the domestic economic base was accentuated by the very uneven development in different sectors of the economy. As one commentator has noted,

> The planning system was not generating the kind of innovations and economic growth that seemed appropriate for the 1960s. The shortcomings appeared particularly acute when compared with the growth in the American, West European and Japanese economies. The prevailing policy of autarky and isolation was only viable on the assumption that Soviet industry could keep pace with (or surpass) the technology being developed in the rest of the world. This it had seemed to be doing at least until the 1960s. But while Soviet technology had proven itself in basic metallurgy, atomic energy, astronautics, and defence, there were embarrassing deficiencies in electronics, computers, sophisticated forms of assembly line production, and, as before, chemicals.[4]

The leadership also recognised that the weaknesses in areas of Soviet industry such as automobile production could only be overcome with the direct help of the West. Covert acquisition of Western technology, a policy made necessary by the US policy of economic denial and by the COCOM restrictions, was insufficient to obtain 'the large infusion of advanced technology that might speed up the country's economic growth'.[5]

The new approach was evident in several sectors, but perhaps most notably in the fifteen-year plan for transportation (1966–80), which envisaged a massive growth in the production of both passenger cars and trucks. Immediate effect was given to this in the Eighth Five Year Plan (1966–70) which vastly increased investment in the automobile industry. Because of Soviet backwardness in this area, however, it was necessary to obtain Western technical assistance – a need that was fulfilled by deals with the Italian car firm Fiat and the French company Renault. Other West European companies were also involved in the modernisation of Soviet factories producing components for the automobile industry.

Another major area of weakness in the Soviet economy was agriculture. Soviet workers in agriculture were far less productive than their American counterparts, and it was clear that progress in this area would depend crucially upon the import of agricultural technologies from the West. The crop failure of 1963 had not only underlined the weakness and unpredictability of Soviet agricultural production but had also marked 'the reversal of Russia's traditional role of an important exporter of wheat and other grains to that of an importer'.[6] Although the Brezhnev–Kosygin leadership gave agriculture a top priority, progress remained elusive, and through the mid and late 1960s the Soviet Union still found it necessary to import grain from Canada. The availability of American grain surpluses also made the United States a natural source for Soviet grain imports. Although the Soviet grain purchases of 1963 had aroused considerable controversy in the United States, in 1969 there were expressions of Soviet interest in further purchases.

In short, the performance of the Soviet economy in the 1960s provided an important incentive for normalising relations with the West. Despite the promise of the Eighth Five Year Plan, economic difficulties became more rather than less acute. The growth of industrial labour productivity dropped from 7.4 per cent to 5.5 per cent. while the quality of goods remained well below those of the West.[7] There were shortages throughout the system, even in areas important to the modernisation of Soviet military power. In 1971, therefore, Brezhnev, who by this time had become the dominant figure in the Soviet leadership, was faced with difficult questions about the direction of the Soviet economy for the next five years.

These questions were closely related to the issue of internal reform. Although Kosygin had been a vigorous advocate of decentralisation in the economy as a way of maximising the benefits from expanded trade with the West, Brezhnev was initially cautious about reform and sceptical about foreign trade. Nevertheless, there were limited reforms in 1965, and it appears that economic decentralisation and foreign trade were, for a few years at least, regarded as complementary. As Brezhnev became more powerful in domestic policy, however, the Soviet Union moved 'closer to substituting Western commerce for the pursuit of major internal reforms'.[8] This is not to imply that Brezhnev was oblivious to the need to revitalise the economy. If the Prague Spring showed what could happen if reform went too far, the revolts in Poland which dislodged Gomulka in 1970 revealed the dangers of doing nothing – and almost certainly had a profound impact on the Soviet leadership. Consequently, Brezhnev attempted to please both the party *apparatchiki* by refraining from major structural reforms, and the consumer by allocating a higher rate of investment to the consumer industries. A rising standard of living and higher defence spending were to be achieved through increased growth and efficiency in the economy as a whole. Increasingly, however, he saw economic growth as vitally dependent on increased trade with the West. Despite opposing earlier plans to increase trade with the capitalist nations, Brezhnev, by the early 1970s, had become the most fervent proponent of expanded commercial and industrial involvement. As he stated, 'There can be no doubt that the expansion of international exchanges will have a favourable effect on the improvement of the work of all our industry.'[9] Although not all members of the Politburo shared this enthusiasm or optimism, it was nevertheless clear by the Congress of 1971 that the Soviet leadership perceived an extremely close link between detente and expanded trade with the West.

If economic factors were important in the Soviet moves to normalise relations with the West, so too was the growing rift with China. Indeed, the widening dispute with the People's Republic of China may have been the most important single consideration impelling the Soviet Union towards an East–West detente, which, it was hoped in Moscow, might lead to an anti-Chinese condominium.

The Sino–Soviet split resulted from a clash of ideological and traditional state interests: the Chinese People's Republic not only challenged Soviet pre-eminence in the international communist movement, but also made significant claims on Soviet territory. Relations had been awkward when Stalin was alive, but they deteriorated markedly after Khrushchev's secret speech of 1956. Khrushchev's denunciation of Stalin, his reformulation of the peaceful coexistence doctrine, and his calls for economic reform at home were condemned as 'revisionist' by Beijing. The denunciation of Stalin was particularly important as it eroded the legitimacy of Soviet domination of the communist bloc. If Stalin had been so wrong, why should other nations put faith in his successors, especially when they lacked direct experience of revolution?

The differences that began to emerge in 1956 were exacerbated by the 1958 crisis over Quemoy. Chinese resentment at the lack of support given by Moscow was matched by Soviet concern over what appeared to be Chinese recklessness. The schism, which continued to develop through the early 1960s entered a new and rather more tense phase in 1964 with a speech by Mao laying claim to portions of Soviet territory. As the Chinese leader stated: 'A 100 years ago they [the Russians] incorporated the territory to the East of Lake Baikal, including Khabarovsk, Vladivostok and the Kamchatka Peninsula.... We have not settled these accounts with them.'[10] This claim to 585,000 square miles of land, ceded by the Quing empire to the Tsar, elicited a massive Soviet military build-up in the area over the following five years. The dozen under-strength Soviet divisions of 1961 were transformed into a more formidable force of twenty-five divisions by 1969, and by 1973 the Soviet union had forty-five divisions on its eastern border.[11] This reveals just how alarmed the Soviet leadership was by Chinese territorial revisionism. Yet this was hardly surprising. The Sino–Soviet border is the longest common border in the world, and is extremely remote from the Soviet capital, with the trans-Siberian railway as the only means of land communication from European Russia. Furthermore, China had a huge army, second in size only to the Soviet Army itself, and a huge population to back it up. This, coupled with China's obvious if still embryonic potential to become a future superpower, inevitably aroused Soviet concerns.

These concerns increased further after the inauguration of the Cultural Revolution in August 1966, but were intensified even more dramatically in the first few months of 1969 as the number of border incidents increased. On 2 March, a large number of Chinese soldiers attacked Soviet frontier guards on Damansky Island, a disputed piece of territory, in the Ussuri River, thereby precipitating a serious escalation. Several dozen Soviet soldiers were killed or wounded. Sporadic clashes erupted along the 4,650-mile frontier during the subsequent months, accompanied by propaganda campaigns in both countries, alerting their populations to the chance of war.

Garthoff has suggested that the Chinese decision to escalate tension on the Sino–Soviet border was a response to the Soviet intervention in Czechoslovakia, and was designed in part to prevent further Soviet military action in Eastern Europe.[12] It may have also been intended to underline the fact that the Brezhnev Doctrine could not be extended to the Chinese People's Republic. Whatever the reason, the incidents of March 1969 seem to have had considerable impact on Soviet decision-makers. Although there is some doubt about the authenticity of reports offered by Shevchenko, the high-ranking defector, his analysis of the effect of the clashes on the Politburo confirms most Western interpretations. In his view, 'the events in Damansky had the effect of an electric shock on Moscow. The Politburo was terrified that the Chinese might make a large-scale intrusion into Soviet territory.'[13] Reports that the Soviet Union contemplated a preventive strike against Chinese nuclear installations have to be treated with caution, but it is clear that Moscow engaged in some highly coercive actions, such as strengthening the bomber force in Siberia and Mongolia and conducting exercises against targets 'made to resemble nuclear facilities in Northwest China'.[14] Whether this was a rehearsal for a strike which was never authorised is uncertain. Such actions may have been intended simply to strengthen deterrence and inhibit the Chinese from further brinkmanship. The possibility that Marshal Grechko did contemplate military action, however, cannot be ruled out. This would explain why there were several Soviet overtures towards the United States probing the American response to a possible Soviet attack on China. William Hyland has even argued that 'the negative American response turned the debate away from an attack'.[15] Whatever the case, Soviet attempts at coercion were accompanied by efforts to defuse the situation through political and diplomatic means. The Politburo sought a cessation of hostilities and the reopening of border negotiations. In late 1969 lines of communication were re-established when Kosygin visited Beijing after Ho Chi Minh's funeral. Although this was an attempt to contain the immediate dispute, substantive differences between the two countries remained unresolved.

Perhaps the most important result of the deterioration of Sino–Soviet relations in 1969 was that it caused the Soviet leadership to look westward. At the Warsaw Pact summit meeting in Budapest in 1969, the discussion was dominated by China, and it was here that Brezhnev formulated his 'Westpolitik'.[16] In this early stage Westpolitik had two main elements – the non-interference of the United States in the event of a Sino–Soviet war, and the stabilisation of relations with Western Europe. There seems to have been some doubt in Moscow at this time about whether to opt for a selective detente with Western Europe or a more comprehensive detente between the two blocs, which would have to go through Washington as well as Bonn. If the Politburo was initially rather sceptical about either the desirability or the feasibility of simultaneously improving relations with the United States and Western Europe, however, this became a matter of great urgency as the Sino–American *rapprochement* began to emerge. China was still backward militarily and economically compared to the Soviet Union, but trade and technology from the West would make it a much more formidable adversary. For the Soviet Union, therefore, detente with the West would not only reduce the threat of conflict on the two fronts but might also hold out some prospect of isolating China and delaying its further military development.

Both the desire for Western trade and the concerns over China impelled Moscow towards detente. To suggest, however, that Moscow was reacting solely to problems is to ignore other factors which from the Soviet perspective made detente appear very attractive. For Moscow, detente was something that had been earned through the attainment of rough strategic parity with the United States. For virtually all of the postwar period, the Soviet Union had been inferior to the United States in strategic arms – an inferiority which, in the aftermath of the Cuban Missile Crisis and Khrushchev's downfall, seems to have been deemed intolerable. Unlike Khrushchev, Brezhnev and Kosygin were intent on establishing the reality of Soviet strength. They seemed to believe that Khrushchev's strategic policy – which was effectively one of minimum deterrence – had failed to provide an adequate basis for Soviet policy towards either China or the United States. It was not surprising, therefore, that Brezhnev, in a key speech in July 1965, announced a major acceleration of Soviet military programmes. In part this may have been a response to the deepening American involvement in Vietnam and increased American defence spending, but it was also significant that it followed the failure of Sino–Soviet talks in November 1964 and February 1965.[17]

There are obvious difficulties in assessing the military budget in the Soviet Union, but it is clear that the collective leadership gave a high priority to the military sector in an effort to end the period of Soviet inferiority. Even official Soviet estimates admit to a rise in defence spending of about 40 per cent between 1965 and 1970. Although this pattern of resource allocation placed considerable strain on the Soviet economy, this was a price that the leadership was prepared to pay in order to maintain Soviet security, develop a significant maritime capability and erode American nuclear superiority. Paradoxically, this build-up offered considerable opportunity for arms control. It is a feature of accords on strategic arms that, for the most part, they ratify the existing balance and add a degree of predictability to the continuing arms race. Agreement is easiest when there is mutual acceptance that some kind of equality already exists, and most difficult when there are inequalities. In 1964 Kosygin rejected President Johnson's proposal for a verified freeze on strategic arms, as this would have frozen Soviet forces into a position of permanent inferiority. By the late 1960s the Soviet Union was much readier to entertain the idea of serious arms control negotiations with the United States. This new enthusiasm for arms control was also the result of a shift in military doctrine which occurred during the years 1966 to 1968. As a result of this doctrinal change, 'avoiding the nuclear devastation of Russia became the governing objective in the strategic hierarchy, constrained only by the need not to lose' in the event that war proved unavoidable.[18] After considerable debate during 1967 and 1968 it was accepted that arms control could contribute to this objective. Furthermore, by this stage Soviet leaders may have seen arms control not only as a way of ratifying Soviet achievements but also as a means of ensuring that the United States did not engage in ambitious strategic modernisation programmes which would once again relegate Moscow to a position of inferiority.

The significance of bilateral arms control negotiations with the United States was political as well as strategic. Negotiations and subsequent agreement would symbolise Soviet status as an equal of the United States. Although considerations of status should not be exaggerated, it does appear that in the late 1960s there was a new sense of confidence in Moscow and a feeling that, at last, it was no longer inferior to Washington. Yet this was a confidence tinged with fragility. Status depends on the perceptions of others, and Moscow badly wanted American acknowledgment of Soviet achievements. Detente in general and arms control in particular may have been regarded as a means of securing this and underlining what the Soviet leadership believed was a fundamental change in both the superpower relationship and the structure of power in the international system. Gromyko expressed the Soviet sense of achievement at the Twenty-fourth Party Congress in 1971 when he stated 'there is no question of any significance which can be decided without the Soviet Union or in opposition to her'.[19] Although offered as a description, this was really a statement of Soviet aspirations.

If Soviet detente policy was in part an expression of newfound, though perhaps superficial, confidence on the part of the Soviet leadership, it was equally a response to opportunities which were developing both in the United States and Western Europe. There was a convergence of differing interests which made possible an unprecedented degree of reciprocity in East–West relations. Moscow, for reasons of its own – to do with the needs of the economy, the challenge from China, the moves towards strategic parity and the need to legitimise its position in Eastern Europe – was anxious to ease tensions and moderate its relationship with the West. This desire coincided with, and was strengthened and encouraged by, a new flexibility on the part of the two key Western powers, the United States and the Federal Republic of Germany. The Soviet relationship with the United States had been evolving in unspectacular but important ways since the Cuban Missile Crisis; the shift in policy towards the Bonn government was more dramatic.

In 1966 the Soviets had rebuffed a diplomatic approach from the Federal Republic seeking better relations. Furthermore, at the Twenty-third CPSU Congress the same year it was alleged that the Kiesinger government was seeking nuclear weapons and presiding over an upsurge of revanchism in West Germany.[20] Five years later, however, the Soviet attitude had changed. When Brezhnev gave the keynote speech at the Twenty-fourth Congress in 1971, he suggested that new prospects in Europe were opening up 'as a result of substantial changes for the better in our relations with the Federal Republic of Germany'.[21] This change reflected the positive Soviet response to the policies pursued by the Brandt government.

Even before Brandt became Chancellor, there were growing diplomatic exchanges between the Federal Republic and the Soviet Union on the possibility of an agreement on a renunciation of force. The prospect of a more cooperative relationship had certain attractions for Moscow: West Germany was a modern industrialised state with much to offer the Soviet Union economically. In addition, Moscow wanted recognition of its position in Eastern Europe and formal German acceptance of the status quo. Yet the negotiations were not without their dangers for Moscow, and in July 1968, shortly before the invasion of Czechoslovakia, they were broken off. At that point the Soviet Union was less interested in improving its relations with Western Europe than with securing its possessions in Eastern Europe.

> The tendencies manifested in Czechoslovakia and Rumania of striking out independent courses in domestic and foreign policy, as well as the willingness shown in some East European states to normalize relations with the Federal Republic, threatened Soviet hegemony and led to tensions within the bloc system ... the Soviet Union ... regarded Bonn's Ostpolitik as one of the causes behind the softening of bloc solidarity, without its having been able to get the West, and the Federal Republic in particular, to confirm the status quo and thus to recognize the Soviet sphere.[22]

In the summer of 1969 the dialogue was resumed as the Soviet Union sought Western acknowledgment of the 'real situation' in Europe.[23] Considerable momentum was given to the negotiations with the election of the Social Democrat–Free Democrat coalition in October 1969. The new Brandt government 'conceived of the normalization of relations with the socialist states of Eastern Europe as an historic mission'.[24] In contrast to previous Chancellors, Brandt was willing to abandon the Hallstein Doctrine and the claim that Bonn should speak for the whole of Germany. He accepted the principle that, although Germany would remain 'one nation', it was a nation divided into 'two states'. Reunification was not abandoned as a long-term aspiration – and Brandt hoped that a reduction of tension between East and West would lead to a gradual lowering of the barriers between the two Germanies. Nevertheless, acting on the assumption that the best way to influence the East German state was not through isolating it but through *rapprochement*, the new government in Bonn went much further than any of its predecessors in accepting geopolitical realities in Europe.

Moscow was extremely receptive to this approach. Not only did it open up new economic opportunities, but it also promised to endow the Soviet position in Eastern Europe with the kind of legitimacy successive Soviet leaders had been seeking since the end of World War II. Furthermore, the trepidation that had been aroused in Moscow by the initial West German moves towards Ostpolitik had diminished significantly by 1969. The promulgation of the Brezhnev Doctrine may have made Moscow less apprehensive about a positive response to Brandt. With the limits of tolerance clearly established in Eastern Europe, an increase in East–West contacts could be contemplated with far greater equanimity.

Whether Moscow also saw in detente an opportunity to divide the United States and its West European allies is more uncertain. French policies in the mid-1960s could well have encouraged such a calculation and the Soviet attempts to convene a European Security Conference which excluded the United States and Canada suggest that this was a major aim of Soviet policy. Yet Moscow seems to have reconciled itself fairly quickly to a situation in which European detente and superpower detente had to proceed along more or less parallel tracks. This is not altogether surprising – although the Soviet leaders were anxious to bring about changes in Europe which worked in their favour, they were constrained by the desire to avoid unmanaged change which might be far less favourable.

The problem with attempting to divide Western Europe and the United States was that success offered not only uncertain benefits but incalculable costs. For all its disadvantages, the American commitment to Western Europe and the United States military presence was preferable to at least some of the conceivable alternatives. If the result of American disengagement was a fragmented Western Europe which could be dominated politically, that was one thing; if it was a more cohesive Western Europe in which the Federal Republic of Germany had an enlarged military role that was something very different – and far less desirable. The dilemma for Moscow was that working too vigorously for the first outcome inevitably carried risks of the second.

The existing situation in Western Europe was less than ideal, of course, but helped to legitimise Soviet dominance over Eastern

Europe. In a period of rapid change or turmoil on the Continent that dominance might be jeopardised. As Lawrence Freedman has argued, 'if NATO broke up in disarray then the resulting turbulence would threaten the strategic and ideological buffer between the USSR and the West which had been the organising concept of all Soviet regional policies since Yalta'.[25] For a Soviet leadership which was in many respects extremely conservative, the existing situation had a comforting familiarity, while the alternatives involved considerable uncertainty. Consequently, prudence and realism combined to encourage Moscow to accept that progress towards a *modus vivendi* in Europe could only be achieved with American involvement.

It is clear then that, in Europe as elsewhere, Soviet detente policy was a response to both constraints and opportunities. The development of this policy, however, was inextricably linked to the decline of collective leadership and the rise of Brezhnev to a position where he was at the very least *primus inter pares*. Initially cautious and even sceptical about pursuing conciliatory policies towards the West, Brezhnev by 1971 was firmly committed to detente with both Western Europe and the United States.

Yet the Brezhnev concept of detente retained an important duality, if not ambivalence. On the one side, the Soviet leader elucidated detente in ways which emphasised the Soviet interest in the easing of tensions and the normalisation of relations:

> Detente means, primarily, the overcoming of the cold war and a transition to normal, smooth relations among states. Detente means a willingness to resolve differences and disputes, not by force, threats or saber-rattling, but by peaceful means at the negotiating table. Detente means a certain degree of trust and the ability to reckon with each other's interests.[26]

On the other side, there was an emphasis on the competitive aspects of detente. Not only would competition continue, but it would actually be made safer as a result of the transition from cold war to detente. Indeed, Brezhnev placed a great deal of emphasis on the possibilities that would open up for Moscow in a period of relaxation, claiming that it would facilitate 'the success of the liberation struggle and the achievement of the revolutionary tasks of the people'.[27]

In short, the Soviet concept of detente embraced competition as well as cooperation. Detente, like peaceful coexistence, was conceived as a dialectical process which would further the cause of international socialism and the cause of peace. This amalgamation of competition and cooperation may simply have reflected confusion in the Soviet mind about the precise nature of detente. Yet this seems unlikely. Rather more persuasive is the possibility that the ideological justifications used to legitimise the new approach reflected pragmatic appraisals in which detente seemed the most appropriate response to constraints and opportunities.

The emphasis on the enduring nature of the competition between rival social systems had a number of advantages which would have been absent had the focus been exclusively on cooperation. There would have been considerable costs to Moscow in a detente which appeared to give priority to stabilising Soviet relations with the United States at the expense of revolutionary movements in the Third World. Such an approach would have alienated nationalist and revolutionary groups which naturally looked to Moscow for support. It would also have undermined the legitimacy of Soviet leadership of the international communist movement, thereby making Moscow vulnerable to the continued political and ideological challenge from China. Another advantage of emphasising the competitive aspects of detente related to Soviet domestic politics. A broad conception which embraced competition as well as cooperation may have been necessary to placate those factions in the Kremlin unhappy about accommodation with the United States. Indeed, the Brezhnev conception of detente, far from being imprecise, may have been a skilful device to establish and maintain a consensus on policies which would otherwise have been subjected to considerable criticism. A third reason for the emphasis on continuing the class struggle and supporting wars of national liberation is that this accorded with the Soviet belief that, as a result of the move towards parity 'the correlation of forces' was shifting decisively in favour of Moscow.

In so far as detente was the product of Soviet achievements, therefore, it was natural that Moscow would prove assertive in pursuing its interests and that this assertiveness would have an ideological dimension. There was also a sense, however, in which Moscow was making clear to the West that there were limits to detente. The Soviet leadership was not attempting to deceive the United States or its allies – and later allegations in the United States that the Soviet Union had used detente to lull the West into a false sense of security do not square with what appears to be considerable transparency and indeed directness in Soviet statements about detente. In the view of one Soviet analyst, the Soviet leaders tried to preclude any American illusions that arms control agreements could be exchanged for Soviet 'guarantees of stability' in the Third World. From the start they emphasised that they would not sit down with the United States to 'decide questions concerning other peoples and countries. They also made clear that, while concluding the agreements on the normalisation of relations with the United States, the Soviet Union nonetheless would continue to support the struggles of the peoples for their social and national liberation.'[28] In short, the problem was not Soviet duplicity. It was simply that the Soviet concept of detente did not coincide with that of the United States.

American Interests and Conceptions of Detente

The Soviet desire for detente with the United States was matched from 1969 by the Nixon administration's commitment to detente with the Soviet Union. The new administration of Richard Nixon saw considerable advantage in attempts to moderate and regulate the superpower relationship. Not only did the administration attempt to engineer a transition from confrontation to negotiation, but under the guidance of the President's National Security Adviser, Henry Kissinger, it also placed its actions within a conceptual framework which was more comprehensive and coherent than anything articulated by its predecessors.

That it was the Nixon administration which crystallised and developed detente as the centre-piece of American foreign policy, however, was rather surprising. Nixon had been a virulent anti-communist and the scourge of domestic liberals, while Kissinger had established his reputation as a leading strategic analyst through a series of prescriptive studies outlining how the United States might develop more effective strategies to contain the Soviet Union. They were not the most obvious figures to embark upon a policy of detente with either the Soviet Union or the People's Republic of China. Their policy can be understood, however, as a response to both short-term imperatives and long-term changes in the international system. The Nixon administration operated in circumstances which compelled a reappraisal of US foreign policy. As Hyland commented,

> Richard Nixon came to office faced with the most disastrous international situation any president had confronted since Pearl Harbor. In the winter of 1969 America desperately needed a new foreign policy and a new strategy to cope with the global power of the Soviet Union. The first priority was to end the war in Vietnam, but to do so while preserving an international position strong enough to deal with both Russia and China after the war ended.[29]

The policy of detente was an attempt to meet both these objectives. Nixon and Kissinger hoped that *rapprochement* with Beijing and Moscow would dilute support for Hanoi, thereby encouraging it to negotiate an end to the war.[30] At the same time the new administration attempted to provide a degree of coherence and continuity in United States policy in a period when the domestic pressures for retrenchment from overseas commitments were almost overwhelming.

When President Nixon took office, he did not bring with him a fully elaborated policy of detente. His approach to the Soviet Union was characterised by improvisation as well as design, and difficulties and setbacks were encountered along the way. For all this, the policy can be understood as an exercise in both damage limitation and opportunity exploitation – and in many respects was a mirror image of Soviet policy. As well as being a strategy for limiting the dangers inherent in the Soviet–American relationship in a period of relative American weakness and Soviet strength, the Nixon administration's pursuit of detente was simultaneously a response to domestic pressures and the demands of alliance management, and an attempt to exploit the opportunities that opened up as a result of the dilemmas and problems which confronted Moscow during the late 1960s and early 1970s.

The fundamental challenge for the new administration was how to maintain America's global role and ensure its continued ability to compete with the Soviet Union even though the domestic base of United States foreign policy had severely eroded. By 1968 the bipartisan consensus in favour of containment which had been forged under Truman and maintained under Eisenhower had disintegrated as a result of the pressures of the Vietnam War. Although there were some defections from the consensus on the Right (for example, by those who advocated a policy of maximum force in Vietnam), the more important defection was that of the liberal Democrats. Not only had this group provided much of the base for cold war internationalism but it had also supported the pre-eminence of the Presidency and a deferential stance by Congress. This changed in the 1960s, especially in the Senate. The Chairman of the Foreign Relations Committee, Senator Fulbright, who had been one of the great defenders of Presidential prerogatives, completely reversed his stance as a result of the intervention of 1965 in the Dominican Republic and Lyndon Johnson's escalation of the Vietnam war. Other Democrats had also become unhappy at the limited congressional role in foreign policy – and were discomfited even more by the Johnson administration's arguments that the Tonkin Gulf Resolution of 1964 had provided a 'functional equivalent' of a congressional declaration of war. This defection from the cold war consensus was apparent during the Johnson administration, but was held in check partly by the loyalty of Democratic senators to a Democratic President and partly by Johnson's skill in dealing with recalcitrant legislators.

The election of Richard Nixon not only removed the constraint of party loyalty but brought into the White House a figure who had long been anathema to the liberals. Furthermore, after his inauguration, Nixon faced a Congress in which both houses remained firmly under the control of the Democrats, in which there was growing sentiment for a reassertion of rights and prerogatives *vis-à-vis* the Presidency, and in which he had little personal popularity.

The predominant mood amongst the liberals was for restriction and retrenchment. Successive Presidents, it was felt, had abused their freedom from congressional restraint and pursued unsustainable global policies. John Kennedy's inaugural address had symbolised a crusading spirit which was shared by many liberals in the early 1960s but which failed to count the costs of American policy. By the time of the inauguration of Richard Nixon that spirit had evaporated, and in the view of many liberal Democrats, the United States was paying too high a price and bearing too many burdens in support of states whose commitment to freedom and democracy was not always self-evident. Containment had become tainted.

The implications of this were felt far beyond the liberals on Capitol Hill. By the late 1960s there was a general sense of exhaustion and disillusionment with overseas obligations, especially those involving the use of the US armed forces, and the desire for retrenchment was powerful. Indeed, there were indications that US policy might be following the familiar historical pattern in which periods of extensive international involvement had resulted in disappointment and disillusionment, and been followed by periods of introversion.[31] The conviction of moral rectitude which had sustained American internationalism throughout the cold war period had been replaced by misgivings about policies which exhibited a serious disproportion between ends and means and which had exacted an unacceptable price in lives and resources.

It was also believed, especially but not exclusively among the liberals, that American policy had become too militaristic, thereby distorting national priorities. National welfare, it was argued, was being sacrificed to the ever-growing demands of national security. It seemed to the critics that little could or would be done to deal with the growing problems of poverty, unrest and urban decay so long as the United States continued its traditional cold war policies.

The new administration, therefore, found itself under considerable pressure to modify American policies. As well as the demands for immediate withdrawal from Vietnam, there were also calls for a scaling down of American commitments elsewhere. Military policies and programmes were subjected to closer and more critical scrutiny than ever before, and weapons systems such as the Anti-Ballistic Missile encountered significant resistance in Congress. Funding for the ABM, in fact, was only secured after a series of extraordinarily close votes.

This opposition to new weapons systems reflected serious and informed concerns about their impact on strategic stability. Indeed, the battle in Congress over the ABM mirrored that which had taken place in the Johnson administration when Secretary of Defense McNamara fought against deployment of a system which, in his view, although technically unsound, would give an added intensity to the Soviet–American competition in armaments. Yet there was also an element of self-flagellation in the American national security debate of the late 1960s and early 1970s. The doubts over US actions in Vietnam helped to undermine the moral certitude that had provided the basis for two decades of cold war policies. If US policy in Vietnam had been so mistaken, perhaps its policies towards the Soviet Union had been similarly misguided.

Such doubts and questions had a profound impact on the eastern establishment which had dominated foreign policy-making for most of the postwar period and done much to sustain the cold war policies of the United States. As Kissinger has noted, by 1969 the establishment was in a state of disarray and demoralisation.

> The war in Indochina was the culmination of the disappointments of a decade that had opened with the clarion call of a resurgent idealism and ended with assassinations, racial and social discord, and radicalized politics .... The collapse of these high aspirations shattered the self-confidence without which Establishments flounder.[32]

The result of all this was uncertainty and lack of consensus over the future direction of US foreign policy. The Truman Doctrine had established the framework for American policy in the postwar period and had set the parameters for the foreign policy debate. Subsequent debate revolved around differences over means; the importance of containment was simply taken for granted. In the late 1960s, however, the debate over foreign and security policy reached a new intensity as the objectives of United States policy were increasingly called into question. The new administration regarded with concern what it saw as the resurgence of isolationist sentiment and a widespread desire in Congress and among the public to abandon America's international obligations. Although many of those who were castigated as isolationists were in fact demanding no more than a 'discerning internationalism', the administration saw itself as holding the line against a new isolationism, and the virtual abandonment of containment.

The disintegration of the consensus, while posing problems for the administration, also offered opportunities. These were increased by the fact that Nixon's reputation as a cold warrior helped to neutralise the Right, which had hitherto acted as a powerful inhibition against any far-reaching reappraisal of American policy. This made it possible for him to initiate a withdrawal from Vietnam, albeit one that was marked by escalatory measures to protect American credibility, and also gave him a freedom of action in relation to both Moscow and Beijing that had been denied to his Democratic predecessors. In the late 1960s and early 1970s there was a unique constellation of circumstances in

American domestic politics – pressures for retrenchment, a weakened Right and a hard-line administration – which provided a permissive environment for an attempt to go beyond the rather tentative and compartmentalised detente of the Johnson administration. On the one side, the forces inhibiting such a move were neutralised, at least temporarily, thereby providing a window of opportunity; on the other, the pressures for retrenchment and reappraisal made it imperative to move through this window.

It was also acknowledged that there might be economic advantages in such a move. By the late 1960s it was clear that the economic resurgence of Western Europe and Japan challenged American hegemony. The United States was suffering from a deteriorating balance of payments, and the pressure on the dollar contributed to demands that the American military presence overseas be considerably reduced. Furthermore, Western Europe in particular had few inhibitions about expanded trade with the Soviet Union and Eastern Europe. In these circumstances, the restrictive stance of the United States seemed both futile and self-defeating. America's competitors had gained access to a lucrative market which government policy denied to American manufacturers. Increasing pressure from American commercial interests for an easing of restrictions, therefore, was inevitable. The rationale for a less restrictive policy was outlined by the Secretary of Commerce in a 1972 government document on the United States–Soviet commercial relationship:

> The increased availability of high technology exports elsewhere rendered some of our original curbs on exports to the Soviet Union increasingly anachronistic. The real loser from these particular constraints would increasingly have been the US producer and worker, not the Soviet consumer or the Soviet economy. There comes a point at which we must face the fact that business is business, and, if it is going to go on in any event, we might as well have a piece of the action.[33]

This more relaxed approach to East–West trade had already been evident in the Export Administration Act of 1969. Important as this was, however, too much should not be made of it. Although the US business community was anxious to increase trade with the Soviet bloc, economic considerations seem to have been less important in the calculations of the Nixon administration than they were in the thinking of the Soviet leadership. Indeed, Nixon and Kissinger saw expanded trade more in terms of its political advantages than its economic benefits: it was an important bargaining lever which could be used to influence Soviet behaviour. Expanded trade might have provided an additional incentive for detente, but was less important than the domestic pressures for reappraisal and retrenchment.

These pressures were reinforced by the imperatives of alliance management. NATO had formally acknowledged the importance of East–West detente in December 1967. The Harmel Report on future tasks committed the members 'to pursue the search for progress towards a more stable relationship in which the underlying political issues can be solved'.[34] Furthermore, it accepted that this was to have a high priority – military security and a policy of detente were regarded as complementary rather than contradictory. The Europeans were anxious for the process of detente envisaged in the Harmel Report to continue, and in view of Nixon's reputation as a cold warrior, were naturally concerned about his election as President. These anxieties were expressed by many of the NATO allies during Nixon's visit to Europe in early 1969. According to Kissinger, most allied governments thought the President 'needed prodding on the desirability of relaxing tensions'.[35] This posed dilemmas for the new administration. As Kissinger summed up the problem:

> If we were perceived to block detente, we would lose the support of our West European allies, who would then speed up their own contacts with the East, with no co-ordinated strategy; they would be too weak to resist simultaneous domestic and Soviet pressures. We found ourselves in the paradoxical position that we would have to take a leadership role in East–West relations if we wanted to hold the Alliance together and establish some ground rules for East–West contacts.[36]

Although Kissinger seems to exaggerate the extent to which the Europeans were pulling a reluctant United States towards detente (after all, the Federal Republic's Ostpolitik was in part an attempt to avoid diplomatic isolation as the United States and France gradually moved towards a less acrimonious relationship with Moscow), it does appear that the White House perceived the alternatives as either a managed detente in which the United States played the central role, or an unmanaged situation in which the Soviet Union, by the selective exploitation of the longing for detente in Western Europe, would be able to drive wedges between the members of NATO.

Domestic considerations and alliance concerns, therefore, worked in the same direction. The vigorous adoption of a detente policy by the new President offered the best chance of restoring consensus at home and maintaining harmony in the alliance. It was also seen as a way of coping with longer-term changes in the international system, the effect of which had been to reduce American predominance *vis-à-vis* both allies and adversaries. During the late 1960s and early 1970s the United States was increasingly aware of the limits of its power. This was evident not only in Vietnam and superpower relations, but also in trade and economic matters. The threat posed by the erosion of American strategic superiority over the Soviet Union was accompanied by a challenge to American economic hegemony from Western Europe and Japan. These changes, and their implications, had been discussed by Kissinger in a study entitled 'Central Issues in American Foreign Policy' which appeared in 1968 and which presaged the analyses, the concepts, and even much of the language that were later adopted by the Nixon administration.[37]

It was not only Kissinger, however, who recognised the need for flexibility and change. Although much of Richard Nixon's career had been based upon his unremitting hostility towards communism both at home and overseas, in an article which he wrote for *Foreign Affairs* in 1967 there were some signs of a more pragmatic approach, especially towards the Chinese People's Republic.[38] Yet Nixon remained suspicious of those groups in American society which, he felt, were insufficiently tough in dealing with America's adversaries. Deep antipathies towards the State Department and the Central Intelligence Agency made him determined to centralise foreign policy-making in the White House. This was perhaps the most important working principle of his administration, and one on which he had the full agreement of his National Security Adviser, Henry Kissinger. Some of Kissinger's most celebrated writings as a Harvard professor had concerned the shortcomings of bureaucracies. On this and on many other issues the President and his major foreign policy adviser were in full agreement. Although Nixon arrived at his conclusions intuitively while Kissinger engaged in a longer process of intellectual and conceptual analysis, there seem to have been few, if any major divergences between the two men. As a result, it was not always possible to discern the source of the major initiatives on foreign policy which took place between 1969 and 1972. Nevertheless, it seems clear that the intellectual rationale for much of the administration's 'grand design' was provided by Kissinger.

Kissinger is sometimes described as a contemporary equivalent of statesmen such as Metternich or Castlereagh, whose achievements he both celebrated and dissected in his doctoral thesis, later published as *A World Restored*.[39] Although such analogies are over-drawn, they make clear that Kissinger was in the European tradition of diplomacy. *Realpolitik*, manoeuvre and calculations of self-interest were, in his perspective, the keys to a successful foreign policy. Less attention was given to a state's internal characteristics than to its foreign policy behaviour. This made possible a pragmatic approach to the Soviet Union which de-emphasised ideological differences, downgraded the need for change in the Soviet system and seized opportunities for specific accommodation.[40] Such an approach was alien to the traditional American approach to international affairs, which was highly moralistic, assumed that there was a natural harmony of interests among the members of the international system and that any state which disturbed this harmony was inherently evil, and saw internal change in the Soviet Union as a precondition for accommodation. In other respects, though, Kissinger was firmly in the American cold war tradition. He accepted that the Soviet Union had to be contained and, like the President, he was acutely concerned over American credibility and toughness: appearances were important in international politics, and the image of the United States held by others would do much to influence their actions.

If Kissinger's approach was a hybrid of traditional European diplomacy and American machismo, he also brought into the administration an acute sensitivity to long-term changes in the international system. Although much attention has been given to his writings on the nineteenth century, the analyses he did shortly before his appointment as Presidential Adviser are perhaps more relevant and revealing. In the 1968 paper referred to above, Kissinger identified several major developments in the international system which demanded a response from the United States. He contended that the world had changed in ways which challenged the pre-eminence of the two superpowers. The existence of military bipolarity had both facilitated and encouraged the development of political multipolarity. Such a trend could not be stopped. Nor was it desirable that it should be:

> If the United States remains the trustee of every non-Communist area, it will exhaust its psychological resources. No country can act wisely simultaneously in every part of the globe at every moment of time. A more pluralistic world – especially in relationships with friends – is profoundly in our long-term interest. Political multipolarity, while difficult to get used to, is the precondition for a new period of creativity. Painful as it may be to admit, we would benefit from a counterweight that would discipline our occasional impetuosity and, by supplying historical perspective, modify our penchant for abstract and final solutions.[41]

This statement contained the seeds of the emphasis on partnership with allies that was to become a key element in the Nixon Doctrine.

Perhaps even more interesting was Kissinger's analysis of relations with the Soviet Union. His starting point was that in the nuclear age 'even enmity is complex'.[42] The proponents of containment, he argued, had not fully understood this, and referred to negotiating from strength without clear ideas about the substantive issues to be negotiated. On the other side, those who adopted a dovish approach were far too ready to accept changes in the tone of Soviet statements as indicative of changes in substance. Kissinger, in contrast, advocated a realistic but positive approach to improving relations. The realism stemmed from his concern – to be repeated frequently during his period in office – that if there was no penalty for intransigence there would be no incentive for conciliation on the part of the Soviet leadership.[43] Furthermore, it was necessary to focus on concrete issues such as intervention in the Third World or the strategic arms race as part of a long-term approach. As he stated, 'peace will not ... result from one grand settlement but from a long diplomatic process, and this process requires some clarity as to our destination. Confusing foreign policy with psychotherapy deprives us of criteria by which to judge the political foundations of international order.'[44] In other words, a realistic foreign policy would accept the Soviet Union as it was and aim at the creation of a less dangerous international order by patient negotiations on concrete issues.

The notion of a legitimate and stable international order was central to Kissinger's thinking. He also acknowledged that, if order was to be created, the United States would have to adjust its attitudes and its policies: a greater willingness to think in terms of power had to be accompanied by an attempt to relate commitments to interests and define positive goals which would elicit the willing cooperation of others. As he stated, 'our conception of world order must have deeper purposes than stability but greater restraints on our behaviour than would result only if it were approached in a fit of enthusiasm'.[45] This is cryptic language of uncertain interpretation. It appeared to recognise that in relations with the Soviet Union the pursuit of stability was necessary but elusive. US policy had to start from the assumption that relations with the Soviet Union would remain competitive. The problem was to contain within bounds the tensions that were liable to be created by that competition. This required, on both sides, policies of restraint and mutual acceptance of the idea of legitimate or permissible behaviour.

This analysis provided the intellectual framework for Kissinger's attempt to adapt US foreign policy to changes in the international system. It also foreshadowed several important themes in the Nixon administration's foreign policy. The idea of co-opting the Soviet Union to become a willing partner in the international order of the 1970s, for example, was to become a key element in the American approach to detente. Perhaps most important of all, though, Kissinger embraced a view of the Soviet Union which allowed for a diplomacy which was both hard-headed and constructive. As one analyst has pointed out, Kissinger's appraisal of Moscow was flexible rather than immutable.[46] He tried to understand both the strengths and the weaknesses of the Soviet Union, its fears as well as its ambitions. If such appraisals were accurate, then it should be possible to design strategies which would influence the Soviet leadership in directions favourable to the United States. Although Kissinger recognised the erosion of American strategic superiority and saw that the postwar position of political and economic primacy was under challenge, he clearly believed that skilful and creative statesmanship could offset increasing American vulnerability. These ideas were reflected in the development of the new administration's policy towards the Soviet Union.

It is often alleged that the Nixon administration's detente policy was misguided and that it accepted too easily both the rise of Soviet power and the decline of American hegemony. In fact, the administration's approach to detente was cautious and realistic. As William Hyland has pointed out, 'it is ironic that Nixon and Kissinger became identified with the policy of detente. Initially, at least, neither saw a prospect for more than a narrow, limited accommodation with the Soviet Union.'[47] Far from rushing into detente, the administration developed its policy with considerable circumspection. Both the President and Kissinger were determined to link the general reduction of tension with specific negotiations on concrete issues.

This determination not to be rushed into an uncritical detente was reflected in the rejection of the idea that there should be a Soviet–American summit meeting between the period of Nixon's election victory and his inauguration. It was also apparent in the early conversations between Kissinger and key Soviet representatives. The Soviet Union was anxious to open talks on arms limitation – a possibility which had been discussed with the Johnson administration but delayed as a result of the Soviet intervention in Czechoslovakia. Although the new President was prepared to talk about arms limitations, he was not willing to do so until the problems had been fully analysed within his administration. Furthermore, Kissinger made clear that the United States wanted to advance along a much broader front than simply arms control. Moscow was expected to observe restraint in various trouble spots, to be helpful in the Middle East, and to facilitate American attempts to extricate itself from Vietnam. In other words, Kissinger wished detente to be comprehensive, not compartmentalised.

This caution was reflected in an exploratory and rather tentative policy, which lasted until May 1971. During this period the administration developed several major strands in its dealings with Moscow. The first was termed 'linkage'. As Kissinger stated,

We insisted that progress in superpower relations should be made on a broad front. Events in different parts of the world, in our view, were related to each other; even more so Soviet conduct in different parts of the world. We proceeded from the premise that to separate issues into distinct compartments would encourage the Soviet leaders to believe that they could use co-operation in one area as a safety valve while striving for unilateral advantage elsewhere.[48]

Kissinger has also argued that the administration attempted to exert leverage on the Soviet Union by making progress towards a settlement in Vietnam a condition for advance in areas of concern to the Soviet Union. For all this, the linkage concept was not yet fully developed. It was cast in general terms rather than given specific application. The idea of using strength in one bargaining area to compensate for weakness elsewhere was clearly an element in the administration's approach, but one that as yet had more impact at the declaratory level than anywhere else. Initially it meant little more than an American insistence on parallel progress across a range of issues. Gradually, though, it crystallised into a more ambitious idea of attempting to 'use Soviet interest in cooperation in some areas – trade and strategic arms limitation, for example – to encourage cooperation in other areas, or at least to encourage Soviet behaviour that was more in keeping with American interests'.[49] The concern with linkage made the administration reluctant to move too far too fast on economic cooperation, until progress had been made elsewhere.

The second concept emphasised by Kissinger and Nixon was that of concreteness. In Kissinger's 1968 analysis and the early conversations with the Soviets it was emphasised that the United States was not interested simply in an improvement in the tone of the relationship. There were specific differences of interest which had to be reconciled if detente was to be anything more than ephemeral. Nixon and Kissinger were not interested in creating a 'spirit of detente'. Such a spirit could prove as transitory as the 'spirit of Geneva' or 'spirit of Camp David' in the 1950s, yet could help to intensify the congressional assault on the defence budget that was already under way. In the event of a deterioration in the superpower relationship, it was important that the United States should not be vulnerable and exposed. The idea of concreteness was designed in part to prevent this and to ensure that substantive sources of tension were dealt with.

The third element in the Nixon administration's approach was triangular diplomacy.[50] Although the breakdown of the domestic consensus made it difficult for the United States to pursue its traditional military policies, the trend towards multipolarity that

Kissinger, along with many other analysts, had identified offered new opportunities which might compensate for this. The Sino–Soviet split was particularly important in this connection. Although this rift had been public since 1960 it reached a new intensity in 1969 as a result of clashes along the Ussuri River. Both Nixon and Kissinger saw these as providing an incentive for Beijing to become rather more conciliatory towards the United States and accordingly began to pursue a more activist diplomacy towards the Chinese People's Republic. These covert moves culminated in the public announcement of Kissinger's visit to Beijing in July 1971.

The development of triangular diplomacy gave the United States a stronger bargaining position *vis-à-vis* Moscow: it added to Soviet incentives to establish a closer relationship with the United States in order to forestall the emergence of a Sino–American alliance. As a result it gave impetus to the development of Soviet–American detente in 1971 and 1972. Indeed, Hyland has argued that 'Soviet–American relations were altered in this period not by a better understanding, or more contacts, but by a raw change in the balance of power.'[51] If the United States, because of the domestic constraints identified above, was no longer able to keep decisively ahead, in traditional military terms, of a Soviet Union which had eroded American strategic superiority, it could compensate for this through diplomatic manoeuvre and by moving towards a more regulated relationship.

A fourth element in the Nixon administration's approach to Moscow was the principle of restraint. This was related to both the ideas of concreteness and linkage. In emphasising restraint, Kissinger, in essence, was demanding that the Soviet Union observe certain limits in its foreign policy. The Soviet government would demonstrate by its deeds whether it was or was not seriously committed to the reduction of tension in superpower relations. In this sense restraint was the natural extension of concreteness: the Soviet willingness to negotiate on specific issues was one of the tests of Moscow's commitment to a genuine detente; Soviet restraint was the other. There was also a close connection with the linkage concept, especially when this was developed more fully and explicitly. What had begun as an insistence on parallelism in different areas of negotiation was broadened to incorporate the notion of inducements and penalties – notions that had been evident in Kissinger's writings in 1968.

This notion of restraint was probably the single most crucial element in the Nixon–Kissinger policy of detente, and can be regarded as a sophisticated form of containment. The Nixon administration's break with past policies, therefore, was not as great as critics suggested. This was obscured partly by the fact that in 1968 Kissinger had severely criticised containment and partly by the impact of the Vietnam war, which rendered it politically impossible to continue the traditional policy of containment through military strength. Yet the objective of preventing Soviet expansionism was not abandoned. Instead of accomplishing this through deterrence and military intervention, the United States would now encourage the Soviet Union to observe a policy of self-restraint, or what Stanley Hoffmann has termed 'self-containment'.[52] The means had changed, but the ends remained what they had been since the promulgation of the Truman Doctrine in 1947. Far from representing the end of containment, therefore, detente appeared to offer a way of maintaining it at a reduced cost. As John Lewis Gaddis has pointed out, detente 'was a means of updating and reinvigorating containment'.[53] The implication is that, in spite of the demands of critics who, as a result of Vietnam, challenged the whole thrust of American cold war policy, the Nixon–Kissinger reappraisal was modest. Innovation in the means of foreign policy disguised a fundamental continuity in objectives.

A second observation about the notion of restraint follows from this. Soviet restraint was vital because the United States was so constrained in its responses – the military option was no longer readily available. By attempting to induce Soviet restraint through economic incentives and implied diplomatic penalties (for example, closer links with China), the United States was attempting to compensate for weaknesses in one area by playing on its strengths elsewhere. Once again this had been foreshadowed by Kissinger's 1968 analysis, in which he noted the growing discrepancy between military power and political influence.[54] It was only a small step from this to attempt to wield more fully the non-military sources of political influence.

A third observation on the notion of restraint is that it was conceived as a permanent indicator of the Soviet commitment to detente. The actions of the Soviet Union would demonstrate either that it was serious about detente, or that it was not prepared to exercise the degree of restraint and responsibility necessary to sustain the detente process. Kissinger hoped that Moscow could gradually be persuaded to behave with restraint, but recognised that this was something that Washington would have to encourage, through both penalties and inducements, and which Moscow would have to prove. It was certainly not something which would happen naturally or which could simply be taken for granted.

There were few illusions in Kissinger's assessment of the Soviet Union. He was not relying on Soviet altruism or goodwill. Although he hoped, by means of appropriate incentives, to create a Soviet vested interest in the continuing observance of restraint, he was conscious of the possibility of failure. And in the event of failure, he thought that the United States would be entitled to the backing of its friends. It was here that American policy towards the Soviet Union connected with the policy towards its allies that became known as the Nixon Doctrine. The notion that America's allies should take a greater share of the burdens and responsibilities of Western security was not new. Burden-sharing had been an issue in the Western alliance from its inception. Furthermore, the idea that the allies should provide the local ground forces for both deterrence and defence while the United States concentrated its efforts on strategic and tactical air power and nuclear weapons was one of the considerations underlying the 'pactomania' of John Foster Dulles. The 'Vietnamisation' programme was the most immediate example of a new division of labour designed to limit the costs of American commitment. In the Atlantic alliance too the pressures for greater burden-sharing by the Europeans became increasingly insistent. They were reinforced by congressional demands for American troop reductions, led by Senator Mansfield and supported by those liberals most concerned about the over-extension of American power.

Perhaps most important of all, outside the NATO area, was the cultivation of regional powers who would act as America's proxies and bear the burden of containment in specific regions. The Shah of Iran, for example, was encouraged to buy large quantities of American weapons and become Washington's 'surrogate gendarme' in the Persian Gulf. The relationship between this process and detente was complex but important. The creation of regional powers was an attempt to ensure that the American retrenchment made necessary by Vietnam would not leave behind a series of political and military vacuums which would virtually invite Soviet expansionism. This process of replacing American power by that of friendly states presupposed Soviet restraint and readiness to maintain detente, at least in the short term. As one analyst has observed,

> American post-Vietnam foreign policy was premised upon the belief that the establishment of a new relationship with the United States' Communist great-power rivals would create a favourable political atmosphere so as to facilitate the orderly devolution of American power to incipient regional powers. The resulting stability along the periphery would, in turn, feed back into the central balance and thereby sustain the momentum of detente through the preservation of mutual trust. In this way, each component of the Nixon–Kissinger strategy – that is, detente and the Nixon Doctrine – would serve as the instrumentality for the achievement of the other.[55]

The implication of all this is that in one sense, at least, Kissinger owed as much to George Kennan, the author of the containment concept, as he did to Metternich, Castlereagh and Bismarck, who are usually held up as the models for his diplomacy. If the ends of American policy were less of a departure from the past than they sometimes appeared, however, there was greater novelty in the means. Kissinger was attempting to encourage Soviet restraint through several mutually reinforcing devices. As well as inducements for good behaviour and penalties for lack of restraint, there was also an attempt to limit the opportunities for Moscow to make unilateral gains and thereby reduce the temptations for it to behave in a manner that was inconsistent with the restraint appropriate to and necessary for genuine detente.

In short, the Nixon–Kissinger policy can be understood primarily as an attempt to minimise the impact of the domestic pressures for retrenchment by co-opting both allies and adversaries into a new foreign policy design. It was both conciliatory and competitive, and was based in large part on Kissinger's understanding of long-term trends in the international system. In the circumstances, it was probably the best alternative available, as it held out the prospect that containment could be maintained and a degree of restraint imposed on Soviet behaviour at minimum cost to the United States and countries dependent on the United States for their security. In essence, the detente strategy was part of an attempt to come to terms with the erosion of the Pax Americana in a world conscious of the growth of Soviet military power: if the United States could no longer maintain an unchallengeable lead in an unrestrained strategic and geopolitical competition, the best alternative was to establish more stringent and extensive rules for that competition. The success of this approach, however, depended crucially on the Soviet Union having a conception of detente which was at least compatible with if not identical to that of the United States.

Assessment

In the late 1960s and early 1970s both superpowers faced problems which impelled them to move towards a less dangerous relationship and to permit compartmentalised cooperation. Yet there was not a comprehensive convergence of interest, and even less of outlook, between Moscow and Washington. The superpowers embraced detente not only for different but also, to some extent, for contradictory or incompatible reasons. Although each side believed that the handling of some of its problems would be easier in conditions of detente, it also believed that detente would make it possible to exploit the problems of the adversary. The difficulties facing each superpower were seen by the adversary primarily as opportunities, giving rise to what might be termed an 'opportunities–constraints dichotomy'.

This dichotomy was perhaps most apparent in the case of China. The Soviet Union saw the deepening Sino–Soviet split as something which at the very least required American neutrality and, if possible, the creation of an anti-Chinese condominium. For the United States, however, the calculations were very different. Triangular diplomacy opened up new opportunities to play off one communist power against the other. The 'China card', which was to be played most explicitly by the Carter administration, was implicit in American policy from the opening with China onwards.

Another area where a similar dichotomy existed was trade. The Soviet Union saw the political relationship with the West as something to be modified, in part at least, for economic reasons. In the Soviet view, trade was mutually beneficial and, since Moscow was seeking collaborative arrangements with, rather than unilateral aid from, Washington, no attempt should be made to attach political conditions. The United States, however, recognising that the Soviet need was greater than its own, believed that trade should be exploited for diplomatic and political purposes. In both these areas Soviet difficulties or constraints were American opportunities.

In other areas, the opportunities–constraints dichotomy worked in the opposite direction. This was particularly true at the strategic level where, as Raymond Garthoff has pointed out, the gradual emergence of parity held 'radically different implications' for the two superpowers.[56] The Soviet Union saw the emergence of strategic parity as 'a tremendous achievement, an unprecedented advance over the inferiority which had characterized the entire two-thirds of a century of Soviet rule', and something which naturally brought with it considerable political benefits. For the United States, however, the erosion of American supremacy was unwelcome and unpalatable. This is hardly surprising:

> parity undoubtedly ... represented a situation of less advantage than in the preceding era of American superiority, an era that encompassed the entire third of a century since its assumption of a continuing active global role at the end of World War II. The United States had not sought its superiority and hegemonic role ... Nevertheless, it had become accustomed to its exercise and fruits.[57]

Although the United States was prepared to concede equality to the Soviet Union in the negotiations on limiting strategic armaments, therefore, it was reluctant to accept that strategic parity brought with it any additional 'political entitlement'.[58]

Implicit in the conceptual basis of the detente policy elaborated by Kissinger – and especially the notion of linkage – was the assumption that Washington could dictate the terms on which detente proceeded. The emphasis on managing Soviet power, disciplining Soviet behaviour and restraining Soviet actions revealed that, in spite of domestic constraints, 'primacy remained an American goal. American leaders were playing bear tamers and would provide the honey and the sticks that would manoeuvre the bear into the stable structure.'[59] The flaw in this was that the Soviet Union had aspirations and objectives of its own which were not easily reconcilable with the stable structure that Kissinger envisaged. Deference to Washington was no longer compulsory for the Soviet Union, and parity would mean little unless it brought increased political influence, especially in areas of instability in the Third World. Moscow wanted its place in the sun, and felt that the United States should acknowledge and accept the Soviet Union as an equal with an equal right to intervene in regional issues.

The tension between Soviet and American conceptions was complete: the Nixon administration saw detente as a means of disciplining Soviet power; Moscow saw it as offering new opportunities for exercising this power – and doing so safely. The situation was complicated by the fact that the new sense of Soviet assertiveness was tinged with self-doubt, the removal of which depended upon the United States, while the decline of American hegemony brought with it a shift in tactics rather than an abandonment of American perceptions of itself as the dominant power in the international system.

In view of these differences of attitude and approach to detente, its decline in the mid and late 1970s is hardly surprising. The detente of the 1970s was flawed from the outset. What is perhaps most remarkable, therefore, is that the interests, objectives and conceptions of detente of the two superpowers overlapped sufficiently to enable them to move from a minimalist detente in the mid and late 1960s to a more far-reaching attempt to regulate and moderate their relationship in the early 1970s. The way in which they did this is the theme of the next chapter.

Notes

1. R. Garthoff, *Detente and Confrontation* (Washington, DC: The Brookings Institution, 1985), p. 38.

2. See A. Ulam, *Dangerous Relations* (New York: Oxford University Press, 1983), p. 61.

3. J. Nogee and R. Donaldson, *Soviet Foreign Policy Since World War II* (New York: Pergamon, 1984), p. 250.

4. M. Goldman, *Detente and Dollars* (New York: Basic Books, 1975), p. 31.

5. B. Parrot, 'Soviet Foreign Policy, Internal Politics, and Trade with the West' in B. Parrot (ed.), *Trade, Technology and Soviet–American Relations* (Bloomington: Indiana University Press, 1985), p. 36.

6. L. Volin quoted in R.B. Porter, *The US–USSR Grain Agreement* (Cambridge: Cambridge University Press, 1984), p. 9.

7. D. Dyker, 'Soviet Industry in its International Context' in C. Keeble (ed.), *The Soviet State* (London: Gower, 1985), p. 76.

8. Parrot, op. cit., p. 40.
9. P. Volten, *Brezhnev's Peace Programme* (Boulder, Col.: Westview Press, 1983), p. 67.
10. Quoted in A. Whiting, 'Sino–Soviet Relations: What Next?' *Annals of the American Academy* (Nov. 1984), p. 143.
11. See Garthoff, op. cit., p. 208.
12. Ibid., p. 203.
13. A. Shevchenko, *Breaking with Moscow* (New York: Knopf, 1985), p. 164.
14. Garthoff, op. cit., p. 209.
15. W.G. Hyland, *Mortal Rivals: Superpower Relations from Nixon to Reagan* (New York: Random House, 1987), p. 26.
16. See *Pravda*, 18 March 1969.
17. H. Gelman, *The Brezhnev Politburo and the Decline of Detente* (Ithaca, NY: Cornell University Press, 1984), p. 80.
18. See M. MccGwire, *Military Objectives in Soviet Foreign Policy* (Washington, DC: The Brookings Institution, 1987), p. 44.
19. Quoted in C.D. Blacker, 'The Kremlin and Detente' in A.L. George, *Managing US–Soviet Rivalry* (Boulder, Col., Westview Press, 1983), p. 125.
20. B. Ponomarev and A.Gromyko (eds), *Soviet Foreign Policy*, vol. 2 (Moscow: Progress, 1980), p. 418.
21. *Current Digest of the Soviet Press 1971*, vol. 23, no. 12, p. 11.
22. H. Haftendorn, *Security and Detente: Conflicting Priorities in German Foreign Policy* (New York: Praeger, 1985), p. 179.
23. Ibid., p. 189.
24. Ibid., p. 192.
25. L. Freedman, 'The United States Factor' in E. Moreton and G. Segal (eds), *Soviet Strategy Towards Western Europe* (London: Allen & Unwin, 1984), p. 94.
26. Quoted in G. Arbatov, *Cold War or Detente?* (London: Zed Books, 1983), p. 12.
27. L. Brezhnev, *Izbrannye Proizvedeniya*, vol. 1 (Moscow: Politizdat, 1981), p. 1.
28. Henry Trofimenko, 'The Third World and the US–Soviet Competition – A Soviet View', *Foreign Affairs*, vol. 59 (1981), p. 1027.
29. Hyland, op. cit., p. 3.
30. Ibid., p. 23.
31. See J.E. Holmes, *The Mood/Interest Theory of American Foreign Policy* (Lexington, Ky.: University Press of Kentucky, 1985).
32. H. Kissinger, *White House Years* (Boston: Little, Brown, 1979), p. 297.
33. P.G. Peterson, *US–Soviet Commercial Relations in a New Era* (Washington, DC: Government Printing Office, 1972), p. 13.
34. The Harmel Report is reproduced as Appendix 6 in *NATO: Facts and Figures* (Brussels NATO Information Service, 1976), p. 336.
35. H. Kissinger, *White House Years* (Boston: Little, Brown, 1979), p. 79.
36. Ibid., p. 94.
37. 'The Central Issues of American Policy' was a contribution to *Agenda for the Nation* (Washington, DC: The Brookings Institution, 1968), and was reproduced in H. Kissinger, *American Foreign Policy* (London: Weidenfeld and Nicolson, 1969). It is cited hereafter as *American Foreign Policy*.
38. R. Nixon, 'Asia After Vietnam', *Foreign Affairs*, vol. 46, no. 1 (Oct. 1967), pp. 111–25.
39. H. Kissinger, *A World Restored* (London: Victor Gollancz, 1977).
40. See Hyland, op. cit., p. 23.

41. *American Foreign Policy*, p. 74.

42. Ibid., p. 85.

43. Ibid., p. 89.

44. Ibid., p. 89.

45. Ibid., p. 94.

46. See H. Starr, *Henry Kissinger: Perceptions of International Politics* (Lexington, Ky.: University Press of Kentucky, 1984), especially pp. 58–9, which compare Kissinger's image of the enemy with that of John Foster Dulles.

47. W. Hyland, *Soviet–American Relations: A New Cold War?* Rand Paper R-2763-FF/RC (Santa Monica, Cal.: RAND, May 1981), p. 22.

48. Kissinger, *White House Years*, p. 129.

49. S. Sloan, *Fundamentals of Nuclear Arms Control: Part VIII – Linkage: Nuclear Arms Control in the Broader Context of United States–Soviet Relations*, Report prepared for the Committee on Foreign Affairs, US House of Representatives by the Congressional Research Service, Jan. 1986 (Washington, DC: Government Printing Office, 1986), p. 5.

50. See Garthoff, op. cit., pp. 199–261.

51. Hyland, *Soviet–American Relations: A New Cold War?*, p. 25.

52. S. Hoffmann, *Dead Ends* (Cambridge, Mass.: Ballinger, 1983), p. 90.

53. J.L. Gaddis, 'The Rise, Fall and Future of Detente', *Foreign Affairs*, vol. 62, no. 2 (Winter 1983/84), pp. 354–77 at p. 359.

54. *American Foreign Policy*, pp. 59–60.

55. R.S. Litwak, *Detente and the Nixon Doctrine* (Cambridge: Cambridge University Press, 1984), p. 54.

56. Garthoff, op. cit., p. 55.

57. Ibid., p. 55.

58. L. Freedman, op. cit., p. 99.

59. S. Hoffmann, *Primacy or World Order* (New York: McGraw-Hill, 1978), p. 46.

4
The Substance of Detente

From 1971 to 1973 the incompatibilities between the Soviet and American approaches to detente were obscured by a superpower dialogue more ambitious, more productive and more positive than anything which had gone before. The attempt to move beyond a minimalist detente had four distinct but reinforcing elements. The first was a major effort to regulate the arms competition between the superpowers through the opening of Strategic Arms Limitation Talks. A second, and often overlooked, facet of this maximalist detente was the attempt to expand the element of cooperation in the superpower relationship so that it embraced not simply crisis management but attempts at crisis prevention or crisis avoidance. The third element was the expansion of East–West contacts, especially but not exclusively trade. For Henry Kissinger in particular, expanded cultural relations and symbolic cooperative ventures in non-political areas such as science and technology were important as a way of giving the Soviet government and the Soviet intelligentsia a vested interest in detente.

The fourth, and in many respects the most important, component of detente was the normalisation process in Europe. The European dimension of detente represented an amalgamation of two separate strands of development as the superpower detente of the early 1970s coincided with the longer, slower, more complex and more sustained search for detente in Europe. Europe had been the main theatre of the cold war, and the attempt to deal with some of the anomalies resulting from the absence of a peace settlement at the end of World War II was long overdue. The German Treaties, the Quadripartite Agreement on Berlin, and the Conference on Security and Cooperation in Europe reduced these anomalies and marked a limited but enduring improvement in East–West relations which lowered the risk of superpower confrontations in the region.

If European detente and superpower detente were reinforcing strands in the developing detente of the early 1970s, their convergence was only temporary. Both de Gaulle's focus on Europe from the Atlantic to the Urals and the West German Ostpolitik predated the Nixon–Kissinger initiatives towards the Soviet Union and China. Having started earlier, the quest for detente in Europe was pursued more tenaciously than superpower detente. It also lasted longer. The high point of detente in Europe was the Helsinki Agreement of 1975. By that time Soviet–American detente was encountering serious difficulties. After the peak of superpower detente was reached at the Summits in Moscow and Washington in 1972 and 1973, there was an erosion of support, especially in Washington. In Western Europe, on the other hand, there was neither the euphoria about detente that existed, if only briefly, in the United States nor the criticism and ultimate rejection of detente that occurred in Washington.

To some extent the American reaction stemmed from unrealistic expectations. What made these so surprising was that the path to superpower detente was not easy. Before looking in more detail at the concrete measures taken by Soviet and American leaders and by European governments, therefore, it is necessary to examine the manoeuvring that took place prior to Nixon's visit to Moscow in 1972.

Slow Progress to the Summit

The movement of the two superpowers from a minimalist to a maximalist detente was tentative and hesitant. Soviet and American concerns and objectives diverged, and the task of reconciling their common desire for a *modus vivendi* with their different preoccupations, vulnerabilities and interests was not easy. On both sides there was also a legacy of distrust from the cold war period. Twenty-five years of hostility tempered only by deterrence could not be dispelled immediately. Furthermore, despite their interests in establishing a more regulated relationship, the superpowers had other interests and objectives, some of which worked against detente.

In the aftermath of the Ussuri River clashes in 1969 between Soviet and Chinese forces, both Washington and Moscow saw new opportunities in Soviet–American relations. Arms control negotiations, which had been discussed for some time, opened in November 1969, and the superpowers appeared to be moving in ways which justified Nixon's rhetoric about the era of negotiation. Difficulties remained, however, and 1970 proved to be a year of mixed fortunes. The United States wanted a summit meeting between Nixon and the Soviet leadership, but the Russians were not responsive. Moscow reluctantly agreed to American and Canadian participation in a conference on security and cooperation in Europe, but its main objective appeared to be the creation of an anti-Chinese alliance, something that the United States was unwilling to accept. Furthermore, several events made a Summit increasingly remote, although significantly they did not interfere with the negotiations on strategic arms control. These events brought to the fore cold war attitudes, especially on the part of Nixon and

Kissinger, who believed that the Soviet Union was looking to take advantage of the domestic travails in the United States. Indeed, in late September 1970 the superpowers appeared to be on the verge of crises over both the Middle East and Cuba.

The Middle East had been a source of concern to the superpowers for some time. Both had important interests at stake in the region, and both had commitments to client states that they were unwilling to disavow. At the same time, there was an awareness of the dangers inherent in the region, and Kissinger occasionally described it as the modern equivalent of the Balkans in which the great powers might be dragged into a confrontation on opposing sides.

In 1970, however, the immediate source of tension was not the Arab–Israeli conflict as such but strife within the Arab world. The Palestinian guerrillas, who had emerged as a formidable force after the failure of the Arab states in the 1967 war against Israel, increasingly used Jordan as a base for their activities. In September 1970 they hijacked and destroyed several planes and compelled King Hussein to move against them. Although the United States provided a display of support for Hussein by reinforcing the Sixth Fleet, this failed to deter a Syrian invasion of Jordan in support of the Palestinians. In response, the Nixon administration considered whether the United States itself should intervene or rely on Israel to do so. The latter option was preferred, and the administration made clear to the Israelis that the United States would try to prevent any Soviet interference – a commitment which was regarded by Secretary of State Rogers as too open-ended.

In the event, the commitment was not challenged. The Soviet Union had been extremely cautious, if opportunist, from the outset and Soviet military advisers had not crossed the border into Jordan with the Syrian forces. Realising the dangers of Israeli intervention, the Soviet Union now pressed the Syrians into withdrawal. In doing this it was simply continuing its cautionary policy. For the Nixon administration, however, the Syrian withdrawal was a vindication of the policy of standing firm. The episode revealed the tendency of both Nixon and Kissinger to see regional conflicts through the prism of Soviet–American relations. From this perspective, demonstrations of resolve were a way of emphasising to the Russians that, despite America's domestic problems, it was still prepared to defend its interests. In fact, as Garthoff has suggested, it was not clear that the Jordan Crisis was a Soviet–American contest, as the Soviet Union was only marginally and indirectly involved.[1] Nevertheless, the episode was seen as a success for tough diplomacy and encouraged the administration to persist in an approach which implied that the rhetoric about the era of confrontation being replaced by the era of negotiation was premature.

Soon after the resolution of the Jordan Crisis, a more direct diplomatic confrontation between the superpowers was precipitated by the American discovery that the Soviets were constructing a submarine base at Cienfuegos in Cuba. The Cienfuegos episode was a curious one in which Soviet motives were far from clear and American intelligence assessments were far from unanimous. Although the establishment of a base would have been a considerable asset to the Soviet Union in terms of logistics, the wider significance of the Soviet move was a matter of some debate in 1970 and has remained so. At the one extreme are critics who see the episode as a 'false crisis' and emphasise that many State Department officials at the time saw the Soviet moves as 'essentially routine fleet exercises'.[2] A more moderate interpretation is offered by Garthoff, who suggests that Moscow was attempting to circumscribe the limits imposed upon the Soviet presence in Cuba in 1962, in the belief that these limits were inappropriate now that American strategic superiority was being replaced by emerging parity.[3] Kissinger, though, saw Soviet actions as a more direct probing of American intentions – demanding an unequivocal response.[4]

In retrospect, it is clear that the challenge was not a frontal one. Nevertheless, had there been no response then Moscow might have been emboldened to further actions. In the event, although Nixon was at first less resolute than Kissinger desired, the administration took a firm stance. There was no attempt to confront Moscow along the lines of 1962, but quiet diplomacy was used to persuade Moscow not to persist in what the United States argued was a violation of the understandings reached as a result of the Cuban Missile Crisis.

The result was that by October 1970 the issue was more or less resolved. Nevertheless, a certain amount of minor Soviet probing continued. Moscow was careful to avoid the visit of a tender with a ballistic missile submarine – which the United States had specifically prohibited in its communications with the Soviet leadership – but tried other combinations until at least May 1971.[5] In doing this Moscow may have simply been exploring the possibilities in a situation characterised by ambiguities about permissible behaviour. It is also possible that the probing reflected uncertainty in Moscow about the extent to which the Soviet Union should commit itself to detente. By the end of the Twenty-fourth Party Congress of March 1971, however, this issue had effectively been resolved: the Congress had ratified Brezhnev's role as *primus inter pares* and the Soviet commitment to detente was firm and unequivocal.

Brezhnev's conception of detente involved not simply a reduction of those tensions which could lead to superpower conflict, but also the Soviet claim to political equality with the United States. For their part, Nixon and Kissinger were determined to safeguard what they regarded as vital American interests. Consequently, the superpower relationship was still subject to strains and tensions. The Indo–Pakistan war in the autumn of 1971 was once again seen by the Nixon administration as a test of will and resolve, which could have repercussions far beyond the immediate problems of the Indian subcontinent. These wider geopolitical concerns about the impact of allowing a Soviet-backed India to dismantle West Pakistan persuaded the administration to 'tilt towards Pakistan', to deploy a carrier task force into the Bay of Bengal and to toy with the idea of cancelling the forthcoming Soviet–American Summit.[6]

It appears, however, that the concerns which animated the President and his National Security Adviser were excessively alarmist: 'The underlying fallacy in Kissinger and Nixon's thinking throughout the crisis is that they persisted in assessing Soviet aims in terms of presumed Indian aims, and vice versa. Moreover, they attributed maximum offensive aims to both', believing, in contrast to the CIA and the State Department, that India, with Soviet support, was intent on destroying West Pakistan.[7] The crisis was also viewed in terms of 'triangular diplomacy', and it was assumed that Moscow was about to grasp the opportunity to humiliate China and thereby undermine the growing Sino–American links. When this did not occur there was a natural tendency to see the outcome as the result of American resolve, when in fact it had more to do with the limited objectives pursued from the outset by both India and the Soviet Union.[8] Indeed, the major Soviet objective may well have been to deter the Chinese from intervening on behalf of Pakistan.

If the war in South Asia threatened the Summit, this was jeopardised even more by US actions in southeast Asia. The American decision to mine Haiphong Harbour in May 1972, just a few weeks prior to Nixon's scheduled visit to Moscow, provoked apprehensions that the Soviet leadership would cancel the Summit. Despite American bombing raids which damaged several Soviet ships in the harbour, the meeting went ahead as planned. This is testimony to the importance the Soviet Union attached to detente in general and to Nixon's visit in particular. Hyland suggests that this was partly a tribute to Kissinger's success in entangling the Soviet Union in a web of negotiations, but resulted even more from the tactical skill of Nixon and Kissinger in triangular diplomacy, and the fact that 'Nixon had already been on his triumphant visit to China'.[9] The Soviet decision to proceed with the Summit also reflected the fact that Moscow was willing to compartmentalise its relations with the United States and move ahead on some fronts despite continuing problems on others. This clearly relieved the Nixon administration, which recognised the symbolic and substantive importance of the forthcoming meeting. Not only did the Moscow Summit represent the desire of both superpowers to go beyond the minimalist detente of the 1960s, but it also offered an opportunity to bring to fruition several sets of negotiations, including those on strategic arms control.

Detente and Arms Control

Although arms control negotiations had long been a feature of East–West relations, they were far more important in the late 1960s and early 1970s than in the past. The Partial Test Ban Treaty of 1963, although far more than a 'clean air bill', was not as central to the superpower relationship as the negotiations on strategic arms which resulted in the agreements of 1972. This is not to denigrate the negotiations which predated the Nixon administration as unimportant. Underlying the Non-Proliferation Treaty (NPT) of July 1968 was a clear linkage between the ideas of 'horizontal' and 'vertical' proliferation: if other states were to respect this treaty and refrain from acquiring nuclear weapons, they would expect the superpowers to display restraint in their strategic programmes. Accordingly, on the day the NPT was signed, the superpowers revealed that they were embarking on bilateral negotiations to limit strategic forces. Although these discussions were postponed as a result of the Soviet intervention in Czechoslovakia in August 1968, the Johnson administration had helped to set the stage for the Strategic Arms Limitation Talks, which were the first negotiations in which participation was confined to the United States and the Soviet Union.

By 1969, therefore, the superpowers had acknowledged that they had a common interest in discussing certain kinds of restraints on strategic forces. This offered the prospect that, although the negotiations would involve hard bargaining, they would not be marred by the gamesmanship and propaganda which had accompanied the disarmament talks of the 1950s. Indeed, conditions in the late 1960s were far more propitious for serious arms control than at any previous time. There were several developments which underlined the coincidence of interests between Moscow and Washington in achieving a limit on strategic arms and facilitated the agreements of 1972.

The first was American willingness to accept that the Soviet Union had become its equal in strategic power. Nixon, in office, repudiated the need for the kind of superiority that he had talked about in the Presidential election campaign of 1968, and by emphasising the notion of sufficiency, made it easier for the United States to accept an agreement which contained certain asymmetries. Sufficiency did not require the United States to match the Soviet Union capability for capability and option for option, and as the head of the US SALT delegation, Gerard Smith, acknowledged, it provided 'the key doctrinal basis for SALT'.[10]

The second development was that both superpowers began to see the strategic arms race as a burden on their economies. The Soviet Union had embarked on a major build-up in the 1960s and may have wanted to allow at least some diversion of resources to economic modernisation – which in the long term was a precondition for competing effectively with the United States in the arms race or anything else. The Nixon administration faced a congressional assault on the defence budget and was anxious, therefore, to restrain a competition in which it was handicapped by Congress. For Washington, mutual restraint was a particularly attractive option when the alternative was unilateral restraint imposed by the domestic opponents of high defence spending.

The third factor which facilitated serious negotiation was the existence of a balance of concerns. The United States was worried primarily over Soviet strategic offensive forces, not least because Washington had levelled off its own deployment of offensive missiles (while opting instead to place Multiple Independently Targeted Re-entry Vehicles (MIRVs) on both ICBMs and SLBMs). For Moscow, in contrast, the major worry was the US Anti-Ballistic Missile (ABM) Programme. The reason for this has been outlined by MccGwire:

> The 1966 decision to work toward the objective of avoiding the nuclear devastation of Russia introduced a new consideration. Nuclear attacks on Russia could not be physically prevented, only deterred, and the credibility of deterrence depended on the certainty that Soviet missiles, once launched, would strike North America. The absence of an effective US ballistic-missile defence system was therefore of much greater importance to the Soviets than any advantage that might be gained from a partially effective ABM system for the USSR. Given the American capacity for making large technological leaps, it was therefore much more important to the Soviets to halt the development of US ballistic-missile defence than to deploy a Soviet ABM system.[11]

Although the ABM was extremely controversial in the United States, was frequently dismissed as a weapon in search of a mission, and barely survived some very narrow votes in the Senate, the potential problems it posed for the Soviet Union provided a useful bargaining chip for the American negotiators. Indeed, Soviet doctrinal concerns were reinforced by the more pragmatic but compelling consideration that in an ABM race the Soviet Union would lose.

Other developments also facilitated the discussions on SALT in the early 1970s. One was the capacity of each superpower to monitor the deployments of the adversary through what were described as 'national technical means'. This, to some extent at least, removed the sensitive issues of verification and inspection from the agenda and allowed the superpowers to reach an agreement which did not require an unattainable degree of trust. There was also a recognition that moves towards a reduction of tensions would be incomplete without at least an attempt to constrain strategic force deployments and thereby make the arms competition more predictable.

These developments provided the preconditions for serious negotiations, but they did not guarantee success. The talks themselves were protracted and difficult. At the outset, both sides were uncertain about whether the negotiations would make substantive progress and were extremely cautious. Furthermore, while the balance of concerns brought the superpowers to the negotiating table, differences in force structures and existing weapons programmes made the issues complex and at times intractable. The two sides had contrasting objectives which could not easily be reconciled. The main preoccupation of the United States was Soviet offensive programmes – which were seen as a potential threat to the survivability of American land-based missiles, and therefore as something to be constrained. The Soviet Union, in contrast,

> wanted an agreement that would stop the US ABM programme, with its potential for triggering a full scale ABM competition, and one that would register American acceptance of strategic parity. They wanted an agreement permitting deployment of a new generation of ICBMs ... and they wanted no inspection in the Soviet Union. Added targets of opportunity were US bases in Europe and the Far East and a long shot possibility of halting or slowing up US MIRV deployments.[12]

Soviet concerns over MIRV, while less intense than those over ABM, were not insignificant.

There were, of course, opportunities in these contrasting concerns for a trade-off between offensive and defensive systems. Whereas the United States wanted an agreement dealing with both offensive and defensive forces, however, the Soviet Union wanted to focus primarily on ABMs, and to leave offensive forces for subsequent discussion. The situation was further complicated by Soviet insistence that any agreement also embrace American Forward Based Systems (FBS) in Europe (that is, the carrier-based and land-based aircraft capable of striking Soviet territory). The Soviet obsession with FBS reflected their desire for what was termed 'equal security'. This notion was difficult to implement, however, because of geographical asymmetries which combined with the requirements of extended deterrence in ways which led the United States to conclude that FBS were non-negotiable.

Another formidable complication was MIRV. Some critics have suggested that the United States missed a major opportunity to achieve strategic stability by not pushing hard for a MIRV ban in SALT.[13] In retrospect even Kissinger has acknowledged that the United States might have been better off had it thought through more carefully the implications of a MIRVed world.[14] Yet not only was this pointed out to him at the time but also there were members of the delegation – most especially Gerard Smith – who at crucial stages argued very strongly that an effort be made to ban MIRVs.[15] The President and Kissinger, however, seemed to regard ABM as much more dispensable, and when the United States did introduce a proposal to ban MIRVs, it contained provision for on-site inspection. This had always been anathema to Moscow, and was clearly a 'joker' designed to ensure Soviet rejection. The inclusion of the inspection clause led the Soviets to conclude, not unreasonably, that Washington was not serious about prohibiting MIRV.[16]

Even if the United States had been more forthcoming, however, it is far from certain that such a ban was attainable. As Gerard Smith acknowledges, the differing levels of development of MIRV made it difficult to reconcile Soviet and American concerns. The American advantage in MIRV – which symbolised American technological prowess – was not something that Washington was eager to sacrifice through agreement to prohibit production and deployment; while for Moscow any ban which prohibited testing had the fundamental disadvantage that it would freeze Soviet inferiority. In addition, there was a serious problem of how a comprehensive MIRV restriction would be verified. The failure to constrain MIRVs, however, may have made Moscow more reluctant to accept any far-reaching restrictions on launcher numbers – which were seen as necessary to offset the US MIRV advantage until the Soviet Union was able to deploy MIRVs of its own.

Another difficulty in the negotiations was the contrasting national styles. The Soviet Union seemed to prefer to respond to US offers than to take initiatives of its own, while for its part the United States sometimes had difficulty in deciding what its own position should be in view of divergent priorities held by differing agencies and departments in Washington. Indeed, at one point in the negotiations the United States had three different proposals for ABM restriction on the table – and even members of the delegation were not entirely clear which option was preferred by the White House.[17] In part, this reflected 'the chaotic state of the American position on ABMs' – a chaos that stemmed from both bureaucratic indecision and the bitter public and congressional debate about the desirability of ABM deployment.[18]

The negotiations were also complicated by the fact that at times they were taking place at two levels. As well as the formal negotiations in Vienna and Helsinki, the superpowers used what was described as the 'back channel' between Henry Kissinger (not yet Secretary of State) and the Soviet Ambassador to the United States, Anatoly Dobrynin. The opening of this channel reflected Nixon's desire to run American foreign policy from the White House. This progressively reduced the role of Secretary of State Rogers, but allowed Kissinger to deal with certain major issues away from congressional and public scrutiny. It has since been defended on the grounds that it offered opportunities for movement in Soviet–American relations that otherwise would not have been available.

Whether this was in fact the case is uncertain and controversial. The conventional wisdom is that the major breakthrough on SALT was accomplished through the 'channel' in the first half of 1971 when, for the first time, the Soviet Union agreed to consider limits not only on defensive systems – for which they had long been pressing – but also a freeze on offensive forces which, significantly, did not include the American FBS. Kissinger emphasises that the breakthrough, which was announced on 20 May 1971, not only accepted that limitations on offensive and defensive forces would be dealt with simultaneously – a major Soviet concession – but contained the essence of the agreement that was finally reached at the Moscow Summit a year later.[19]

More critical assessments of the 'channel' and the May 'breakthrough' have been made by several participants and analysts. Smith has emphasised that the seeds of the May 1971 deal were apparent before the end of 1970 but were hampered by the administration's reluctance to give the SALT delegation sufficient flexibility to respond to Soviet hints of compromise.[20] Although resentful at being saddled with instructions which were rendered nonsensical by the Kissinger–Dobrynin talks, Smith nevertheless accepts that the May 1971 accord was significant. But in his view, the price that was paid was high. Kissinger's solo diplomacy gave a political impetus to the negotiations but at the expense of a considerable loss of clarity. Apparently Kissinger had emphasised the need for limitations on the Soviet ICBM force but had been much more casual about SLBM restrictions – an omission that was both strategically significant and politically unwise in view of Soviet construction programmes. In response to a question from Dobrynin about whether SLBMs were to be included in the freeze on offensive systems, Kissinger apparently responded that the United States was prepared to have it either way, thereby changing the position which the United States had been pressing for almost a year. In Smith's view this was lone diplomacy at its worst:

> There is no evidence to indicate that this major change in SALT policy was ever considered in advance by anyone except Kissinger – and perhaps not even by him. It may well have been a random answer of a fatigued and overextended man who did not realise the immense significance of his words. It was to take a lot of effort and expenditure of bargaining power to redeem these words and restore the earlier US position that SLBMs must be included in any SALT agreement.[21]

Kissinger may have also made other concessions on non-related issues. It has been argued, albeit on the basis of largely circumstantial evidence, that whereas Kissinger's account emphasises Soviet concessions resulting from the implicit linkage between SALT and the negotiations on Berlin, the real impetus to progress on SALT came from American promises of increased trade with the Soviet Union.[22] This charge is impossible to verify. What is certain, however, is that the subsequent negotiations were made more difficult for the United States because of Kissinger's vagueness on both the SLBM issue and the relationship between the negotiations on defensive weapons and those on offensive systems. Kissinger had succeeded in persuading the Soviets to accept that limits on defensive forces had to be accompanied by constraints on offensive systems, but had paid little attention to the nature of the constraints that would be imposed, even assuring Dobrynin that the modernisation and replacement of Soviet forces would be permitted. There were also question marks about the sequence of the negotiations on defensive and offensive forces.

The immediate issue for the summer of 1971, however, was the ABM. The delegations suggested a variety of possible limits, without moving very much closer to agreement. At one stage the American delegation proposed a total ban on ABMs, but although there were indications of Soviet interest, the offer was withdrawn. Nevertheless, accord was reached on two matters which, although peripheral to SALT, were far from insignificant – upgrading the Direct Communications Link between the superpowers, and agreeing on measures to reduce the risk of nuclear war by accident. These helped to give the negotiations some sense of movement in a period when the differences between the two sides still loomed large. The announcement on 12 October 1971 that President Nixon would visit Moscow the following spring added a sense of urgency to the negotiations. Both sides continued to posture on ABM, but by early 1972 the main difficulties revolved around the agreement on strategic offensive forces.

A significant move towards a final agreement allowing each side two ABM sites – one around the National Command Authority and one to protect ICBMs – was made on 15–16 April 1972, when the delegations were on a visit to Lapland. The Tundra conversations, in which Raymond Garthoff played a key role for the American side, covered most of the details and were accepted as the basis for agreement by both Washington and Moscow.[23]

On offensive forces, however, it was another intervention by Kissinger which proved decisive, as once again the formal negotiators were ignored in favour of high-level diplomacy. On 20–24 April, Kissinger was in Moscow for discussions about Nixon's forthcoming visit. His instructions were to focus primarily on Indochina and persuade Moscow to put pressure on North Vietnam – which had recently launched another major offensive – to be more forthcoming in the peace negotiations. Nevertheless, Kissinger also engaged the Soviet leadership on arms control. The details of the ABM agreement – as worked out in the Tundra talks – were presented by Brezhnev and accepted by Kissinger, apparently without any realisation on his part of the role that the US delegation had played.[24] If the discussions on ABM merely ratified what had been accomplished elsewhere, Kissinger succeeded in re-establishing agreement on the inclusion of SLBMs in the offensive limitations, albeit with a ceiling (950 SLBMs on sixty-two submarines) which, despite Kissinger's claims to the contrary, did not significantly curtail the Soviet building programme. When the Verification Panel met in Washington to discuss these terms which were embodied in what was termed the 'Brezhnev paper', Gerard Smith's objections to the high ceiling were overruled in a somewhat brutal manner by President Nixon.[25]

If Smith and other members of the delegation had reservations about the second Kissinger intervention they were also unhappy about the way in which the final details of the package were hammered out in a frenzied series of negotiations occurring simultaneously at Helsinki and at the Moscow Summit. The picture that emerges is one of considerable confusion in which issues were dealt with on both sides by policy-makers who lacked the knowledge and expertise required. The issues involved in these final days and hours of SALT One were concerned with detail rather than principle. Nevertheless, two matters in particular were significant: one was the question of precisely which submarines were to be included in the freeze; the other concerned modernisation and replacement, and in particular what constituted a heavy missile. The first of these issues was settled in a way relatively favourable to Moscow, while the second remained essentially unresolved.

The Soviet Union rejected the American position that any missile significantly larger than the Soviet SS-11 be considered a 'heavy missile', only to have the United States place its understanding of this in a unilateral statement to accompany the Interim Agreement – even though Washington had intelligence estimates that the impending Soviet replacement for its SS-11, the SS-19, was a larger missile. This failure to establish a mutually accepted definition of a heavy missile was crucial, as the Interim Agreement prohibited the replacement of light missiles by heavy missiles. In these circumstances, allegations that Soviet deployment of the SS-19 violated the Accord were difficult to avoid. They were made inevitable by a White House briefing to congressional leaders in June 1972, in which Kissinger overstated the constraints imposed on Soviet modernisation and replacement programmes by the Interim Agreement.[26]

The flaws and imprecisions, however, did not prevent either Kissinger or the members of the SALT delegation from feeling a considerable sense of achievement with the package of measures that was both finalised and unveiled at the Moscow Summit. This package consisted of an Anti-Ballistic Missile Treaty restricting each superpower to the deployment of two sites. In the common understandings attached to the ABM Treaty it was agreed that the sites had to be at least 1,300 kilometres apart, and that one was permitted around each national capital and the other around an ICBM field. Each site was limited to 100 interceptors. The Treaty also prohibited the development, testing and deployment of ABM systems or components which were 'sea-based, air-based, space-based, or mobile land-based'. There were restrictions on location of early-warning radar and on upgrading missiles, launchers or radars to give them an ABM capability, while a common understanding acknowledged that 'ABM systems based on other physical principles' would be subject to discussion within the Standing Consultative Commission set up to oversee the implementation of the Treaty and to deal with compliance issues. There were provisions for periodic reviews, while either side could withdraw from the Treaty at six months' notice if vital national interests required it.

The ABM Treaty was accompanied by an Interim Agreement on Offensive Missiles, establishing limits on both ICBMs and SLBMs. The ceilings were unequal, with the United States restricted to 1,054 ICBMs and the Soviet Union permitted to deploy up to 1,618 land-based missiles. At the same time, either side had freedom to mix from land to sea and could increase the number of SLBMs if it was prepared to dismantle its older ICBMs. The threshold figure for the Soviet Union before this dismantling process had to begin was 740 SLBMs. Under the freedom to mix arrangement the Soviet Union was permitted 950 SLBMs on sixty-two submarines, but to reach this had to give up 210 ICBMs. The United States was allowed 710 missiles on forty-four submarines. The agreement was of five years' duration, and it was acknowledged by both sides that there would be follow-up negotiations designed to establish more permanent limits on offensive forces. The Standing Consultative Commission established by the ABM Treaty would also oversee the implementation of the Interim Agreement on Offensive Arms and deal with any compliance problems that might arise.

Judgment on these accords has been mixed. Yet the very fact that the superpowers reached agreement against a background of continued differences elsewhere was itself a considerable achievement. As well as the Jordanian Crisis, Cienfuegos and the Indo–Pakistan war, there were two other episodes which highlighted the growing Soviet interest in detente in general and SALT in particular. The first was the American invasion of Cambodia; the second, the bombing and mining of Haiphong Harbour. The lack of reaction by the Soviet SALT delegation to American actions in Cambodia was what convinced their American counterparts that the Soviet Union was serious about the arms control negotiations. The lack of response to the attack on Haiphong was even more striking. As Smith notes, 'The silence about Vietnam was deafening.... Apparently SALT was to take priority. This was linkage in reverse'.[27] Although Nixon and Kissinger constantly emphasised linkage, on both these occasions it was Soviet willingness to compartmentalise relations with the United States which allowed the arms control talks to continue and to culminate in the agreements of May 1972.

What, though, of the agreements themselves? There are three major criticisms which have been directed at the 1972 accords. The first contends that the limitations imposed were not severe enough since neither superpower was forced to make significant sacrifices. In this somewhat sceptical assessment, the ABM Treaty, was 'a classic case of both sides agreeing not to build something that neither side wanted but that each would have probably ended up building in the absence of an agreement'.[28] Nor was the Interim Agreement much better, as this imposed quantitative limits but left qualitative developments unconstrained.

A second, more discriminating critique argues that the ABM Treaty was a considerable achievement in preventing a vicious new spiral to the arms race which would have complicated and intensified the competition in offensive forces. The Interim Agreement, on the other hand, was in certain respects 'a crucial failure'.[29] The limitations imposed on the United States were marginal and those on the Soviet Union inconsequential.[30] The failure to prevent MIRV deployments was, from an American point of view, particularly unfortunate. In a strategic environment in which MIRVs were unconstrained, the heavier Soviet missiles would pose an increasing threat to American strategic forces. The lack of restrictions on MIRVs was seen in 1972 as necessary compensation for the Soviet numerical advantage in launchers. A few years later it began to look very different as the Soviet Union followed the United States in the large-scale deployment of MIRVs.

It was at this stage that the critique of those who were unhappy about the consequences to the arms race of the Interim Agreement coalesced with the argument of a third group of critics whose main concern was what they regarded as the one-sidedness of the accord on offensive systems. The more immediate complaints of this group, though, focused on the unequal ceilings, and it was contended that the United States had unnecessarily conceded advantages to the Soviet Union. In fact, the Nixon administration had conceded a good deal to the Joint Chiefs of Staff, whose price for supporting the Interim Agreement was an acceleration of the Trident and other strategic offensive programmes.

Despite these criticisms, the achievements of the 1972 accords should not be overlooked. The ABM Treaty might have headed off a competition in weapons that neither superpower really wanted, but without the treaty that competition would have been intense. Furthermore, the superpowers had begun a serious dialogue about the shape and size of their strategic forces. Although the arms control process was imperfect, it was preferable to a wholly unrestrained competition. The commitment to continue this process was evident in the creation of the Standing Consultative Commission which not only institutionalised the dialogue but also provided an important forum for the examination of the complaints about non-compliance that would inevitably arise.

Although arms control in itself did not, and could not, guarantee a comprehensive detente, SALT One and the ABM Treaty contributed significantly to the detente of the early 1970s. The attempt to regulate the competition in armaments and ensure that it did not lead to uncontrollable tensions fitted perfectly into Kissinger's managerial concept of detente. The 1972 accords also reflected the Soviet concern that the risks inherent in the competition between the superpowers should be kept within limits, and in particular that steps be taken to reduce the risk of nuclear war. Equally important for Moscow was the fact that SALT One ratified strategic parity and provided a visible embodiment of Soviet superpower status. Yet it was in the United States that the arms control achievements were oversold, largely because of Nixon's electoral concerns. President Nixon's rhetoric in the aftermath of the Moscow Summit helped to generate unrealistic expectations about arms control. SALT One was presented as a major achievement of the era of negotiations and as a symbol of mutual restraint. When the expectations were not met, there was inevitably a sense of disillusionment, and the symbol became somewhat tarnished. Something similar occurred with the attempt to establish a set of 'rules' for crisis avoidance.

From Crisis Management to Crisis Prevention

A key element in the detente process was an attempt by the super-powers to move from 'confrontational competition' to 'collaborative competition' and to replace improvisation in crisis management by a code of conduct designed to avert crises.[31] At the Moscow Summit of 1972 and the Washington Summit of June 1973 the superpowers tried to establish understandings designed to regulate the competition which, they recognised, could not be eliminated from their relationship.

The initiative in this was taken by the Soviet Union, which proposed that the Moscow Summit result in a Declaration of Principles about the superpower relationship. Kissinger was prepared to accept the declaration but not the wording proposed by Moscow. After stalling for a time, Kissinger seems ultimately to have decided that there was little to lose, so long as the United States insisted on language that reflected its own conceptions of an appropriate basis for the further development of detente. The initial Soviet proposals were redrafted by Kissinger and his aide Helmut Sonnenfeldt in ways designed to ensure that American ideas were incorporated into the document and that the unacceptable elements in the Soviet proposal were excised. The one exception to this was the Soviet emphasis on 'peaceful coexistence'. This was allowed to remain, and Nixon and Kissinger 'contented themselves with introducing into the same document their own principles of international restraint' in the expectation that this would effectively neutralise or negate the peaceful coexistence clause.[32]

The Basic Principles Agreement (BPA) signed at the Moscow Summit has since been dismissed in the United States as either a rhetorical flourish designed only to give the Summit greater domestic appeal or else as no more than a device to establish a code of behaviour which could be invoked whenever the United States wished to condemn Soviet behaviour. While both considerations may have played some part, the BPA can best be understood as a genuine, if flawed, attempt by the superpowers to establish rules of behaviour which would minimise the likelihood of superpower confrontations. As Kissinger noted in a press conference in Kiev just after the Summit, the Declaration 'was intended to mark the transformation from a period of rather rigid hostility to one in which, without any illusions about the differences in social systems, we would try to behave with restraint and with a maximum of creativity in bringing about a greater degree of stability and peace'.[33] The Soviet Union seems to have had a similar understanding of the Basic Principles. Although Soviet

policy-makers and analysts constantly emphasised that there would
be no end to the class struggle and that Moscow would continue to
support wars of national liberation, there was also a recognition of the
importance of avoiding direct confrontations with the United States.
As one Soviet commentator wrote, 'the main thing ... is not merely
to extinguish military conflicts after the hostilities have started, but to
prevent the emergence of the sources of war, to defuse the explosive
situations before they break out'.[34]

The Agreement on Avoiding Incidents at Sea was a specific
application of this superpower concern with crisis prevention and was
another acknowledgment of common interest between Moscow and
Washington. Initially suggested by the United States in 1967, the idea
of negotiations on naval incidents was revived by the Soviet Union in
1970. The American position was formulated in an inter-agency group
chaired by Herbert Okun, and in October 1971 the negotiations began
in Moscow, with high-ranking delegations from both sides. With provisions to regulate dangerous manoeuvres, restrict harassment, increase
communications at sea, and facilitate consultations and information
exchanges, the Agreement was formally signed at the Moscow Summit
in 1972.[35] Subsequently, there was a marked reduction in the number
of incidents, and the accord was widely regarded as a success. This
is not entirely surprising: unwanted incidents are in the interest of
neither side. Furthermore, an agreement on specifics of this kind
is easier to monitor and uphold than the more general codes of
conduct enshrined in the Basic Principles Agreement. In fact, the
BPA was supplemented in 1973 by an Agreement on the Prevention
of Nuclear War. The initial Soviet objective was to get agreement
that neither superpower would use nuclear weapons against the other
– a declaration which would have profoundly affected American
alliance obligations. Partly because of this alliance dimension the
United States consulted Britain. Thomas Brimelow, an official in the
Foreign and Commonwealth Office – which throughout this period
held a cautious view of the emerging detente and was concerned
that Washington should neither overbuy nor oversell the degree of
change in the superpower relationship – played a key role, along with
Kissinger's aides, in redrafting the document. These efforts succeeded
in blunting the Soviet move and securing an accord which developed
some of the ideas enshrined in the BPA.

Together, these declarations established four main precepts to
be observed by the superpowers. The first was that they should
both act so as to prevent situations developing which might cause
'a dangerous exacerbation of their relationship' and provoke military
confrontations. The second was that they should refrain from the
threat or use of force not only against each other but also against

each other's allies. The third obligation was that, if situations arose involving the risk of nuclear conflict, they were to 'engage in urgent consultations with each other and make every effort to avert this risk'. The fourth principle committed the superpowers to exercise restraint in their relationship and to negotiate in order to settle differences by peaceful means. Perhaps even more important, it also acknowledged that efforts by either side to obtain 'unilateral advantage at the expense of the other, directly or indirectly', were incompatible with the notion of restraint in their relationship.[36]

These principles, which are sometimes described as a charter for detente, reflected an attempt to specify the kind of restraints that were both appropriate to, and necessary for, the maintenance of detente. Yet they were problematic from the outset. The emphasis on common interest and mutual understanding obscured the differing aspirations and objectives of the two sides. For Washington, the agreements were an attempt to express formally Kissinger's ideas about the need for restraint in Soviet foreign policy as a prerequisite for a stable international order. For their part, the Soviet leaders probably saw the agreements less as a set of self-denying ordinances than as a token of American willingness to accept Moscow as an equal, with an equal say in regional disputes and their settlement.[37]

Future misunderstandings might have been avoided if the superpowers had thought more seriously about how the accords might be implemented in circumstances where one or both were involved in regional conflict or instability. In the event, not only did Moscow and Washington fail to engage in follow-up discussions, but there was no policy planning by either side on how the principles would be applied and what obligations they imposed in practice. At the same time, no one in the Nixon administration regarded the agreements as self-enforcing. It was accepted that they would have to be buttressed by a system of rewards and punishment. One of the rewards was increased trade, and it is to the economic aspect of detente that attention must now be given.

Detente and East–West Trade

East–West trade was to prove one of the most controversial aspects of the superpower detente in the 1970s. Expanded trade between the superpowers was one of the slowest areas to develop during the period of high detente in the early 1970s and was also one of the earliest casualties of the attack on detente that was launched in the United States. The main reason for its tardy development was Nixon and Kissinger's belief that trade with Moscow could be an important bargaining lever in obtaining concessions on political issues. There was also continuing concern that the Soviet Union might exploit certain kinds of trade and technology transfer for military purposes. Because of this the administration was reluctant to go too far too fast in expanding trade. In April 1970 Henry Ford announced in Moscow that the Ford Motor Company was considering a Soviet offer to participate in the building of a giant truck-manufacturing plant in Kazan, intended to produce 150,000 trucks a year. As a result of administration pressure, and public opposition to the deal by Secretary of Defense Laird, the Soviet offer was rejected. The same hard line was evident in November 1970 when the Commerce Department announced that the sale of a million-dollar oil-refining plant to Poland had been suspended, while the following month the United States complained to the British Prime Minister, Edward Heath, about Britain's plans to sell computers to the Soviet Union. The result of this restrictiveness was that in 1971 the Soviet Union did four times as much business with Japan and nearly four times as much with Germany as with the United States. Soviet–British trade was three times as large as Soviet–American trade, while France and Italy had double the American level.

In 1971, however, US policy began to undergo a significant shift. There were still reservations about helping the Soviet Union in the construction of heavy trucks, and in September 1971 the Mack Truck Company, apparently under some pressure, cancelled an agreement to supply $750 million worth of equipment for a Soviet truck-manufacturing plant. Increasingly, though, the Nixon administration adopted a more liberal approach. There were sound economic reasons for this. With the United States suffering from unprecedented balance of trade problems, the Soviet market began to appear extremely attractive. Probably more important, however, was the improvement in political relations symbolised in the May 1971 breakthrough on SALT. Initially, expanded trade had been held out as an incentive for the Soviet Union to exert a moderating influence on North Vietnam and to exhibit restraint in the Middle East. Although the American desire for Soviet assistance in disengaging from Vietnam would continue to have some influence on the speed with which commercial relations were normalised, it does seem that in the spring of 1971 there was a major change in the administration's approach, and there was a new and important linkage between SALT and trade. How explicitly the connection was made in the Kissinger–Dobrynin channel is uncertain. What is clear, though, is that the breakthrough on SALT, at the very least, encouraged the administration to adopt a much more liberal trade policy. On 1 June the Department of Commerce announced that it had approved licences for the export of $85 million worth of truck-manufacturing equipment to Moscow, while on 10 June it was announced that President Nixon had removed grain from the list of items needing licences before they could be exported to the Soviet Union. The President also suspended the requirement that half of all grain shipments be made in American vessels. This decision on shipments caused problems with the maritime unions – both threatened jobs and ran up against the visceral anti-communism which had hindered Kennedy's efforts to liberalise trade with the Soviet Union in the early 1960s. When Kissinger failed to placate the unions, the task was passed to Nixon aide Charles Colson, who, by making concessions on other issues, was more successful.[38]

Over the next few months Soviet–American trade began to develop considerable momentum. This went hand in hand with the improvement in political relations: in September 1971 the Four Power Agreement on Berlin was signed, while the following month Nixon's plan to visit Moscow in May 1972 was made public. In November it was announced that, for the first time since 1964, grain sales to the Soviet Union had been approved. The Soviet Deputy Minister of Trade visited the United States, and emphasised that the Soviet Union not only wanted Most Favoured Nation (MFN) status from the United States but was actively looking for American companies to participate in joint ventures with Moscow. Later in the month the Secretary of Commerce, Maurice Stans, led a delegation to Moscow to explore the major problems inhibiting Soviet–American commercial relations. These included the old Lend-Lease debts dating back to World War II, tariff treatment and credits.

The issue of Soviet–American trade was now clearly and openly on the superpower agenda, and further meetings were held in January 1972 to explore ways in which this trade might be increased. In early April negotiations began in an attempt to settle the Lend-Lease problem, and Secretary of Agriculture Earl Butz visited Moscow to discuss the possibility of a Soviet–American agreement on grain purchases. In May 1972, Soviet Minister of Foreign Trade Patolichev visited the new Secretary of Commerce, Peter Peterson, a meeting which established a basis for further negotiations. In spite of all this activity the May 1972 Summit did not include a formal trade agreement. One possible explanation for this is that the issues were proving more intractable than anticipated; another is that the United States had deliberately slowed the negotiations in response to events in Vietnam. Nevertheless, progress was made, and the Basic Principles Agreement – which Nixon described as a 'road map' – acknowledged the importance attached by both sides to the further development of economic and commercial ties.

Washington and Moscow were both anxious to establish long-term arrangements and created a Joint Commercial Commission with a mandate to negotiate an overall trade agreement which included

MFN status, arrangements for credit and provisions for the reciprocal establishment of business facilities. Rapid progress was made, and after the first meeting of the Commission, Peterson issued a report entitled 'US–Soviet Commercial Relationships in a New Era', which set out in very positive and optimistic terms the benefits which would accrue to the superpowers from expanded trade. It was not surprising, therefore, that at its second session in October 1972, the Joint Commercial Commission reached a formal agreement, which was announced simultaneously with an agreement on settling the Lend-Lease debt.

The Trade Agreement provided for large Soviet orders for American 'machinery, plant, and equipment, agricultural products, industrial products and consumer goods'. In addition, commercial offices were to be opened in Washington and Moscow, and other steps were taken to facilitate contacts between American companies and the Soviet Union. The agreement also committed the United States to grant the Soviet Union MFN status and thereby treat Soviet exports in a non-discriminatory manner. Separate from the Trade Agreement, but of equal if not greater importance, were arrangements for large-scale credit facilities for the Soviet Union. Moscow had opted for a 'development strategy based on a level of capital imports from the West' that made 'debt accumulation inevitable'.[39] Credits were essential to Soviet industrial investment: they would help to compensate for the shortages of hard currency and make possible the purchase of Western technology that was necessary if the Soviet Union was to overcome the sectoral weaknesses in its economy. Accordingly, the President determined that it was in the American interest for Eximbank to facilitate transactions with the Soviet Union. Agreement was also reached to open forty ports in each country to the merchant ships of the other.

As a result of these agreements the climate for Soviet and American trade was made far more propitious, and during 1972 and 1973 a number of important deals were signed involving companies as diverse as International Harvester, General Electric, Pepsi-Cola, Caterpillar Tractors and Occidental Petroleum. The Washington Summit in June 1973 gave a further boost to commercial contacts, and the superpowers set a target of $2 to $3 billion of trade over the next three years. Joint ventures in the area of oil and gas exploration appeared particularly attractive. 'With the Soviets' increasing need to turn to their rich but difficult-to-tap reserves in western Siberia, American export strengths matched Soviet import priorities.'[40] The Nixon administration was anxious to secure access to Soviet energy sources, and rejected any notion that this would compromise American security. Two major projects – North Star and Yakutsk – were envisaged in which American companies would assist in the exploitation of Soviet gas deposits.

Payment would be made at least in part by deliveries of liquified natural gas to the United States.[41]

In order to facilitate this commercial expansion, a US–USSR Trade and Economic Council composed of 200 US firms and 100 Soviet organisations was established with offices in New York and Moscow. Not surprisingly the result was a significant increase (in absolute terms) in Soviet–American trade over the next few years, even though this trade remained a small percentage of the total trade for either country. Although much was later to be made about the export of high-technology items which, it was contended, helped the Soviet defence effort, the importance of this tended to be exaggerated. As one analysis completed towards the end of the 1970s noted, 'by world trading standards, high technology products do not dominate in exports to communist countries, are not large in volume, and are not experiencing any marked shift in relative importance'.[42]

The most immediate effect of the new accord on expanding trade was grain sales. The expectation of the Nixon administration was that this would help to strengthen public support for detente in the United States, and Secretary of Agriculture Butz did much to encourage such sales by promoting credit arrangements with the Soviet Union. In the event, the grain sale backfired on the administration and eroded rather than extended domestic support for detente. Soviet grain purchases, which in July 1972 had been heralded as the beginning of a new era in US–Soviet commercial dealings, helped to drive up prices for the American consumer and as a result became extremely unpopular.

Using the negotiating resources available to a centralised economy, Soviet representatives were able to conclude a series of independent and separate deals with merchants such as Continental Grain, while effectively concealing the extent of their involvement in the grain market, at least from the grain companies themselves.

> The Soviet purchases were made confidentially and early in the season before prices adjusted to the sudden leap in demand. At the same time, global food production declined amid poor weather conditions worldwide. The outcome was a major disruption of the American agricultural market, with consequences reverberating through the economy: grain prices shot up leading to increases in the cost of food; the rising costs gave a general impetus to inflation; national grain reserves were depleted; and the US Treasury paid large grain companies 333 million dollars in export subsidies and dispensed over 46 million dollars in shipping subsidies to help move the grain to the USSR.[43]

Senator Jackson described the episode as 'one of the most notorious government foul-ups in American history', and it was popularly characterised in the United States as 'the great grain robbery'.[44]

It appeared that the administration, at the very least, had been guilty of several intelligence failures which had enabled Moscow to exploit its credit facilities and manipulate the American market. In fact, the administration may have been more aware of the extent of the failure of the Soviet grain harvest in 1972 and the consequent need for massive grain imports than was believed. Not only were there reports from the US Embassy in Moscow about the huge crop failure in the Soviet Union, but there were also indications that the Soviet Union was engaged in large purchases from the Continental Grain Company and other large merchants. The Central Intelligence Agency produced two reports to this effect in August 1972, and although the bulk of the purchases had already been made by then, the reports imply that there was a closer monitoring of the events than was generally assumed.

Even Kissinger acknowledges that the United States was outmanoeuvred, and had 'subsidised the deals at a time when the Soviet Union quite literally had no other choice than to buy our grain at market prices or face mass starvation'.[45] Nevertheless, the kind of Soviet dependence that, in one sense at least, was symbolised by the grain deal was something that he had been striving to bring about. As one analyst has observed:

> Kissinger was ... more than a little interested in establishing a grain linkage to detente. The perennial efforts of farm bloc and the US Department of Agriculture to sell more grain converged with his desire to engage the Russians on as many fronts as possible, to create linkages between economics and politics, and to give the Soviet leadership a long term vested interest in continuing their 'dialogue' and 'relationship' with the United States.[46]

For all this, the episode took some of the glitter off detente, and it was clear that in the future the Soviet–American grain trade would have to be regulated far more carefully.

If there were problems over grain there were still considerable expectations in both Moscow and Washington about the future potential of Soviet–American commercial exchanges. The United States, in the words of one report, had gone 'from hostility and indifference in the 1950s and 1960s to euphoria in the early 1970s'.[47] Its approach was based on desire for economic gain and on the hope that trade would help to stabilise and perpetuate detente. As the Secretary of Commerce put it, 'Improvement in political relationships is a prerequisite for improved economic relationships but, once in place, economic ties create a commonality of interest which in turn improves the climate for further progress on the political side.'[48]

The Soviet Union may have had similar expectations about the moderating impact of trade on the ruling classes in the West. It is also likely that Brezhnev overestimated the beneficial effects on the Soviet economy of increased trade with the West in general and the United States in particular. In the event, his expectations were never properly tested. Soviet–American trade did increase, especially in agriculture (where a long-term agreement on grain sales was reached in 1975), manufactured goods and machinery. Structural differences between the economies and political developments in the United States, however, inhibited the full development of commercial relations between the two superpowers. Most Favoured Nation status and credits – which were essential in order to finance Soviet purchases from the United States and the creation of joint ventures – became politically controversial issues in the United States. The agreements on expanded trade which were made between 1972 and 1973 were made by the Soviet government and the Nixon administration; their implementation, however, depended crucially on the concurrence of the US Congress – and it was here that the plans for expanded trade ran into serious trouble.

Other areas in which the superpowers in 1972 and 1973 agreed to collaborate were far less controversial. Perhaps the most visible of these areas of functional cooperation was space exploration. This culminated in the Apollo–Soyuz Mission in July 1975 which involved a highly symbolic docking of the Soviet and American space capsules. Less visible but quite extensive and important cooperative ventures were also initiated in medicine, environmental protection and conservation, and scientific and technical exchanges. Although the deterioration in the Soviet–American political relationship in the second half of the 1970s eventually undermined the effectiveness of these exchanges, they do seem to have benefited both societies.[49] Much more important, though, was the success of detente in Europe, where the achievements were considerably greater and more enduring.

Detente in Europe

Detente in Europe was assisted by superpower detente, but stemmed in part from different impulses and had a different cast. The major Western participant in promoting detente in Europe was Bonn rather than Washington. Indeed, it was the conjuncture of Brezhnev's Westpolitik and Willy Brandt's Ostpolitik which provided the key to the process of normalisation in the early 1970s. Yet this process was not simply a consequence of policy decisions. The political division of Europe that was both cause and consequence of the cold war could not prevent the continuation and development of trade and cultural links between Eastern and Western Europe. If the superpowers were natural adversaries in a bipolar system, Europe was a continent which had been artificially and arbitrarily divided. It is not surprising, therefore, that during the 1960s there was a gradual but distinct increase in contacts between Eastern and Western Europe. The result was that, at one level, detente 'developed naturally, involving countries and peoples more than political acts and institutions'.[50]

Yet detente also developed with an acute sense of limits and constraints. If the aim of West European proponents of detente was to encourage the trend towards a lowering of the barriers between the blocs, there was nevertheless a recognition that politically there could be no change in the status quo. In the immediate future, there was no alternative to the security and political framework established in the rival alliance systems. It was Western, and especially West German, acceptance of this fact that provided the basis for a *modus vivendi* in Europe. At the same time, the policies initiated in the name of detente reflected Western aspirations to promote greater liberalisation in Eastern Europe, and more comprehensive links between East and West. In a sense, this provided what might be termed the 'hidden agenda' of European detente – an agenda which led one French analyst to suggest that cold war in Europe had been replaced by a 'hot peace' in which defensive rhetoric hid revisionist aspirations.[51]

These aspirations, however, were essentially long term. A more immediate problem for the Brandt government, which came to power in 1969, was to ensure that West Germany did not become diplomatically isolated. Brandt was concerned that unless Bonn abandoned its cold war policies the Federal Republic would be regarded as 'the last of the cold warriors, the opponents of change and thus perhaps the world's trouble-makers'.[52] In fact, Nixon and Kissinger became anxious that Brandt might go too far too fast, thereby enabling Moscow to engage in a 'selective detente' which would undermine Western unity. Because the German Chancellor was manifestly determined to move towards the normalisation of relations with East Germany, however, Nixon and Kissinger accepted that the best course was to go along with this process while taking action to ensure that Western interests were protected and the cohesion of the Atlantic alliance was maintained.

In December 1969, at a meeting of NATO Foreign Ministers, the United States was successful in obtaining allied agreement on a formula which postulated parallel progress on a range of outstanding issues. As Kissinger later put it,

> We made agreement on a European Security Conference conditional on progress in talks on Berlin and in Soviet–German negotiations. Ostpolitik was being embedded in a matrix of negotiations that enhanced the bargaining position of the Federal Republic but that also set limits beyond which it could not go without an allied consensus.[53]

Although the idea of a multilateral detente was clearly in the air, progress at this stage of the normalisation process was mainly bilateral, with Brandt's new policy providing the impetus.

On 28 November 1969, West Germany signed the Non-Proliferation Treaty – something which the Soviet Union had effectively made a precondition for Ostpolitik. With this constraint – which was as much symbolic as substantive – accepted, Ostpolitik moved forward fairly rapidly. On 12 August 1970, the Moscow Treaty between the Soviet Union and the Federal Republic was signed. Hailed in *Pravda* as an 'acknowledgement by realistic forces in the West of post-war realities', the Treaty provided for the mutual renunciation of force, and the recognition that all borders in Europe – including the Oder–Neisse line and the frontier between East and West Germany – were inviolable. Bonn thereby confirmed the division of the German nation into two states and its acceptance of the loss of prewar German lands in the east to Poland and the USSR. Whatever Brandt's long-term aspirations, therefore, his immediate actions ratified the status quo. Although this was not easy for a state which had clung tenaciously to the hope of reunification, the Chancellor presented the Treaty as the product of a new realism in the Federal Republic's foreign policy. As he put it: 'Nothing was lost with this Treaty that was not gambled away long ago.'[54] At the same time, Brandt clearly hoped that detente in Europe would lower the barriers between East and West and thereby contribute to German reunification in the long-term. In effect, he relegated an unattainable political objective to the status of a long-term aspiration.

For all this the Treaty represented a major accomplishment by Brezhnev, especially as it envisaged increased economic relations between the Federal Republic and the Soviet Union. Yet the agreement had implications which went well beyond the bilateral relationship between Moscow and Bonn. As well as the achievement of a *modus vivendi* on the German question, the Moscow Treaty 'symbolized the waning of the cold war, the settlement of the unfinished postwar agenda' and, 'the inauguration of the detente era' in Europe.[55] It opened the way for the normalisation of relations with other East European countries, and its accomplishments were consolidated by the Warsaw Treaty of December 1970 between the Federal Republic and Poland. This confirmed the agreement made between Moscow and Bonn concerning Poland. The Oder–Neisse line was recognised and all claim given up to the territories of Silesia and Pomerania. At the same time, borders were regarded as inviolable rather than unalterable (as the Soviets wanted), thereby allowing for change by peaceful means.

Progress was also made on the status of Berlin. Although this was related to Ostpolitik, the Berlin negotiations were the responsibility of what were still technically the four occupying powers. This gave the United States an opportunity to exert greater leverage upon the normalisation process in Europe. The Nixon administration was able to engage the Soviet Union in a series of exchanges through the Kissinger–Dobrynin channel. It quickly became clear in these discussions that Moscow was anxious to obtain agreement on Berlin in order to ensure that the Bundestag ratified Brandt's Eastern Treaties – something that Bonn had made dependent upon 'a satisfactory settlement of the situation in and around Berlin'.[56] As Kissinger noted, 'Because it was inherent in Ostpolitik that its tangible advantages appeared to be one-sided – after all, Bonn was accepting the division of its country in return for nothing more than improvements in the political atmosphere – a favourable Berlin agreement had to supply the quid pro quo.'[57]

The result was that Moscow had to make concessions in two areas. As well as acquiescing to Western demands that access to the city be guaranteed by the Soviet Union and not East Germany, it also had to accept the close political ties between the Federal Republic and West Berlin. The Soviet negotiating position underwent several reversals as Moscow retreated from concessions that it had already given, a development which suggests that, during the run-up to the Party Congress of March–April 1971, there was internal controversy over the detente policy. After the Congress had given its support to Brezhnev's peace policy, however, the pace of the negotiations began to intensify in April and May 1971. Furthermore, in April 1971 Kissinger established a series of private or back-channel contacts between Federal Republic State Secretary Egon Bahr and the Soviet and American Ambassadors in Bonn, which greatly facilitated progress. Most of June was spent by Soviet, American and West German negotiators in drafting the text of the accord, and in July 1971 – just after Kissinger's visit to Beijing –

compromise was finally reached on an acceptable text. The agreement was of considerable significance:

> Whereas before there had existed no legal basis for civilian access at all, procedures for it were now spelled out in meticulous detail.... Whereas before the Soviet Union had washed its hands of Berlin access, claiming that it took place at the sovereign discretion of the East Germans, it now guaranteed it. The Federal presence in West Berlin was slightly reduced – essentially with respect to activities that had never been recognised by the allies, such as the quadrennial election of the Federal President. But the Soviet Union had accepted the principle that ties between the Federal Republic and Berlin could be 'maintained and developed' – thus providing a legal basis for strengthening economic and cultural ties between Bonn and Berlin. The accord empowered West Germany to represent Berlin in international agreements or bodies and enabled Berliners to travel on West German passports. In sum, the agreement implied and brought about a substantial improvement in the lives and safety of Berlin's population.[58]

The back-channel negotiations were clearly of crucial importance in obtaining this agreement. Yet Kissinger downplays the contribution that was also made by the British and French negotiators. The accord reached in the back channel had to be fed into the formal four-power negotiations – and had to face close scrutiny in the American State Department, which had been bypassed for much of the discussions. Nevertheless, the agreement was formally signed on 3 September 1971. The deal was effective: the Soviet Union had accepted the status quo in Berlin; and West Germany and its allies, at one level at least, had accepted the status quo in Europe.

Other agreements followed which elaborated the deal. A transit traffic accord was initialled on 12 May 1972, and this opened the way for negotiations about the basis of future relations between the Federal Republic and the German Democratic Republic. In August 1972, talks began in Berlin on what was to become, on 21 December 1972, the Basic Treaty between the two Germanies. The negotiations were not easy, as Bonn faced a fundamental dilemma: it 'had to recognize *de facto* the emergence of two German states on German soil ... and at the same time to keep open *de jure* the German question by means of a number of compromise formulations'.[59] The agreement established special relations between the two Germanies below the *de jure* level of recognition and involved an exchange of permanent missions but not embassies. At the same time it allowed the admission of both states to the United Nations on an equal footing. Underlying the agreement, however, were fundamental differences of conception. Brandt wanted *rapprochement* as a means of transforming the East German state and lowering the barriers to reunification, whereas the

German Democratic Republic wanted only *rapprochement* – which was to be accompanied by continued demarcation between the two states.[60] It is not surprising, therefore, that the Basic Treaty aroused considerable controversy within the Federal Republic, where critics argued that Bonn had made too many concessions. In spite of this domestic controversy the Treaty was clearly a major step towards normalisation in Europe. With the Czechoslovakia Treaty of 1973 – which renounced the Munich Treaty and therefore all claims to the Sudetenland – the normalisation process between West Germany and its Eastern neighbours was more or less complete.

The impact of this is difficult to overestimate. The process of normalisation succeeded in reducing tension in an area and over issues which had done much to nourish the cold war in the late 1940s and in the period from 1958 to 1962. Not surprisingly, there were continued differences over West Berlin as Bonn attempted to develop its ties with the city, while the East attempted to restrict the links. Nevertheless, the position of the city was made less anomalous and perhaps less vulnerable as a result of Ostpolitik. Brandt's policy also helped to increase the human contacts between the two parts of Germany and benefited Bonn economically as exports to the Soviet Union increased very substantially.

In the process, however, the Federal Republic developed a vested interest in relaxation of tension, which meant that when superpower detente came under pressure in the late 1970s, there was an attempt by Bonn to insulate the progress that had been made in Europe from the broader deterioration in East–West relations. The selective detente that Kissinger had been so anxious to avoid was once again to become apparent. Yet too much should not be made of this. The divergences were in part an inevitable consequence of Bonn's increased maturity and independence in foreign policy. All this was still in the future, however. The more immediate result of Ostpolitik was that it gave impetus to broader attempts at normalisation, symbolised most graphically in the Conference on Security and Cooperation in Europe (CSCE), and somewhat less notably in the negotiations on mutual force reductions.

Although the idea of a pan-European Security Conference had been floated by Moscow since the mid-1950s, the Western powers were reluctant to embark on such a venture. From the mid-1960s the proposal was pushed more vigorously by the Soviet Union, but NATO remained non-committal. The alliance placed more emphasis on negotiations for mutual and balanced force reductions – negotiations which were given an added urgency by congressional pressures for unilateral American troop cuts in Europe. After a period in which the two blocs engaged in a dialogue through communiqués

– with both affirming their commitment to exploring possibilities for negotiation – the Soviet Union accepted that American involvement in the detente process in Europe was inevitable. The Berlin Agreement and the achievements of Ostpolitik provided an additional impetus for multilateral negotiations. There was also agreement that the security conference and the force reduction negotiations would go forward together. Gradually, however, NATO's insistence on what was termed 'parallelism' was dropped as it became clear that the very existence of the force reduction talks in Vienna had helped to head off Senator Mansfield's attempt to bring about large reductions in the American presence in Europe.

What is rarely emphasised is that the Soviet Union connived in what was essentially a charade to maintain the status quo in Europe. In May 1971, when the Mansfield Amendment on troop cuts was being considered by the Senate, Brezhnev made a speech applauding the idea of negotiations on mutual force reductions, and thereby ensured the defeat of the proposal. Although it is often assumed that this was simply the price Brezhnev was prepared to pay in order to obtain the more important goals involved in the security conference, such an interpretation does not adequately explain the fact that Soviet enthusiasm for force reduction negotiations seemed to increase in line with the pressure from the US Senate for unilateral American action.

The more convincing explanation, therefore, is that this was another example of the Soviet Union preferring the existing situation – which helped to legitimise the Soviet military presence in Eastern Europe – to possible alternatives. In the event the negotiations on mutual and balanced force reductions reaffirmed the status quo. The talks, which finally opened in Vienna in 1973, bogged down in 1976 in a dispute over data, with the two sides presenting divergent assessments of the conventional military balance. Although they continued into the 1980s and yielded a variety of proposals, the negotiations became secondary. Their inception in 1973 was obviously a step forward for detente and provided a military counterpart to Ostpolitik and CSCE. Nevertheless, detente in Europe subsequently went ahead despite the impasse in Vienna. The main forum was the CSCE.

Preparations for the CSCE began in November 1972, and the proceedings opened in Helsinki in July 1973. The Conference and its outcome can best be understood as a multilateral version of the Ostpolitik, the overall effect of which was to strengthen and legitimise the achievements of Brandt's policies. Thirty-five states participated in the Conference – with the neutrals and non-aligned joining the members of the two blocs – which culminated in a Final Meeting in Helsinki from 30 July to 1 August 1975.

The Helsinki Final Act, as it was known, consisted of three main 'baskets' or sets of agreement. Basket One, dealing with security issues consisted of a declaration on the principles to govern relations between the participants. It emphasised the importance of sovereignty and self-determination, the non-use of force, the inviolability of frontiers, the principle of non-intervention in internal affairs, and respect for human rights and fundamental freedoms. There were also provisions for modest confidence-building measures involving advance notification of manoeuvres. Basket Two dealt with cooperation in economics, science and technology and the environment, and expressed the desire for increased trade between East and West Europe. Basket Three of the Final Act dealt with humanitarian cooperation and contained provisions relating to the free flow of people, information and ideas. It was also agreed that the process would be continued in follow-up meetings.

These provisions were the result of a series of compromises between the Soviet objective of legitimising its position in Eastern Europe and the desire of the West to promote greater liberalisation and to keep open the possibility of change. Although there was general acceptance of the inviolability of frontiers (a term in international law relating specifically to the non-use of force), the Soviet attempt to incorporate stronger language such as 'untouchability' or 'immutability of frontiers' was rejected. In the words of the British Foreign Office, 'neither the declaration, nor any other part of the Final Act, consecrate the political or territorial status quo in Europe. Indeed, the theme of peaceful change is evident in many of the conference texts.'[61] If the wording was fully in accord with Western preferences, however, the First Secretary of the German Democratic Republic, Erich Honecker, could still claim that the inviolability of frontiers was 'the decisive point' and that the provision for peaceful change was 'without practical relevance'.[62] This East German reaffirmation of the principle of *Abgrenzung* or demarcation highlighted the limits of Ostpolitik.[63] Nevertheless, the Western position was strengthened by the emphasis in Basket Three on the free flow of information, people and ideas, an emphasis designed to encourage the long-term evolution of the societies of Eastern Europe in ways which Bonn and its allies desired.

In other words, both sides could claim to get something out of Helsinki. Moscow had not obtained the *de jure* acceptance of its position in Eastern Europe but it had a more formal acknowledgment by the West of the *de facto* position. At the same time the West had obtained agreement on principles which in some respects ran counter to the Brezhnev Doctrine. By providing a charter on human rights, it had established a bench mark against which Soviet practices could be assessed. Furthermore, the Helsinki Final Act, by acting as a surrogate peace settlement, gave the process of normalisation in Europe a degree of irreversibility. At a fundamental level it did not change security relationships in Europe. The alliance system remained intact, and both blocs still saw military strength as the key to security. Yet by dealing on a multilateral basis with issues which had remained outstanding since World War II, the CSCE provided an additional layer of stability and restraint in what was already a stable if far from satisfactory situation. As well as helping to defuse East–West tensions in Europe, the CSCE also established the principle, through the inclusion of Confidence Building Measures, that there were steps which could be taken to enhance the security of both sides. The acknowledgment that security in Europe is reciprocal was psychologically of considerable importance.

Nor should Basket Two of the Final Act be ignored. The emphasis on economic cooperation not only acknowledged the developments which had already taken place in East–West trade in Europe, but also encouraged the further growth of commercial links between the two blocs. Trade between the Soviet Union and Western Europe increased far more than that directly between the superpowers, with Soviet–West German economic links increasing at a particularly rapid rate. Furthermore, European trade with the Soviet Union was not subject to the ups and downs that characterised US–Soviet trade. American exports to the Soviet Union were particularly volatile: they 'fluctuated often, severely, and principally for political reasons'.[64] European exports did not. Yet the contrast was not simply between political and economic conceptions of trade: if American trade policy was marked by the dominance of politics over economics, the Europeans were also sensitive to political considerations and regarded the growth of trade as a positive development which created a healthy degree of interdependence between the blocs. The United States, in contrast, became apprehensive about what it regarded as the creation of dangerous dependencies on Moscow. Although such concerns greatly exaggerated the extent of West European trade dependence on the Soviet bloc, they became increasingly pronounced throughout the 1970s as superpower relations deteriorated. They reflected a broader divergence between Western European and American attitudes towards detente which was apparent by the time of the Helsinki Final Act, and increased thereafter.

Responses to Helsinki in the West ranged from critics who saw it as a victory for the Soviet Union to much more positive commentators who regarded it as a substantial achievement in reducing tensions in Europe. Although both East and West Europeans were positive, they tended to focus on different aspects of the Final Act. The contrast between the Soviet and American emphases was even starker. Whereas, for Brezhnev, the Declaration had achieved acceptance of the status quo and was seen in Moscow as a major political achievement, President Ford focused on the obligations that it placed upon the Soviet Union to observe human rights. This divergence was symptomatic not only of the differing aims of the two superpowers in Helsinki, but also of the fact that by 1975, superpower detente was already in trouble.

Assessment

The four elements of detente – arms control, codes of conduct, trade, and normalisation in Europe – were mutually reinforcing. They were inextricably connected by Kissinger's concept of linkage, which gave the disparate elements an overall coherence. The connections, however, went beyond American tactics. The fact that there were several distinct strands in the detente of the early 1970s meant that even when there were difficulties in reaching agreement on one issue, there could still be movement elsewhere. Furthermore, accommodation in one area had a positive impact on the overall relationship and helped to create a sense of progress which improved the atmosphere and made it easier to get agreement elsewhere. This gave the moves towards detente considerable momentum. If the connections between the various elements of detente appeared to be a source of strength, however, they also proved to be a source of weakness. Because it was so broadly based, detente required careful and systematic management, and was vulnerable to anything which undermined the capacity of the American and Soviet governments to provide this leadership. Furthermore, when one element started to go wrong, this had an adverse impact on the whole fabric, as it proved difficult to insulate other areas. Linkage may have contributed to the rise of detente, but was also to contribute to its decline. The most important interaction was between continued superpower competition in regional conflicts and developments in American domestic politics. This became discernible in 1973 only a few months after Brezhnev had visited Washington for the second major detente summit. The occasion was the October war in the Middle East. The relationship between this episode and Soviet–American detente is the theme of the next chapter.

Notes

1. R. Garthoff, *Detente and Confrontation* (Washington, DC: The Brookings Institution, 1985), p. 86.

2. S. Hersh, *The Price of Power* (New York: Summit Books, 1983), p. 253.

3. Garthoff, op. cit., pp. 76–7.

4. H.A. Kissinger, *White House Years* (Boston: Little, Brown, 1979), pp. 632–52.

5. Ibid., p. 651.

6. Ibid., pp. 842–914, especially pp. 913–15.

7. Garthoff, op. cit., p. 267.

8. Ibid., p. 277.

9. W.G. Hyland, *Mortal Rivals* (New York: Random House, 1987), p. 51.

10. G. Smith, *Doubletalk* (New York: Doubleday, 1980), p. 24.

11. M. MccGwire, *Military Objectives in Soviet Foreign Policy* (Washington, DC.: The Brookings Institution, 1987), p. 242.

12. Ibid., p. 125.

13. Hersh, op. cit., pp. 150–6.

14. Ibid., p. 155 (see note).

15. Smith, op. cit., especially ch. 4.

16. Garthoff, op. cit., p. 136.

17. Ibid., p. 150.

18. Hyland, op. cit., p. 49.

19. Kissinger, op. cit., pp. 810–23.

20. Smith, op. cit., p. 235.

21. Ibid., p. 229.

22. Hersh, op. cit., p. 353 and pp. 343–8.

23. Garthoff, op. cit., pp. 154–5.

24. Ibid., p. 155.

25. Ibid., p. 166.

26. Ibid., p. 174.

27. Smith, op. cit., p. 383.

28. R. Barnet, *The Giants* (New York: Simon & Schuster, 1977), p. 102.

29. Garthoff, op. cit., p. 189.

30. Ibid., p. 187.

31. The terms are used by George Breslauer in 'Why Detente Failed: An Interpretation' in A.L. George, *Managing US–Soviet Rivalry* (Boulder, Col.: Westview Press, 1983), pp. 319–40.

32. A.L. George, 'The Basic Principles Agreement of 1972: Origins and Expectations' in ibid., pp. 109–10.

33. H. Kissinger, Press Conference in Kiev, 29 May 1972 (USIS official text), p. 3.

34. H. Trofimenko, 'The Third World and the US–Soviet Competition: A Soviet View', *Foreign Affairs*, vol. 59 (Summer 1981), p. 1039.

35. For a fuller account, see S.M. Lynn-Jones, *Avoiding Confrontation at Sea: The 1972 US–Soviet Agreement on Naval Incidents*, Harvard Project on Avoiding Nuclear War, Occasional Paper Series, no. 2 (Boston, Mass.: Kennedy School of Government, May 1984).

36. These agreements are discussed more fully in George, op. cit.

37. See H. Kissinger, *Years of Upheaval* (London: Weidenfeld & Nicolson, 1982), pp. 278–86.

38. Hersh, op. cit., p. 346.

39. See *Issues in East–West Commercial Relations*, A Compendium of Papers submitted to the Joint Economic Committee, Congress of the United States, 12 Jan. 1979 (Washington, DC: Government Printing Office, 1979), p. 180.

40. B.W. Jentleson, *Pipeline Politics: The Complex Political Economy of East–West Energy Trade* (London: Cornell University Press, 1986), p. 136.

41. See ibid., pp. 139–42.

42. *Issues in East–West Commercial Relations*, p. 39.

43. R.B. Porter, *The US–USSR Grain Agreement* (Cambridge: Cambridge University Press, 1984), pp. 6–7.

44. Quoted in ibid., p. 6.

45. Kissinger, *White House Years*, p. 1270.

46. D. Morgan, *Merchants of Grain* (London: Penguin, 1980), p. 200.

47. Peter S. Peterson, Secretary of Commerce, *US–Soviet Commercial Relationships in a New Era* (Washington, DC: Government Printing Office, Aug. 1972), p. 13.

48. See Roger Morcton, Secretary of Commerce, *The United States Role in East–West Trade: Problems and Prospects* (Washington, DC: Government Printing Office, Aug. 1975).

49. N. Jamgotch (ed.), *Sectors of Mutual Benefit in US–Soviet Relations* (Durham, NC: Duke University Press, 1985).

50. Garthoff, op. cit., p. 122.

51. P. Hassner, 'Detente: The Other Side' in *Survey*, vol. 19, no. 2 (Spring 1973), pp. 76–100.

52. W. Brandt, *People and Politics* (London: Collins, 1976), p. 167.

53. Kissinger, *White House Years*, p. 412.

54. Quoted in H. Haftendorn, *Security and Detente* (New York: Praeger, 1985), p. 199.

55. A. Stent, *From Embargo to Ostpolitik* (Cambridge: Cambridge University Press, 1981), p. 154.

56. Quoted in Haftendorn, op. cit., p. 210.

57. Kissinger, *White House Years*, p. 824.

58. Ibid., pp. 830–1.

59. Haftendorn, op. cit., p. 230.

60. P. Windsor, 'The Role of Germany' in S. Windass (ed.), *Avoiding Nuclear War* (London: Brassey's Defence Publishers, 1985), p. 89.

61. See *Selected Documents Relating to Problems of Security and Cooperation in Europe, 1954–77. Miscellaneous No. 17 (1977)*, Cmnd. 6932 (London: HMSO, Sept. 1977).

62. M. Rutherford, 'Summit Underlines East–West Splits', *Financial Times*, 31 July 1975.

63. See Windsor, op. cit.,

64. Jentleson, op. cit., p. 159.

5
Detente and the Middle East War of 1973

The Middle East war of October 1973 provided the first real test for superpower detente. It also revealed unforeseen difficulties in the attempt to expand the area of superpower cooperation to embrace crisis prevention as well as crisis management. Part of the problem was the lack of genuine superpower agreement on what constituted permissible behaviour in a period of detente. The understandings on crisis prevention reached at the Moscow and Washington Summits combined the American desire for restraint with the Soviet desire for equality. Not surprisingly, therefore, the two superpowers did not agree fully on the scope of crisis prevention. The United States was concerned with prohibiting Soviet military intervention in the Third World, and consequently had a much more extensive concept of crisis than a Soviet leadership concerned only with avoiding situations which, in its judgment, contained a serious risk of war between the superpowers.[1] Whenever tempting opportunities arose for Moscow to change the correlation of forces in its favour, and to do so safely, then, in its view, military action was legitimate.

These differences of approach and expectation were obscured by creative ambiguity on both sides. Although this made agreement possible, it stored up trouble for the future. Because the accords of 1972 and 1973 lacked precision, the obligations they imposed offered considerable latitude for differences of interpretation and expectation. There was no attempt, for example, to specify the level or timing of consultation which was required. Moreover, terms such as 'restraint' were inherently imprecise, and encouraged conflicting judgments about whether or not superpower actions were consistent with their obligations. The lack of consensus on the nature of restraint led inexorably to charges 'that the understandings were being violated and that detente was being betrayed.'[2]

Another problem was that the accords depended for their effectiveness on the willingness of the two superpowers to subordinate other objectives to their desire to avoid increased tension. This posed dilemmas for the superpowers, especially the Soviet Union, in dealing with allies and clients. The more the Soviet Union appeared willing to compromise its objectives and limit its support for anti-Western forces in the Third World, the more vulnerable it became to charges that it was compromising its ideological mission for the sake of detente. The concern with heading off such criticisms – from domestic opponents of detente and from Beijing, as well as from pro-Soviet governments and revolutionary movements in the developing world – may, in part at least, explain the number of Soviet statements emphasising the obligation to support wars of national liberation despite detente. Rhetoric was not always enough, however, and on occasion Moscow found itself unable to refuse more tangible support for anti-Western forces in the Third World, even though this caused problems with the United States. Although the commitment of both superpowers to the Basic Principles may have been serious, therefore, it was manifestly not absolute. Not only did each superpower regard the restraints as more applicable to the adversary than to itself, but both felt it necessary to balance them against – and on occasion subordinate them to – interests and objectives related more directly to the continued competitive elements in their relationship.

An additional problem with the crisis prevention regime was the implicit assumption that the superpowers were in complete control of their allies. Such an assumption was both questionable and harmful: the adversary was blamed for the actions of its clients when in fact it may have had little control over these actions. Patron–client relations are complex, and at times it is uncertain who is manipulating whom to do what. There is also a curious ambivalence about the relationship between the respective clients of the two superpowers and that between the superpowers themselves. On the one hand, conflict between the clients may be a surrogate for direct superpower confrontation; on the other, such a conflict almost invariably carries with it considerable potential for superpower involvement on opposing sides, with attendant dangers of escalation. While the dangers of what could be termed a 'catalytic crisis' work in favour of a restrictive attitude towards clients, the role of these states as superpower 'proxies' works against restraint. Once again, this suggests that agreement on crisis prevention can only be partial rather than comprehensive and qualified rather than absolute.

Another consideration pointing to the same conclusion is that crises cannot be understood solely as dangers to be avoided. Crises often have positive as well as negative functions: they may, for example, be the only way of resolving diplomatic log-jams. Furthermore, there are occasions when taking risky actions and creating a sense of urgency is necessary to sensitise the adversary to one's interests or concerns. The problem is that such actions will be seen as incompatible with the crisis prevention regime, thereby undermining confidence in the regime and eroding even limited trust between the superpowers.

In spite of these limitations, the accords of 1972 and 1973 created certain expectations in Washington about future Soviet behaviour. Although it has been claimed that these expectations were disingenuous since there was no serious code of conduct for behaviour in the Third World, this goes too far.[3] The problem was not the absence of a code of conduct, but the fact that the inherent flaws and ambiguities in this code were not fully understood. The expectations which were generated in the United States were understandable, if somewhat naïve. These expectations were put to the test in October 1973, and according to many accounts of the crisis, Soviet behaviour fell short of the standard of restraint expected. Complicity in the Arab preparations for war, a massive re-supply effort and preparations for direct intervention were cited in the indictment against Moscow. Yet such criticisms of Soviet conduct, while not baseless, underestimate the dilemmas faced by Moscow and ignore the attempts made by the Soviet leaders to act in ways which limited damage to detente.

The Outbreak of War

The Middle East war of 1973 subjected detente to strains that neither superpower wanted and that both would have preferred to avoid. The clients of the superpowers, however, have interests which often depart from those of their patrons. This was certainly the case in October 1973 when Egypt and Syria, acting in concert, launched a two-front offensive against Israel. Underlying President Sadat's initiative was a desire not only to restore Egyptian self-respect which had been so badly damaged in the 1967 war, but also to consolidate his domestic position. Sadat may have also been the prisoner of his own rhetoric: having described 1972 as the year of decision and then done nothing, his credibility could only be restored by dramatic action. The point about all these objectives was that they did not require the defeat of Israel. In this sense, Sadat did not go to war in 1973 in order to achieve victory. This may have been one reason why both the Americans and the Israelis, assessing the probability of hostilities in terms of the traditional military objectives of victory or defeat, were caught by surprise.

Sadat's decision to initiate hostilities seems to have been a very personal one. Yet it was also a protest against Soviet–American detente. Nasser's strategy had been to compensate for Israeli superiority at the local level by raising the Arab–Israeli conflict to the superpower level.[4] Detente undercut this strategy and placed the problems of the Middle East on the back burner.

> 'Sadat wanted to bring the Middle East situation back to center stage in superpower relations ... The superpowers Sadat realised, held the key to a political solution but were willing to see the 'no war, no peace' situation continue indefinitely as long as it kept the Middle East from becoming a source of friction in an otherwise increasingly relaxed superpower relationship. Only through a resumption of the war could Sadat break this attitude.[5]

Far from encouraging this decision, the Soviet Union may have tried to restrain the Egyptian President. Yet, there were limits to Moscow's influence in Cairo. The expulsion of Soviet advisers by Sadat in 1972 had been a setback to Soviet ambitions in the Middle East provoked in large part by Moscow's tardiness in supplying Egypt with the weapons it wanted. The reconciliation, in early 1973, between Sadat and a Soviet Union anxious not to suffer a further deterioration of its position in the Arab world was both an example of 'reverse influence' (that is, from client to patron) and a precondition for an Egyptian attack on Israel. Although the Soviet Union still refused to supply Egypt with the MIG-23s it had long demanded, other restrictions on weaponry, including SCUD missiles, were eased and Sadat was able to go ahead with preparations for war.

In spite of the February reconciliation, Soviet–Egyptian relations remained difficult. The period from February to October 1973 was 'one of recurrent strains ... rather than concerted preparations for war'.[6] The relationship at this stage was a very uncomfortable one for Moscow. By expelling advisers in 1972 Sadat had changed the balance between patron and client and faced Moscow with a dilemma of exclusion from the region or identification with Egypt on terms established by Cairo. In the aftermath of the reconciliation, therefore, the basic problem for Moscow was that it was affected by Egyptian actions but had no effective mechanism for controlling Egyptian policy.[7]

If Moscow was a reluctant rather than an enthusiastic participant in Sadat's plans to go to war, however, its resolve to stand by its ally may have been significantly strengthened as a result of events elsewhere. The overthrow of the government of Salvador Allende in Chile in September 1973 was a setback for Soviet hopes that detente might facilitate a peaceful road to socialism in Third World countries, especially Latin America. Alleged American involvement in the coup against Allende made it difficult for the Soviet Union to continue with its claims that 'the transition from confrontation to stable peaceful coexistence makes it harder for the aggressive neo-colonialist quarters to impose their diktat on the newly-emerged national states'.[8] Even so, the immediate Soviet response to the overthrow of Allende was restrained. This was partly because the Soviet Union had maintained its distance from Allende, displaying a tacit respect for the US sphere of influence in Latin America and an explicit awareness of the limits of Soviet power. The fact that the Soviet press was less critical than the American press of the role of the Nixon administration in the coup also suggests that Moscow attached considerable importance to the maintenance of superpower detente.

Yet events in Chile had intensified the dilemmas associated with detente. In so far as detente was a matter of controversy within the Soviet Union, then Allende's accession to power had been a useful argument in its favour, while his overthrow could only strengthen the arguments of the critics. Also important were the international repercussions. As Glassman has noted: 'Radical elements in the Middle East as well as in other areas of the Third World had already criticised detente as a betrayal of the "progressive" movement. The overthrow of Allende would undoubtedly lead to further questions.'[9] It also exposed the major weakness of Soviet detente policy in the Third World: a Soviet commitment to restraint could very easily undermine Moscow's appeal to allies and clients. Soviet support for Sadat, reluctant as it was, therefore, may have been intended to demonstrate to critics that Moscow was unwilling to sacrifice the interests of its allies for the sake of superpower accommodation.

Even if the Soviet resolve had not been strengthened by events in Chile, however, it is difficult to see what Moscow could have done other than support Egypt. Once the decision was made to retrieve Soviet influence in the region by repairing relations with Sadat, Moscow was effectively committed to Egypt's plans. This posed problems, of course, in terms of Soviet obligations to 'consult' with the United States about situations likely to 'exacerbate' the superpower relationship. One interpretation of Soviet behaviour suggests that Moscow's response to this dilemma was simply to ignore the obligations under detente: 'the Soviet leaders failed to inform the United States of the coming war despite an explicit agreement to do so reached at the 1972 Brezhnev–Nixon Summit'.[10] If the Soviet Union did not provide tactical warning of the Arab attack, however, it did provide a degree of strategic warning – to which, for a variety of reasons, Washington failed to respond.

From May 1973 onwards the Soviet leaders revealed to Nixon and Kissinger that they were having difficulty in restraining their Middle East allies and that there was a significant danger of war in the region. This was made clear to Kissinger during a pre-Summit visit to Moscow, and the same theme was reiterated at the June Summit, especially in an apparently spontaneous late-night discussion between Brezhnev and Nixon at San Clemente.[11] Nixon seems to have treated Brezhnev's anxieties in a somewhat cavalier, if not irresponsible, manner. Soviet warnings were dismissed as heavy-handed attempts to compel Washington to exert pressure on Israel to withdraw from the occupied territories, when in fact they were a serious indicator of Soviet concern over its inability to control the situation in the Middle East.[12] The mistakes, of course, were not only at the top. If Nixon and Kissinger dismissed Soviet concerns, other warning indicators were disregarded within the intelligence community. This was partly because of what one former official has described as conceptual biases: 'a deliberate, rationally planned war was simply implausible in the light of military realities'.[13] It was also a result of the close links between the Israeli and American intelligence services. The Israelis operated on the basis of what later became known as the 'conception' – a conviction that the Egyptians would not initiate hostilities until they had offset Israeli military superiority. This complacency was contagious. American intelligence estimates in May 1973 suggested that war might occur 'soon' in the Middle East.

> This estimate was supported by information which came in during September from America's excellent monitoring system ... and SAMOS satellites. The Israeli intelligence was alerted but dismissed the forecasts of war; in turn the American intelligence community's evaluation of the extensive indicators that had been picked up was heavily influenced by the opinion of its Israeli opposite number.[14]

The implication of all this is that the failure to appreciate the force of Soviet warnings was part of a much broader intelligence failure. For their part, Soviet policy-makers continued to warn that the Middle East could erupt at any time. In late September Gromyko outlined the dangers in an address to the UN General Assembly, and repeated his concern in discussions with President Nixon at the White House a few days later.

Soviet awareness of Sadat's determination to go to war, however, was not matched by awareness of the timing of the impending offensive. Although Sadat had apparently decided on 10 September that the Soviet Union had to be given advance notice of the Egyptian action, this was kept very short. The Soviet Ambassador in Egypt was provided with a somewhat opaque message for Brezhnev on 1 October, and two days later was told that Egypt and Syria were planning military action. It was not until the next day, however, that Assad of Syria informed the Russians that the attack was set for 6 October. It seems, therefore, that the Soviet Union itself had little tactical warning that the Middle East was on the verge of hostilities.

There was, of course, still time for consultation with Washington had Moscow desired. Informing the United States of what was in the offing, however, would have given advance warning to Israel and thereby undermined the element of surprise which was so important to Sadat's military plans. Even so, the Soviet Union engaged in a highly visible evacuation of its personnel from Syria and Egypt, diverting some civilian planes to help in the operation. It is possible that this was meant to warn Washington of the impending war. Garthoff tends to discount this possibility, but it may be significant that Moscow did not take steps to conceal the evacuation.[15] Had American intelligence operators and policy-makers been less insensitive to the possibility of an Arab attack for limited gains, Soviet moves would have provided a degree of tactical warning. At the very least, they suggest that Moscow was not averse to the United States obtaining some advance notice. Furthermore, when hostilities did begin, Moscow may have hoped that the evacuation would be seen in Washington as a clear signal of the Soviet desire not to get directly involved. This somewhat ambivalent approach by Moscow was evident in the war itself, as Moscow buttressed its clients with massive arms supplies while engaging in negotiations with the United States to bring about a cease-fire.

Superpower Competition and Cooperation in the War

During the hostilities both superpowers were intent on maintaining the detente relationship, but they were also concerned with obtaining other objectives that carried some risk to this relationship. The Soviet Union, while anxious to avoid a direct confrontation with the United States, wanted to consolidate its position in the Arab world. US objectives were more complex. As well as preventing the Israelis from being defeated, Kissinger was anxious to manoeuvre diplomatically so that Egypt would increasingly look to Washington rather than Moscow for support. The American stance was also complicated by the fact that Nixon was deeply entangled in Watergate.

Although the actions of the two superpowers were influenced by developments on the battlefield, their initial reactions owed as much to the 1967 Arab–Israeli war as to the situation they found themselves confronting in 1973. The Soviet Union, fearing that its clients would be defeated, was anxious to obtain a cease-fire, whereas Washington, 'expecting a repeat of the Six Day War', was more complacent.[16] Nor was the United States too concerned about Soviet behaviour. Kissinger met with Dobrynin on several occasions and messages between Brezhnev and Nixon were conciliatory in tone.

As pressure mounted on both superpowers to initiate arms shipments to offset the losses incurred by the belligerents through unprecedented attrition rates, much of this initial good will was dissipated. On 9 October, the United States took a decision to begin a limited re-supply of arms to Israel using El Al planes. A Soviet decision seems to have been made around the same time although Moscow was much quicker in dispatching the arms supplies. This was partly because of bureaucratic wrangling in Washington. In order to minimise the visibility of American involvement and thereby avoid alienating moderate Arab states, consideration was given to chartering civilian airlines for the re-supply. This turned into a fiasco and on 13 October a full-scale airlift using American military planes began. The delay, however, may not have been completely accidental. While bureaucratic and organisational difficulties almost certainly played some part in what was a substantial logistical exercise, there have been suggestions that Secretary of State Kissinger was primarily responsible for the hold-up and was using the arms issue to bring Golda Meir in line with American policy.[17] One analyst has claimed that from 10 to 12 October there was a divergence between the American and Israeli positions: 'The United States wanted an early cease-fire. Israel wanted arms in sufficient quantity to ensure a military victory. Over the next two days, the United States moved slowly on arms for Israel as a form of pressure to induce the Israelis to accept a cease-fire in place.'[18] Although Kissinger has rejected these allegations, such an approach was consistent with his overall strategy.

Whatever the case, a more positive American response soon became necessary. The Soviet airlift (which Kissinger described as 'moderate' rather than massive) together with a more conciliatory attitude to the cease-fire by Israel and the rejection of a cease-fire by Sadat prompted a full-scale American re-supply effort beginning on 13 October.[19]

> The main considerations underlying this stage of the Nixon–Kissinger strategy were to convince Sadat that a prolonged war of attrition, fuelled by Soviet arms, would not succeed, and to demonstrate to the Kremlin that the United States was capable of matching Soviet military deliveries to the Middle East. Above all, for the sake of the American position globally and in the region, Soviet arms must not be allowed to dictate the outcome of the fighting.[20]

By 15 October, this danger was past as the military situation began to swing in favour of Israel – a development which prompted Kosygin's trip to Cairo from 16 to 19 October. Although there was a certain cynicism in Soviet behaviour in that its interest in a cease-fire was prompted by the deteriorating position of its clients, this was matched by the cynicism of the American stance which now seemed quite content to procrastinate while Israel improved its military position. In any event, Kosygin's success in getting Sadat to agree to a cease-fire was followed by an invitation for Kissinger to fly to Moscow for consultations on the terms of such an agreement.

The visit to Moscow from 20 to 22 October coincided with increasing domestic turmoil in the United States over Watergate. Furthermore, Kissinger suggests that President Nixon complicated his task by informing Brezhnev that he had full authority to negotiate and then sending him a message to be presented orally to Brezhnev to the effect that the United States and Soviet Union should jointly 'determine the proper course of action to a just settlement, and then bring the necessary pressure on our respective friends for a settlement'.[21] This message conflicted with Kissinger's priorities, which were 'to separate the cease-fire from a postwar political settlement, and to reduce the Soviet role in the negotiations that would follow the cease-fire'.[22] The desire of the Secretary of State to pursue 'exclusionary diplomacy' was clearly uppermost, with the result that he omitted to deliver the message, concentrating instead on the terms of the cease-fire. The Soviet desire for a cease-fire was evident in the alacrity with which the American draft of a UN cease-fire resolution was accepted. This was relayed to Washington and then accepted rather grudgingly by the Israelis, who were angry that they had been presented with a *fait accompli* by the two superpowers acting in concert. In agreeing to the UN resolution, however, they took the opportunity to request that Kissinger return from Moscow to the United States via Israel.

There followed what Kissinger has described as 'a tense visit to Israel'.[23] One result of this was that, either inadvertently or deliberately, Kissinger gave the Israelis the impression that they still had an opportunity to improve their position.[24] In the event, Israeli actions went further than Kissinger either anticipated or wanted, and on 23 October it became clear that the cease-fire of the previous day was beginning to unravel. The position of the Egyptian Third Army – which was surrounded – was becoming increasingly perilous. Although the Security Council passed Resolution 339 reaffirming the initial cease-fire and urging the parties to return to the previous lines, the scene was becoming set for a brief but intense Soviet–American confrontation which seemed totally alien to the spirit of detente.

This confrontation was a result of the initial success of Washington and Moscow in imposing a cease-fire together with their incomplete control over Israeli and Egyptian compliance. The cease-fire, engineered as it was by the superpowers, made the situation at once more stable and more dangerous. By elevating the crisis to the superpowers level, the more refined crisis management practices developed over 30 years and formalized by detente made resolution more likely ... At the same time, the superpowers were now placed in the position of having to guarantee directly the cease-fire and by implication, the behavior of their historically unruly clients. Developments that might occur on the battlefield, even after the cease-fire was implemented, could no longer be artificially segregated into a level of crisis removed from detente. This was to have a profound effect in the course of the subsequent 72 hours.[25]

On 24 October the Israelis, possibly responding to a breakout attempt by the Egyptian Third Army, further improved their position and intensified the sense of alarm in Cairo which had been generated by the breakdown of the first cease-fire. Since the superpowers had taken on responsibility for the cease-fire these developments precipitated a series of abrasive exchanges between them.

The Confrontation of 24–25 October

Of all the Soviet actions during the Middle East war, none had quite so much impact on American opinion as the Brezhnev message to Nixon on the night of 24 October threatening unilateral Soviet intervention in the Middle East. The message, which Senator Henry Jackson described as 'tough' and 'brutal' and which others have interpreted as an ultimatum, had greater impact because it was accompanied by apparent preparations for direct military intervention by Soviet forces.[26] Not only did this aspect of Soviet behaviour appear inconsistent with detente, but it was also in direct contravention of the agreement not to use force or the threat of force against an ally of the other superpower. Yet when considered against the events which preceded it, the Soviet stance appears to be the result of desperation rather than ambition. It was not the preferred option for Moscow, and almost certainly reflected the belief that Kissinger had behaved with considerable duplicity.

The Soviet threat of intervention was essentially a response to the predicament of the Third Army and the panic in Cairo. Sadat, on 24 October, sent messages to both superpowers requesting that they send forces to ensure that the cease-fire was implemented. Initially private, these requests were repeated in public. In response, the Soviet Union made clear that it would support a UN Security Council Resolution acceding to Sadat's request.

Kissinger's reaction was one of horror. As he put it,

> We were not prepared to send American troops to Egypt, nor would we accept the despatch of Soviet forces. We had not worked for years to reduce the Soviet military presence in Egypt only to cooperate in reintroducing it as a result of a UN resolution. Nor would we participate in a joint force with the Soviets, which would legitimize their role in the area and strengthen radical elements. Anti-Soviet moderates like Saudi Arabia, the Emirates, Jordan and Kuwait might well panic at this demonstration of US–Soviet cooperation. The Soviet force might prove impossible to remove; there would be endless pretexts for it to intervene at any point against Israel, or against moderate Arab governments.[27]

Although some of these concerns were understandable, Kissinger was endowing a limited Soviet proposal with a significance it did not have. In his earlier discussions with Moscow he had emphasised that the superpowers had a joint responsibility for bringing an end to hostilities. Now that this was being put to the test it was rejected as a bid for condominium. Although it is understandable that Kissinger did not want Soviet and American forces in close proximity in a volatile military situation, his concern about the introduction of Soviet forces would have been more readily explicable had there never been a large Soviet military presence in Egypt. His rejection of the Soviet proposal, therefore, seems to have resulted from his belief that joint intervention might spoil the opportunity to encourage a long-term shift in Egyptian policy away from Moscow.

Whatever the reason, the rejection of the proposal for joint action faced Moscow with the kind of dilemma it had been anxious to avoid – protecting the interests of its clients was now only feasible by measures which increased the risk of confrontation with the United States. Yet the Brezhnev message, despite its tone, was not intended as a direct threat to Washington. It is better understood as an attempt by Moscow to communicate its concern over the apparent insensitivity of the United States to Soviet interests. It was also a loud protest at Kissinger's failure to restrain the Israelis – a failure which made it appear that Moscow had been taken to the cleaners.[28] Kissinger's claim that the Brezhnev letter was 'one of the most serious challenges to an American President by a Soviet leader' reflected not simply its content but the fact that it coincided with domestic difficulties faced by Nixon in the aftermath of the dismissal of the Watergate special prosecutor Archibald Cox.[29] Garthoff's assessment that 'Brezhnev was appealing to Nixon and Kissinger rather than challenging them' is more persuasive.[30] Kissinger focused on the opportunities that were open to the Soviet leaders; in Moscow, though, the situation was seen in terms of damage limitation.

In order to be effective, however, the appeal had to take dramatic form. Furthermore, the message from Brezhnev warning that the Soviet Union would take unilateral action in the event that the United States found it impossible to act jointly with Moscow, seems to have been accompanied by preparatory actions designed to facilitate such an intervention if necessary. The extent of these preparations is a matter of considerable uncertainty. It has been argued, for example, that Kissinger misinterpreted Soviet actions and that 'the Soviets never really intended to send their airborne units to the fighting zone. They knew that these units were not fit to engage in an Arab–Israeli war.'[31] The problem with this, however, is that it assumes that Soviet intervention would have been primarily a military act, when in fact the preparations (and any subsequent action) were essentially political in character. Furthermore, Soviet airborne troops could have been flown into Egypt without necessarily being introduced into the fighting zone. A Soviet presence in Cairo, while doing nothing to save the Third Army, would at least have set limits to any subsequent Israeli advance. This is not to claim that the Soviet Union was intent on taking such a step. Any intervention would have been a last resort. The preferred Soviet course was clearly for the United States to restrain the Israelis, thereby making Soviet action unnecessary.

For American decision-makers on the night of 24 October, however, the signs looked ominous. Although all seven Soviet airborne divisions had been on alert since 11 or 12 October, there were unconfirmed reports that at least one of these divisions had moved on to a higher alert status and that preparations for imminent departures were visible. The cessation of the Soviet airlift of supplies, which had earlier been seen as a positive step, was now interpreted very differently. 'A large portion of the Soviet airlift fleet could not be located by US intelligence systems, electronic intercepts indicated that Soviet flight plans for the next day were being changed, and certain "communications nets" showed a surge in activity, indicating that a major change in Soviet operations could be expected soon.'[32] It is sometimes suggested that American concerns were intensified by reports that a Soviet ship which had passed through the Bosphorus on 22 October and was heading for Egypt, was emitting radioactive material and might therefore be carrying nuclear weapons. Whether these reports actually reached the White House on or before the night of 24 October is not entirely clear.[33] If they did, then undoubtedly they contributed to the sense of crisis. But even if they were not fed into American calculations, there was still sufficient uncertainty to generate a strong sense of urgency amongst American decision-makers. As one of the participants in the Washington Special Action Group (WSAG) convened by Kissinger to discuss the situation commented, the Soviets 'had the capability, they had the motive, and the assets (i.e., transport aircraft) had disappeared from our screen'.[34] In these circumstances, it was clear to the WSAG that the United States had to respond, if only to clarify the limits of what it regarded as tolerable behaviour. Furthermore, precautionary actions were deemed necessary in case the Soviet Union followed through its warnings and did intervene directly.

A major element in the American response was a series of visible military measures that would be immediately apparent to Soviet intelligence. American strategic forces were placed on a DEFCON 3 alert, fifty to sixty B-52s were moved from Guam back to the continental United States, US naval forces in the Mediterranean were augmented, and perhaps most significantly, the 82nd Airborne Division was placed on standby. These preparatory moves had a dual purpose: they were intended to deter Moscow from direct intervention by signalling that the United States would respond strongly to such a move; in the event that the signals failed they would enable the United States to launch a rapid counter-intervention.

These actions were supplemented some hours later (5 a.m.) by a formal reply to the Brezhnev message that had so alarmed Kissinger. The message, which was passed to Moscow through Dobrynin, warned Brezhnev that unilateral action could have 'incalculable consequences'.[35] It was not wholly negative, however. As well as invoking the spirit of the 1973 Agreement on the Prevention of Nuclear War, it also contained a proposal that a small number of Soviet observers be allowed to monitor the cease-fire. By referring to the prompt implementation of the cease-fire, the note also acknowledged that the Soviet messages had succeeded in heightening American sensitivity to Soviet concerns. In addition, the United States sent a message to Sadat which encouraged the Egyptians to replace their request for superpower intervention with a proposal for a UN 'international force'. Perhaps most important of all, however, the United States compelled the Israelis to ease the position of the Third Army. In other words, as well as attempting to deter the Soviet Union from intervention, Washington also took steps to render that intervention unnecessary. In this connection, the alert was an advantage in that it enabled the United States to put more pressure on Israel without seeming to act under duress.

This mixture of firmness and conciliation was apparent in Kissinger's press conference at noon on 25 October. Although warning about the dangers of transplanting great power rivalry into the Middle East, Kissinger also made clear that the Soviet Union had not taken any irrevocable action and that the United States was not seeking confrontation with Moscow.[36] Within a few hours Brezhnev sent another message confirming that he had despatched seventy Soviet representatives to observe the implementation of the cease-fire. Further pressure still had to be exerted by the United States on Israel to relieve the position of the Third Army, but apart from this the crisis was effectively over.

Although the nuclear alert had contributed to this outcome, the political climate engendered by Watergate led to allegations that it was a ploy to divert attention from Nixon's domestic problems. In fact, Nixon had played a minimal role, simply ratifying the decision made by the Washington Special Action Group under the guidance of Kissinger. Where Watergate might have had some effect, however, was in convincing Kissinger that dramatic action was needed to demonstrate to Moscow that the United States was not paralysed by internal difficulties and was capable of a decisive response when challenged. The alert can best be understood, therefore, as a major element in a package of measures designed both to deter and to reassure the Soviet Union. The approach was classic crisis management.

Questions remain, however, about the extent to which the behaviour of the superpowers was compatible with detente, and especially with the principles of crisis prevention that had been enunciated at the 1972 and 1973 Summits.

The Middle East War and Superpower Detente

The events of October 1973 can be understood as both a challenge to and a vindication of detente. They were a challenge in two senses. In the first place, both the outbreak of the war and the actions of the Israelis after the cease-fire revealed clearly the difficulties the superpowers confronted in translating detente into regional stability. They had to contend with intractable and potentially uncontrollable clients with interests, preoccupations and ambitions that diverged significantly from their own. Furthermore, for Egypt at least, superpower detente was unwelcome, limiting as it did President Sadat's options and inhibiting Soviet support. Because of their continued geopolitical rivalry, however, the superpowers saw advantage in 'surrogate competition'.[37] The desire to preserve the detente relationship and avoid direct confrontation had to be balanced against the need for both Washington and Moscow to demonstrate that they remained reliable patrons. The result was that during the war the superpowers became 'reluctant adversaries ... driven on a collision course by their respective allies'.[38]

The second and closely related way in which the war posed a challenge to detente was that both superpowers took actions which appeared inconsistent with a commitment to relax tensions, and thereby gave ammunition to those who favoured tougher policies towards the rival superpower. This was especially the case with the events of 24 and 25 October when each began to believe that the other was acting in bad faith. The Soviet leaders seem to have concluded that Kissinger had double-crossed them, while Kissinger saw Soviet communications and actions as a frontal challenge encouraged by the belief that the Nixon administration could no longer act decisively. In fact, as Sagan has pointed out, Moscow wanted Washington to act with greater authority and decisiveness – in restraining the Israelis.[39]

The crisis revealed the potential for misunderstanding and misperception inherent in superpower involvement in regional conflicts. It also weakened detente, especially in the United States. 'Although it would be going too far to say that the detente was dealt a mortal blow by the October War, the relationship between the two sides was never the same thereafter.'[40] This was all the more ironic because the codes of conduct for crisis prevention were observed to a surprising degree. In so far as these principles can be understood as a general injunction demanding restraint, they were remarkably successful. Both superpowers behaved with considerable prudence and managed to avoid incidents despite large-scale re-supply efforts into a highly volatile region. Furthermore, they exhibited considerable caution in their naval activities in the Mediterranean. Although Soviet naval forces moved into positions from which they could launch an attack against the Sixth Fleet, this may have been a result of standard operational procedures rather than a deliberate exercise in risk-taking or an attempt at intimidation. Admiral Worth Bagley, the Commander-in-Chief US Naval Forces Europe, later acknowledged that Soviet naval forces were not particularly aggressive. 'It looked as though they were taking some care not to cause an incident. On the whole, their overt posture was restrained and considerate.'[41] In addition to exhibiting such caution, Moscow and Washington cooperated, albeit uneasily, in bringing about a cease-fire, thereby fulfilling the injunction that they act so as to prevent situations liable to cause 'a dangerous exacerbation of their relationship'. These achievements were impressive, and cast doubt on claims that the superpowers, especially the Soviet Union, blatantly disregarded the 'rules of behaviour' that they had recently formulated.

One element in the agreements of 1972 and 1973, however, was that Moscow and Washington should refrain from the threat of force against each other and against each other's allies. The events of 24 and 25 October seemed to violate this 'rule'. Yet the measures initiated by the superpowers had something of a ritualistic quality about them and were not nearly so dangerous as they appeared. The confrontation was very far removed from that which had taken place in Cuba eleven years earlier. It is significant, for example, that neither side attempted to achieve a *fait accompli*. What appeared as preparations for military action were essentially substitutes for direct intervention. Nor should Moscow's preparations be seen as an attempt by the Soviet Union to 'obtain unilateral advantage' at the expense of the United States – something that the superpowers had declared incompatible with the principle of restraint. On the contrary, Moscow at the end of the war was less concerned with obtaining 'unilateral advantage' for itself and its allies than with minimising the unilateral disadvantages resulting from Israeli military actions after the cease-fire. The United States was less restrained: the whole thrust of Kissinger's diplomacy was designed to exclude the Soviet Union from the postwar settlement and thereby gain a major advantage for the United States in the continued geopolitical competition. Suggestions that the United States was playing by a set of rules to which the Soviet Union was indifferent, therefore, are not persuasive. If anything, the asymmetries of behaviour were in the other direction.

The implication of all this is that the reappraisal of detente which began in Washington in the aftermath of the war was, by and large, unwarranted. The statements made by Kissinger and by Soviet leaders claiming that superpower behaviour during October 1973 vindicated the improved relationship were far more appropriate. This was rarely acknowledged in the American debate, however, and from the October war onwards, detente was in political trouble. The hostility towards it was intensified by Soviet–American competition elsewhere in the Third World.

Notes

1. See A. George, *Managing US–Soviet Rivalry* (Boulder, Col.: Westview Press, 1983), for a fuller analysis.

2. R. Garthoff, *Detente and Confrontation* (Washington, DC: The Brookings Institution, 1985), p. 338.

3. R. Menon, *Soviet Power and the Third World* (New Haven: Yale University Press), p. 11.

4. We have benefited from discussions with Avi Shlaim, St Antony's College, Oxford, on this point.

5. C.S. Shoemaker and J. Spanier, *Patron–Client State Relationships* (New York: Praeger, 1984), p. 140.

6. G. Golan, *Yom Kippur and After* (Cambridge: Cambridge University Press, 1977), p. 44.

7. I. Smart, 'The Superpowers and the Middle East', *The World Today*, vol. 30 (Jan. 1974), pp. 4–15.

8. *New Times*, no. 36, Sept. 1973.

9. J. Glassman, *Arms for the Arabs* (Baltimore, Md.: Johns Hopkins University Press, 1975), p. 118.

10. R.O. Freedman, 'Detente and US–Soviet Relations in the Middle East during the Nixon Years (1969–74)' in D.W. Sheldon (ed.), *Dimensions of Detente* (New York: Praeger, 1978), p. 105.

11. R. Garthoff, *Detente and Confrontation* (Washington, DC: The Brookings Institution, 1985), p. 365 and H. Kissinger, *Years of Upheaval* (Boston: Little, Brown, 1982), pp. 296–8.

12. See ibid.

13. W. Quandt, *Decade of Decisions* (London: University of California Press, 1977), p. 168.

14. See A. Shlaim, 'Failures in National Intelligence Estimates: The Case of the Yom Kippur War', *World Politics*, vol. 23, no. 3 (April 1976), p. 361.

15. Garthoff, op. cit., p. 367.

16. Kissinger, op. cit., p. 491.

17. Garthoff, op. cit., p. 369 note 37.

18. Quandt, op. cit., p. 179.

19. Kissinger, op. cit., p. 500.

20. Quandt, op. cit., p. 184.

21. Kissinger, op. cit., p. 551.

22. Ibid.

23. Ibid., p. 559.

24. Garthoff, op. cit., pp. 371–2.

25. Shoemaker and Spanier, op. cit., p. 167.

26. Garthoff, op. cit., p. 386.

27. Kissinger, op. cit., p. 579.

28. B. Blechman and D. Hart, 'The Political Utility of Nuclear Weapons: The 1973 Middle East Crisis' *International Security*, vol. 7, no. 1 (Summer 1982), pp. 132–56 at p. 136.

29. Kissinger, op. cit., p. 583.

30. Garthoff, op. cit., p. 383.

31. E. Karsh, 'The Myth of Direct Soviet Intervention in an Arab Israeli War', *Journal of the Royal United Services Institute for Defence Studies* (Sept. 1984), pp. 28–32 at p. 31.

32. Blechman and Hart, op. cit., pp. 137–8.

33. We are grateful to Galia Golan for a helpful discussion on this point.

34. Blechman and Hart, op. cit., p. 139.

35. See Ibid., p. 141, for the text.

36. Kissinger, op. cit., pp. 594–5.

37. Shoemaker and Spanier, op. cit., p. 184.

38. S. Sagan, 'Lessons of the Yom Kippur Alert', *Foreign Policy*, no. 36 (Fall 1979), pp. 160–77 at p. 161.

39. Ibid, p. 170.

40. George, op. cit., pp. 150–1.

41. See *US News and World Report*, 24 Dec. 1973, p. 28.

6
Superpower Detente and Competition in the Third World

The demise of detente is often attributed to Soviet activism in the Third World especially in Africa. By the end of the 1970s the dominant view in Washington was that Moscow had used detente as a cover to build up its military capabilities and to embark upon a course of unremitting expansionism: although the Soviet Union may not have had a master plan, Moscow consciously and deliberately launched a geopolitical offensive designed to undermine Western influence throughout the Third World. This was interpreted as part of a Soviet quest for global dominance inspired by Marxist-Leninist ideology. Soviet statements themselves gave credence to this interpretation. At the Twenty-fifth Party Congress in 1976, for example, Brezhnev acknowledged the crucial Soviet role in the 'development of a world-wide revolutionary process'.[1] The Soviet Union had always preached revolution, but there now appeared to be a much closer congruence between Soviet words and actions.

It was also believed in Washington that Moscow's extensive involvement in Third World conflicts reflected a Soviet willingness to take high risks: prudence and caution were no longer necessary now that the Soviet Union had neutralised the American nuclear advantage. Emboldened by strategic parity, the Soviet Union used its newly developed power projection capabilities to provide logistic support for Cuban combat forces in what became an effective pattern of 'cooperative intervention'.[2] Cuban involvement, it was claimed, guaranteed outcomes favourable to Moscow and ensured that Soviet gains were significant and enduring. 'The USSR had been involved militarily in local conflicts before ... but the magnitude, scope and apparent success of its efforts in the 1970s were perhaps without precedent.'[3]

Inevitably, this led to allegations in Washington that Moscow was breaking the rules of detente – and violating the crisis prevention regime which had been established during the detente of the early 1970s. The restraint which was appropriate to detente – and which the United States expected as a result of the Basic Principles Agreement and the Agreement on the Prevention of Nuclear War – was simply not evident in Soviet conduct. Despite lip-service to the principle that neither superpower should attempt to obtain 'unilateral advantage' at the expense of the other, Soviet actions, it was argued, subordinated the relationship with the United States to revolutionary activism and displayed a ruthless opportunism which the United States believed was incompatible with detente and ultimately destroyed it.

In spite of the comprehensiveness of this indictment, there are several outstanding questions about detente and superpower involvement in the Third World in the 1970s. Some stem from ambiguities in the rules of detente. Was Soviet behaviour incompatible with these rules as mutually understood or simply as interpreted by the United States? There are also questions about US behaviour: if the crisis prevention regime failed, was it simply a result of Soviet transgressions or did the United States also breach the codes of conduct? Were American policies as restrained, as circumspect and as consistent with the crisis prevention injunctions as is often suggested? Is the asymmetry argument – that Moscow sought unilateral advantage while Washington exhibited unilateral restraint – really valid?

In attempting to answer these questions the analysis focuses primarily on the struggle for power in Angola in 1975 and 1976, and the conflict between Ethiopia and Somalia in 1977 and 1978. Other areas of Soviet involvement, most notably the Yemen and southeast Asia, intensified the fears about Soviet ambition and irresponsibility and are also briefly considered. The final section of the chapter offers an overall appraisal of Soviet and American behaviour and its compatibility with detente.

Superpower Detente and the Angola War

If superpower detente had barely survived the Middle East war of 1973, developments in Angola in 1975 posed a further challenge. Soviet and Cuban involvement in Angola not only provided domestic critics of detente with new ammunition but also led Henry Kissinger himself to question the relationship that he had done so much to establish. Moscow's apparent willingness to exploit opportunities for unilateral advantage resulting from regional instabilities, even when this jeopardised detente, was regarded as a symbol of a new assertiveness which added a disturbing element to superpower relations.

The opportunities in Angola arose partly because of events in Europe. In April 1974 a military coup in Portugal overthrew the Caetano regime. The new government moved quickly to grant independence to its African colonies. Problems arose in Angola, however, because there were three major revolutionary movements, divided largely along ethnic and geographical lines. The rivalry among them was intensified by personal antipathies among the leaders, as well as by their links with other governments.

The Front for the National Liberation of Angola (FNLA), led by Holden Roberto, had its roots in the Bakongo community in northern Angola, and was strongly supported by Zaïre's President Mobutu and by Beijing. A second group, the National Union for the Total Independence of Angola (UNITA), led by Jonas Savimbi, had a strong political base in the Ovimbundu people – the largest single ethnic group. The third faction, the Popular Movement for the Liberation of Angola (MPLA), led by Dr Agostinho Neto, a Marxist, had its strength in the urban poor in Luanda and the 1.3 million Mbundu people of the hinterland. The MPLA was the recipient of Soviet, Cuban and East European aid. It also had broad support from the Portuguese Left and, after the coup, from the Portuguese Armed Forces Movement.[4]

Faced with competing factions, the Portuguese, together with the Organisation of African Unity, attempted to ensure that there was an orderly devolution of power in Angola. Strenuous efforts were made to bring the factions together. The Alvor Accord of 15 January provided for a transitional government in which the three movements would share power with the Portuguese until 11 November, the date set for independence. Elections were to be held in October to determine the composition of the new government. The animosities among the three movements, however, militated against a peaceful transition to independence. Fighting broke out in Luanda in February and escalated in March and April. By July, the MPLA had not only consolidated its position in and around Luanda but also had gained control over many of the provincial areas. In the following months, however, the position of the MPLA deteriorated. The FNLA and UNITA buried their differences in order to launch concerted counter-offensives against MPLA-controlled territory, while in October, 1,500 to 2,000 South African troops added their weight to the counter-offensive. The results of this intervention were short-term military gains for UNITA and FNLA but a loss of political and diplomatic support in the rest of Africa. By early November much of the southern part of Angola had been wrested from the MPLA, but this did not prevent Neto from proclaiming the existence of the People's Republic of Angola on 11 November. Furthermore, around the middle of November, the MPLA, supported by Cuban troops, turned the tide of battle once again. South African forces began to withdraw, and the FNLA was forced to retreat into Zaïre. By the end of January 1976 there were around 10,000 to 12,000 Cubans fighting alongside the MPLA, and except for sporadic guerrilla activity by UNITA forces in the south, the war was over. An increasing number of states recognised the MPLA as the legitimate government of Angola, and in April it was admitted to the United Nations. As far as the United States was concerned the outcome was victory for Soviet and Cuban intervention. Yet a close analysis of American policy suggest that Washington had inadvertently helped to legitimise that intervention.

US Policy towards Angola

American policy towards Angola in 1975 and 1976 was characterised by mistaken assumptions, inadequate intelligence, bureaucratic rivalry and ineptitude, inefficient implementation and, finally, by a decisive congressional intervention which completely undermined the Ford administration's policy. These shortcomings can be traced back to National Security Study Memorandum 39, completed during the first year of the Nixon administration. This review of American policy towards southern Africa concluded that African insurgent movements did not offer viable alternatives to continued colonial rule. Portuguese resolve to uphold its position was not questioned.[5] After the 1973 Middle East war underlined the importance of the Azores in facilitating the American re-supply of Israel, the United States was particularly anxious to maintain good relations with Portugal and gave little attention to the nationalist aspirations of the Portuguese colonies.

Consequently, the coup in Portugal and the moves towards the independence of Angola caught the United States unprepared. The result was a policy which was insensitive to local conditions and 'marked by a notable lack of careful planning, only sporadic high level attention, and remarkably loose implementation'.[6] In the evolution of this policy, several key decisions stand out.[7] The first is that of the 'Forty Committee' (that is, the Committee of the National Security Council set up to authorise and oversee covert operations) in January 1975 to provide $300,000 to the FNLA for political activities although not for military aid. The CIA had supplied Roberto with money and arms from 1962 until 1969. The decision to 'reactivate' him in January 1975 has been severely criticised, yet was simply a legitimisation of activities initiated by the CIA in 1974 without the approval and possibly even the knowledge of the Forty Committee.[8] Perhaps because of this, the January decision was made with little assessment of its possible consequences: it 'was made almost casually, as a routine matter, in part because of past ties with the FNLA, and certainly without any apprehension whatsoever that it might prove to be the first step on a slippery slope'.[9] This decision helped to lock the United States into a competitive approach to the war: it both reflected and intensified the tendency to impose an East–West framework upon a conflict that was deeply rooted in indigenous conditions. The MPLA's Marxist label, together with the fact that it had been receiving support from Moscow, was sufficient to generate American opposition. Conversely, the close links between the FNLA and Mobutu, who was one of America's closest allies in Africa, made Roberto a natural client for Washington. In addition, the January decision ruled out certain options which would have served the United States better. Washington

> might have acted expeditiously to forestall competition with the Soviets, modestly improve its diplomatic position in Africa, and even to encourage conciliation in Angola. In particular, the United States might have mustered its diplomatic forces and encouraged the OAU to take up a continuing role as political arbiter, thereby minimising the hazards of large-scale external intervention.[10]

At the time, however, these options were given scant attention and deemed less attractive than continued covert action. Consequently, the United States provided little support for the Alvor Accord and did not attempt, until too late, to invoke the 1972 and 1973 understandings on crisis prevention.

Nor was this the only mistake. Little consideration was given to the way in which American support for the FNLA might be perceived in Moscow. It was assumed that the Soviet Union would simply accept the advantages accruing to the FNLA as a result of American assistance. 'Soviet involvement on behalf of the MPLA was seen as minimal, lukewarm, and hesitant.'[11] What Washington failed to realise was that it had 'stumbled into a Sino–Soviet dispute'.[12] The competition with China, which supported the rival factions, gave Soviet support for the MPLA a degree of significance that was simply not appreciated in the United States. Consequently, American policy-makers failed to anticipate that their political aid to the FNLA would help to provoke Moscow into increasing its military aid to the MPLA.

They also seemed to be unaware of Soviet disillusionment with detente. In the aftermath of the Middle East war Moscow was effectively excluded from the region. Kissinger now appeared to be pursuing an active if low-key policy in Angola, and it was difficult, therefore, for the Soviet Union to refrain from a firm response. Furthermore, there were few incentives for Soviet restraint. The expected benefits for Moscow from trade with the United States had not been forthcoming because of congressional legislation linking expanded trade to the issue of Jewish emigration. This congressional action was not a cause of Soviet involvement in Angola; it simply meant that there were few incentives for Moscow to impose a self-denying ordinance and exhibit the kind of restraint which Kissinger wanted – especially when Kissinger himself seemed unwilling to act with similar restraint. If the United States was unaware of the Sino–Soviet dimension in Angola, it was equally insensitive to the effect of its own actions on Moscow.

In short, the January decision of the Forty Committee was based on several reinforcing misperceptions. William Hyland, however, has dismissed the argument that this decision was a fatal step as nonsense.[13] He is certainly correct to emphasise that the amount of aid involved was minimal. Nevertheless, it is crucial not to ignore 'the tyranny of small decisions'.[14] Despite the casual way it was made, the January decision established the policy framework; subsequent discussion focused largely on implementation. Until the congressional intrusion into the policy-making process in December, there was no serious attempt to reconsider the wisdom of covert intervention. Objections from the State Department were effectively overruled in July 1975, when a series of high-level meetings within the executive branch resulted in a substantial programme of military aid to the movements fighting against the MPLA.

The July decision was in many respects an elaboration of that made six months earlier. Once again the CIA pressed hardest for further American involvement, even though this was a tacit acknowledgment that the high expectations which generated the earlier package of aid to the FNLA had been unwarranted. Whereas the earlier decision had been made almost by default, however, by July the question of American involvement in Angola had become the focus of considerable internal debate, sparked largely by Nathaniel Davis, former Ambassador to Chile and one of the people blamed (wrongly as it happened) for the fall of Allende. Davis had been confirmed as Assistant Secretary of State for African Affairs in March, and after reviewing the Angolan issue concluded that enlarging the covert aid programme should be avoided: there was a high probability of disclosure, which in the American political climate of the mid-1970s could prove disastrous.[15] He also expressed doubts about American ability to compete effectively with Moscow, arguing that the United States would be unable to do more than 'commit limited resources and buy marginal influence'.[16] In addition, Davis warned about becoming linked with Savimbi, whose search for arms was leading him towards South Africa which 'had expressed interest in providing financial assistance'.[17]

These views were reiterated and embellished in the report of an inter-agency task force on Angola, which appeared in June. The committee, chaired by Davis, concluded that an increased diplomatic effort was preferable to further military involvement, which would simply provoke greater Soviet efforts on behalf of the MPLA. It favoured using private approaches or public pressure to persuade Moscow to reduce its involvement. At the same time, it argued, the United States should work with Tanzania, Zambia and Zaïre to reduce the flow of arms into Angola. In this way the competition could be shifted back to the political arena, thereby providing more opportunity for a black African solution to be found to a black African problem.

These recommendations were not accepted by Secretary of State Kissinger and other leading figures. There were several reasons for this. The first was Kissinger's concern with American credibility. This had been evident over the Cienfuegos base in 1970 and in the India–Pakistan war of 1971, as well as in the Middle East conflict of October 1973. If anything, it was even stronger in the summer of 1975 because of the fall of Saigon to the North Vietnamese. Kissinger and President Ford were anxious to demonstrate that the United States was still capable of decisive action. Furthermore, the Mayaguez incident, when American forces were used to secure the release of Americans seized by Cambodia, had shown that assertiveness could elicit domestic support. The administration was also under pressure from critics in Congress to adopt a tougher stance towards Moscow. When combined with Kissinger's continued complacency about the depth of the Soviet commitment, these considerations militated against the diplomatic or 'hands-off' options identified by Davis. It was also suggested that Davis himself was not giving sound advice – 'still smarting from the trauma of Chile, he was terrified of having anything to do with another crisis'.[18] Perhaps most important of all, though, was the fact that the July decision was made against the background of a growing crisis in Portugal itself: 'The interaction of the two crises – in Lisbon, where a Communist success appeared imminent, and in Angola, where the indigenous communists also seemed about to prevail – was decisive.'[19] This linkage certainly increased American sensitivity to events in Angola. Yet, in one sense, the linkage was a false one. The two situations were very different both in their origins and seriousness. A communist Portugal would have posed difficult problems for NATO; an MPLA victory in Angola would hardly be decisive. Furthermore, the American policy in Portugal helped to avert a communist victory whereas in Angola it contributed to the success of the MPLA.

Despite a lack of credibility with Kissinger and the National Security Council staff, Nathaniel Davis did not give up easily. Davis prepared a series of memos on 12, 14, 16 and 17 July in an attempt to influence the decisions of the Forty Committee, which was considering the CIA Action Plan for further covert aid. The rejection of his advice not only led to his resignation but also revealed the dominance of the global strategists over the area specialists.[20] Local and regional considerations were set aside in favour of an approach which saw the issue primarily in terms of geopolitical competition between the superpowers.

If global considerations were decisive in the July decision to embark on a $30 million programme of covert assistance to the FNLA and UNITA, these were reinforced by at least one local factor

– the favour which Mobutu enjoyed in Washington. Regarded as one of America's most important allies in Africa, Mobutu emphasised the dangers to Zaïre that would stem from a victory of the pro-Soviet faction in Angola, and seems to have played skilfully on American concerns about Soviet influence in southern Africa.

The purpose of the programme initiated by the Forty Committee in July, however, remains ambiguous. It is not clear whether Kissinger intended the aid programme simply to restore the position of the FNLA and UNITA, thereby opening the way for a compromise settlement, or saw it as an opportunity to bring about the defeat of the MPLA. The account by John Stockwell of the CIA task force on Angola suggests that in the summer of 1975 there was a 'no win' policy.[21] He is highly critical of this, arguing that at this stage the war was on such a small scale that if the United States had introduced advisers and tactical air support it could have defeated the MPLA before the Soviet Union could react. Hyland suggests that this evaluation was suppressed by the CIA, which thereby 'sabotaged its own plan and operation'.[22] Although he acknowledges that Kissinger had not clarified American objectives sufficiently, he also contends that 'The CIA had never pressed the issue of American aims and tactics.'[23] Furthermore, whereas Kissinger wanted to act quickly, 'the actual programme was the opposite: slow and incremental. It was maddening how inept the CIA was in finding and dispatching military equipment.'[24]

For Hyland, the problem was one largely of poor implementation. Although this might have hampered American policy, however, there were more fundamental flaws. Stockwell's assumptions about the possibility of quick victory were probably as over-optimistic as those in the CIA Paper presented to the Forty Committee in July. This Paper claimed that a $40 million programme would match Soviet aid to Neto, and reveals that one of the recurrent mistakes of American policy during this period was to underestimate the Soviet commitment to the MPLA.

The other mistake was to become too closely associated with South Africa. There has been much speculation that South African involvement was the result of American encouragement. Yet Stockwell, who is generally highly critical of American policy in Angola, denies this. If South Africa came into the war for its own purposes, though, it did so in the expectation that the United States would welcome its involvement. This was certainly the case as far as the CIA was concerned. Although no formal decision was made, 'coordination was effected at all CIA levels and the South Africans escalated their involvement in step' with that of the United States.[25] The consequences of this were far-reaching: it delayed the military victory of the MPLA, but legitimised the Soviet and Cuban intervention in the eyes of other African states.

Soviet Policy towards Angola

Soviet involvement in the Angola war was a continuation of its traditional policy of support for national revolutionary movements in the Third World. The difference in 1975 was that Moscow was both less inhibited and more effective than in the past. The lack of inhibition stemmed partly from the Soviet conception of itself as a superpower equal to the United States. Strategic parity meant very little unless accompanied by a right to intervene militarily in the Third World as the United States had done throughout the cold war. This does not mean that the Soviet Union was prepared to take high risks. During the mid-1970s the likelihood of superpower confrontation was minimal as American opinion in the aftermath of the Vietnam war effectively prohibited the United States from direct military involvement in the Third World. This represented an important shift in the 'correlation of forces' in Moscow's favour. Soviet scholars, in a judgment probably shared by the political leadership, concluded that American domestic paralysis offered the Soviet Union opportunities to determine the outcome of regional conflicts, and to do so with impunity.[26]

Although there were several novel features in Moscow's approach to the Angola war in 1975, the Soviet Union had supported Neto since 1964 when his visit to Moscow was followed by Soviet arms and military training. Further visits in 1966, 1967, 1970 and 1971 helped to cement the relationship, as did the MPLA's commitment to Marxism. As a result of a dispute within the MPLA, Soviet arms deliveries were suspended in 1973, but resumed in October 1974. By the end of 1974 the total aid to the MPLA provided by the Soviet Union since the early 1960s had reached a level of around $54 million.

If there were important elements of continuity in Soviet policy, there were also major elements of improvisation. Policy 'evolved incrementally in reaction to the internal dynamics of the conflict as well as to the courses charted by other external actors'.[27] Soviet initiatives exploiting new opportunities in Angola were combined with reactive elements in Soviet policy designed to ensure that the MPLA had at least some part in the government of Angola after independence. The balance between these elements changed as the situation in Angola changed. In late 1974 and the spring of 1975, Soviet policy was designed to ensure that the MPLA remained a major force in Angola. Had the Soviet Union failed to increase the level of support for the MPLA, it would have left the field to the FNLA and permitted a victory for its

Chinese and American backers. Moscow may·have been especially sensitive to further Chinese gains at Soviet expense. As Legum has observed, 'The collapse of the Portuguese dictatorship in April 1974 initiated a new phase in the Sino–Soviet struggle, with the Chinese initially making far the greater gains, particularly in Mozambique and in consolidating their relations with Tanzania and Zambia.'[28] If it was to halt 'the rising Chinese tide', therefore, Moscow had little alternative other than to act decisively.[29] The Chinese factor was also relevant to Soviet–American relations. Although Moscow may have been concerned about the possibility of provoking a tacit alliance between Washington and Beijing, it could not seek an agreement with the Ford administration on mutual non-involvement as this would have left the Chinese with a free hand. In these circumstances, increased Soviet support for the MPLA was deemed essential. Even with the additional aid, the Soviet Union remained anxious about the MPLA's prospects, and in the early months of 1975 supported the Alvor Accord, probably on the basis that this offered Neto the best chance of participation in the future government of Angola.

Accordingly, the Soviet news media dropped their propaganda against the FNLA and UNITA. As the Accord broke down and fighting intensified, Soviet military aid to the MPLA increased. Whereas earlier supplies had come through intermediary states, the new batch of arms was delivered directly to Angolan ports. 'Available evidence suggests that in the months of April, May and June alone, two Yugoslav ships, four Soviet ships, and two East German ships delivered arms to Luanda. Other heavy equipment was shipped and airlifted by the Soviets to Pointe-Noire in Congo-Brazzaville and to Guinea, where it was either reshipped or airlifted to MPLA bases ... on the Angolan coast or to Luanda.'[30] Between April and October, twenty-seven shiploads and thirty to forty air supply missions took place.[31]

Equally if not more significant was the arrival in Angola in May and June of 230 Cuban military advisers to assist the MPLA. This was in response to an MPLA request for direct help – a request which stemmed from the inexperience of its forces in handling modern weapon systems, and which may have been prompted by a Soviet unwillingness to go beyond the supply of arms. It is also possible that Moscow suggested to the MPLA leadership that they approach the Cubans. Whatever the case, the request was met sympathetically, partly because the links between Cuba and the liberation movements went back to the early 1960s, and partly because Castro sensed an opportunity to further his own revolutionary mission.

Equipped with Soviet weapons and Cuban advisers, the MPLA was able to improve its position, thereby precipitating the decision by the

Forty Committee in July. By August outside forces were engaged on all sides. Zaïre had committed several paratroop companies to the FNLA while South African troops had moved into Angola to protect the Cunene Dam complex, which supplies Namibia with electricity. Furthermore, by then the MPLA had suffered several reverses. This loss of momentum together with concerns over Chinese–American collusion, and the possibility of large-scale South African intervention seems to have prompted another Soviet reappraisal during August 1975.

The result was a decision to intervene much more actively in support of the MPLA. There may well have been the same kind of incrementalism in this decision that had characterised the US policy review in July. Having already invested considerable resources in Angola, the Soviet Union was reluctant to withdraw. The only real alternative, therefore, was to increase the level of support, a decision which may have been encouraged by the Soviet assessment of American policy. Kissinger had hoped that increased assistance to the FNLA would signal American determination to the Soviet Union, but the covert and limited nature of the aid may simply have revealed the limits of American involvement. Sufficiently engaged to alarm Moscow, the United States was not committed enough to pose a serious prospect of a direct superpower confrontation. As Valenta has summarised it:

> In August 1975, the MPLA situation was viewed by the Soviets as precarious, and the imminence of a massive South African intervention as very real. The stakes in Angola were high, the risks relatively low. The Soviets appear to have perceived American policy-makers as operating under multiplying domestic constraints, and they probably believed that a Soviet–Cuban intervention would not provoke a strong US response.[32]

These considerations may have been strengthened by domestic factors, especially the forthcoming Twenty-fifth Party Congress.[33] A strong stand on Angola would disarm critics claiming that detente was a one-way street favouring the United States, would give substance to ideological statements denying incompatibility between detente and wars of national liberation, would provide 'an occasion for regaining momentum in world politics following the setbacks in Chile, Egypt and Portugal', and would polish 'the USSR's tarnished image as leader of the world revolutionary movement'.[34]

The other consideration was the availability of Cuban combat forces. Cuban involvement was one of the most important developments of the war, and one which particularly angered not only the critics of detente in the United States but also the architect of detente, Henry Kissinger. Consequently, much discussion has revolved around the nature of the Soviet–Cuban relationship.[35] One interpretation is that the Cubans were little more than Soviet surrogates and that Havana was acting on the direct orders of Moscow rather than according to its own precepts and in pursuit of its own objectives. This is plausible. Cuba's economic dependence on the Soviet Union gave Moscow considerable influence over Havana. If Cuban troops provided the cutting edge of Soviet involvement in Angola, however, this was advantageous to Castro as well as to Moscow. Although Castro emphasised international solidarity with oppressed peoples in Africa, the Cuban role in Angola did not stem solely from revolutionary altruism. Castro was bidding for a leadership role among the non-aligned nations, as well as attempting to establish himself as a key link between African nations and the Soviet bloc in a way which would increase his leverage with both. These external considerations may have been reinforced by internal factors. According to some reports, the Minister for the Armed Forces, Raul Castro, provided much of the impetus for Cuban military involvement in Africa, seeing this as a way of enhancing the status and prestige of the armed forces within Cuba. More generally, successful military activities overseas would help to compensate for the disastrous state of the Cuban economy.

In short, there were persuasive reasons for Cuba to respond positively to requests for help from the MPLA. The Cubans themselves have always claimed that this was an independent decision, and that Moscow was informed afterwards rather than consulted beforehand. If Cuba was not simply a surrogate for the Soviet Union, however, there was clearly a convergence of interests between them. Without Soviet logistic support the large-scale introduction of Cuban forces into Angola would have proved impossible.

In late September 1975, Soviet and East German ships began arriving in Angola with Cuban combat troops. On 11 November, the day independence was declared, the FNLA and Zaïrean forces were routed in the Quifangondo valley about 20 kilometres from Luanda. The use by the Cubans of 122 mm rockets proved decisive and heralded the final phase of the war for the FNLA and Mobutu's forces. South African and UNITA forces continued to advance for some weeks, but then they too began to retreat as the combined weight of Soviet arms and Cuban forces proved overwhelming.

This left the MPLA in a dominant position. The Chinese had ceased to support the FNLA in October, partly because of the movement's ineptitude, but also because Beijing feared being tainted by association with South Africa. Rather than opting for a similar withdrawal, the United States attempted to escalate its involvement, and in the last few months of 1975 and early 1976 Angola became a major problem in Soviet–American relations. Although it did not develop into a full-blown confrontation, the Soviet and Cuban involvement – and the success it had – placed considerable strain on detente.

Angola and Superpower Detente

Until the autumn of 1975 Angola, despite the connection with events in Portugal, was little more than a sideshow for the United States. The increased presence of the Soviets and Cubans, however, endowed the conflict with greater significance. Garthoff has even suggested that 'The American stake in the Angola conflict was not threatened by the Soviet–Cuban involvement on the other side, it was created by it.'[36] This is something of an exaggeration. The American programme of covert aid had already given the United States a stake in the outcome. Nevertheless, the American involvement had been covert and there was still an opportunity for a graceful exit. Instead of this, Kissinger adopted a two-pronged approach as part of what Alexander George has described as a 'complex damage-limitation strategy'.[37] One element in this strategy was a public and private campaign designed to get Moscow to refrain from further assistance to the MPLA. This was accompanied by efforts to keep the other factions in the war. Both strands encountered major difficulties.

The campaign to induce greater Soviet restraint began with a Kissinger speech in September complaining that the involvement of extra-continental powers was 'inconsistent with the promise of future independence'.[38] By November, Kissinger's statements had become much more direct, and included remarks about the threat to detente posed by Soviet actions in Angola. In a speech in Detroit on 24 November, Kissinger warned that

> The United States cannot be indifferent while an outside power embarks upon an interventionist policy – so distant from its homeland and removed from traditional Russian interests. The Soviet Union still has an opportunity for a policy of restraint which permits Angolans to resolve their differences without outside intervention. We would be glad to cooperate in such a course. But time is running out. Continuation of an interventionist policy must inevitably threaten other relationships.[39]

The following day at a press conference the Secretary of State argued that Soviet actions were difficult to reconcile 'with the principles of coexistence that were signed in 1972'.[40] In language reminiscent of that used by Nathaniel Davis in the internal debates in July 1975, Kissinger claimed that it was necessary to find an African solution to an African problem.

Similar messages were apparently being conveyed to Moscow in private. Kissinger had raised Angola with Dobrynin on 29 October (before the Cubans had a decisive impact) and discussed it further with the Soviet Ambassador on several occasions in November. By the end of that month, however, the United States was still awaiting 'a conclusive reply' to the concerns it had conveyed to Moscow.[41] This was hardly surprising. The superpowers had been competing in Angola throughout the year and Kissinger had not objected to Soviet involvement, preferring to continue the competition. Now that the Cuban card had been played he was attempting to change the rules and 'to convert the competitive game into a cooperative one'.[42] But the considerations which had encouraged Soviet involvement had not disappeared. Furthermore, by this stage the Soviet commitment had taken on a momentum which was difficult to reverse. For Moscow to have accepted a change in the ground rules in December

> would have required the USSR both to forego the advantages it had gained and to undertake to persuade the Cuban forces to withdraw from Angola. Not only did the United States lack sufficient leverage – either in threats or in promises – to persuade the Soviets to accept the US proposal, the costs to Moscow of appearing to back away from victory in Angola and of pressuring the Cubans to do the same would have been substantial.[43]

After recognising the MPLA as the legitimate government of Angola, the Soviet Union could hardly accept arrangements for a coalition government. A strategy which might have worked in the middle of 1975 was no longer feasible by November and December 1975.

Yet the Soviet Union was not oblivious to American concerns. On 9 December Dobrynin responded to the earlier American complaints in a meeting with Kissinger, and the following day President Ford formally proposed to the Soviet Union that it support a negotiated settlement. There is some circumstantial evidence that Moscow took this seriously, and from 9 December to 25 December the Soviet airlift of supplies to Angola was halted. During this period, however, the other strand of American policy was derailed. The covert support that had been given since July had been provided out of the CIA's Contingency Reserve Fund. By November this was virtually exhausted. Even so, the CIA produced a new set of options identifying three programmes, costing around $30, $60 and $100 million respectively. In an attempt to stay in the competition in Angola with a limited investment, the administration chose the smallest programme, and went to Congress with a request for $28 million for further covert aid in Angola.

In the circumstances of late 1975, several factors militated against congressional approval of this relatively trivial sum. The first was concern that the incrementalism that had led the United States into Vietnam was being repeated in Angola. Although Kissinger denounced parallels between Vietnam and Angola, in Congress the analogies were as compelling as they were inescapable. The second problem was that the request came against a backdrop of damaging revelations about CIA activities. In addition, Senator Clark of Iowa, the Chamber's leading expert on Africa, was extremely unhappy about American involvement in Angola and especially the tacit collaboration with South Africa. Along with Senator Tunney of California – who was looking for an issue to give him greater prominence and thereby help his impending re-election campaign – Clark led the opposition to American involvement in the Angolan war.[44] Attention focused on the Defense Appropriations Bill, which included the funds for the CIA. On 17 December, Senator Tunney introduced an amendment to the bill prohibiting any of the funds being used for further covert aid in Angola; on 19 December, this was passed by 54 votes to 22. On 27 January, the House reaffirmed the position of the Senate by a vote of 323 to 99. It was the initial Senate action, though, which was decisive.

The extent to which the cessation of the Soviet airlift reflected a serious reappraisal in Moscow is not clear. In the aftermath of the Senate vote, however, the Soviet Union was less inhibited. The airlift was resumed and its scale increased. In early January 1976 Moscow began to use two Aeroflot IL-62s to transport Cuban troops to Luanda at a rate of 200 a day. Over the next few months the number of Cubans in Angola reached a level of somewhere around 20,000. The United States could do little in response. 'Deprived of military leverage, the Ford Administration clung to the hope that the leverage of rhetoric might restrain Soviet behaviour.'[45] There were a few other options available. An embargo on grain sales could have been initiated by the administration, but would have been very costly for President Ford in an election year, and was effectively ruled out in his speech to the American Farm Bureau Federation on 5 January 1976. This speech is testimony to the weakness in American policy. Ford emphasised that 'the Soviet attempt to take unilateral advantage of the Angola problem' was 'inconsistent with the basic principles of Soviet–American relations', but made no effort to impose penalties for what was presented as a breach of the 1972 and 1973 understandings.[46] This reflected a fundamental flaw in the linkage strategy. Linkage worked best when the benefits were one way and when the costs of withdrawing them did not hurt the United States as well as the Soviet Union. Grain sales, though, were as important to the American farmer as to the Soviet Union, and could not readily be withdrawn. Furthermore, the United States did not have a monopoly: in the event of an embargo Moscow could go elsewhere for its grain supplies.[47]

The other possibility open to the administration was to delay the arms control talks. As a result of a Brezhnev invitation in November 1975, Kissinger had initially intended to go to Moscow in December for a further round of discussions about SALT. This was postponed until January 1976 largely because of the administration's difficulties in working out an agreed position. The invitation itself, however, may have symbolised a Soviet desire to insulate progress in arms control from superpower differences over Angola. Kissinger sympathised with this, and prior to the visit made several statements denying that the limitation of strategic arms was a favour the United States had granted to the Soviet Union 'to be turned on or off according to the ebb and flow of our relations'.[48] Even so, he raised the issue of Angola in Moscow, but found Soviet leaders unresponsive to American concerns.

The administration fumbled for an appropriate response to this rebuff and ended up with the worst of all worlds. It was impossible to effect a change in Soviet policy, yet that policy was increasingly pilloried: 'American policy-makers seemed intent upon escalating the consequences of not doing something after they knew that nothing would be done.'[49] The warnings that Soviet action were inconsistent with detente were too late and too contrived (in view of American involvement) to have much impact in the Soviet Union. In the United States, though, they fuelled the growing disillusionment with detente, thereby adding yet one more to the series of mistakes and miscalculations made by Kissinger and Ford.

Was this American domestic reaction justified? Did the Soviet Union flout the rules of detente and disregard the principles of crisis prevention established in 1972 and 1973? This was Kissinger's claim, and he suggested to a Senate Subcommittee that 'the efforts of the Soviet Union and Cuba to take unilateral advantage of a turbulent local situation where they never had any historical interests' were

> a wilful, direct assault upon the recent constructive trends in US–Soviet relations .... Angola represents the first time since the aftermath of World War Two that the Soviets have moved militarily at long distance to impose a regime of their own choice. It is the first time the US has failed to respond to Soviet military moves outside their immediate orbit.[50]

These comments reflected Kissinger's frustrations with Congress almost as much as his disillusionment with Moscow. The sense of grievance has been reaffirmed by Hyland in his description of the Soviet Cuban intervention as 'a gross violation of the so-called rules of superpower engagement'.[51] He claims that

> the United States had scrupulously avoided direct involvement in Angola, to the point that the actual clandestine operations were hampered. So even a small Cuban intervention seemed to go beyond the implicit rules, and its eventual size made a mockery of any such superpower rules not to seek unilateral advantage.[52]

This argument is both persuasive and disingenuous. It is persuasive in the sense that direct Cuban involvement had not been anticipated when the codes of conduct were drawn up and was clearly a major new

development in the Soviet–American competition. It is disingenuous in
that the restraint exhibited by the United States stemmed from domestic constraints rather than an imperative to observe a code of conduct
for detente. Both sides were playing a competitive game; it was simply
that the Soviet Union played it far more effectively than did the United
States. Moscow did not behave in accordance with the crisis prevention
accords of 1972 and 1973, but neither did Washington. Intelligence
sources in Washington in late 1975, suggested that what had happened
in Angola was 'a standard action-reaction cycle'.[53] This is compelling.
The implication is that Kissinger's actions in Angola contributed to the
very predicament that his detente policy had been designed to avoid.
The United States had attempted to establish a code of conduct that
would compensate for its inability to compete effectively against the
Soviet Union in the Third World. In 1975 Kissinger ignored this,
and became embroiled in a competition which was then stymied by
the very domestic constraints to which he had been sensitive when
formulating the detente policy. Having rejected the non-competitive
options in July, later complaints about Soviet competitiveness were
ineffective. No effort was made to invoke the Basic Principles until
much too late: Angola does not seem to have been discussed between
the superpowers until October 1975, and there were no joint efforts
to impose a cease-fire or find a cooperative solution to the conflict.

Whether the Soviet Union would have been responsive to
American preventive diplomacy in early or mid-1975 is uncertain.
Even at this stage, there were incentives for Moscow to deepen its
involvement. Furthermore, Soviet spokesmen consistently emphasised
that their actions in Angola were not incompatible with detente. As
one Soviet journal in January 1976 noted:

> No one seeks to deny that the Soviet Union and other socialist
> countries render moral and material assistance to the Angolan people
> and its vanguard, the MPLA ... As for the contention voiced from time
> to time, even by responsible Western government leaders, that this policy
> does not accord with the spirit of detente, it only testifies to a false
> understanding of the meaning of detente which never implied and cannot
> imply giving a free hand to aggression.[54]

Such sentiments reveal once again the conflicting conceptions of
detente. The Soviet Union was concerned primarily with avoiding
situations likely to result in direct military confrontation between
the superpowers – a danger which never really existed in Angola –
but was anxious to advance its interest where the risks were lower.
Nevertheless, concerns about diplomatic isolation and an African
backlash at outside intervention might have made the Soviet leaders
responsive to a diplomatic approach by Washington. In the event,

these consequences were avoided. American policy, together with South African involvement, legitimised Soviet and Cuban intervention in a way that Moscow alone could never had done.

If American policy was counter-productive, the Soviet stance was short-sighted. Moscow seemed oblivious to the effect of its actions on American support for detente. The use of the Cubans as 'proxies' caused profound concern in the United States, and it was not coincidental that a few months after the Cuban build-up in Angola, President Ford, under pressure from the Republican Right, banned the word 'detente' from his political vocabulary. This was silent testimony to the effect of Angola on superpower relations. Despite this, the Soviet Union failed to appreciate the impact of its activities and allowed its involvement in the Horn of Africa to become another source of friction in relations with the United States.

The Superpowers and the Horn of Africa

Because of its strategic location the Horn of Africa has traditionally been an area of great power competition.[55] The cold war was no exception to this pattern, and the United States became involved with Ethiopia in 1953, developing a communication station at Kagnew which became an important part of its world-wide communication network. Soviet links with Somalia were established in the early 1960s but were strengthened in the early 1970s, partly as a result of growing superpower naval competition in the Indian Ocean. The Soviets were granted use of military facilities at the northern port of Berbera, which was strategically placed to support their patrols in the Indian Ocean. Despite this, superpower competition in the region was sufficiently restrained that it did not affect the development of detente. In 1977 and 1978, however, the Horn became a bone of contention between the United States and the Soviet Union. Regional instability, stemming from Somalian irredentism and Ethiopian weakness, coupled with the ability of the local powers to manipulate their patrons, placed considerable strain on superpower detente.

Somali irredentism can be traced back to independence in 1960. Territorial demands on the Ogaden in Ethiopia became more vociferous when Siad Barre became President of Somalia in 1969. In the mid-1970s growing internal pressure on Siad Barre to act over the Ogaden coincided with instability and weakness in Ethiopia. In September 1974, the Ethiopian emperor, Haile Selassie, was deposed and replaced by a military committee, the Derg. Instability continued and in February 1977, Lieutenant-Colonel Mengistu Haile Mariam seized power. His repressive policies, however, only succeeded in worsening the situation. Nationalist guerrillas had been fighting for independence in the northern province of Eritrea since 1961, but as political disaffection overtook all sectors of society, including the army, they proved more difficult to control. By 1977 the Ogaden was also causing grave concern to the government, and fears arose that Ethiopia might disintegrate completely.

In July, large numbers of regular troops invaded Ethiopia. The Somalis made impressive gains in the early stages of the war, and by the end of September most of the Ogaden had been seized. To make matters worse for the Derg, secessionist guerrillas in Eritrea were also capturing key towns and ports. Ethiopia appeared to be on the verge of collapse. Nevertheless, the Ethiopian Army did not disintegrate and by October the Somali offensive had stalled. Large-scale transfers of Soviet equipment to Ethiopia together with the introduction of Cuban troops in November 1977 reversed the military situation. By January 1978, the Somalis were forced to retreat and in March they finally agreed to withdraw from the occupied territory. Having secured the eastern flank, the Ethiopians then moved against the Eritreans, and with Soviet assistance the towns and ports were recaptured by July 1978. This sequence of events caused considerable concern in Washington. To understand the reasons for this it is necessary to examine the role of the superpowers in the Horn of Africa prior to the war in the Ogaden.

Superpower Involvement

After the military coup of 1969 which brought Siad Barre to power, Somalia was proclaimed a socialist republic and given a more pro-Soviet orientation. Relations between Somalia and the Soviet Union were cemented in 1974 with the signing of a Treaty of Friendship and Cooperation. Following an agreement in 1976, Moscow provided considerable military aid to Somalia. In addition to the supply of arms, some 2,400 Somali military personnel were trained in the USSR, while up to 1,000 Soviet military advisers were assigned to work with the Somali Army.[56] Before the Ogaden war, therefore, Somalia was not only one of Moscow's staunchest allies, but also appeared to be one of its most important clients in the Third World.

In contrast, Ethiopian relations with the United States were becoming more distant. This was a gradual process, and even after the overthrow of Selassie, military aid from the United States continued. In fact, from 1974 to 1976 it actually increased despite the socialist orientation of the new regime. Washington was eager to encourage the pro-Western elements in the Derg, and hoped that military aid would discourage the Ethiopian leadership from seeking military assistance from Moscow.[57] The Mengistu coup, however, forced the United States to reconsider its policy, and in April 1977 – largely in response to human rights violations – a total ban was imposed on all military sales to Ethiopia. This was made easier by the decline in Ethiopia's strategic importance. Technological innovation had rendered the Kagnew communications facility largely redundant, and had the Soviets not been establishing a presence in Somalia, the United States might have withdrawn from Ethiopia much earlier. 'But in the mid-1970s, this meant leaving the Soviet Union unchallenged in the Horn at a time the United States was increasingly worried about Soviet penetration in Africa.'[58] Mengistu's takeover, however, and his subsequent anti-American stance made American disengagement inevitable.

As the West reduced its commitment to Ethiopia, the Derg turned to the Soviet Union. The first approach to Moscow had been made in December 1974, but did not go beyond preliminary soundings.[59] In 1975 both sides made a more concerted attempt to improve relations. Yet even at this stage Moscow was still cautious about supplying arms. Gromyko openly stated that he feared such moves could harm the relationship with Somalia, revealing that Ethiopia was more enthusiastic for a military alliance than the Soviet Union.[60] In spite of Soviet reservations, in December 1976 a secret arms deal was arranged which was said to be worth about $100 million for second-line equipment such as T-34 tanks. This agreement was signed on condition that Ethiopia sever its remaining ties with the United States.[61] The Mengistu coup ensured this, and it has been suggested that the Soviet Union made the delivery of military aid depend upon Mengistu's seizure of power.[62] Moscow was certainly very prompt in recognising the Mengistu regime and made rapid moves thereafter to strengthen the Soviet–Ethiopian relationship. In May 1977 the two countries agreed on an arms deal worth up to $500 million for more modern weapons.[63]

This deal provided a further impetus to Somali military action. Although it angered the Somalis, they also realised it would take time before the Ethiopian Army adapted to Soviet equipment and made up for the loss of military aid from Washington. This was yet another reason why mid-1977 offered opportunities for a Somali offensive which were both unprecedented and likely to diminish in the future.

The Soviet Reversal of Alliance in the Horn

In spite of improved relations with Ethiopia, Moscow was reluctant to abandon Somalia, and maintained a large contingent of advisers there even after the invasion. It is difficult to believe, therefore, that the Soviets were unaware of Somali preparations to seize the

Ogaden. Furthermore, the weapons provided by Moscow appeared to give Somalia a capability beyond that required for defensive purposes. From this, some analysts have inferred that the Soviet Union may have actually encouraged the Somali invasion in order to gain pre-eminence in Ethiopia.[64] Yet there is more evidence to suggest that Moscow attempted to restrain the Somalis in the belief that peace in the Horn would best serve Soviet interests. The Cubans in March, and the Soviets in April proposed a peace plan in which Ethiopia and Somalia would sink their differences and form a Federation (or progressive alliance) of Marxist states in the Horn. This Federation would include Ethiopia, Somalia, South Yemen and Djibouti, and allow substantial autonomy for the provinces of the Ogaden and Eritrea. It is unclear whether Moscow really expected this ambitious proposal to be taken up. It does appear, though, that the Soviets believed they could control the Somali leadership and prevent an attack on the Ogaden. They actually expressed this view to Mengistu in April 1977, a fact he reminded them of in September.[65] Although these assurances proved worthless, Moscow still remained reluctant to condemn Somalia outright and come to the aid of Ethiopia.

At the outset of the war, major arms deliveries from Moscow to Somalia ceased, but shipments of light arms and spare parts continued, albeit at a reduced level.[66] Mengistu was outraged at this apparent duplicity, and rebuked Moscow at a press conference on 18 September, suggesting that it might be guilty of 'complicity with the reactionary Mogadishu regime'.[67] This may have contributed to the termination of all arms deliveries to Somalia from Moscow. Nevertheless, it was only after Somalia unilaterally abrogated the Treaty of Friendship and Cooperation on 13 November that Moscow gave up altogether on its erstwhile ally and intervened massively on the side of Mengistu. Although Siad Barre appeared to hope that this final break with Moscow would persuade Washington to supply arms, these hopes were not fulfilled.[68]

The Soviet aim seemed to be some form of exclusionary policy in the Horn not entirely dissimilar to that of the United States in the Middle East. Moscow wanted to ease out Washington and become the decisive external power. This policy did not work because the Soviets underestimated the level of regional tension and overestimated the level of Somali dependence and Soviet ability to restrain Somalia. In the event, the invasion of the Ogaden compelled Moscow to make a choice between Somalia and Ethiopia. Faced with an inescapable choice, Moscow found Ethiopia a more attractive ally than Somalia. It was twice the area, its population nine times greater, and its GNP eight times larger. Furthermore, the military bases at Massawa and Assab would compensate for the loss of Berbera.

Nevertheless, Moscow resented the loss of Somalia.[69] Soviet President Nikolai Podgorny might even have paid for it with his job. Podgorny focused on African affairs, and he knew the Somali leader well. His visit to Mogadishu in July 1974, when the Treaty of Friendship and Cooperation was signed, marked the high point in Soviet–Somali relations. When Podgorny returned in April 1977 with the Soviet peace plan, his visit was a failure. The following month he was dropped from the Presidency and ousted from the Politburo.[70]

The Soviet Union explained its switch of clients with the claim that, having done 'everything possible to prevent the armed conflict breaking out', it was compelled to side 'with the victim of aggression'.[71] Moscow justified its behaviour in terms of international law and Article 3 of the OAU rules which permit military aid for a country to defend itself.[72] Moscow emphasised its desire for peace 'based on reciprocal respect ... for sovereignty, territorial integrity, inviolability of frontiers and non-interference in one another's internal affairs'.[73] There is something rather spurious about these justifications. Hard-headed strategic considerations were almost certainly decisive in Soviet calculations. Nevertheless, they coincided with legal norms which had particular appeal within the African context and effectively legitimised the Soviet and Cuban intervention. Not surprisingly, Moscow placed considerable emphasis on its observance of these norms.

The air- and sea-lift of military supplies to Ethiopia represented the biggest Soviet build-up of weapons and manpower since the October war of 1973 in the Middle East, exceeding the military assistance given to Angola in 1975. By the end of the war there were between 12,000 and 17,000 Cuban troops in Ethiopia as well as 1,000 Soviet military advisers.[74] In addition, Soviet military advisers were crucial in organising the Ethiopian counter-offensive against Somali forces in the Ogaden.

For its part, the United States had little influence over the dispute. Nevertheless, Washington began to fear that the USSR could vastly increase its influence in the area and enforce its 'progressive alliance' on the Horn by military means where diplomacy had failed. The oil routes to the West would be jeopardised by such an outcome, and Iran, supported by Saudi Arabia, stated that it would not stand idly by if Somalia were invaded.[75] American concerns over the possibility of such an invasion were clearly communicated to the Soviet Union.

In the event, the Ethiopians and the Cubans regained the Ogaden but did not cross the border into Somalia. Mengistu, again with Soviet aid, was then able to turn against the Eritreans. Although the Soviet Union had supported the Eritreans in the past, it defended its action in helping to suppress the wholly indigenous secessionist movement in terms of the need to consolidate the Marxist–Leninist revolution.

Perhaps more significant for Moscow, however, was the strategic importance of the province. Guerrillas had largely immobilised the port of Massawa and were posing a threat to the other main Eritrean port, Assab. Significantly, however, Cuba refused to participate in the suppression of the Eritrean rebels. Cuba's vice-president, Carlos Rafael Rodrigues, stated that the Derg had no authority to use Cuban troops in Eritrea, and admitted to helping the Eritreans 'in their fight for self-determination'. He also demanded a political, not a military, solution to the problem.[76]

Although the Eritrean issue posed dilemmas for the Cubans and Soviets, the support for Ethiopia, combined with the policy of restraint and the respect for Somali territory, won general African support, and could not be portrayed by the United States as a contravention of international law. Indeed, although the Soviet Union had intervened directly, it had not acted irresponsibly. Nevertheless, Soviet behaviour sparked off a considerable debate in the United States about the implications both for American policy and for superpower detente.

American Reactions and Superpower Detente

Much American commentary portrayed Soviet behaviour in the Horn of Africa in terms of Machiavellian diplomacy and geopolitical ambition. Soviet explanations were dismissed as disingenuous, and Soviet and Cuban involvement in a regional conflict was once again held up as a violation of detente. Henry Kissinger, now out of office, was particularly strident in his criticism. He contended that the conflict was not about local or regional issues and dismissed the question of who initially crossed the border as insignificant.

> The first thing to notice is that Soviet equipment went first to Somalia, a country that had put forward claims on the territory of all its neighbouring states; Soviet equipment was thus guaranteed to be used in an expansionist way. And then when that equipment was used for the precise purpose that Somalia had always asked for it, the Soviet Union switched sides and became the defender of that territory which its own equipment had initially threatened. And 17,000 Cuban troops and a billion dollars' worth of equipment went into Ethiopia. It is too cynical to be asked to accept the proposition that what is involved here is the unselfish Soviet desire to respond to the appeal of a sovereign country. The Soviet purpose is geopolitical; to outflank the Middle East, to demonstrate that the US cannot protect its friends, to raise doubts in Saudi Arabia right across the Red Sea, in Egypt, in the Sudan and in Iran.[77]

This interpretation had powerful adherents within the Carter administration. Nevertheless, the contention that Moscow imposed its own design on events in the Horn presumes a greater capacity to manipulate events than is warranted. There is no sense in Kissinger's analysis of either the dilemmas that were faced by Soviet leaders anxious to avert a military clash between the regional actors, or of the limited control Moscow was able to exert over its clients. This is not to deny that the Soviet Union displayed a ruthless opportunism in its policies or that the pattern of 'cooperative intervention' with Cuba proved very effective. Yet American policy also contained elements of opportunism and competitiveness. Washington was not averse to weaning Somalia from its Soviet alignment, and initially viewed the rise in tension between Ethiopia and Somalia – which placed Moscow in an awkward position – with 'public neutrality but private pleasure'.[78] Furthermore, although allegations that Washington precipitated the Somali invasion are overstated, the United States may have inadvertently encouraged the Somalis to move against Ethiopia.

In April 1977, after Washington had cut ties with Ethiopia, *Time* suggested that President Carter wanted his administration 'to move in every possible way' to obtain Somali friendship.[79] On 16 June 1977 the Somali Ambassador met the President and discussed the possibility of military aid. Carter pointed out the difficulties, but agreed to explore the possibility of assistance from America's allies. Rightly or wrongly, the Somalis interpreted this as a positive response. In addition, Siad Barre's American doctor was reportedly told by a State Department official that the US government was 'not averse to further guerrilla pressure in the Ogaden'.[80] The Somalis were even more encouraged when, on 1 July, Vance announced that the United States would 'consider sympathetically appeals for assistance from states which are threatened by a build-up of foreign military equipment and advisers on their borders, in the Horn of Africa and elsewhere in Africa'.[81] A State Department spokesman went further, and said that the Somalis had been informed that 'we are prepared in principle to provide arms in cooperation with other nations they have approached'.[82] Other countries such as France, Britain, West Germany, Iran and Pakistan were reported to be involved.

Assistant Secretary for African Affairs Richard Moose later dismissed these American 'assurances' as far too abstruse to encourage any 'prudent man' to launch an offensive.[83] Similarly, Vance has contended that the American response to Somali requests for aid was deliberately limited to helping its allies provide defensive equipment. Nevertheless, Siad Barre clearly, if erroneously, expected Western support for his Ogaden campaign. When evidence reached the White House of the invasion, however, the United States made clear that the agreement in principle to provide arms could not be implemented while Somalia was involved in the Ogaden. This decision was imparted to the Somali President on 4 August, but was only made public on 1 September, when a State Department official said: 'We have decided that providing arms at this time would add fuel to a fire we are most interested in putting out.'[84] This turnaround was described by the Somalis as a 'betrayal'.[85]

If a limited increase in tension in the Horn served US interests, Washington, deliberately or inadvertently, gave Somalia the impression that it could count on American support. In the event, the United States proved unwilling to give military aid to an aggressor. Yet its earlier stance may have sent confusing signals which encouraged Somali ambitions.[86] At the very least, the United States failed to take steps to prevent the outbreak of war in the Ogaden. This may have been a missed opportunity for superpower cooperation:

> The United States did not have a favored candidate to win the conflict ... while the Soviet Union had an interest in reconciling Somali and Ethiopian positions and in preventing an open conflict between them. It would therefore appear that a concerted American–Soviet effort to dissuade Somalia from attacking Ethiopia might well have succeeded.[87]

The problem, though, is that this underestimates regional tensions, the pressures on Siad Barre to act, and the ability of the local powers to manipulate their patrons, while it overestimates the capacity of the superpowers to impose their will on client states.

In the event, superpower cooperation was not put to the test in the first half of 1977. Mutual suspicion and short-term calculations of advantage made a joint exercise in regional crisis prevention impossible. After the Soviet intervention, however, there were tentative moves in this direction. In December 1977, Carter wrote to Brezhnev proposing collaboration to prevent disputes in Africa from escalating into major international conflict involving the superpowers.[88] This initiative came late – long after the Somali invasion and the Soviet air- and sea-lift – partly because Carter may have been reluctant to propose collaboration soon after his much-criticised attempt at superpower cooperation in a Middle East peace settlement. For its part the Politburo was suspicious of any renewed attempt at superpower collaboration. Nevertheless, in January 1978, Gromyko proposed joint US–Soviet mediation on the conflict in the Horn. This offer, only revealed five years later in Brzezinski's memoirs, was rejected by the US as an attempt to establish a condominium which would legitimise the Soviet presence in the region.[89]

Diplomatic contacts between the superpowers continued, and Moscow was warned privately but unequivocally about the damage that Soviet and Cuban involvement was causing to Soviet–American relations. 'High level information from the Soviets indicated that restraining the Ethiopians and ending the crisis was the course they were trying to follow.'[90] Whereas the USSR was preoccupied with ensuring a Somali withdrawal and re-establishing central authority in Ethiopia, Washington remained concerned that Moscow might enforce a 'progressive alliance' on the Horn by military means. The Soviet and Cuban military intervention was certainly in excess of that needed to eject the Somalis. Yet this does not mean that the Soviets intended going further. The large-scale presence enabled Moscow to maintain control over all aspects of the military campaign and ensure that an East–West crisis was not provoked through Ethiopian mismanagement.

Because of the uncertainty over Soviet intentions, the Carter administration emphasised the importance attached to the territorial integrity of Somalia. Deputy Director of the National Security Council David Aaron was sent to Ethiopia to warn Mengistu not to let the Cuban troops cross the border into Somalia.[91] Similar warnings were given in public, with Vance emphasising that a crossing of borders 'would present a new and different situation'.[92] A week later, the President reaffirmed this tough line when he said that an invasion of Somalia would be 'a very serious breach of the peace endangering even worldwide peace'.[93]

These public warnings were reiterated in private communications between the superpowers. On 14 February at an important meeting between Vance and Ambassador Dobrynin, the Secretary of State demanded

> a firm commitment that neither Ethiopians nor Cubans would cross into Somalia. Dobrynin replied that the Ethiopians had given the Soviets such an assurance. Further, Raul Castro had said during his recent visit to Moscow that the Cubans had no intention of moving into Somali territory. Moscow also said it would support a cease-fire in conjunction with Somali withdrawal, peace negotiations, and the territorial integrity of both states. The Soviets made clear, however, that a Somali withdrawal was an essential precondition.[94]

Although this was not the first pledge that the Soviet Union had provided – Dobrynin had given Brzezinski a similar assurance as early as December 1977 – it was of considerable importance. Through public statements and private diplomacy the superpowers succeeded in establishing the limits of American tolerance and the limits of Soviet ambition.

In one sense, therefore, efforts at crisis prevention were successful. Although Garthoff suggests that the conflict in the Horn was 'a further setback to development of rules of the game of superpower geopolitical competition in the Third World' because no attempt was made to apply them, this is too harsh.[95] Attempts at crisis prevention through diplomatic consultation, though belated, were made. The two superpowers may have increased tension in the Horn prior to the outbreak of hostilities, but they then acted with greater responsibility to prevent a regional crisis becoming global. The United States refused to deliver arms to either side throughout the war; the Soviet Union only began the air- and sea-lift after the United States had made its non-participation in the conflict clear; and Moscow did not enforce its optimum goal of a Marxist Federation. These were only limited victories for the policy of superpower collaboration, but were not negligible. They were achieved partly because at this stage the United States had a concrete and realistic goal, which was articulated clearly and unequivocally. The Soviets accepted the American position, and were able to deliver on their assurances. Nevertheless, this 'success' was insufficient to pacify critics of Soviet policy both within the Carter administration and outside.

According to the critics, the United States had acted with restraint while the Soviet Union had taken advantage of American adherence to the rules of detente. Brzezinski epitomised this standpoint: for him, as for Kissinger, the key issues were geopolitical, and he dismissed as preposterous the idea that the Soviet Union was acting out of a 'strange territorial legalism'.[96] In Brzezinski's view, Soviet and Cuban respect for Somali territory was less significant than the large military presence in Ethiopia which increased the momentum of Soviet advances in the Third World. Furthermore, Soviet actions in the Horn were important as a test of strength for the United States and in particular for President Carter. Consequently, quiet diplomacy was an inadequate response to the challenge. US action – either through the use of linkage as a lever to influence Soviet behaviour in the Horn – or through a more direct show of force was essential. Brzezinski wrote a series of memoranda to the President urging linkage. Vance strongly opposed this and was particularly averse to any linkage between Soviet behaviour in Africa and negotiations on strategic arms control. He felt that most of the proposals would adversely affect American interests yet have little impact on Soviet actions. The issue not only remained unresolved but indeed became public, with Brzezinski warning that 'linkages may be imposed by unwarranted exploitation of local conflict for larger international purposes' and Vance denying that there was any linkage 'between the SALT negotiations and the situation in Ethiopia'.[97]

Similar differences were evident over a proposed military response to the crisis. According to Vance, the NSC staff became interested in the early months of 1978 in employing some form of military option: among the actions considered were large-scale US naval deployments to the area; US air cover for Somali forces if the

Ethiopians and Cubans crossed the border; and military aid to Somalia (and even the Eritrean rebels) through proxies, to 'tie down the Soviets and Cubans in a bloody and inconclusive struggle'.[98] Such moves would have isolated America from its NATO allies and the OAU, and, consequently, evoked little support in the administration. Nevertheless, Brzezinski remained convinced of the need for a show of force, and on 21 February, at a meeting of senior foreign policy and national security officials, proposed deploying a carrier task force to the region and encouraging friendly states to supply Somalia with weapons which did not originate from the United States. The underlying rationale – as it had been in Angola for Henry Kissinger – was that Washington should not be perceived as passive or weak in the face of Soviet and Cuban actions.

Other members of the administration were not persuaded by these arguments. Secretary of Defense Harold Brown opposed the carrier task-force option on the grounds that it would irrevocably commit American prestige in a situation where the United States had very limited control over the outcome. If Somalia was subsequently invaded and Siad Barre overthrown, it would be perceived as a defeat for the United States. Vance and Brown were also opposed to a show of force that was essentially cosmetic: 'If our bluff was called and we were not prepared to use our planes, the credibility of future carrier task force deployments would be compromised.'[99]

Although Brzezinski was not persuasive in private, his public statements revealed the discord within the administration. Not only was this politically damaging, but the statements themselves were characterised by Vance as 'shooting ourselves in the foot'. 'By casting the complex Horn situation in East–West terms, and by setting impossible objectives for US policy – elimination of Soviet and Cuban influence in the Horn – we were creating a perception we were defeated, when, in fact, we were achieving a successful outcome.'[100]

In retrospect, Brzezinski's fears seem exaggerated and unnecessary. If the Soviet action in the Horn was part of a coherent Third World offensive, it was, at best, a partial success. The benefits were minimal. The 'progressive alliance' was not formed, while a former ally, Somalia, was lost to the Americans – a loss formalised in 1980 when the Somalis granted the United States access to military bases in return for military aid. Although Ethiopia is the dominant state in the Horn and strategically more significant than Somalia, it has proved a drain on Soviet resources rather than a major geopolitical asset. The nationalist guerrillas have not been silenced, and both Cuban and Soviet help has been needed to suppress nationalist movements since 1978. In other words, in the Horn of Africa there has been no significant shift in the correlation of forces in favour of the Soviet Union.

Both the resolution of the conflict and subsequent events vindicated the stance taken by Vance rather than that of Brzezinski. In the aftermath of the war, the Carter administration initiated an intensive review of Soviet policies and American options in the Third World. According to Vance, this study

> led most participants to reject the grand design interpretation of Soviet behaviour. It concluded that Soviet policy in Africa could best be described as an exploitation of opportunity, an attempt to take advantage of African conflicts to increase Soviet influence. This view did not, of course, make Soviet behaviour any more tolerable, but it did suggest that we should deal with each problem in its own context and not as a local battle in a global East–West geopolitical struggle. Most participants also agreed that African nationalism was strong enough to preclude permanent Soviet domination and that the best strategy for protecting our interests was to help bring about peaceful solutions to African conflicts.[101]

This assessment focused on the limitations as well as the achievements of Soviet power in the Third World.

To critics worried about what they saw as a continuing pattern of Soviet expansionism, such an appraisal seemed too complacent. The increasingly dominant view within the United States was that events in the Horn were a major defeat for Washington and for detente. The expectation that detente would restrain Soviet ambitions contrasted starkly with the efficiency and success of Soviet and Cuban military activities. Consequently, some critics went further and concluded that detente, by lowering defences and weakening the commitment of anti-Soviet forces in the West, was actually encouraging the Soviet expansionist drive. Brzezinski's view that detente was effectively destroyed in the Ogaden became the accepted orthodoxy in Washington. But is this orthodoxy compelling?

The Soviet Union, the Third World and Superpower Detente

American concerns about Soviet activism in the Third World stemmed partly from the sheer scale and extent of Soviet involvement. The ventures in Africa were all the more disconcerting because they appeared to be part of a wider pattern in which Soviet allies and clients engaged in regional aggression. Soviet arms were important, for example, in the victory of North Vietnam over the South in 1975. Furthermore, soon after the Soviet–Vietnamese Treaty of Friendship and Cooperation was signed in 1978, Vietnam invaded Kampuchea. Although Washington shared the general aversion to the Kampuchean government of Pol Pot, Vietnam was characterised as another Soviet 'proxy', whose military actions were sponsored directly by the Soviet Union.

The proxy thesis was equally important elsewhere. The incursions by Katangan forces based in Angola into the Shaba Province of Zaïre in March 1977 and May 1978 were attributed by President Mobutu to the Cubans. On the second occasion this interpretation seems to have been accepted by the Carter administration, which condemned both Cuban and Soviet involvement, even though there was little evidence of complicity let alone participation. In the end, the criticism became simply that the Cubans had done nothing to prevent the incursions. Nevertheless, the administration had once again contributed to the notion that the Soviet Union was embarked on a sustained offensive in the Third World which directly challenged Western interests.

This interpretation was reinforced, albeit in a way not entirely justified, by events in North and South Yemen.[102] In 1978 there was a series of assassinations of political leaders in the two Yemens. Among those killed was President Rubyi of South Yemen, who appeared to be moving increasingly in a pro-Western direction but who was overthrown and executed before this process could be consolidated. Although this seems to have resulted primarily from the internal power struggle, the United States interpreted it as a result of Soviet machinations. Consequently, the Carter administration attempted to improve ties with North Yemen, but was not prepared to meet its request for arms. After border clashes between the two Yemens in February 1979, the restraints were discarded and Carter expedited a large arms transfer – partly to reassure Saudi Arabia about American protection and partly in the hope that this would bring North Yemen firmly into the Western camp. A few months later, North Yemen finalised an even larger arms deal with the Soviet Union. The American attempt to use it as a surrogate to balance Soviet-supported South Yemen had failed. 'Instead the United States was used by the North Yemeni, and then left high and dry as they saw greater opportunities in balancing Soviet and Saudi influences.'[103] If Washington had been out-smarted by the local actors, however, it was tempting to use Moscow as a scapegoat.

By this time, Brzezinski's claim that the Soviet Union was embarked upon a major geopolitical offensive in what he termed the 'arc of crisis' had become a dominant theme in Washington. Yet, as one analyst has observed, the arc of crisis 'was one of those intellectual constructs that may dramatize a threat but that hardly contribute to clear thinking. It lumped together a series of internal and external conflicts ... of the most disparate sort reflecting a variety of sources, many of which ... had little to do with US–Soviet competition.'[104] To the extent that there was an 'arc of crisis', it was not created by the Soviet Union. 'The numerous upheavals in this period resulted not from a change in Soviet policy but from the underlying conditions of international politics.'[105] Detente coincided with a period of considerable turbulence in the Third World during which fourteen revolutions occurred.[106] Most of these stemmed from the remnants of the decolonisation process and were primarily indigenous in origin. They were accompanied by a series of local and regional disputes which had little connection with one another. Even so, the turbulence helped to erode superpower detente.

In the first place, it strengthened critics of detente in the United States who believed that the Soviet Union was not only exploiting but actually fomenting much of the instability. Soviet involvement in widely differing geographical areas encouraged the conclusion that Moscow was embarked on a far-reaching geopolitical offensive. The analysis of the crises in Angola, the Horn of Africa and the Yemen suggests that such conclusions are over-simplistic. Nevertheless, they were compelling to Brzezinski who, like Kissinger before him, tended to impose a superpower framework on events which were primarily local or regional in character. Partly because of the weakness of the Presidency during and after Watergate, the traditional preoccupation with credibility was intensified. This led both Kissinger and Brzezinski to interpret events in the Third World as challenges to the United States even when they were nothing of the kind, and to hold Moscow responsible not only for those things it did but also for events and actions over which it had little control.

A second consequence of Third World turbulence was that it made the codes of conduct of 1972 and 1973 appear a dismal failure. These codes depended for their success on the superpowers being able to impose their conception of appropriate behaviour on regional actors – which in the event proved extremely difficult. Yet it was alleged that Moscow had systematically undermined Western interests in spite of the agreement not to seek 'unilateral advantage'. This kind of allegation was inherent in accords which were simultaneously very general and very stringent. By creating expectations that were unrealistic the accords made allegations of Soviet betrayal and duplicity almost inevitable. Revolutionary change and regional conflicts in the Third World, though, provided the occasion for such allegations.

The third way in which the upheavals of the 1970s contributed to the demise of detente was that they brought to the fore the competing conceptions held in Washington and Moscow. The American notion of restraint had never sat comfortably with either the Soviet concept of peaceful coexistence or Moscow's expectations about political equality. The instability in the Third World during the mid and later 1970s revealed not just a lack of comfort but a more fundamental incompatibility.

A fourth way in which the instability undermined detente was that it offered the Soviet Union unprecedented opportunity for advancing its interests in the Third World. During the 1970s Moscow *was* more active than ever before. Its power projection capabilities made this possible, but the real catalyst was political change in both the Third World and in the United States which provided favourable conditions for Soviet intervention. If Moscow had no grand design, it nevertheless displayed considerable opportunism and an ability to shape events in its favour. This is not to imply that the United States ceased to compete. Although Washington found it impossible to match the Soviet Union and Cuba in terms of military intervention, it continued the competition by other means. Immediately after the Moscow Summit in 1972, the United States, together with Iran, began to provide covert support to the Kurds in Iraq, even though Iraq had only just signed a treaty of friendship and cooperation with the Soviet Union. Kissinger's 'exclusionary diplomacy' in the Middle East was another example of a competitive American policy – and one which proved immensely successful. Even the US failure in Angola did not occur because Washington failed to compete; it was simply that the United States was hamstrung by domestic pressures while the Soviet Union and Cuba were not. The results in the Horn of Africa were mixed. The crisis was not America's finest hour, but neither was it a disaster. Elsewhere, it was local considerations as much as the role of the Soviet Union that proved decisive. If Moscow had considerable success, it remained acutely aware not only of the constraints on American policy which provided a relatively permissive environment but also of American competitiveness, a fact that was reinforced in Angola when Moscow found itself facing what it construed as a Sino–American alignment.

It is also worth emphasising that throughout this period the Soviet Union remained circumspect in its behaviour. Activism was one thing; risk-taking was another. Indeed, the Soviet willingness to take risks had not significantly increased despite the attainment of strategic parity. For the most part the risks were low because of the domestic inhibitions on the United States. Even so, the desire to avoid direct confrontation with the United States remained a salient factor in Soviet calculations. Indeed, this was one of the great advantages of 'cooperative intervention' with the Cubans. Soviet advisers were present, but it was the Cubans who actually engaged in hostilities. 'Such a division of labour reduced the danger of a military encounter between the superpowers in Africa, while also making it easier for the USSR to disengage if such an encounter threatened to occur.'[107] Although Soviet behaviour was not high-risk in the sense of provoking superpower confrontations, it was not without political risk. Yet Moscow does not seem to have appreciated the extent to which its actions would erode American support for detente. This may have been partly because it did not see a shift in American behaviour from competition to collaboration, and accordingly believed that its own competitive policies were equally acceptable. Whatever the reason, Soviet policy appeared to be based on a curious blend of realism and idealism: 'the realism of accepting East–West competition as inevitable' was combined with the idealism of believing that this competition 'would not impair detente'.[108] The idealism, though, was badly misplaced, resting as it did upon a failure to appreciate the extent to which the United States consistently exaggerated its stakes in Third World conflicts.[109] The Soviet Union also failed to understand the interplay between the dynamics of Soviet actions in the Third World and the dynamics of American domestic politics.

Notes

1. See W.G. Hyland, *Soviet–American Relations: A New Cold War?* R-2763-FF/RC (Santa Monica, Cal.: Rand Corporation, May 1981), pp. 42–3.

2. S.T. Hosmer and T.W. Wolfe, *Soviet Policy and Practice Towards Third World Conflicts* (Lexington, Mass.: Heath, 1983), ch. 8.

3. B. Porter, 'Washington, Moscow and Third World Conflict in the 1980s' in S. Huntington (ed.), *The Strategic Imperative* (Cambridge, Mass.: Ballinger, 1982), p. 253.

4. For a fuller account of the three movements and their strengths and weaknesses, see J. Marcum, 'Lessons of Angola', *Foreign Affairs*, vol. 43, no. 3 (April 1976).

5. See ibid., p. 408.

6. For a fuller analysis, see A. George, *Managing US–Soviet Rivalry* (Boulder, Col.: Westview, 1983), p. 203.

7. A useful and critical attempt to disentangle the key decisions taken in Washington can be found in A. Gavshon, *Crisis in Africa* (London: Penguin Books, 1981), pp. 228–57.

8. J. Stockwell, *In Search of Enemies* (London: André Deutsch, 1978), p. 67.

9. George, op. cit., p. 202.

10. Marcum, op. cit., p. 414.

11. George, op. cit., p. 203.

12. G. Bender, quoted in ibid., p. 204. The importance of the China factor is also emphasised in C. Legum, 'The Soviet Union, China and the West in Southern Africa', *Foreign Affairs*, vol. 54, no. 4 (July 1976), pp. 745–62.

13. W.G. Hyland, *Mortal Rivals* (New York: Random House, 1987), p. 137.

14. We are grateful to Professor Joseph Frankel for this term.

15. N. Davis, 'The Angolan Decision of 1975: A Personal Memoir', *Foreign Affairs*, vol. 57, no. 1 (Fall 1978), pp. 109–24.

16. Ibid.

17. Ibid.

18. Hyland, *Mortal Rivals*, p. 137.

19. Ibid., p. 135.

20. G. Bender, 'Angola, the Cubans and American Anxieties', *Foreign Policy*, no. 31 (Summer 1978), pp. 3–30 and p. 4; see also George, op. cit., pp. 207–9.

21. Stockwell, op. cit., p. 158; see also George, op. cit., p. 210.

22. *Mortal Rivals*, p. 140.

23. Ibid., p. 139.

24. Ibid., p. 141.

25. Stockwell, op. cit., p. 188.

26. On the views of the scholars, see R. Menon, *Soviet Power and the Third World* (New Haven: Yale University Press, 1986), p. 31.

27. A. Klinghoffer, 'The Soviet Union and Angola' in R.H. Donaldson (ed.), *The Soviet Union in the Third World: Successes and Failures* (London: Croom Helm, 1981), pp. 97–124 at p. 121.

28. Legum, op. cit., p. 749.

29. C. Ebinger, 'External Intervention in Internal War: The Politics and Diplomacy of the Angolan Civil War', *Orbis*, vol. 20, no. 3 (Fall 1976), pp. 669–99 at p. 688.

30. J. Valenta, 'The Soviet–Cuban Intervention in Angola 1975', *Studies in Comparative Communism*, vol. 11, nos 1 and 2 (Spring/Summer 1978), pp. 3–33 at p. 11.

31. B. Porter, *The USSR in Third World Conflicts* (Cambridge: Cambridge University Press), 1984, p. 160.

32. Valenta, op. cit., p. 25.

33. See ibid., for a fuller discussion.

34. Ibid., p. 21.

35. The following discussion has benefited considerably from K. Hawthorn, 'The Role of the Cubans in Africa' (University of Southampton, June 1982), Undergraduate dissertation presented to the Department of Politics.

36. Garthoff, *Detente and Confrontation* (Washington, DC: The Brookings Institution, 1985), p. 521.

37. George, op. cit., p. 212.

38. Quoted in Garthoff, op. cit., p. 521.

39. Kissinger, *Address to the Economic Club of Detroit*, 24 Nov. 1975 (USIS official text, 25 Nov. 1975).

40. See J. Steele, 'Kissinger warns: detente at stake in Angola', *Guardian*, 26 Nov. 1975.

41. See George, op. cit., pp. 210–12; and D. Binder, 'US stays out of Angola, Kissinger says', *New York Times*, 29 Nov. 1975.

42. George, op. cit., p. 212.

43. Ibid., p. 218.

44. See N. Livingstone and M. Von Nordheim, 'The United States Congress and the Angola Crisis', *Strategic Review*, vol. 5, no. 2 (Spring 1977), pp. 34–44.

45. Porter, op. cit., p. 173.

46. See P. Shabecoff, 'Ford bars cutoff of grain to Soviets in Angola dispute', *New York Times*, 6 Jan. 1976.

47. See D. Healy, *The Grain Weapon*, Centrepieces, no. 1 (University of Aberdeen: Centre for Defence Studies, Spring 1982).

48. Quoted in 'Mission to Moscow', *New York Times*, 17 Jan. 1976.

49. Marcum, op. cit., p. 419.

50. Quoted in Gavshon, op. cit., p. 227.

51. *Mortal Rivals*, p. 142.

52. Ibid., p. 143.

53. O. Johnston, 'US move in Angola seen as spur to Russia', *International Herald Tribune*, 29 Nov. 1975.

54. Quoted in Gavshon, op. cit., p. 225.

55. For a good discussion of superpower involvement see S.M. Makinda, *Superpower Diplomacy in the Horn of Africa* (London: Croom Helm, 1987).

56. M. Ottaway, 'Superpower Competition and Regional Conflicts in the Horn of Africa' in R.C. Nation and N.V. Kauppi (eds), *The Soviet Impact in Africa* (Lexington, Mass.: Heath, 1984), p. 173.

57. *Hearings before the Subcommittee on Foreign Relations, United States Senate, 94th Congress on US Relations with Ethiopia and the Horn of Africa* (Washington, DC: Government Printing Office), especially pp. 114–23.

58. Ottoway, op. cit., p. 174.

59. Porter, op. cit., p. 192.

60. Ibid., p. 193.

61. Ibid., p. 193. See also R.B. Remnek, 'Soviet Policy in the Horn of Africa' in R.H. Donaldson, op. cit., p. 125.

62. Porter, op. cit., p. 194.

63. Remnek, op. cit., p. 126.

64. P.B. Henze, *Communist Ethiopia – Is it Succeeding?* (Santa Monica: Rand Corporation, Jan. 1985), pp. 18–19.

65. Remnek, op. cit., p. 135.

66. Ibid., p. 138.

67. *Washington Post*, 27 Sept. 1977.

68. Garthoff, op. cit., p. 639.

69. See L.C. Napper, 'The Ogaden War' in George, op. cit., p. 244.

70. *New York Times*, 8 June 1977. Garthoff, op. cit., pp. 631–2, offers another interpretation of Podgorny's dismissal.

71. *TASS*, 18 Jan. 1978; and *Soviet News*, 24 Jan. 1978.

72. Ibid., and *Soviet News*, 9 Aug. 1977.

73. *Soviet News*, 24 Jan. 1978.

74. There are many differing estimates on the size of the Soviet air- and sea-lift to Ethiopia. See, for example: Hosmer and Wolfe, op. cit., p. 392; Garthoff, op. cit., p. 638; and *Observer*, 22 Jan. 1978.

75. *Christian Science Monitor*, 23 Jan. 1978.

76. *Observer*, 12 March 1978.

77. Quoted in Gavshon, op. cit., p. 273.

78. *New York Times*, 8 June 1977.

79. *International Herald Tribune*, 27 July 1977.

80. *Newsweek*, 26 Sept. 1977. See F. Halliday and M. Molyneux, *The Ethiopian Revolution* (London: Verso, 1981), for a more detailed examination.

81. See Makinda, op. cit., pp. 116–17.

82. *Newsweek*, 26 Sept. 1977.

83. Ibid.

84. *New York Times*, 2 Sept. 1977.

85. *New York Times*, 3 Oct. 1977.

86. See Makinda, op. cit., pp. 114–17.

87. Garthoff, op. cit., p. 646.

88. Z. Brzezinski, *Power and Principle* (New York: Farrar, Straus & Giroux, 1983), p. 180.

89. Ibid., pp. 180–1.

90. C. Vance, *Hard Choices* (New York: Simon & Schuster, 1983), p. 86.

91. *Mortal Rivals*, p. 221.

92. *New York Times*, 11 Feb. 1978.

93. *New York Times*, 18 Feb. 1978.

94. Vance, op. cit., p. 87.

95. Garthoff, op. cit., p. 653.

96. Brzezinski, op. cit., p. 186.

97. Garthoff, op. cit., p. 650.

98. Vance, op. cit., p. 86.

99. Ibid., p. 87.

100. Ibid., p. 88.

101. Ibid., p. 91.

102. The brief analysis here rests heavily upon Garthoff, op. cit., pp. 654–60.

103. Ibid., p. 660.

104. R.H. Johnson, 'Exaggerating America's Stakes in Third World Conflicts', *International Security*, vol. 10, no. 3 (Winter 1985–6), pp. 32–68 at p. 62.

105. M. Shulman, 'US–Soviet Relations and the Control of Nuclear Weapons' in B. Blechman (ed.), *Rethinking the US Strategic Posture* (Cambridge, Mass.: Ballinger, 1982), p. 82.

106. F. Halliday, *The Making of the Second Cold War* (London: Verso, 1983), p. 92.

107. Menon, op. cit., p. 144.

108. Ibid., pp. 32–3.

109. See Johnson, op. cit., for a fuller analysis.

7

American Domestic Politics and Detente

Superpower rivalry in the Third World was not a novel feature of Soviet–American competition. During the latter half of the 1970s, however, it not only developed a new intensity but also became an issue in the American domestic debate over detente. As a result, the window of opportunity for an improvement in US–Soviet relations which had opened as a result of Vietnam was gradually but decisively closed. To understand why this occurred it is necessary to examine the different phases in the domestic debate which preceded the abandonment of the policy established by Nixon and Kissinger.

The first phase was one in which Nixon, Ford and Kissinger failed to legitimise detente as a necessary and enduring feature of US policy towards Moscow. In the second phase, there was a collision between two contrasting approaches to world politics – one based on a continuing *modus vivendi* with Moscow as simply one element in a US foreign policy designed to bring about a new world order, and the other emphasising both the dominance of the Soviet–American relationship and the unremitting hostility of the Soviet Union towards the West. This collision provided the occasion for the most fundamental debate since the late 1940s about the nature and purpose of US foreign and security policies. It was also a major political battle to determine the future shape of these policies, and one from which those who rejected superpower detente – at least as it was conceived and implemented during the 1970s – emerged victorious. This victory was possible because of the earlier failure to establish a domestic consensus in favour of detente.

Obstacles to Consensus on Detente

One of the ironies of the 1970s is that the very trends in American domestic politics which had enabled Nixon and Kissinger to embark on a detente policy also undermined its implementation. The domestic reaction against the Vietnam war had made detente both necessary and feasible; yet it also unleashed forces which complicated the conduct of America's Soviet policy. One of the most important of these forces was a resurgent Congress. Throughout the cold war, Congress had been extremely deferential to the President. A threatening international system had promoted a kind of Democratic Caesarism based on the assumption that on national security matters the executive knew best

– an attitude symbolised by the Tonkin Gulf Resolution of 1964. Yet the disastrous escalation of the US involvement in Vietnam which this Resolution facilitated undermined the legitimacy of what critics increasingly began to term 'the Imperial Presidency'.[1] The erosion of the national consensus on foreign policy ended the period of congressional abdication and made legislators less willing to accept Presidential control and direction. By destroying the myth of Presidential infallibility in foreign policy, Vietnam also encouraged a much more intrusive congressional role in foreign policy-making.

The new assertiveness was symbolised by measures such as the War Powers Resolution, designed to restrict Presidential power and ensure that in future Congress was fully consulted on the use of force and American military commitments overseas. It was also evident in congressional demands for a larger 'peace dividend' as the Nixon administration reduced the American presence in Vietnam. The congressional assault was directed at procedures and policies closely associated with the cold war, yet, ironically, was encouraged by the disappearance of the crisis atmosphere that had characterised American policy during the 1950s and 1960s. Without the sense of permanent danger, the centrifugal forces in the American political system were allowed completely free rein. Furthermore, the exercise of congressional prerogatives could not be restricted to correcting past mistakes. New departures initiated by the Nixon administration came under congressional scrutiny and were subjected to congressional challenge. Legislative intrusions into the policy making process were particularly damaging to the Nixon–Kissinger detente strategy, predicated as it was on the assumption of strong centralised control within the executive. The most vulnerable element in Kissinger's conception was the idea of linkage. The manipulation of carrots and sticks required congressional acquiescence and in some cases congressional approval, but Congress proved intractable, and difficulties arose over both the provision of inducements for Soviet good behaviour and the imposition of penalties for Soviet bad behaviour. In other words, the American political system of the 1970s was not conducive to the implementation of the Nixon–Kissinger detente strategy.

This was particularly the case after Watergate. The crisis of Presidential authority in 1973 and 1974 and what Kissinger terms 'the disintegration of the White House' severely impeded the conduct of US foreign policy.[2] It made it difficult to establish and maintain a consensus within the executive branch let alone outside. Prior to Nixon's June 1974 visit to Moscow for his third Soviet–American summit, for example, there was considerable pressure from the Pentagon for an uncompromising stance in the SALT Two negotiations. At a meeting of the National Security Council on 20 June 'Secretary of

Defense Schlesinger presented the Pentagon's proposal. It amounted to an unyielding hard line against any SALT agreement that did not ensure an overwhelming American advantage. It was a proposal that the Soviets were sure to reject out of hand.'[3] Nixon clearly favoured the stance adopted by Kissinger in his battle with the Secretary of Defense, but his travails over Watergate made it difficult for him to impose his preference on a recalcitrant cabinet officer. In view of all this it was hardly surprising that the Summit was far removed from the triumph of the President's visit to Moscow in 1972. Nixon returned empty-handed, and the failure to make further progress on strategic arms control not only made detente appear increasingly vulnerable but underlined the isolation of the White House.

Kissinger has provided a graphic account of the bewilderment and frustration evident in the White House as the revelations undermined executive authority and allowed the challenge to the Imperial Presidency to go much further than anticipated in the early 1970s. By the late 1970s it appeared that the Imperial Presidency had been replaced by an imperilled Presidency.[4] Watergate had created a power vacuum at the centre of the political system which was not filled for the remainder of the decade. Nevertheless, it is a mistake to attribute all the problems associated with the detente policy to Watergate. The difficulties were inherent in a system which makes a virtue out of political fragmentation. It was not the 1970s which were the aberration but the cold war period, in which the injunction that politics should stop at the water's edge overrode the traditional pluralist approach to foreign policy.

The cold war policy framework, the systematic efforts to mobilise support for containment, and the symbolism associated with US policy inhibited change. But by the late 1960s and early 1970s conditions had altered in ways which encouraged the establishment of US–Soviet detente. The opportunity to embark on new policies, however, did not guarantee that these policies could be sustained. Much depended on the skill of the administration in presenting and justifying them, as well as on their outcome. The problem of legitimising detente in a highly pluralist system combined with political expediency to encourage tactics of political salesmanship which brought short-term success but created long-term problems. Detente was oversold.[5]

The overselling of both threats and remedies is a recurring feature of American politics, and it is not surprising that detente was presented as a major departure in the superpower relationship.[6] Although neither Nixon nor Kissinger had any illusions about the Soviet Union, and recognised that superpower competition would continue, they never-theless claimed too much for detente. Nixon especially was guilty of this. Although his exaggerated rhetoric was sometimes accompanied by more cautious statements acknowledging the continued conflicts of interest between East and West, the overall impression conveyed by the administration was one of considerable optimism that the struggles of the cold war were over. By implying that the superpower relationship was being fundamentally transformed, the administration simply stored up future problems. When the promised transformation did not take place and abrasive clashes of interest between the superpowers occurred – as they were almost bound to do – a backlash was inevitable and would have occurred even without Watergate.

Had the administration been aware of this danger it still might not have been able to avoid oversell given the exigencies of electoral politics. Considerable oversell took place in the months prior to the Presidential election of 1972 when Nixon used the openings to both Beijing and Moscow to present himself as a man of peace – even though the United States remained deeply entangled in Vietnam. The failure to secure peace in Indochina placed a premium on detente – especially in view of the McGovern campaign for the Presidency with its appeal to 'bring America home'.[7] Yet, if detente was oversold, it was accompanied by a continued emphasis on the importance of American military strength. The administration suggested that McGovern, who had recommended a $30 billion reduction in the US defence budget, would be unable to negotiate successfully on arms control with an adversary who respected strength and firmness but would exploit any weakness in the American position. Nixon's search for negotiated agreement was contrasted with McGovern's preference for what was caricatured as unilateral disarmament. The challenger, it was asserted, would make the United States the second strongest power in the world.

The Nixon campaign was both shrewd and effective, at least in the short term. Detente was heralded as a considerable achievement – but one that only Nixon could sustain. The conclusion of the US–Soviet Trade Agreement in October 1972 provided a further boost to the President, as did predictions that peace in Vietnam was very close. Nixon's re-election was assisted by McGovern's own ineptness, but was not a victory by default. Nixon was able to use both his 'statesman' image in foreign policy and the positive trends in the economy in a manner which helped to ensure a landslide.

There were already signs in the election, however, that the second term would have its share of problems. The disclosures over Watergate, although they did not yet implicate the President, cast a cloud over the re-election. Furthermore, there were indications that the policy of detente itself would come under pressure. During the campaign, McGovern, in a deliberate attempt to win back the Jewish vote – which Nixon's support for Israel was weaning away from the Democrats – demanded that increased East–West trade be made dependent on Soviet liberalisation of Jewish emigration. This marked the beginning of a defection from detente by the liberals, who were one of its natural constituencies – a development that was all the more important because it coincided with a conservative assault, which Nixon, weakened by Watergate, would find difficult to withstand. In a very prescient commentary a few days before the election, James Reston claimed that the President was in danger of winning re-election 'under circumstances that will hound and defeat him in the next four years'.[8]

If some of the problems besetting Nixon's detente policy during his second term were the result of unique political circumstances, the difficulties of mobilising a consensus in favour of detente were exacerbated by the style of the administration's diplomacy – a style that was well suited to the initiation of detente but far less appropriate to its subsequent development and legitimisation. Nixon and Kissinger were masters of secret diplomacy and had a flair for the dramatic which made detente good domestic theatre. The centralisation of decision-making power in the White House which facilitated this also caused problems. Consensus-building is easier the larger the number of individuals and groups which feel they have a stake in the consensus, and if policy is to endure beyond its original architects, it must have an institutional rather than simply a personal base. This was something that Nixon and Kissinger neglected to build. They became so bound up with the short-term tactics of detente that they mortgaged its long-term future. Even supporters of the detente policy became uneasy about the centralised and secretive way in which it was formulated and implemented. Yet Kissinger never understood how alien his style was to the traditional American approach to foreign policy, and may have believed that the secrecy surrounding his activities could be maintained indefinitely.[9] With the crumbling of Presidential power, the reaction set in.

The problem of mobilising and maintaining support for detente, however, was not simply one of hyperbole or style. Dan Caldwell has argued very persuasively that a more fundamental problem was Nixon and Kissinger's failure 'to relate the policy of detente to important American beliefs and values'.[10] Yet this was not simply a shortcoming of the administration. American traditions and attitudes militated against any easy and lasting acceptance of detente no matter how skilfully it was presented.

Part of the problem was the nature of detente. The concept was European in origin, and Kissinger himself was too obvious a practitioner of European *Realpolitik* for the taste of many Americans. It was not only the secretive style which was alien but a lack of clear moral purpose. The concept of detente was an abstraction and one which did not sit easily with a people which, at least up until Vietnam, had a sense of exceptionalism and of mission. If Vietnam had destroyed the moral certitudes of American life, and demolished the myths by which the United States had sustained itself throughout the cold war, there was still a need to fill the vacuum. But Kissinger seemed to put nothing in its place beyond a policy of expediency – and one which seemed more interested in cultivating relations with America's major adversary than with its major allies. The detente policy suffered from moral ambiguity in a period when the United States was undergoing a trauma because its actions in Vietnam seemed so far removed from the moral purposes and principles that the nation espoused. In such circumstances, detente could hardly be more than an interim measure.

It is not clear that Kissinger himself ever fully understood the nature of the domestic political problem, seeing it primarily as a matter of educating the public 'in the complexity of the world we would have to manage'.[11] As he observed, 'the proposition that to some extent we had to collaborate with our adversary while resisting him found a constituency only with great difficulty; the emotional bias was with the simpler verities of an earlier age'.[12] To some extent this comment misstates the problem. Although the cold war was clear cut and detente was a more complex notion, the problem was not simply a lack of sophistication in the audience. The simpler verities of which Kissinger is so contemptuous reflected deep-rooted assumptions in American political life, and went to the heart of the American self-image. As one analysis of American myth observed: 'Notions of America as the "redeemer nation" ... came to pervade the culture even before the proclamation of universally applicable political, social, and economic ideals in the Declaration of Independence. America was the leader of the Forces of Light and its enemies necessarily the Forces of Darkness.'[13] This attitude, prevalent throughout American history, had been powerfully reinforced by the symbolism associated with the cold war. The architects of detente were never able to provide symbols of the new policy which had anything like the same power, appeal or durability.

In the early 1970s black and white images of the world were replaced by shades of grey. This was not to last, though. And once again Vietnam comes into the picture. If US actions in Vietnam had temporarily dented the American self-image, the end of the conflict, in which Soviet arms loomed large, did nothing to improve American images of the Soviet Union. Soviet-made tanks rolling into Saigon in 1975 evoked memories of Soviet repression in Hungary and Czechoslovakia – and Kissinger's 'peace with honour' had become an example of the appeasement that the United States had been intent on avoiding. It was not the complexity of the detente relationship with Moscow which made it unacceptable, but the moral ambivalence inherent in cooperating with an adversary whose own behaviour – both internally and externally – was so far removed from the ideals which the United States, in spite of Vietnam, still represented.

Although a respite in the conflict with Moscow was initially welcomed, the transformation from an adversary relationship to the ambiguities and ambivalences of detente was painful – especially when it was initiated not out of magnanimity but out of weakness. The Soviet Union as supplicant was tolerable; the Soviet Union as equal was not. Indeed, an approach which seemed to depend for its success not on the restraining influence of American power but on Soviet self-restraint did not rest easily with those whose experience and upbringing taught that Moscow could not be trusted and that it understood only American military might.

The critics of detente were helped immeasurably by the very developments in American politics which had made detente necessary in the first place. The challenge to Presidential pre-eminence had been led by liberals anxious to disengage from Vietnam, but the consequent breakdown of the foreign policy consensus provided an opportunity for conservatives who remained distrustful of the Soviet Union to challenge the new policy. Many of these conservatives had been supporters of the American involvement in Vietnam. Having lost this battle they turned their attention to the issue of Soviet–American relations, on which their arguments were stronger, more compelling, and attuned to the traditional American approach to international politics, which emphasised moralism rather than *Realpolitik*. The political skill of the leading critics of detente was also important.

Henry Jackson and Detente

The key figure in the campaign against detente was Senator Henry Jackson. A Democrat from Washington state, Jackson was a formidable critic whose appeal stemmed partly from the fact that he combined liberalism on domestic matters with a fundamental conservatism on national security issues. Inherent in his assessment of superpower relations was a profound pessimism about the ability of the United States to deal effectively with Moscow in a period of detente. De Tocqueville's assertion that the United States had few of the qualities necessary for the effective conduct of foreign policy underlay many of Jackson's concerns. The irony is that Kissinger, who is sometimes condemned as a theorist of American decline, actually had great faith in his ability to manipulate Moscow. Jackson, in contrast, seems to have felt that the United States could only compete effectively if the competition was unequivocal. He also believed that the Soviet commitment to detente was superficial, and consequently argued that detente was a fraud perpetrated on the United States by a Machiavellian adversary and a gullible and misguided White House.

Jackson's attitudes were reinforced by a staff in which Richard Perle and, to a lesser extent, Dorothy Fosdick were the key figures. Hardliners with an innate scepticism about detente, both were extremely efficient and effective political operators, while Perle had an expertise on strategic and arms control issues which was rarely matched by other legislative aides. Kissinger has claimed that Jackson had one of the ablest – and most ruthless – staffs he ever encountered in Washington, and Jackson and Perle in particular provided a formidable combination.[14] Their opposition to detente was intense and enduring: not only did they initiate the anti-detente campaign in the early 1970s but they were also there to ensure its final victory in the SALT Two debate of 1979. By then the anti-detente coalition was much stronger. Yet this was in part a tribute to their effectiveness. Perle has since claimed that detente was an experiment which failed.[15] This is disingenuous: the Jackson campaign did not give the experiment a chance.

As leaders of the opposition to detente, Jackson and Perle started from a strong position. They had well-placed allies not only in Congress but also within the executive branch itself. Indeed, the fight over detente in Washington which began in the first half of the 1970s can perhaps best be understood as political warfare between two competing networks.[16] Jackson and Perle were at the heart of a network of people who were hostile to detente. Their allies in the executive branch included Admiral Zumwalt, Chief of Naval Operations, General Ed Rowny, who was to become the representative of the Joint Chiefs of Staff on the SALT Two delegation, and on certain key issues, James Schlesinger Secretary of Defense during 1973–5. One commentator has suggested that Schlesinger was 'Jackson's man' in the national security bureaucracy.[17] This is an exaggeration in that Schlesinger was an analyst rather than an ideologue. Nevertheless he shared Jackson's concerns over Soviet military programmes and an antipathy towards Henry Kissinger. His successor, Donald Rumsfeld, was even more hostile to the continuing SALT negotiations, and according to one former official 'the more Rumsfeld took hold, the more he turned hard right'.[18] The hard-line position within the administration was strengthened by the allegiance of other key officials such as James Wade in the Office of Secretary of Defense, and Fred Ikle and John Lehman at the Arms Control and Disarmament Agency. Paul Nitze, until his resignation from the SALT negotiating team in 1974, was yet another influential figure concerned over both the general detente policy and the specifics of the American arms control position. The anti-detente network also included George Meany, head of the AFL-CIO, a visceral anti-communist and a strong supporter of Jackson. The arguments of the coalition found a sympathetic outlet in the Evans and Novak column in the *Washington Post*.

From his base in the Senate, and with a network of sympathisers and supporters in place, Jackson was able to launch a series of assaults on the Nixon–Kissinger policy. He chose issues and arguments which had widespread appeal and thereby made his challenge all the more formidable. One of the first salvos in what was to become a recognisable pattern of political warfare was against the Interim Agreement on Offensive Arms. Jackson was unhappy about the unequal ceilings which permitted the Soviet Union to have more launchers than the United States. Accordingly, he introduced an amendment to the ratification resolution on the Interim Agreement specifying that in any future accord there must be equal ceilings on Soviet and American forces. Rather than confronting this challenge, the Nixon administration – perhaps to strengthen its bargaining position in future negotiations with Moscow as well as defuse the immediate opposition in the Senate – opted to work with Jackson. Negotiations between John Lehman, then on the NSC staff, and Richard Perle resulted in a softening of the proposed language, although it still asserted the American right to equal ceilings. Jackson was prepared to make concessions because he needed the administration's support for the Amendment to pass. With this support secured, his amendment was approved on 14 September 1972 in a 56 to 35 split.[19]

This was not the only Jackson victory. In the aftermath of Nixon's re-election, there was a purge at the Arms Control and Disarmament Agency and the whole SALT One team was sacked. Although the impetus for this seems to have come from Jackson, Nixon and Kissinger seemed content to acquiesce in a move which rid them of officials who had not always been as amenable as the White House desired. Even so, the appeasing of Jackson in 1972 may have been a major tactical blunder by an administration which at that time was virtually unassailable, as it encouraged further intrusions into the arms control process by the Senator.

In June 1974, as the administration debated its negotiating stance prior to Nixon's visit to the Soviet Union, Jackson launched another assault. As well as advocating proposals that differed significantly from those of the administration, he accused Kissinger of making secret agreements in SALT One which were advantageous to the Soviet Union. His recommendations were strengthened by a letter from Schlesinger which effectively endorsed the Senator's approach and distanced the Secretary of Defense from the administration. If this was a clear sign of the disarray during the closing weeks of the

Nixon Presidency, the acrimonious and suspicious atmosphere created by Watergate also helped give credence to Jackson's allegations about a secret deal. Kissinger's refutation of what he regarded as 'fantasy' was emphatic, but suffered from the fact that the charges were simple and the rebuttals complex.[20] The result was that 'the explanations ... never quite caught up with the charges'.[21]

Jackson's assault on arms control with the Soviet Union continued throughout the 1970s and contributed to a process of politicisation in which SALT was transformed from the private concern of a narrow elite into a highly controversial public issue. The issue, however, was not arms control *per se*. The argument that Moscow was cheating went beyond the specifics of SALT and struck at detente itself. Always implicit and sometimes explicit in Jackson's campaign against SALT was the question whether it was possible to have meaningful cooperation with a state which cheated on agreements. What was ostensibly an assault on arms control was in fact an attempt both to vilify the Soviet Union and to discredit detente. This became even more obvious in the summer of 1975 when public and congressional concerns over Soviet violations were intensified by an article in *The Reader's Digest* written by former Secretary of Defense Melvin Laird. Although there were few cases of clear violations of SALT, the controversy was important because it contributed to a belief that the Soviet Union could not be trusted and that US detente policy, including its arms control policy, was naive and misguided.

Jackson's campaign against SALT culminated in the challenge to SALT Two in 1979. It was helped by Soviet activities in the Third World – activities which were interpreted by Jackson and other critics of detente in the worst possible light. This was evident as early as the Middle East war of 1973, which brought together several issues – Israel, American security and the Soviet Union – on which Jackson was strong.[22] Although there were several aspects of Soviet behaviour prior to and during the war which were, at best, ambivalent in their relationship to detente, Jackson offered a worst case interpretation. The Soviet threat to intervene was presented as a reflection of Soviet ambition rather than Soviet fears, and the image of an implacable adversary ready to exploit any hint of American weakness was re-established. This interpretation was validated to some extent by the comment of President Nixon – attempting to establish his indispensability and thereby mitigate the effect of Watergate – that the episode was the most serious Soviet–American confrontation since the Cuban Missile Crisis.

The importance of the Middle East war for the Jackson–Perle campaign against detente can hardly be overestimated. Even many of those who had been sympathetic to the Nixon–Kissinger policy were disillusioned, and one commentator has suggested that in the aftermath of the war anti-communism became respectable once again.[23] Editorials in the *New York Times* and the *Washington Post*, which had tended to be sympathetic towards detente, echoed Jackson's criticisms of Soviet actions. If detente did not seem illusory – as Jackson was claiming – it appeared to be more limited than its proponents contended. As a result of the war there was a subtle but important change in the continuing argument over detente. Until October 1973 the critics had been fighting a rearguard action against an administration which had more or less defined the terms of the debate. Soviet actions during the war, together with the subsequent energy crisis, placed the proponents of detente on the defensive.

As a result of the war, Jackson also found himself with important new recruits. The Jewish community in the United States is not monolithic. Nevertheless, important elements within it seem to have concluded that Israeli freedom of action had been restricted by Soviet–American cooperation in ending the war. Consequently 'American confrontation with the Soviet Union, or at least a relationship based more on competition than on detente, was seen as offering greater assurance of American support' to Israel against its Arab neighbours.[24] The effect of this was twofold. In the first place, the Nixon administration lost the support of a constituency which, given its traditional liberalism, might have been expected to provide strong backing for superpower detente. Second, a group of important opinion leaders had concluded that neither US nor Israeli security would be enhanced by the maintenance of detente – and was prepared to campaign vigorously in favour of a hard-line policy by the United States.

The Jewish community was not only hostile to the Soviet Union because of its support for the enemies of Israel; it was also unhappy about the Soviet treatment of its Jewish population, particularly the restrictions on emigration. Consequently, Jackson and Jewish leaders worked very closely in an attempt to press the Soviet Union into liberalisation of its emigration policy. Expanded trade between the United States and the Soviet Union was made dependent upon changes in Soviet emigration practices. Legislation to this effect – which eventually became known as the Jackson–Vanik Amendment – was first introduced in October 1972, and became a major issue in American policy-making for the next two and a half years.

Jackson, although obviously sincere in his concerns over Soviet Jewry, had discovered an issue which enabled him to combine expediency and principle. His campaign is explicable partly in terms of his ambition to obtain the Democratic nomination for the Presidency in 1976. Initially, it brought him closer both to George Meany and organised labour and to American Jewry which has traditionally been important to the finances and electoral fortunes of the Democratic Party.[25] Yet the campaign also reflected deep-rooted beliefs: by linking Jewish emigration and expanded trade, Jackson was attacking a policy which not only seemed oblivious to Soviet domestic repression but also provided trade and technology to America's major adversary. His efforts were designed not only to improve human rights practices but also to embarrass Moscow and derail detente.

Jackson's campaign won the support of those who disliked detente and those who disliked repression. He provided an issue on which liberal and conservative groups coalesced. Although liberals were generally sympathetic towards detente, they could hardly be oblivious to human rights violations. Crusading anti-communism as manifested in the Vietnam war had become anathema, but Jackson offered a substitute which was not only less painful than military intervention, but also skilfully enabled the United States to retrieve the moral high ground it had lost in Vietnam. Jackson himself had continued to support the Vietnam war, and his campaign on Jewish emigration reflected the same crusading moralism which had buttressed not only the Vietnam involvement but American policy throughout the cold war. By reasserting this moralism, Jackson was offering a frontal challenge to the amoral *Realpolitik* of Henry Kissinger.

Jackson's opportunity arose partly because of the Nixon administration's mistakes. At the outset, 'the Nixon administration ... avoided any serious discussion' with congressional sponsors of the amendment to link emigration to Most Favoured Nation status.[26] It was only in September 1973, when Andrei Sakharov, a leading Soviet dissident, wrote an open letter to the US Congress urging support for Jackson's amendment to the Trade Bill, that the administration began to respond more vigorously.

During 1974 an intricate series of trilateral negotiations took place in which Kissinger attempted to mediate between Henry Jackson and the Soviet leadership. Although the Soviets in March 1973 had waived the 'exit tax', the imposition of which had aroused much anger in the United States, Jackson dismissed this as no more than a 'first step' and demanded reassurances that increasing numbers of Jews would be allowed to emigrate.[27] Gradually a formula was devised whereby Kissinger and Jackson were to exchange letters setting out their understanding of the Soviet position. Kissinger's letter, based on talks with Dobrynin and other Soviet officials, provided reassurance about Soviet practices. Jackson's response, however, went much further, and the administration retreated from its commitment to send a second letter to the Senator affirming his understanding of the Soviet commitment. Despite this, agreement was reached on the procedure, and on 18 October 1974 there was a formal exchange of letters at the White House. This was followed by a press conference, dominated by Jackson, in which the Senator claimed not only that Moscow had capitulated but that the benchmark figure for Jewish emigration was 60,000 per year.

The Soviet leadership had hitherto been conciliatory – as well as waiving the exit tax, it had allowed Jewish emigration to swell to almost 35,000 in 1973 – but was unwilling to tolerate a public and humiliating intrusion into its internal affairs. On 26 October, Kissinger was presented in Moscow with a letter signed by Gromyko which protested against the distortion of the Soviet position, reaffirmed that the matter 'was entirely within the internal competence' of the Soviet state, and disavowed any acceptance of specific numbers of Jewish emigrants.[28] Kissinger, for the moment, kept this letter secret in the hope that the October 18 agreement would make it possible to finesse the issue. His subsequent testimony before the Senate Finance Committee on 3 December has been described as 'the quintessence of ambiguity' and was clearly an attempt to maintain the fiction of a compromise on the linkage between Most Favoured Nation status and Jewish emigration.[29]

The fiction, however, could not hold much longer. Part of the reason was that the congressional restrictions on trade were more stringent than anticipated. As well as the Jackson Amendment to the Trade Act, an amendment was attached to the Export-Import Bank Bill limiting the extension of credits to the Soviet Union by the Bank to $300 million over the next four years. This amendment had initially been introduced by Senator Stevenson who, according to one of his aides, did not approve of Jackson–Vanik and was anxious to find a substitute.[30] If the proposal was intended as a political compromise, however, it was also an attempt to reassert the role of Congress in the extension of credits. Because it was on a separate legislative channel it took on a momentum of its own – lack of coordination within Congress meant that both pieces of legislation were passed, thereby adding a further set of restrictions to the expansion of Soviet–American trade.[31] The final version of the Export–Import Bank legislation also included a sub-ceiling of $40 million as the maximum which could be devoted to the financing of Soviet fossil-fuel exploration projects. The administration also failed to forestall the introduction and approval of an amendment to the Trade Bill introduced by Harry Byrd of Virginia, which imposed a $300 million ceiling on loans to Moscow from all agencies of the US government, and was therefore, even more restrictive than the Stevenson Amendment.

The Soviet response had been foreshadowed by the Gromyko letter, and on 18 December, Moscow released this letter. On 10 January 1975 the Soviet Union made clear that it was unwilling to accept the conditions contained in the legislation. Four days later Kissinger announced that the 1972 Trade Agreement would not go into force, thereby tacitly acknowledging that one of the main pillars of Soviet–American detente was in ruins.

The significance of this episode is difficult to overestimate. In one sense Jackson's victory was pyrrhic. The Senator had overplayed his hand and Jewish emigration declined rather than increased. Furthermore, by supporting the passage of the Trade Act, Jackson had alienated Meany.[32] Nevertheless, Jackson's campaign had undermined both the style and substance of the Nixon–Kissinger foreign policy. In terms of style, it highlighted the gap between an approach which demanded strong, centralised control and the rampant pluralism of the American political system in the 1970s – as a result of which the Nixon administration was unable to deliver on its part of the detente bargain. The substantive change symbolised by the trade restrictions was, if anything, even greater. Jackson–Vanik was a major defeat for an approach to Soviet–American relations, which focused only on Soviet external behaviour and ignored its internal conduct. Jackson's legislation symbolised the reassertion of the moral impulse in American foreign policy which was to continue in the human rights campaign of Jimmy Carter and the vehement anti-communism of the Reagan administration.

It is also tempting to see Jackson–Vanik as representing the demise of linkage – the carrots were no longer there, and a crucial element in the Kissinger approach to the Soviet Union was in tatters. Rather than destroying linkage, however, Jackson had transformed it – in at least three ways. The administration was concerned primarily with inducing restraint in Soviet foreign policy; Soviet internal politics, if not wholly irrelevant, were at most a matter for quiet diplomacy. Jackson, in contrast, wanted to use linkage to change Soviet domestic policies. His version of linkage 'touched the fundamental basis of the regime' and, as such, was unacceptable to Moscow.[33] The second difference was between private and public forms of linkage: the administration emphasised quiet diplomacy; Jackson's linkage policy was 'big, political and noisy'.[34] The third contrast was between positive and negative forms of linkage. The administration wanted expanded trade as a reward for Soviet good behaviour in the recent past and an inducement for Soviet good behaviour in the near future. Jackson, in contrast, 'used trade overtly and as a weapon, a stick, not as a carrot. He withheld something the Soviet leaders thought America had already pledged.'[35] The result was that Kissinger's attempt to create a 'web of interdependence' which would give the Soviet Union a vested interest in restraint was blocked. The victory of Jackson's version of linkage meant that the more sophisticated approach of Kissinger could not be put to the test – the Soviet Union would have nothing to lose if it failed to behave in accordance with Kissinger's conception of restraint. Yet, in a sense, the administration had created its own vulnerability: Jackson did not invent linkage, he merely hijacked a notion that had been devised by the Nixon administration itself. The effect in Moscow, though, was to cast doubt on the United States as a reliable partner in detente.

The Weakness of the Pro-Detente Forces

The success of Jackson's campaign revealed just how limited American enthusiasm for detente actually was. It also revealed the weakness of the supporters of detente. Although the National Association of Manufacturers and other business organisations campaigned against restrictions on Soviet–American trade, they were vulnerable to allegations that they were placing commercial gain above moral principle. Consequently, American business was reluctant to become too exposed on the detente issue.

The grain merchants were constrained as a result of the 'great grain robbery' of 1972, and, in any event, were given some comfort by the long-term grain agreement of 1975. Consequently, they had neither the will nor the need to lobby for detente. Other areas of business and commerce were sensitive to allegations that they were supplying an adversary with 'high technology' and thereby jeopardising American security. In addition, there was a general concern that the Soviet Union, because of its centralised political and economic system, would invariably obtain the better deal in any negotiations. The worries of organised labour that the opening up of Soviet–American trade would increase unemployment in the United States was yet another inhibition.

By the mid-1970s, therefore, American business was reluctant to press the case for expanded trade too strongly. Once detente was under pressure, business executives were nervous that it might collapse, exposing firms trading with the Soviet Union to attack from the labour unions, the press and the congressional critics of detente. Consequently, a low profile seemed preferable, and no attempt was made to stem the rising tide of criticism against detente. As one analyst of the American business community in the 1970s has suggested, there was

> a total absence of any well defined sense of political direction. Despite their worry and frustrations over recent trends in the political atmosphere and US government policy, executives on the whole had no clear concept of a political role for individual companies or the United States business community in national debates over US–Soviet economic and political issues.[36]

Although one natural constituency for detente was unable and unwilling to fight to save it, the struggle over Jackson–Vanik had highlighted the partial defection of the liberals in Congress who in the mid and late 1960s had become advocates of military retrenchment, arms control and accommodation with Moscow. Liberal support for detente was mitigated in part by antipathy towards the President who had initiated it, as well as the secretive manner in which it was conducted. Liberals also disliked the Soviet political system as intensely as did conservatives. For detente to be made palatable, therefore, it had to be accompanied by a political offensive designed to ameliorate the worst features of Soviet politics. In this connection, the Jackson concept of linkage and the emphasis on human rights can be understood as 'a psychological exercise that Americans perform on themselves'. It was 'a way for them to conduct business with the Soviet Union while overcoming their distaste at having to do so'.[37] The problem, though, was that this did enormous harm to detente.

Neither the caution of American business nor the ambivalence of the liberals would have mattered too much had the President been stronger. But, as suggested above, Watergate had created a vacuum at the centre of the American political system. Nixon increasingly became preoccupied with his political problems, and there was growing suspicion that his foreign policy initiatives were diversions. His resignation and the accession to the Presidency of Gerald Ford did little to improve the situation. Although Ford initially reiterated his commitment to detente, the challenges to it intensified during 1975 and 1976.

There were several reasons for this. One was the superpower competition in Angola during 1975 which culminated in a congressional veto on further covert aid to the American-supported factions. This challenge, led primarily by liberals concerned about another Vietnam, took away the stick of American opposition to Moscow and effectively left the Soviet Union free to increase its involvement in Angola – a development which further eroded American support for detente.

An even more important domestic challenge to the Ford–Kissinger foreign policy came from the Republican Right. Until 1975–6 the main assault on detente had come from Jackson, and although he had fashioned a bipartisan majority on the Jewish emigration issue, on most other foreign policy issues Republicans had remained loyal to the White House. Increasingly, though, there were signs of unrest. Nixon's departure meant that the Right was no longer neutralised by the President's reputation as a hard-liner, and that conservative Republicans were free to express reservations about detente. Their suspicions about Gerald Ford were intensified by his appointment of Nelson Rockefeller as his Vice President, by his deference to Henry Kissinger on foreign policy issues, and by his initial commitment to the maintenance of detente. The firing of Secretary of Defense Schlesinger – which was widely if erroneously portrayed as a victory for Kissinger and for detente – together with Ford's refusal to invite Alexander Solzhenitsyn to the White House, confirmed these suspicions, while the fall of South Vietnam and the Soviet and Cuban intervention in Angola heightened conservative antipathies towards Moscow. The result was that Ford, under challenge for the Republican nomination by Ronald Reagan, felt compelled to ban the word 'detente' from his political vocabulary. His attempt to decrease his vulnerability to the Right, however, was not entirely successful. The detente policy was subject to ridicule, and Reagan claimed that its main accomplishment was 'the acquisition of the right to sell Pepsi-Cola in Siberia'.[38] It was also claimed that the Ford and Nixon administrations had allowed American power to decline to a level where the United States had become 'Number Two in a world where it is dangerous – if not fatal – to be second best'.[39] Although Ford was able to stave off the Reagan challenge, the Republican Convention forced him to adopt much of Reagan's foreign policy plank.

The same kind of pressure was apparent in the Team B episode which took place in 1976. CIA estimates of the strategic balance were relatively sanguine, but were not allowed to go unchallenged. In June, George Bush, the Director of Central Intelligence, appointed a team of outside experts to consider the accuracy of official CIA analyses of the Soviet threat. Team B was composed of critics of detente and SALT such as Paul Nitze, General Daniel Graham, former head of the Defense Intelligence Agency, and Harvard Professor Richard Pipes. Basing its assessment on worst-case assumptions about Soviet intentions, the panel arrived at worst-case assumptions about Soviet capabilities. 'The net result was to contribute to a general popular impression that the United States had been complacent over a build up of Soviet military capabilities and in judging Soviet intentions under detente.'[40]

Both this episode and the internecine struggle in the Republican Party in 1976 symbolised the failure of the Nixon and Ford administrations to establish a consensus about detente. This was also apparent in the contest between Ford and Jimmy Carter for the Presidency. Whereas the Republican attack on detente was based on conservative internationalism, Jimmy Carter, the Democratic candidate, and a clear product of nominating politics, attacked detente from a liberal perspective.

Carter's campaign, of course, did not focus wholly on foreign policy. He emphasised that he was not part of the Washington establishment, which, in the climate of cynicism engendered by Watergate, turned his inexperience into an asset.[41] In so far as he dealt with foreign policy and defence, however, his comments seemed designed to appeal to all factions. Discontent with *Realpolitik* was rife on the Right as well as the Left and Carter's campaign offered to restore a sense of moral purpose to American foreign policy. The Republicans were criticised both for being outmanoeuvred on detente and for failing to move ahead fast enough with arms control. At the same time Carter promised that he would cut the defence budget by up to $7 billion: more moralism was to be accompanied by less militarism. Carter was proposing a tougher ideological stance *vis-à-vis* the Soviet Union, while still planning to cooperate with Moscow on arms control. His approach blended expediency and conviction. The emphasis on human rights reflected deeply felt concerns, but was also intended to tap the rich vein of moralism which had been evident in the Jackson campaign on Jewish emigration.

The effect of all this, however, was to cast further question marks over the future of detente. The attack from the Republican Right had been reinforced by the assault from the Democrats, and by the end of 1976 it was clear that the policy enunciated by Nixon and Kissinger had few supporters left. Yet it was not certain what would replace it. The next four years were to provide the answer.

The Carter Administration and the Restoration of the Cold War Consensus

The 1976 election campaign placed detente in limbo; if it was to be revived Soviet–American relations would require judicious management. Yet the Carter administration was philosophically and politically ill-equipped for such a task. At the same time, the novel and difficult circumstances of the mid 1970s should not be overlooked. As one commentator has observed, 'Carter was perhaps all too faithfully a man of the season – the season of confusion in US foreign policy goals following the country's misadventure in Vietnam.'[42] Containment through traditional military means had been discredited, containment through detente appeared untenable, and it was not certain what could replace either of these policies. The administration had to formulate a new foreign policy against a background of economic uncertainty caused by rising oil prices. It also had to operate in a domestic environment in which consensus was absent and debate over foreign policy and national security was increasingly polarised. 'The establishment, which once helped keep things together, was now replaced by foreign policy activists who ferociously tore the fabric apart.'[43] In addition, Congress was both assertive and fragmented, making the task of coalition-building an immensely difficult one. It was also a Congress in which conservative Republicans such as Jesse Helms were no longer constrained by loyalty to a President of the same party – and in which conservatives of both parties were increasingly dominant.

In other words, any President in the second half of the 1970s would have confronted immense and possibly insuperable problems in establishing a viable domestic base from which to formulate and implement a coherent and effective foreign policy. Yet Carter's own personality and philosophy compounded the problems, as did his choice of key advisers who disagreed fundamentally on central issues of policy.

During the election campaign Carter, of necessity, had been all things to all men, and subsequently appeared to vacillate between different approaches to foreign policy. Seyom Brown has suggested that there are both charitable and uncharitable explanations for the 'many faces of Jimmy Carter': an uncharitable explanation is that the President

> had no deeply held views of his own and was simply a politician attempting to secure the support of diverse factions in the body politic.... A charitable explanation is that Carter, faithful to the country whose values he was attempting to embody, was a complex person, whose own deep impulses and commitments were sometimes at cross purposes, particularly when it came to concrete policy implications, and that the various approaches he appeared to vacillate between were indeed facets of the real Jimmy Carter.[44]

The more charitable explanation is persuasive since Carter also came to office with a clear set of principles and preferences, if not a detailed set of policies. His blend of religious conviction and Wilsonian idealism placed him nearer the McGovern wing of the Democratic Party than the Jackson wing. Carter was also influenced by his participation in the Trilateral Commission – a select group of businessmen, academics and members of the foreign policy elites from North America, Western Europe and Japan concerned with promoting greater cooperation between the advanced industrialised nations. This brought him into contact with members of the foreign policy community such as Zbigniew Brzezinski, Cyrus Vance, George Ball, Paul Warnke and McGeorge Bundy, as well as the founder of the Commission, David Rockefeller. Many, although not all, members of the Commission were former cold warriors who had reassessed their positions as a result of Vietnam.

This reassessment was also evident in the work done by the Council on Foreign Relations during the mid and late 1970s.[45] Indeed, it is possible to discern in the activities of the Council and the Commission four main themes, all of which were evident in the policies of the new administration. The first was considerable scepticism about the continued utility of military power. This was a direct result of Vietnam where the gap between American military capabilities and political influence had been immense. It was reinforced by the activities of OPEC, which highlighted the importance of non-military sources of influence. The increasing distribution of power and influence in the international system provided a second major theme. The third element in this new approach was the rejection of the superpower competition as the dominant element in American foreign policy. Indeed, the Council on Foreign Relations made explicit that its major research effort, entitled the 1980s project, 'sought to break out of the narrow outmoded boundaries of the cold war' and provide a general reappraisal of world politics.[46] The assumption was that the Soviet Union would not have a major role in shaping the international system of the 1980s and consequently need not be the central concern of US foreign policy. The fourth theme was the counterpart of this relegation of the Soviet Union to a secondary role: instead of the Soviet threat, emphasis was placed on economic concerns and problems of world order such as nuclear proliferation and human rights, which were assumed to be the dominant issues for the future.

Carter's experience with the Trilateral Commission not only helped inform his views on foreign policy, but also provided him with the people to fill key positions in his administration. Cyrus Vance, his Secretary of State, and Zbigniew Brzezinski, his National Security Adviser, were both active in the Commission. Although neither of these appointments was particularly controversial, other Carter choices were. His nomination of Theodore Sorensen as Director of the Central Intelligence Agency had to be withdrawn and Paul Warnke's appointment as head of the Arms Control and Disarmament Agency also proved highly controversial. The Jackson Democrats, along with other conservatives, were particularly aggrieved that the office of Secretary of Defense was not filled by either James Schlesinger or Paul Nitze.

Conservative anxieties about the character of the new administration were intensified by the influx of liberals to influential positions through the foreign affairs bureaucracy.[47] Although controversy focused on a small number of key individuals, it was a crucial battle for the soul of the new administration, and one which accentuated the internecine struggle within the Democratic Party. In fact, the exclusion of the Jackson Democrats was a major tactical blunder and exposed the administration to constant criticism and powerful opposition: 'many of those excluded worked against the Carter foreign policy through the Committee for a Democratic Majority and the Committee on the Present Danger'.[48] Other disaffected Democrats such as Norman Podhoretz, the editor of *Commentary*, added their weight to criticism of the new liberal orthodoxy on foreign policy.

The result was a fundamental debate about the future of American foreign policy. The Carter administration arrived in office with a world view very different from that of the previous administration, and in many respects very different from that of any other administration since 1945. Although there were differences of emphasis among Carter, Vance and Brzezinski, at the outset they appeared to share a 'liberal internationalist image of a complex global community' and were intent on devising policies appropriate to the new reality of an interdependent world.[49]

This liberal internationalism conflicted with the conservative internationalism dominant among both the Jackson Democrats and the majority of Republicans. The differences were of understanding and prescription. The conservative critique of the Carter administration, together with a set of alternative policy prescriptions, was elaborated most fully by the Committee on the Present Danger, a group which was established in March 1986 mainly by Democrats unhappy about the state of Soviet–American relations and especially trends in the strategic balance. Prominent figures in the Committee included Eugene Rostow, Paul Nitze, Norman Podhoretz, Dean Rusk, Clare Booth Luce, Admiral Zumwalt and Richard Allen. Many of those involved had already expressed anxieties about detente, so in one sense the Committee represented nothing new. Yet the coalescing of the opposition to both Soviet–American detente and to liberal internationalism was highly significant. Perhaps the most important figure in the CPD was Paul Nitze. A renowned hard-liner, who had been the principal author of NSC-68 in 1950, Nitze had resigned from the SALT delegation in 1974 and was to become probably the most important single figure in providing an alternative philosophy on Soviet–American relations to that promulgated by the Carter administration.

The differences between the Carter administration – at least as it enunciated its position in 1977 and 1978 – and the CPD were profound. Although much of the debate focused on Soviet military capabilities, the argument went well beyond differing threat assessments. In essence, the administration and the Committee formulated two competing paradigms about the contemporary international system and the nature of power within it.

The Carter administration, reflecting its intellectual origins, saw the international system as highly pluralistic and complex. The system was conceived as one in which no single state could dominate. Bipolarity was effectively a thing of the past, as power was widely diffused among the member states and varied from issue to issue. The nature of the system also determined the problems and objectives of American foreign policy. A narrow focus on superpower relations was believed to be anachronistic, while military security was only one among several objectives. Interdependence was seen as a fact of life in the latter half of the 1970s, and the administration was more concerned with the health of the global economy, with development in the Third World, and with promoting regional order and stability through restrictive policies on arms transfers than with the Soviet Union. Moscow was regarded both as a potential partner in an ambitious arms control enterprise and as a target of American human right policies. Human rights were described by Brzezinski as 'an idea whose time has come', and the administration's prime aim appeared to be promoting world order rather than containing the Soviet Union.[50] This more than anything else set Carter apart from his predecessors. Since 1947, administrations had differed in the means they adopted to contain the Soviet Union, but all had accepted containment as the major objective. The Carter administration, in contrast, attempted to transcend containment.

For the President, the relegation of containment was a doctrine of hope rather than despair and of strength rather than weakness. In a sense, Carter was trying to change the agenda of world politics: the focus would hitherto be on areas where the United States could still provide leadership. This was most evident in the President's address at Notre Dame University in May 1977. The theme was one of renewal, and the tone was optimistic. As the President stated,

> Being confident of our future, we are now free of that inordinate fear of communism which once led us to embrace any dictator who joined us in that fear.... This approach failed, with Vietnam the best example of its intellectual and moral poverty. But through failure we have now found our way back to our own principles and values, and we have regained our lost confidence.[51]

Underlying this confidence was the belief that although the United States had been forced to come to terms with the loss of hegemony, Moscow's ability to influence the international system was even more limited than that of Washington. Both superpowers were constrained by complexity, but the United States was stronger than the Soviet Union economically, politically and morally, while in military terms there was rough parity. The implication was that the United States could afford to 'reduce the profile and even the substance of Soviet–American relations'.[52] Instead of being the centre-piece of American foreign policy, the Soviet Union was to be marginalised. Where this was not possible, it was hoped that Moscow might cooperate with the United States both in arms control and ameliorating regional tensions. For a while in 1977 the administration even called for a reconvening of the Geneva Conference on the Middle East under Soviet and American auspices. Had this been implemented, it would have nullified Kissinger's 'exclusionary diplomacy' in the region. That it was even contemplated was castigated by critics as evidence of the administration's naïvety. Yet it was also a sign of the administration's confidence in its ability to provide leadership and to co-opt the Soviet Union into an equally responsible role.

The assumption that Moscow was willing to cooperate on a range of issues was accompanied by the belief that it was also willing to accept strategic parity and did not aim for superiority. Carter and Vance were relatively sanguine about the Soviet threat. Brzezinski, even at the outset, was somewhat more sceptical, and contended that Moscow was becoming more assertive in its behaviour and was aiming to replace the United States as the dominant power in the international system.

Brzezinski did not fully share the prevailing assumptions of the Carter administration, and these assumptions were rejected in their entirety by the CPD. The Committee differed from the administration in its appreciation of the international system, the predominant issues and problems within it, the strength of the United States, and the capabilities and intentions of the Soviet Union.

For Paul Nitze and his colleagues the fundamental element in the international system was the same as it had been since 1945 – Soviet–American competition. In their view the world was still bipolar and the relationship between Moscow and Washington was effectively zero sum – what was good for the Soviet Union was bad for the United States and vice versa. Consequently, the key issues were not about 'world order' but national and international security. Whereas the administration believed that military power was increasingly irrelevant to the problems of the late twentieth century, the CPD argued that it still retained a crucial role in contemporary international politics. The historical references for these conclusions were very different. The administration was influenced by the Vietnam war, which had revealed very clearly the limits of military force; the members of the CPD were much more impressed by the Cuban Missile Crisis – which had shown the effectiveness of coercive diplomacy – and were worried about the possibility of a 'Cuban Missile Crisis in reverse' with the United States being compelled to back down.[53] According to the Committee, such an eventuality was becoming more likely.

In its initial policy statement the Committee began with the contention that the United States was 'in a period of danger', and added that the danger was increasing.[54] It also rejected the idea that the danger could be dealt with through arms control. This approach, in the CPD's view, had resulted in American restraint without Soviet reciprocity. Even so, it was argued, there was insufficient awareness of the danger or of the urgent need for higher defence spending.

This was closely related to another point of contrast with the administration: whereas the President suggested that the United States was able to provide leadership, the Committee emphasised American weakness. Nitze and his colleagues had far less faith in the American ability to exercise influence in the international system than did the Carter administration. In this sense their assessment was similar to that of Jackson and Perle. Yet they also offered a remedy – 'a conscious effort of political will to generate higher levels of military spending'.[55] Without this, the United States would not only allow the Soviet Union to gain a potentially decisive strategic advantage but would become Number Two in the world. This argument would subsequently be developed into the 'decade of neglect' thesis which contended that in the 1970s the United States unilaterally opted out of the arms race and allowed the Soviet Union to obtain strategic superiority.

American restraint was all the more disturbing to the Committee because of its assessment of Soviet intentions. Whereas the administration emphasised the limits on Soviet power and was sanguine about Soviet policies, the CPD claimed that the Soviet Union was engaged in a systematic effort to acquire 'visible preponderance' in military terms and would attempt to translate this into political dominance. 'The principal threat to our nation, to world peace, and to the cause of the human freedom is the Soviet drive for dominance based upon an unparalleled military build-up.'[56] The Soviet objective was still world domination; the military build-up which went well beyond the need of Soviet self-defence was evidence of this. Indeed, it was suggested in some of the Committee's publications that the build-up was reminiscent of that of Nazi Germany in the 1930s.[57] The Committee's position was perhaps best encapsulated in its claim that 'The pressures of Soviet imperial ambition, backed by a military build-up without parallel in modern history, are threatening the world balance of power on which our ultimate safety as a nation depends.'[58] As for detente, it was dismissed as an aspiration rather than a reality: 'the notion that there has been a change for the better in Soviet–American relations since 1972 is persiflage, or worse – a figment of political imagination.'[59]

The contrast between the appraisal presented by the administration and that offered by the CPD and other conservative internationalists could hardly have been more stark. The differences, though, were of political as well as intellectual importance. The outcome of what was effectively a battle to determine the future direction of American security policy would do much to shape the pattern of Soviet–American relations in the late 1970s and early 1980s. In the event the battle was won by the CPD. There were several reasons for this.

One of the advantages of the CPD was the clarity and simplicity of its message. The parallels between Nazi Germany and the Soviet Union were reminiscent of cold war thinking and evoked responsive echoes in both the public and Congress. Part of its message was that the only thing holding the Soviet Union in check was the countervailing power of the United States. As this was increasingly neutralised by Soviet advances, particularly its increased capability for hard target kill, so Moscow would become more assertive and willing to take higher risks. Future Soviet behaviour was seen as simply a function of the strategic balance – the United States had to recognise that Soviet advantages in throw-weight and counterforce capability would inevitably be translated into political gains. The message was as powerful as it was crude. It was based on a reductionist view of the Soviet Union and on projections of Soviet capabilities which were essentially founded on worst-case thinking.[60] As one analyst has observed,

> the period of peril theory is a self-contained system of thought. If its basic assumption of technological determinism and its projections of Soviet capabilities are accepted there is almost no way in which it can be invalidated. The argument therefore has a powerful persuasive appeal. Its ramifications are derived in a seemingly logical way. No knowledge of Soviet history or the complex structure of Soviet goals and motivations is required.[61]

Furthermore, the solution to the problem is also readily available: by following the prescriptions of the Committee, the threat could be forestalled.

The CPD presented a picture of the Soviet Union which was not only difficult to disprove but which fitted in with the assessment which had predominated until the late 1960s. In addition, the arguments advanced by the Committee were redolent of cold war symbolism and appealed to deep-rooted American values and traditions. The contention that the United States was becoming Number Two was especially potent for a nation based on competitive individualism and one which had enjoyed hegemony in the international system for much of the postwar period. Despite emphasising the dangers which confronted the United States, however, the CPD offered a counsel of hope rather than despair. If Americans woke up to the threat and made the sacrifices necessary, then the danger would be averted. Implicit in this argument was the notion that by an act of will the United States could regain its status as the dominant power in the international system. This contrasted starkly with President Carter's rhetoric, which increasingly emphasised not American leadership and strength of purpose – as it had done at the outset – but the need to cope with complexity and come to terms with the limits of power. Carter played into the hands of the critics as he seemed to offer pessimism and defeat rather than the regeneration he had initially promised.

The CPD was also very successful in placing itself within the bipartisan tradition which had guided American policy up until the late 1960s. The public statements of members harked back to Truman and Acheson, and it was emphasised that the Committee was simply trying to restore the foreign policy consensus that had been created in the 1940s. This was a skilful argument, which implied that the detente policies of Nixon and Kissinger and the 'world order' concerns of Carter were both aberrations from mainstream American foreign policy. The Committee was able to establish this because of the eminence of its leading members. Long experience and detailed knowledge made Nitze and Rostow authoritative in their pronouncements. This was all the more significant because it contrasted with what appeared to be a lack of authority by the Carter administration itself.

What really gave the Committee's interpretation added credence, though, was Soviet involvement in the Third World. As pointed out in the previous chapter, Moscow's activities were more ambiguous than is often suggested. The impact on the American political debate of the latter half of the 1970s, however, was anything but ambiguous. For the Carter administration Soviet and Cuban involvement in the Horn of Africa was an embarrassing complication. It was impossible to downgrade the profile of Soviet–American relations when the Soviet profile and presence were being extended in the Third World. For the CPD, Soviet and Cuban activities provided confirmation of their fears and underlined the need for the United States to compete more vigorously. Consequently, the burden of proof was placed not on the critics but on those who believed either that superpower relations had become secondary or that it was possible to place the emphasis on the cooperative rather than the competitive elements in this relationship. For all this, the Carter administration seemed unwilling or unable to take the necessary action and mobilise support for the anti-Soviet policies which the CPD was demanding.

The result was that the administration appeared to be pursuing objectives which, in light of the Soviet challenge to American interests, had little relevance. This may have been inevitable: geopolitical rivalries were not high on the administration's list of priorities. Yet it is hard to escape the conclusion that the Carter administration contributed to the success of the Committee's campaign, not only through ineptness but also because some of its own policies played into the hands of the hard-line critics. This was especially true of the human rights campaign. Carter's emphasis on Soviet violations of human rights and his support for individual dissidents had adverse consequences for detente. It affected the tone of the relationship and made the Soviet Union sceptical about the Carter administration's commitment to improved relations. The impact of the human rights campaign in the United States itself was even more significant. Carter continued the process initiated by Jackson of restoring a sense of morality and self-righteousness to US foreign policy. This undermined much of the residual support in favour of continued detente: if the Soviet Union was as repressive as Carter's campaign implied, then a policy of detente was inappropriate. The President's moralistic approach contributed to the tendency to portray superpower relations as a Manichaean struggle between democracy and totalitarianism, and thereby unwittingly strengthened the analysis and prescriptions offered by the CPD. American self-righteousness was meaningless unless accompanied by military strength; while Soviet repressiveness made Soviet geopolitical ambitions even more disconcerting.

Part of the problem was that the administration did not seem willing to follow through this logic. Yet too much can be made of the Carter administration's weakness on defence. A large part of the problem was image. Here the contrast with the Nixon administration is very sharp. Throughout his period in the White House, Nixon emphasised the need to maintain American strength. In fact, defence spending declined during the Nixon years. Under Carter, defence spending went up but there was no rhetorical accompaniment to ensure that the President obtained credit for this. Part of the reason was that during his campaign Carter had pledged to cut defence spending. In office, he concluded that this was not a sensible option, but attempted to redeem himself with his liberal supporters by cutting back on the defence budget projections of the Ford administration. Although he actually increased spending beyond the level of the Ford administration, his campaign rhetoric was difficult to live down. Furthermore, the President's personal preferences were clearly in favour of slowing procurement, especially of strategic capabilities. In March 1977, Secretary of Defense Harold Brown claimed that there was 'no reason for immediate or grave alarm about our ability to deter major military actions by the Soviet Union'.[62] The contrast with the assessment that had been presented by Team B and was now being offered by the CPD could hardly have been greater.

It was underlined by the announcement on 30 June 1977 that President Carter was cancelling the acquisition of the B-1 bomber. Although the new manned bomber had for several years been a symbolic target of congressional liberals concerned with reducing defence spending, Carter's decision seems to have been based primarily on considerations of cost effectiveness. In the President's judgement, B-52s armed with air-launched cruise missiles were preferable in the short term, while 'stealth' technology offered a more capable and less vulnerable long-term substitute. The problem, though, was that the new technologies designed to make aircraft invisible to radar were still secret, and Carter felt unable to explain the rationale behind his decision. Even so, the public presentation of the decision could have been handled better. As Cyrus Vance later acknowledged,

> more attention should have been given to finding ways to soften the impact of this decision on congressional and public attitudes about the administration's commitment to a strong defence. One option might have been to seek some Soviet concession in SALT in return for canceling the B-1. Another might have been to announce that the administration intended to design a more advanced follow-on bomber for the 1990s, using ALCM-armed B-52s simply as a stop gap.[63]

In the absence of either of these, the decision confirmed the fears of those who felt that the administration was not reliable on defence. Consequently, it proved one of the most 'politically costly decisions' of the Carter Presidency.[64]

The belief that Carter was not taking the challenge to American security seriously enough was reinforced in 1978. The defence budget for fiscal year 1979 slowed down the development of the MX missile, while the Navy's shipbuilding programme suffered a 20 per-cent cut in funding below that of the previous year. Indeed, the Carter projections of naval strength were well below what the Navy regarded as a high risk option. Even Congress was dissatisfied with the administration's approach and added funds to the defence budget for a fifth nuclear-powered carrier, only to have the bill vetoed by the President.

Even more damaging than the fight over the carrier was the announcement in April 1978 that the President had decided to defer production of the enhanced radiation weapon or neutron bomb. Although Carter had not been as vacillating as his critics contended, what appeared to be an abrupt reversal on the issue not only discredited him with his NATO allies but added further to the domestic criticisms of the administration. 'Political opponents of the administration linked the ERW with the B-1 to charge wrongly that the administration was engaged in unilateral disarmament.'[65] The crusading moralism on human rights seemed increasingly vacuous as it was accompanied by what many critics claimed to be an imprudent neglect of American military capabilities. Not only was President Carter never able to overcome these charges, but his references to the limits of American power and the subsequent claim that the United States was suffering from 'malaise' only strengthened assertions that the administration was ill-equipped to manage American foreign and security policy.

In fact, the administration began to move away from its initial preoccupation with 'world order' and back towards a much more traditional foreign policy. Problems arose, however, because the leading figures in the administration differed in both the pace and scope of their reassessments. The one who moved the most – and in a sense defected to the opposition – was Brzezinski. One of his critics has discerned in Brzezinski an 'enduring penchant for fashionable issues and concepts that are adopted or discarded in the light of changing circumstances' as well as an 'unbecoming reliance on the intellectual cliché of the moment'.[66] A more charitable judgment is that, although Brzezinski had been a leading figure in the Trilateral Commission, he was a cold warrior in trilateral clothing – and, while jumping on and off fashionable bandwagons, was fairly consistent in his concern over the Soviet challenge.

In Brzezinski's view, the superpower relationship had gone through several distinct phases in which either Moscow or Washington had held the upper hand.[67] Furthermore, the mixture of cooperation and conflict in the relationship was also something which varied at different times. The latter half of the 1970s was a phase in which the Soviet Union was still on the upswing and was becoming increasingly assertive. In these circumstances, instability and change in the Third World offered unprecedented opportunities for Moscow to extend its influence. If the United States was to halt the momentum of Soviet geopolitical expansion, therefore, it was necessary not only for the Carter administration to acknowledge that the competitive elements in the relationship were once again coming to the fore but also to take a firm and unequivocal stance in this competition. Early demands that detente be more comprehensive and more reciprocal were, in Brzezinski's view, not met by Moscow. Consequently, the continued pursuit of detente was increasingly inappropriate for the United States.

Secretary of State Vance, like Brzezinski, recognised the mixture of conflict and cooperation in superpower relations. The main difference was that he was less impressed by the Soviet capacity to obtain enduring advantage from turbulence in the Third World. For Vance, this was another lesson of Vietnam. Developing states were highly nationalistic and, having thrown off one set of imperial masters, were unlikely to subordinate themselves willingly to Moscow. The contention that the pluralism and complexity of the Third World made it resistant to outside intervention was not accepted by Brzezinski. Although he did not hold to a simple bipolar conception of the international system, he saw the Third World as a major arena of superpower competition and was, therefore, much more apprehensive than Vance about indigenous instability. Consequently, much of the intellectual argument focused on the nature of change in the Third World. 'Brzezinski, Vance and Carter all accepted global complexity and the inevitability of change. Carter and Vance were prepared to see the beneficent side of change. Brzezinski beheld change as conflict and turmoil from which the Soviet Union stood to gain.'[68] This was reflected in Brzezinski's statements of late 1978 and 1979 that regional instabilities and the 'disintegration of political fabric in some regions of the world' had combined with increased Soviet military power to produce an 'arc of crisis'.[69]

In policy terms the argument centred on the concept of linkage. Brzezinski's notion of comprehensive detente – which was not very different from Kissinger's initial emphasis on the need for parallel progress across a range of issues – made him reluctant to compartmentalise issues. He also tended to emphasise what might be termed 'denial linkage', and claimed that the United States should not give the Soviet Union the arms control agreement it wanted unless Moscow was restrained in its behaviour in the Third World. Vance, in contrast, believed that attempts to regulate the strategic relationship between the superpowers were sufficiently important that they should not be derailed by the inevitable geopolitical competition.

Yet there was a sense in which linkage was not a matter of choice. Domestic support for arms control depended in large part on the overall climate of relations between the superpowers. As the competitive elements of the relationship came to the fore, so there was increasing support for the thesis of the CPD that the United States, instead of relying on arms control, should rebuild its military strength as rapidly and as decisively as possible. Only if this was done would it be possible to deter the Soviet Union from further adventurism of the kind it had embarked upon in Angola and the Horn of Africa.

The Soviet and Cuban involvement in Ethiopia, in particular, had a profound impact on American opinion, and Brzezinski's claim that SALT was 'buried in the sands of the Ogaden' was politically compelling.[70] Yet Brzezinski's own contribution to this was significant. By emphasising Soviet geopolitical restraint as a prerequisite for the continuation of arms control negotiations, Brzezinski had not only legitimised the use of linkage by those who were opposed to both detente and arms control, but offered what one former official described as an invitation to 'extremists in our body politic ... to pre-empt ... with a harder line than reality merits'.[71] Nor did Carter help. By asserting that although linkage was not the policy of the administration but something imposed by Soviet actions, the President undermined the efforts of Cyrus Vance to insulate SALT from the broader deterioration of Soviet–American relations. This effort may well have been doomed to failure in any event. But it seems clear that the administration, in this as in other things, contributed to its own difficulties.

Throughout 1978 the differences between Vance and Brzezinski were readily apparent, and the President seemed to oscillate between them. The fundamental divisions in the administration and the inability of Carter to impose a consistency and coherence on policy towards the Soviet Union proved profoundly debilitating.

In a major address on US–Soviet relations at Annapolis in June 1978 the President offered the Soviets the choice between cooperation or confrontation. The memoirs of Vance and Brzezinski relating to this speech are as divergent as the recommendations that went into it. Brzezinski claims that the confrontational elements in the speech were Carter's own.[72] Vance has offered a different version of events, suggesting that the speech drew on both his draft which 'emphasized the complex nature of the US–Soviet relationship and the need for lowering political tensions on a reciprocal basis' and the more confrontational draft provided by Brzezinski.[73] Whatever the exact details of the drafting, however, Vance is certainly correct about the outcome. Carter in effect attempted to reconcile incompatible recommendations. 'The end result was a stitched-together speech. Instead of combating the growing perception of an administration rent by internal divisions, the image of an inconsistent and uncertain government was underlined.'[74]

In spite of this disarray, it was clear that the administration was gradually moving away from the issues of world order back to the security concerns inherent in Soviet–American relations. This movement, however, was uneven and clearly a matter of internal debate within the administration. The result was that, politically, the administration obtained the worst of all worlds. Not only did it fail to get credit for its increasing toughness in dealing with the Soviet Union and its growing emphasis on restoring American military strength, but such actions as it did take were deemed inadequate. Yet by moving in the direction demanded by such critics as Paul Nitze and the CPD, the President effectively legitimised and strengthened their demands. In a sense, the Carter administration, as a result of domestic pressures, its internal divisions, and Soviet actions, inadvertently went a long way towards conceding the battle to the opponents of detente. By accepting, if only tacitly, the dominance of Soviet–American relations over issues of world order, it allowed the CPD to set the agenda of the debate over foreign policy and national security.

While this was a tactical mistake it may have been unavoidable. The trend of opinion in the country was clearly becoming more conservative, with the result that the emphasis on world order was increasingly out of tune with the national mood. As Gaddis Smith has noted, Carter 'had the good fortune to ride into office on the waning hour of a vaguely anti-military tide of public and congressional opinion and the bad luck to take office just as that tide turned'.[75] Indeed, the most fundamental problem for the administration was how to legitimise liberal policies in what was an increasingly conservative nation. In contrast, the arguments of the CPD evoked a positive response at the level of public and congressional opinion.

This conservative trend was inimical to detente. It simultaneously weakened the proponents of detente and strengthened the critics. It also accounts for many of the difficulties with which the Carter administration had to contend. The Carter era was in many respects an anomaly, and is best understood as a liberal interregnum in a period of conservative politics. The administration came to power largely because of what has been termed the 'Watergate warp'.[76] This interrupted a conservative revival in American politics which right-wing commentators themselves trace back to the Goldwater defeat of 1964. This revival was given added momentum in the first half of the 1970s by what was widely accepted as the failure of liberal policies, and the disintegration of the New Deal coalition which had been the mainstay of the Democratic Party since the 1930s. Part of what occurred in the 1970s was simple reaction, especially in domestic policy, to what was seen as the excesses of the 'Great Society' programmes of the 1960s and the pacifism and permissiveness, associated with the McGovern wing of the Democratic Party. It was also a result of shift in electoral geopolitics away from the northeastern strongholds of traditional liberalism to the more conservative south-west. The shift in the centre of gravity of American politics was bound up with an ideological shift of immense importance.

The rise of the Right had several distinct but mutually reinforcing strands. One of the most important was the emergence of neo-conservatives – intellectuals and former Democrats disillusioned with liberal prescriptions in domestic and foreign policy. Figures such as Norman Podhoretz, a vigorous member of the CPD, Jeane Kirkpatrick, Daniel Moynihan and Irving Kristol not only helped make conservatism 'intellectually respectable', but also 'interesting and relevant'.[77] They also provided severe indictments of both Kissinger and Carter's polices towards Moscow, denying that there could be any fundamental accommodation between liberal democracies and communist totalitarianism.

The writings of the more prominent neo-conservatives were buttressed through the 1970s by the rise of new conservative think-tanks. With money from industrialists such as Joseph Coors and Richard Mellon Scaife, heir to the Mellon banking fortune, institutions such as the American Enterprise Institute, the Institute for Foreign Policy Analysis and the Heritage Foundation were established to provide conservative analysis and prescription to counter that available to liberals through more well-established bodies such as the Brookings Institution. The 1970s also saw several older think-tanks such as the National Strategy Information Center and, more importantly, the Georgetown Center for Strategic and International Studies, attain greater prominence. Almost invariably these institutions took a robust approach towards the Soviet Union. They provided reinforcement for the kinds of concerns enunciated by the CPD, and for the most part were unsympathetic to the Carter administration.

Although it had an important new intellectual dimension, however, the conservative movement of the 1970s was also populist in orientation. The rise of the New Right was well orchestrated by certain key individuals such as Richard Viguerie (who perfected computerised mailing lists as a fundraising and lobbying device), Paul Weyrich, of the Committee for the Survival of a Free Congress, Howard Phillips of the Conservative Caucus, and John Dolan, creator of the National Conservative Political Action Committee (NCPAC). Under such leaders the New Right became a powerful influence in American politics. Feeding on what one former member of the movement described as 'backlash politics', the conservative leaders were able to establish 'an institutionalized, disciplined, well-organized and well-financed movement of loosely knit affiliates' which gained considerable support from blue-collar workers and American house-wives.[78] The 'angry style' of the leadership encouraged and was intensified by popular resentment against big government, elitism, northeastern dominance of American politics, and by a reaction against what was seen as a growing assault on traditional values as a result of increased tolerance of homosexuality and abortion.[79] For much of the New Right, therefore, 'politics was analogous to a crusade which demanded the energy and conviction of a zealot'.[80]

In view of this, it is not surprising that the rise of the New Right was closely associated with the revival of religious fundamentalism and the emergence of groups such as the Moral Majority under the leadership of Jerry Falwell. The increasing importance of religion had been evident in Jimmy Carter's emphasis in 1976 on his life as a 'born-again Christian', an emphasis which won Carter a surprisingly large percentage of the Baptist vote.[81] The disillusionment which followed Carter's reluctance to place social and moral issues on his legislative agenda facilitated what was in many respects an amalgamation of the New Right and religious fundamentalism – one that was engineered by the close links between Falwell and figures such as Weyrich and Phillips.

The implications of all this for the debate over detente were profound and far-reaching – and once again worked in ways which favoured the CPD and worked against attempts to maintain detente. The rise of the New Right strengthened and reinforced the anti-communism which is endemic in American political culture. Richard Viguerie, for example, advocated the abandonment of all arms control restraints and the restoration of American nuclear superiority over the Soviet Union with as much vigour as he advocated opposition to busing and abortion.[82] Indeed, the crusade against permissiveness and decay in American life and the crusade against the Soviet Union went hand in hand. Both foreign policy and domestic policy were seen as 'one giant battleground for the struggle between good and evil which rages in all realms: moral, religious, social, spiritual and political. There is no room in fundamentalism for differing social perspectives or political systems. Compromise is sin.'[83] From this perspective, detente, whether the Kissinger variety or the Carter version, was anathema. Kissinger lacked the moral credentials, while Carter lacked the expertise to compete effectively on behalf of the free world. If the rise of the New Right is explicable in terms of the politics of resentment, then much of that resentment was directed against the Soviet Union.

The rise of the Right was also important because of its impact on Congress. Although both the House and Senate became more conservative, the change was particularly marked in the upper chamber. In the early 1970s the Senate had been the most liberal institution in the American government; by the late 1970s it was the most conservative. Indeed, the Carter administration was under severe pressure from the Senate – in which the New Right was represented by such figures as Jesse Helms – to take a much tougher line with Moscow in the Third World and to do more to ensure that the United States could not be subject to nuclear coercion by a Soviet Union possessing strategic superiority.

The rise of conservatism clearly worked in favour of the CPD and its attempt to restore something akin to the traditional cold war consensus in the United States. Yet both the crusading politics of the New Right and the rejection of detente had psychological as well as political roots. The 1970s was a traumatic decade for the United States, in which the main themes of foreign policy could readily be construed in terms of defeat or decline. The impact of Vietnam and other foreign policy defeats was compounded by considerably reduced economic growth. This was caused partly by the rise in oil prices, partly by the increased competitiveness of Western Europe and Japan, and partly by the inevitable decline in American heavy industry. If the causes were structural, the effects on the American national psyche were nevertheless considerable. The relatively poor economic performance – with inflation and the growth in unemployment overshadowing the modest rate of economic growth – contributed to a sense of national malaise.

The Carter administration offered no way out of this. The protest against the Panama Canal Treaties, finally concluded in 1978 after years of negotiation, although carefully orchestrated by the New Right, was significant of the growing mood of unrest with what was increasingly seen as the defeatism of President Carter. This mood was inimical towards detente. The decade of detente and the decade of decline seemed inseparable. Furthermore, the growing frustration manifested itself in a xenophobic nationalism in which the Soviet Union became the scapegoat for many of the ills that had fallen on American society. Conversely, the restoration of American power and prestige *vis-à-vis* Moscow was seen as a means of overcoming malaise. Rather than coming to terms with the limits of a complex world, the American public and Congress reverted to the orthodoxies which had prevailed prior to 1968. This was not entirely surprising. The rebuilding of American military strength 'redolent as it was of a past era of US greatness, subsumed and displaced the frustrations brought on by the recession' and the other American reverses of the 1970s.[84] The CPD, which was essentially backward-looking, was more in tune with American needs at the end of the 1970s than was the Carter administration. Consequently, the struggle over the future of US foreign and defence policies was decided in favour of a traditional cold war orientation. The Kissinger attempt to pursue containment through detente and the Carter administration's attempt to transcend containment had both proved unacceptable. In short, the American foreign policy debate of the 1970s led to the rejection of detente. The extent to which a similar development occurred in Moscow is addressed in the next chapter.

Notes

1. See A. Schlesinger, *The Imperial Presidency* (Boston: Houghton Mifflin, 1973).

2. For Kissinger's analysis of the impact of Watergate on detente, see H.A. Kissinger, *Years of Upheaval* (Boston: Little, Brown, 1982), pp. 122–7 and 979–80.

3. R. Nixon, *Memoirs* (London: Arrow Books, 1978), p. 1024.

4. See T.M. Franck and E. Weisband, *Foreign Policy by Congress* (New York: Oxford University Press, 1979).

5. T. Lowi, 'Making Democracy Safe for the World' in J. Rosenau (ed.), *The Domestic Sources of Foreign Policy* (New York: Free Press, 1967), p. 315.

6. See R. Garthoff, *Detente and Confrontation* (Washington, DC: The Brookings Institution, 1985), p. 29.

7. See P. Jenkins, 'Come Home America', *Guardian*, 7 Aug. 1982; and R. Semple, 'McGovern unit says defence can be cut', *New York Times*, 22 Sept. 1972.

8. J. Reston, 'The Nixon Paradox', *New York Times*, 3 Nov. 1972.

9. We are indebted to Murray Marder, formerly of the *Washington Post* for this point.

10. D. Caldwell, *American–Soviet Relations from 1947 to the Nixon–Kissinger Grand Design* (Westport, Conn.: Greenwood, 1982), p. 98.

11. Kissinger, op. cit., p. 981.

12. Ibid.

13. J. Hellman, *American Myth and the Legacy of Vietnam* (New York: Columbia University Press, 1986), p. 6.

14. Kissinger, op. cit., p. 985.

15. Address to the Conference on Communism and Liberal Democracy in London, 19 March 1985.

16. We are grateful to Larry Smith for the 'networks' concept.

17. A.M. Cox, *The Dynamics of Detente* (New York: Norton, 1976), p. 153.

18. W.G. Hyland, *Mortal Rivals* (New York: Random House, 1987), p. 156.

19. See A. Platt, *The US Senate and Strategic Arms Policy, 1969–77* (Boulder, Col.: Westview, 1978), pp. 26–9, for a fuller account.

20. Kissinger, op. cit., p. 1150.

21. Garthoff, op. cit., p. 423.

22. L. Gelb and A. Lake, 'Washington Dateline: The Age of Jackson?', *Foreign Policy*, 14 (Spring 1974), pp. 178–88.

23. G. Will, *Washington Post*, 19 Feb. 1974.

24. Garthoff, op. cit., p. 406.

25. P. Stern, *Water's Edge* (London: Greenwood Press, 1979).

26. W. Korey, 'Rescuing Russian Jewry: Two Episodes Compared', *Soviet Jewish Affairs*, vol. 5, no. 1 (1975), pp. 3–19.

27. Stern, op. cit. Ch. 4 provides a detailed account of the trilateral negotiations.

28. See ibid., pp. 168–9, for the text of the letter.

29. Ibid., p. 174.

30. See comments by S.J. Marcuss in *The Premises of East–West Commercial Relations*, a Workshop sponsored by the Committee on Foreign Relations, US Senate and Congressional Research Service, Library of Congress, Dec. 1982 (Washington, DC: Government Printing Office, 1983), p. 71.

31. Ibid., p. 72.

32. Stern, op. cit., p. 197.

33. Ibid., p. 201.

34. Ibid.

35. Ibid.

36. W.F. Kolarik, 'A Model for the Study of International Trade Politics: The United States Business Community and Soviet–American Relations' (Kent State University: Ph.D. dissertation, 1981), p. 409.

37. S. Talbott, 'Social Issues' in J. Nye (ed.), *The Making of America's Soviet Policy* (New Haven: Yale University Press, 1984), pp. 183–205 at p. 200.

38. Quoted in G. Ford, *A Time to Heal* (New York: Harper & Row, 1979), p. 373.

39. See ibid.

40. R. Garthoff, op. cit.

41. G. Smith, *Morality, Reason and Power* (New York: Hill & Wang, 1986), p. 28.

42. S. Brown, *The Faces of Power* (New York: Columbia University Press, 1983), p. 460.

43. I. Destler, L. Gelb and A. Lake, *Our Own Worst Enemy* (New York: Simon & Schuster, 1984), p. 20.

44. Brown, op. cit., p. 454.

45. R.D. Schulzinger, *The Wise Men of Foreign Affairs: The History of the Council on Foreign Relations* (New York: Columbia University Press, 1984), ch. 8.

46. See ibid., p. 226.

47. Destler, Gelb and Lake, op. cit., p. 97.

48. Ibid., p. 116.

49. See J. Rosati, 'The Carter Administration's Image of the International System: The Development and Application of a Belief System Framework' (American University: Ph.D. dissertation, 1983).

50. See ibid., p. 155, for the Brzezinski comment.

51. Quoted in ibid., p. 156.

52. Garthoff, op. cit., p. 565.

53. See C. Tyroler II, *Alerting America* (Washington, DC: Pergamon Brassey's, 1984), p. 41.

54. Ibid., p. 3.

55. Ibid., pp. 3–4.

56. Ibid., p. 3.

57. Ibid., p. 13.

58. Ibid., p. 29.

59. Ibid., p. 30.

60. R. Johnson, 'Period of Peril', *Foreign Affairs*, vol. 61, no. 4 (Spring 1983), pp. 950–70.

61. Ibid., p. 951.

62. G.C. Wilson, 'Brown Convincing Congress Soviet Threat is Overstated', *International Herald Tribune*, 16 March 1977.

63. C. Vance, *Hard Choices* (New York: Simon & Schuster, 1983), p. 58.

64. Ibid., p. 57.

65. Ibid., p. 96.

66. S. Serfaty, 'Play It Again, Zbig', *Foreign Policy*, no. 32 (Fall 1978), pp. 3–21 at p. 6 and p. 7.

67. See Z. Brzezinski, *The Competitive Relationship* (New York: Research Institute on Communist Affairs, Columbia University, 1972).

68. D.S. McLellan, *Cyrus Vance* (Totowa, NJ: Rowman & Allanheld, 1985), p. 35.

69. Rosati, op. cit., p. 172.

70. See Brzezinski, *Power and Principle* (New York: Farrar, Straus & Giroux, 1983), p. 189.

71. Brian Atwood quoted in M. Marder, 'In Wrestling the Russian Bear, Even the Basic Rules are in Dispute', *Washington Post*, 1 Jan. 1981.

72. Brzezinski, *Power and Principle*, p. 320–1.

73. Vance, op. cit., p. 102.

74. Ibid.

75. Smith, op. cit., p. 48.

76. K. Phillips, *Post-Conservative America* (New York: Random House, 1982), p. 63.

77. Ibid., pp. 43–5; for a useful and balanced analysis of the neo-conservatives, see G. Peele, *Revival and Reaction* (Oxford: Oxford University Press, 1984), pp. 19–50.

78. A. Crawford, *Thunder on the Right* (New York: Pantheon, 1980), p. 5.

79. Peele, op. cit., p. 9.

80. Ibid.

81. Phillips, op. cit., p. 91.

82. R. Viguerie, *The New Right: We're Ready to Lead* (Falls Church, Va.: The Viguerie Company, 1980), especially pp. 133–54.

83. Quoted in Peele, op. cit., p. 79.

84. F. Halliday, *The Making of the Second Cold War* (London: Verso, 1983), p. 110.

8

Soviet Domestic Politics and Detente

The Soviet domestic debate about detente was in some respects the reverse of that which occurred in Washington. At the outset, detente was not seriously challenged in the United States, but became increasingly controversial throughout the 1970s – the policy preceded the debate. In Moscow, in contrast, the main debate seems to have taken place in the late 1960s and early 1970s as Brezhnev was moving towards the formulation of his Westpolitik. Once the policy of detente was established and legitimised at the Party Congress in 1971, it was pursued in a relatively coherent and consistent manner and was not subjected to a fundamental reappraisal of the kind which occurred in the United States. There were difficulties early on in gaining approval for the policy, and there was almost certainly a continuing review of the costs and benefits of detente. For the most part, however, the consensus seemed to be remarkably firm.

There are two major reasons, one conceptual and one political, why Soviet detente policy was more resilient and more sustainable than that of the United States. In the first place, the Soviet concept of detente was broadly based: it acknowledged, and to some extent extolled, the benefits of cooperation yet did not preclude competition. Detente in Soviet thinking was not an either–or concept, as it increasingly seemed to be in the United States. In a sense, there was something in it for everyone. Detente did not represent a diminution of Soviet concerns over national security or an abandonment of support for national liberation struggles. Furthermore, the fact that detente was in large part a product of Soviet achievements gave it considerable appeal.

In addition to a robust conceptual basis, detente in the Soviet Union was formulated and implemented within a relatively stable political framework. The changes in the composition of the decision-making elite which marked US policy during the 1970s were largely absent in Moscow. There were, of course, changes in leadership, but these generally involved the demotion of particular individuals who had been critical of Brezhnev's polices and the promotion of those who were more sympathetic. This continuity of leadership gave Soviet foreign policy the kind of coherence, stability and legitimacy that US policy lacked. This is not to claim that the Soviet Union is a monolith or that there was complete unanimity on important foreign policy issues. The detente policy was not immune from controversy, and, on occasion,

US officials were able to detect that enthusiasm for Soviet–American negotiation was not uniform. Yet there were few, if any, signs in the 1970s that there was anything like as fundamental a reassessment of detente policy in Moscow as there was in Washington.

The lack of uniformity in Moscow together with the fact that Soviet policy-makers represent particular organisations and interests, has led some analysts to identify several competing groups within the foreign policy debate. One commentator has even described Soviet foreign policy-making in terms of the competition between three distinct factions: the 'moderate internationalists' who favour detente, East–West trade and arms control; the 'Leninist internationalists', who emphasise the need to create propitious conditions for national liberation struggles; and a 'nationalist group', which is highly suspicious of the West, favours autarky, and regards military power as the only effective guarantor of Soviet security.[1] Although such an approach has attractions, it is not without problems. The most fundamental difficulty is the imposition of a Western pluralist model where it may not be applicable. The distinctions themselves are not entirely clear-cut, and it would be possible, for example, to combine moderate internationalism with Leninist internationalism. Furthermore, Soviet leaders would not necessarily identify themselves as members of these factions, and the difficulties become particularly acute when an attempt is made to locate specific individuals within a particular group. Brezhnev, for example, could be fitted into each of the factions at various points throughout his career.

The other problem with using a pluralist model to explain Soviet foreign policy-making is that it misrepresents the nature of the policy debate in Moscow. Such debate as there is comes from the top downwards and is contained within strictly defined limits. If these are transgressed too overtly then the culprits are excluded from the inner circle of decision-making and relegated to a minor role in the policy-making process. The closed nature of Soviet policy-making and the fact that differences are discussed within a much narrower political framework than in the United States, however, cannot conceal the fact that there were important developments in Soviet politics and policy-making during the 1970s. There is some evidence, for example, that during the latter half of the decade Brezhnev's control over foreign policy began to weaken – a process which accelerated as his health deteriorated. The re-emergence of collective leadership, however, seems to have had only marginal effects on policy, and there is little evidence of a concerted effort by opponents of detente to overthrow Brezhnev's policies.

In short, debates and disputes persisted throughout the period, but were circumscribed in scope, content and intensity. Yet there were several occasions during the 1970s when even the most ardent proponents of detente among the Soviet leadership must have questioned whether the policy was reaping the benefits they had anticipated. This has led some Western analysts to suggest that there was a marked shift in Soviet foreign policy from 1974 onwards.[2] This can easily be exaggerated since there does not seem to have been any major alteration in the way the Soviet Union approached detente. Nevertheless, in 1974 the Soviet leadership had to begin the difficult and rather painful process of coming to terms with the possibility that it would not achieve some of the objectives it was pursuing through detente. American legislation linking increased trade to Jewish emigration revealed the difficulties Moscow faced in dealing with a government based on the separation of powers.

From the Soviet perspective, the changes in American politics and policies during the 1970s must have been highly disconcerting. Not only did these changes mean that successive administrations were unable to deliver on bargains already made with Moscow, but that Washington initiated policies which, at the very least, seemed incompatible with Soviet expectations about detente. The Soviet Union found the United States an unpredictable and unsatisfactory partner in detente. Furthermore, the kinds of question marks that were raised in Washington about detente being a one-way street in favour of the adversary almost certainly had some echoes in Moscow. Yet it does seem that the Soviet Union still regarded detente as preferable to any alternative and never rejected or abandoned it in quite the same way as did the United States.

The Rise of Brezhnev

After the tumultuous years of Khrushchev, the Soviet elite sought a period of stability and consolidation. Consequently, Brezhnev was chosen in 1964 as First Secretary and two years later at the Twenty-third Party Congress took the title of General Secretary. It was hoped that stability could be further enhanced by restricting the power of the new party leader through the imposition of collective leadership. By the turn of the decade, however, Brezhnev was able to escape the stricter confines of collective leadership to emerge as *primus inter pares*. But even in this position, his power never approached that of his predecessors, and throughout his term of office he had to govern by consensus rather than rule by diktat.

If Brezhnev operated through consensus, he was also extremely skilful in manipulating the nomenklatura system. Two influential rivals, Podgorny and Shelepin, were demoted at the Central Committee plenum of December 1965, and the following year, Brezhnev successfully manoeuvred some of his protégés into important posts. Chernenko, for example, took over the General Department, which dealt with personnel policy and administration for the secretariat. Kirilenko was shifted into the secretariat to replace Podgorny, and proved to be one of Brezhnev's closest allies for many years. In the late 1970s such patronage became so blatant that a group of his supporters was nicknamed 'the Dnepropetrovsk mafia', after a town in the Ukraine where Brezhnev himself had once been First Secretary.[3] In the 1960s, however, he had to act more cautiously until he had established a firm base of support among the major Soviet institutions. He succeeded in this by adopting a conservative stance on policy, consistently supporting the military and, initially at least, distancing himself from economic and political reform.

The Twenty-third Party Congress of 1966 generally applauded the Brezhnev style of cautious orthodoxy. There had been plans to rehabilitate Stalin at the Congress. Although these were shelved at the last minute, this did not mark any relaxation of the anti-dissident campaign which had started with the Daniel–Sinyavsky trial of 1965.[4] Indeed, the Congress focused only to a limited extent on future policy, and its main task appeared to be the legitimisation of the new leadership. Although Brezhnev's position was strengthened, his victory was only partial as the Congress also expressed its support for collective decision-making.

A more important opportunity for Brezhnev to consolidate his position as Party leader came two years after the Congress. In Prague in the spring of 1968 Czech reformists were threatening the leading and guiding role of the Party. After initial reluctance, Brezhnev sided with Shelest and supported military intervention – an action which firmly established his conservative credentials.[5] This may well have served to comfort the military and the party ideologues in Moscow when Brezhnev began to escape the restrictions of collective leadership. By then Brezhnev was not only emerging as the dominant figure but also was increasingly taking an interest in foreign policy. In a more dominant position inside the Politburo, Brezhnev was well placed to respond positively to offers of detente from the West.

At the outside, though, there was no unanimity on the need for *rapprochement*. Walter Ulbricht of East Germany led the opposition to Brandt's Ostpolitik, and enunciated positions which evoked sympathy and support from within the top echelons of the Soviet elite. Some Soviet officials in the autumn of 1970 expressed reservations about the Soviet position on the German question, while Soviet journalists abroad were surprisingly critical of the treaties themselves. All these statements of discontent were quickly dismissed by official sources as unauthorised. Nevertheless, it seems likely that without at least some support from within the Politburo itself – probably led by Shelest – Ulbricht would not have survived in office as long as he did. In the event, he was dismissed in May 1971. It is not coincidental that this action took place after Brezhnev's Peace Programme was formally accepted by the Twenty-fourth Party Congress.

Brezhnev faced opposition over his policy towards the Federal Republic of Germany, and he also encountered difficulties in his attempts to establish a more conciliatory approach towards the Americans and a more flexible stance on arms control. This became most apparent to the West in the delays and reversals of policy in the late 1960s and early 1970s. In June 1968, for example, Andrei Gromyko announced to the Supreme Soviet an interest in arms control negotiations only eight days after a *Pravda* article had rejected an appeal from President Johnson for broad US–Soviet cooperation.[6] Similar signs of division and disarray were evident as the Soviet Union began to move towards the era of negotiations with the Nixon administration. The most obvious example of this was the Soviet delay in responding to the United States on the opening of arms control negotiations.

As an increasingly dominant leader with sound conservative credentials, however, Brezhnev was able to win over or conciliate enough of the critics and sceptics to end this period of apparent indecision and embark upon serious negotiations with the United States. Yet the Peace Programme he unveiled at the Twenty-fourth Party Congress only emerged after considerable manoeuvrings behind the scenes. Care was also taken with the way in which it was portrayed. In order to establish its legitimacy, the Peace Programme was presented to the Congress not as a novel departure but as a continuation of traditional Soviet foreign policy. Emphasis was placed not on the novel features of Soviet detente policy but on the way in which Western governments had accepted the necessity for *rapprochement* with the Soviet Union. The legitimisation process was further assisted by the fact that growing Soviet military strength had, from the Soviet perspective, been a crucial factor in the US desire for negotiations. Furthermore, Brezhnev consistently expressed his support for increased military power, ideological conformity at home and the national liberation movements in the Third World. None of these measures was regarded as in any way incompatible with detente. By the same token, they did not preclude detente. This was evident in the conciliatory remarks made by Brezhnev at the Twenty-fourth Party Congress, and directed at the United States and West Germany. Although the departure in Soviet policy represented by the Peace Programme was limited, therefore, it was far from insignificant. Its importance is underlined by the fact that it was also a shift which at least some members of the Soviet elite continued to resist.

Their resistance was minimised by the fact that Brezhnev, for the most part, was not replacing old policies with new but was initiating a more gradual process in which new departures were grafted onto existing policies and programmes. Arms control, for example, was not regarded as an alternative to Soviet military strength but as something which ensured that the gains which had accrued from the increase in Soviet capabilities would not suddenly be rendered void by another American technological leap. The rationale was almost certainly hard-headed and practical. Indeed, Brezhnev never reversed his strong commitment to the military: defence spending continued to grow throughout his term of office, albeit at a lower rate in the latter half of the decade.

Nevertheless, he did not succeed completely in stifling opposition. Prior to the Twenty-fourth Party Congress the military press expressed considerable concern over arms control. The military newspaper, *Krasnaya Zvezda*, published a number of editorials stressing the need for military strength to execute the international mission of the armed forces.[7] Shelest, in his report to the Ukrainian Party Congress, strongly supported the defence lobby. He was alarmist about Western intentions, and he alone of all first secretaries went out of his way to justify the invasion of Czechoslovakia.[8] Furthermore, Grechko, the Defence Minister, delivered a similarly hard-line speech which seemed to contrast sharply with that of the General Secretary. Although Grechko was confident of the Soviet Union winning any future superpower conflict, he raised the spectre of aggressive action by NATO against the USSR, and concluded that there was an urgent need to continue the build-up of Soviet military strength.[9] In such circumstances, Brezhnev had to proceed cautiously and with a minimum of disruption.

Although Brezhnev remained constant in his commitment to military power, the shift in his position was far more pronounced on other issues, especially East–West trade. During the Czech crisis of 1968, Brezhnev had opposed any extension of trade with the West and extolled the virtues of autarky.[10] By the time of the Twenty-fourth Party Congress in 1971, he had been converted to the opposite point of view. In part, his earlier opposition can be understood as a tactical manoeuvre to isolate Kosygin who was an early advocate of East–West trade. Furthermore, although Brezhnev's conversion seems to have been genuine, embracing Kosygin's position may have helped to conciliate erstwhile opponents. There was, after all, a precedent for this in the way in which in 1956 Khrushchev, having displaced Malenkov, embraced his ideas on peaceful coexistence.

Both arms control and East–West trade excited considerable debate before and after the Twenty-fourth Party Congress, but the issue which most exercised the minds of the Soviet elite was resource allocation. The plan to shift resources from heavy to light industry aroused considerable opposition. The Congress was postponed, largely because of disagreements on this matter, while Shelest made no secret of his opposition to the plan. At his Republic Congress in the Ukraine immediately prior to the main Congress in Moscow, he expressed pride in the 'special attention devoted to heavy industry' in the Ukraine.[11] Nor does he seem to have been alone in his opposition, as is testified by the fact that even the General Secretary's report to Congress was censored, in an otherwise verbatim report in *Pravda*, when he referred disparagingly to the 'metal eaters'.[12] Despite all the disagreements, Brezhnev appeared to emerge victorious, and the controversial shift in resource allocation was formally agreed at the Congress. Although Brezhnev won the battle, he did not, however, win the war. The commitment to light industry was never realised in practice, and at the following Congress in 1976 there was a reversal to traditional priorities.

Brezhnev's temporary victory on resource allocation, together with the promulgation of the Peace Programme at the Congress, suggest that the new policy framework had been established and endorsed. Yet the issue was far from closed. Even Gromyko, thought by many to be one of the architects of Soviet detente policy, was cautious on the matter of Westpolitik in his Congress speech. He made no mention of Brezhnev's Peace Programme, and it was only in September 1971 at the UN General Assembly that Gromyko announced this as official policy.

Nevertheless, Brezhnev was able to consolidate his position and advance his policies during the following year. In the summer of 1971 the Politburo accepted the idea of a superpower summit. Once more this decision proved highly controversial, with Shelest again Brezhnev's most outspoken critic. Matters were almost certainly brought to a head by American involvement in southeast Asia. The Vietnam war created considerable difficulties for the supporters of detente in Moscow, and these were exacerbated when Nixon ordered the mining of Haiphong harbour only two weeks before the proposed Summit. The Summit went ahead, however, and the main loser was Shelest. During the Summit he was removed from his post as First Secretary of the Ukraine. Although Shelest had been critical of Politburo policy on a number of issues, the timing of his dismissal strongly suggests that his opposition to detente and to the Summit was the crucial element in his downfall.

Brezhnev was able to demote Shelest, but he was not yet in a strong enough position to remove him altogether. In spite of losing his position as First Secretary of the Ukraine, Shelest (in what was a unique arrangement) remained a full member of the Politburo for another year. With his power base removed, however, he was in a very vulnerable position. His successor, Shcherbitsky, a close ally of Brezhnev, undermined his position even further. Perhaps most important in Shelest's final departure, though, was the fact that detente appeared to be providing tangible benefits to the Soviet Union. The Summit which he had so vigorously opposed produced significant accords on arms control as well as the Basic Principles Agreement, a document which appeared to enshrine American acceptance of the Soviet Union as an equal. In these circumstances, Shelest's isolation was inevitable. With Shelest's dismissal from the Politburo in June 1973, Brezhnev's hold on power and his control over policy seemed unassailable.

The first half of 1973 was probably the high point of detente for the Soviet Union, and it also found Brezhnev at the height of his power. The April Central Committee plenum provided ample evidence of this. Not only was detente described in fulsome terms but it was stated officially for the first time that the process had reached an 'irreversible stage'.[13] A major Politburo reshuffle also took place at the plenum. Key figures on foreign policy, including Defence Minister Grechko and Foreign Minister Gromyko, were promoted to full membership of the Politburo. These changes were seen by many as further evidence of the Soviet commitment to detente. Nevertheless, the presence of Grechko – a somewhat sceptical supporter of detente and a loyal representative of the military establishment – on the major decision-making body in the Soviet Union must have been reassuring to the more orthodox elements in the Soviet elite.

The Emerging Challenge to Detente

Brezhnev had won much support for his detente policy because of its tangible gains for the Soviet Union. Yet from the autumn of 1973 onwards Soviet detente policy was once again under domestic pressure. The crisis centred on two crucial aspects of policy: regional issues and East–West trade. Set-backs in both these areas made Brezhnev's policy more vulnerable to criticism, although they did not lead to a full-scale reappraisal.

Despite some earlier set-backs in Egypt, the problems really began in Chile in September 1973, when Allende's democratically elected government was overthrown by a military coup supported by the United States. The Pinochet coup caused a stir throughout the communist world, and led to allegations that the Soviet Union could have done much more to protect the Allende government. Allende himself did not expect a military commitment from the Soviet Union. Nevertheless, he visited Moscow shortly before the coup in the hope of winning substantial economic aid. His reception was decidedly lukewarm, possibly because the Soviet Union was unwilling to extend its foreign aid commitments at a time when there were growing concerns over the performance of the domestic Soviet economy. Outside the Soviet Union, however, there was a tendency to attribute Soviet reticence to detente, and it was suggested that Moscow was more interested in improving relations with the United States than with helping its Third World allies. This argument was presented most forcibly by Beijing, but was also crucial in the thinking of President Sadat.

The Pinochet coup also cast doubt on the Soviet theory that a peaceful road to socialism was possible even in areas like Latin America which was in the American sphere of influence. On the one occasion that this had occurred, Soviet policy-makers believed they had acted with circumspection but that the United States had taken advantage of the goodwill engendered by superpower detente and supported the violent overthrow of a Soviet ally in the Third World.[14]

The impact of the coup on subsequent Soviet foreign policy behaviour is not entirely clear. The Soviet media tended to describe the overthrow of Allende as an internal affair which should not affect superpower relations. Moreover, Brezhnev continued to commend the peaceful road to socialism in the Third World. In February 1974, for example, the General Secretary visited Havana. While pledging continuing support for Cuba, he also criticised violent means of achieving socialism.[15] On the other hand, as discussed in Chapter 5, there may well have been a connection between the coup in Chile and a more opportunistic Soviet policy in the Middle East.

While Chile provoked the beginning of a reassessment in Moscow, the Middle East war of October 1973 may well have taken this further. Detente did not prevent the superpowers from coming closer to direct confrontation than at any time since the Cuban Missile Crisis of 1962. Furthermore, in the peace process that followed, Kissinger was very active in excluding Soviet participation, and succeeded in drawing Egypt away from Moscow and into a much closer relationship with Washington. This was an extremely serious loss for the Soviets in an area of considerable strategic interest. Kissinger's unilateral action also showed to any in the Politburo who doubted it that the United States, despite its recent set-backs in Vietnam, was still able to compete actively with the Soviet Union in the Third World.

Conclusions drawn in Moscow over the events in the Middle East were mixed. The overall effect, however, was to confirm the existing preferences of the leading members of the Politburo rather than to generate a major political realignment. Those who had been cautious and sceptical became even more wary; those who had supported detente continued to do so, if with slightly less enthusiasm. Grechko, who was pessimistic about the future of superpower relations, suggested, not surprisingly, that the events in Chile and the Middle East had highlighted the continuing need for Soviet military strength and combat preparedness.[16] The majority in the Politburo, however, including Brezhnev and Kosygin, kept faith with the process of detente, partly on the grounds that this had helped to localise the conflict.[17] This was easier because expectations were low: even the proponents of detente were sensitive to the limits of superpower cooperation on regional issues. In spite of the Basic Principles Agreement and the Agreement on the Prevention of Nuclear War, the Soviet rhetoric on national liberation movements remained vigorously competitive. On the issue of East–West trade, however, expectations were considerably higher – and the disappointments were correspondingly greater.

When the US–Soviet Trade Agreement was signed in 1972, Soviet leaders portrayed it as the start of a new era in superpower relations. The link to Jewish emigration imposed by the American Congress, however, seriously complicated matters. In spite of the fact that Henry Jackson appeared to be interfering in Soviet internal affairs, Moscow attempted to comply with the demands of Congress. At the height of detente in March 1973, the emigration tax was lifted and the rate of Jewish emigration peaked at 35,000 in that year. Furthermore, the Soviet Union, in September 1973, signed the UN Covenant on Human Rights, which included articles on the right of emigration. These concessions did not placate Jackson, and Congress passed several measures restricting US–Soviet trade. Moscow was opposed to all these measures, but the Stevenson Amendment may have been particularly important in the progressive disillusionment with Washington. It seriously hindered Brezhnev's ambitious plans for import-led growth in the Soviet Union, and was probably a major factor in the Soviet decision to abrogate the Trade Agreement.

The impact of the restrictive measures was all the greater in Moscow because the Congressional success was unexpected. Kissinger, at this stage, was relatively satisfied with Soviet foreign policy behaviour, and he clearly underestimated congressional support for the amendments. The misperception was transferred to Moscow, where Soviet leaders initially interpreted the proposed legislation as little more than electioneering. The back channel which had been useful in the past did not function nearly so effectively on an issue in which Kissinger was not in complete control. As a result, the Ambassador to Washington, Anatoly Dobrynin, was reprimanded by Moscow for not reporting the threat early or accurately enough, while Soviet faith in the ability of Henry Kissinger to manage the domestic base of detente was severely dented.[18]

Even so, there were no signs that Moscow wanted to abandon detente or that it wanted the weakening of the Nixon administration. In contrast to American intrusions into Soviet domestic affairs, Moscow treated Watergate with remarkable restraint. The Soviet press said nothing about the crisis until the summer of 1973, and when the story finally broke in Moscow, there was considerable sympathy for President Nixon. In a content analysis of both Western and Soviet newspapers, one analyst found that *Pravda*, closely followed by *Izvestiya*, was the newspaper most supportive of the President's position.[19] When Nixon at last resigned in 1974, the immediate response in Moscow was to see the Watergate scandal as part of a deepening plot by the American Right to undermine superpower detente.[20]

The Soviet attitude towards Watergate was revealing in several ways. Not only did it highlight the centrality of detente in Soviet thinking about foreign policy, but it also revealed Soviet fears that the right-wing, anti-detente faction was gaining strength in American politics. It may have also been intended to signal to Washington that, under conditions of detente, there should be no interference in the internal affairs of the other superpower. Perhaps most important of all, it exposed the difficulties faced by Moscow in attempting to understand the nature of the American system. The Deputy Procurator General of the USSR, M.P. Malyarov, described the Watergate scandal as 'a demagogic trick ... all this is meant just as show, it will end in nothing if only Nixon shows determination. That's their democracy – just a hocus pocus.'[21] The top Party officials may have had a rather more sophisticated view, but Brezhnev still called Nixon's opponents 'senseless', while Gromyko said that Watergate was 'really about nothing'.[22] Despite the apparent sophistication of Soviet academics and officials, it appears that they failed to appreciate the fundamental nature of the constitutional crisis generated by Watergate.

Such misjudgements stemmed largely from the differences in ideology and political structure between the two societies. Given the much greater concentration of power in Moscow, it is hardly surprising that Soviet decision-makers were not able to come to grips with the turbulent and unpredictable nature of the American policy process. The result was a tendency to interpret the failure of the Nixon and Ford administrations to deliver on their commitments as evidence of bad faith, when in fact it was simply an expression of American pluralism. This was significant because it fed back into the domestic debate in the Soviet Union, and contributed to Soviet disillusionment with the United States.

Soviet observers were badly mistaken in ascribing Watergate to a right-wing conspiracy in the United States. Their concern that the Right was gaining in strength and looking to bring down detente, however, was more soundly based. Consequently, Nixon's resignation was greeted with apprehension, and there was considerable relief when

Gerald Ford not only pledged to continue the policy of detente but also retained the services of Henry Kissinger.[23] Despite increasing problems over human rights – Alexander Solzhenitsyn was exiled in February 1974 – progress continued to be made in arms control. The Vladivostok Accord of November 1974 seems to have been greeted with considerable optimism by the Soviet political leadership. It seems, however, that the Soviet military was more cautious and ambivalent about the Accord, and by the end of 1974 Brezhnev had used up a good deal of political capital in maintaining the momentum of detente. Consequently, when it became clear that Congress would pass both the Jackson–Vanik and Stevenson Amendments, Brezhnev was unable to save the US–Soviet Trade Agreement of 1972. At the December 1974 Central Committee plenum, it was decided to abrogate the treaty, thereby removing one of the central planks of Brezhnev's Westpolitik. Clearly, detente had become more problematic. Even so, it remained important in Soviet calculations.

The Consensus Maintained

In the months that followed the crucial December 1974 Central Committee plenum, there were intermittent rumours that Brezhnev would either resign or be deposed. These rumours were fuelled by the disappearance of the General Secretary from public view for two months. The most probable reason for Brezhnev's low profile was ill-health, but in March 1975 François Mitterrand, the French socialist leader, was asked at short notice to postpone his proposed visit to Moscow, and an emergency meeting of the Central Committee was called. It seems clear that, at this stage, Brezhnev was coming under increasing pressure, mainly from Shelepin.[24] After the meeting, however, it was announced that Shelepin had been dropped from the Politburo. While the significance of this should not be exaggerated – Shelepin's influence had been declining since the mid-1960s – it helped to re-establish Brezhnev's pre-eminence after a period of doubt and confusion. Although rumours persisted that Brezhnev might choose the impending CPSU Congress to announce his retirement, these were finally stilled by a bravura performance at the Congress.

Some analysts, especially Harry Gelman and Peter Volten, explain the events of 1974–5 in terms of crisis and fundamental reappraisal.[25] They also suggest that out of this period of turmoil there emerged a new, more limited concept of detente based on a less conciliatory attitude towards Washington, a clear differentiation between the United States and Western Europe, and a more vigorous policy in the Third World. Furthermore, it is argued, Brezhnev was forced to accept the change as the price for staying in office.[26]

There are several problems with this interpretation. The first concerns the exact nature of this more limited conception of detente. It is far too simplistic to claim that the Soviets adopted a harder line on all aspects of East–West relations. Detente, after all, had never represented any diminution of Soviet military strength or a weakening of support for national liberation movements. Soviet military programmes and heightened activity in the Third World do not of themselves indicate that a more limited concept of detente had been adopted. Nor is it adequate to suggest that Moscow continued to pursue a cooperative relationship with Western Europe while adopting a more hostile approach to the United States. There was an element of differentiation, as was evident in the emphasis on the Helsinki Final Act and on increased trade with Western Europe. Yet this should not be exaggerated. The United States was deeply involved in the CSCE process, while the Soviet emphasis on trade with Western Europe was in part a response to the actions of the American Congress. In other words, arguments that collaborative detente were replaced by a more competitive detente are not persuasive. Superpower detente after the December 1974 reassessment, as it had done from the outset, combined cooperation and conflict. Despite problems in Soviet–American relations ranging from human rights to competition in the Third World, the Soviet Union attempted to be fairly conciliatory on arms control and welcomed the signing of SALT Two.

This suggests an alternative explanation for Soviet behaviour in the latter half of the 1970s. What changed was not Soviet policy but the international context. The framework established by Brezhnev remained intact, but Soviet actions became more confused, reactive and opportunist in response to developments in Washington and events in the Third World. This explains why, at some times and on some issues, the Soviets appeared to go out of their way to be conciliatory to the United States, while at other times and on other issues Moscow displayed considerable insensitivity to American concerns. Yet, there was nothing radically new or different about this: the Soviet concept of detente had always been sufficiently ambivalent to allow this kind of mixture. There is little to suggest, therefore, that there was a conscious shift of approach or explicit reordering of priorities by the Kremlin.

The analysis of superpower competition in the Third World outlined in the previous chapter gives credence to this second view. Although there was no conceptual change, however, there was a change in the tone of Brezhnev's statements. Yet there is no obvious incompatibility between the idea of a consistent policy framework and the possibility that for internal reasons Brezhnev was forced to adopt a slightly tougher line after 1974. Indeed, the very fact that Brezhnev emphasised Soviet gains in the Third World may have been intended primarily to placate domestic critics of detente who complained that it was becoming a one-way street in favour of Washington. Rather than implying the abandonment of the initial detente policy, it can be understood as an attempt to reaffirm its legitimacy.

Brezhnev's report to the Twenty-fifth Party Congress, which began in February 1976, placed more emphasis on continuity than on change in detente policy, but also displayed a stridency which intensified Western concerns about Soviet activities in the Third World. In his report, Brezhnev was far more cautious than in some earlier statements about the prospects for superpower detente. In a five-and-a-half-hour speech, he dismissed the achievements of Helsinki and Vladivostok in under six minutes. The General Secretary was particularly concerned about the rise of right-wing circles in the United States and the threat they posed to detente, but seemed to view detente in Europe with greater optimism, describing the gains there as both durable and tangible.[27]

Despite this harsher tone towards the United States, Brezhnev by no means relinquished all references to a cooperative relationship. Indeed, in certain sections of his report he appeared more conciliatory than at the previous Congress, placing considerable emphasis on the firm intention of the United States and the Soviet Union 'to settle differences and disputes not by force, not by threats or sabre-rattling, but by peaceful means'.[28] At the same time Brezhnev vigorously defended the intervention in Angola, declaring that the Soviet Union acted according to its 'revolutionary conscience'.[29] He went on to link the victory of the MPLA and similar successes in the Third World with the process of detente which had created 'more favourable conditions for peaceful and socialist and communist construction'.[30] Indeed, on the Third World the 1976 Report to Congress went further than that of 1971. At the Twenty-fourth Party Congress, Brezhnev had not devoted a discrete section to the question of national liberation movements, and had treated the whole issue with restraint, despite American involvement in Vietnam. In 1976, in contrast, he dwelt at length on this question and provided a roll-call of the states which had recently joined the socialist commonwealth. The tenor of the speech was triumphant.

Yet the report did not mean that Moscow was intent on securing international revolution by military means. On this issue the language of the 1976 Congress was not very different from that used earlier in the 1970s. Brezhnev continued to support the thesis of a peaceful road to socialism. The key point was simply that Soviet rhetoric and Soviet practice on national liberation movements had come more closely into line.

The argument that there was a fundamental shift in Soviet detente policy after 1974 assumes that the Soviet leaders were aware that their actions in the Third World would have a detrimental effect on the relationship with the United States, and simply saw this as a price that had to be paid for geopolitical gains. There are grounds, however, for suggesting that the American reaction was simply underestimated. There are several reasons why this might have occurred. In the first place, the Soviet Union had been prepared to establish detente in a period when the United States was extremely active in the Third World – in 1972 Moscow had allowed the Summit to proceed in spite of the American mining of Haiphong harbour. The Soviet rejection of linkage had facilitated Nixon's visit to Moscow which provided one of the high spots of detente. It was natural for the Soviet leaders to assume, therefore, that there was no incompatibility between detente and support for national liberation movements. They had made this clear to the United States from the outset, and repeated it in relation to specific contingencies such as Angola. A second reason for underestimating the American reaction was that Washington itself appeared to be behaving in a competitive way. A third reason was that the Soviet Union did not fully understand the changes which were taking place in American politics, and expected the 'Vietnam syndrome' to focus American attention inwards rather than onto the Third World.

It was only later that the Soviet leaders began to realise the extent to which their activities in the Third World had eroded American support for detente. A growing awareness of this may have been reflected in the setting up of a department on the Third World in the prestigious US and Canada Institute in Moscow towards the end of the 1970s. It was certainly evident in the more downbeat presentation of the national liberation issue at the Twenty-sixth Party Congress in 1981 when Brezhnev insisted that the Soviet Union was not interested in the 'export of revolution'. At the time of the Twenty-fifth Party Congress in 1976, however, the leadership may well have believed that the furore in the United States would blow over very quickly and would not fundamentally affect the relationship with the United States.

The desire of the Soviet Union to maintain detente was perhaps most evident in relations with Western Europe, which, economically, had become even more important to Moscow as a result of the impasse over expanded trade with the United States. The importance attached to the European dimension – and in particular the Soviet desire to legitimise the status quo in Europe – was evident in the Conference on Security and Cooperation in Europe. Talks on the CSCE process had appeared to be deadlocked on the issue of human rights, but as a result of Soviet concessions on the inclusion of Basket Three, the negotiations were concluded in August 1975. The Helsinki Final Act brought Moscow many benefits – especially in terms of security and economic cooperation. Nevertheless, the inclusion of human rights represented a major concession from the Soviets, particularly as it came so soon after the problems with the Jackson–Vanik amendment. Although this revealed an eagerness on Moscow's part to continue with detente, it also created difficulties in the relationship with Western Europe. Despite the earlier concessions, the Soviets made little effort to abide by the non-binding regulations on human rights in Basket Three. Indeed, some figures, such as the Marxist dissident Roy Medvedev, believe that Moscow actually tightened up on intellectual dissidence in the late 1970s.[31] One obvious example of this was the harassment of the independent monitoring group set up by Yuri Orlov to assess the compliance of its government with the Final Act. All members of this group were arrested or otherwise neutralised by the time of the first follow-up conference in 1977. Such flagrant abuse of the CSCE process dampened the atmosphere in Europe, and the follow-up conferences in Madrid and Belgrade were acrimonious and unproductive.

The pattern on human rights, however, was not uniformly bleak. Some efforts were made by Moscow to comply with certain aspects of Basket Three. For example, information from the West – either in the form of newspapers or radio transmissions – was more widely available in the Soviet Union. Cultural and scientific exchanges were also increased. Perhaps most interesting of all, the rates of emigration from the Soviet Union reached their highest level in this period. For example, the number of Soviet Germans allowed to emigrate peaked at over 9,000 in 1976 and 1977, while the number of Armenians allowed to leave trebled in 1979 and almost doubled again in 1980. Most significantly, the number of Soviet Jews allowed to emigrate, having declined from 35,000 in 1973 to well under half that number in 1975, 1976 and 1977, climbed again to 29,000 in 1978 and reached over 50,000 the following year.[32]

Although the Soviet record on Jewish emigration was more mixed than is sometimes suggested, the Soviet leaders still viewed the election of Jimmy Carter with some trepidation. Carter was an unknown quantity, but a central theme of his election campaign was the need for a return to moralism in politics. There were hopes in Moscow that Carter would moderate his views in office, but he continued to pursue a vigorous policy on human rights issues. Carter held an audience in the White House with the Soviet *émigré* Bukovsky – an action which contrasted with that of Ford, who, on Kissinger's advice, had decided not to meet Solzhenitsyn. But it was President Carter's letter to Sakharov – who won the Nobel Peace Prize in 1975 – which really upset the Soviets. It prompted Brezhnev to write to Carter, saying he would 'not allow interference in our internal affairs', and that he regarded Sakharov as 'a renegade who proclaimed himself an enemy of the Soviet state'.[33]

Other aspects of Carter's foreign policy were more palatable to the Soviet leaders. They welcomed his attempt to bring the Soviet Union back into the peace process in the Middle East. When this policy was quickly reversed, however, it began to cause deeper mistrust of his motives inside the Kremlin. Indeed, Carter must have been an inordinately difficult President to deal with. The divisions and reversals which characterised his administration almost certainly made him appear as a very unreliable partner in detente. During the second half of Carter's Presidency, the Soviet press began to portray him as an opponent of detente. The contrast with the earlier treatment of Nixon could hardly have been more stark. Although this change in press coverage revealed an increased level of acrimony in superpower relations, it was also an indication of Soviet frustration with an administration whose vacillations were as puzzling to Moscow as they were to the American people. As President Carter – largely in response to Soviet activities in the Third World and political pressures in the United States – moved from the 'world order' agenda to a hard-line policy towards Moscow, so Soviet dissatisfaction increased. Particularly troubling for Moscow was the emergence of Brzezinski to a dominant position, and especially the way in which he played the 'China card'. For the Soviet Union, Washington's China policy was the negation of one of the key elements of detente. From the outset detente had been seen in Moscow as a way of dealing with the threat from China. The maximum aim was the establishment of a Soviet–American condominium directed against China; the minimum objective was to prevent Sino–American collusion. Yet, under the Carter administration, not only did Washington and Beijing begin to move much closer but also their cooperation seemed to have a pronounced anti-Soviet bias. The visit of Brzezinski to China in May 1978 was picked up by Soviet commentators as being of particular importance, and as signifying 'a sharp zigzag in the policy of the Carter administration from a relatively considered and even-handed triangular diplomacy to a single-minded pro-Peking and anti-Soviet orientation'.[34] The establishment of full diplomatic relations between China and the United States, the visit of the Chinese leader, Deng Xiaoping, to Washington in January 1979, and the subsequent Chinese invasion of Vietnam all intensified Soviet concerns and cast further doubt on the American commitment to superpower detente. Although these doubts were to be put on one side for the Vienna Summit and the signing of SALT Two in June 1979, they were intensified by the American debate over the Treaty.

It is clear, therefore, that in the mid and late 1970s detente entered a spiral of decline. Mutual mistrust and antagonism increasingly dominated the superpower relationship. The question arises as to why Brezhnev allowed this to happen to a policy and a process with which he was so closely identified. One possible explanation is that in the latter half of the 1970s Brezhnev was less dominant in the formulation of Soviet foreign policy than he had been in 1972 and 1973. Proponents of this view point to the rise of Defence Minister, Marshal Grechko, a man less supportive of detente, who, in the immediate aftermath of the December 1974 Central Committee plenum assumed a higher public profile. There were even some suggestions by Western observers that shortly before his death in April 1976 Grechko was number two in the Kremlin. The rise of anti-detente forces inside the Kremlin, however, can easily be exaggerated. Grechko's replacement, Ustinov, was not only a civilian and close to Brezhnev, but was also a strong proponent of detente. Furthermore, in 1976 the Soviet commitment to arms control was reaffirmed, something which again casts doubt on the argument that, as a result of domestic pressure, Brezhnev moved away from detente.

Superficially, Brezhnev's power appeared to be growing in this period. He was able to surround himself with his protégés, to assume the Presidency in 1977 and to shower himself with medals. This concern with the trappings of leadership, however, may have coincided with a weakening of Brezhnev's control over the policy-making process. Because of ill-health, he was able to work only short hours and make fewer public appearances. Furthermore, Gromyko emerged as an increasingly influential figure on foreign policy in the late 1970s, and Brezhnev clearly had to operate within the confines of a more collective form of decision-making in which the consensus was moving further against concessions or self-denying ordinances simply to maintain detente. At the same time, the decline of Brezhnev should not be exaggerated. Brezhnev has appropriately been described as the 'artful synthesiser', and it seems likely that his synthesis reflected the concerns of his colleagues.[35] Yet he almost certainly shared these concerns, and there is little evidence that he was forced into actions he would have preferred to avoid. Moreover, to the extent that Brezhnev's power did decline this did not cause the decline of detente. There was certainly no abrupt abandonment of Soviet detente policy. What does seem to have happened, however, is that considerations relating to the maintenance of detente began to figure less prominently in Moscow's calculations. This became particularly important in the latter half of 1979 when the Soviet leadership was wrestling with the Afghanistan problem. By then, however, much of the American body politic, although not yet the Carter administration, had effectively rejected detente. The fundamental shift away from detente took place in Washington, not Moscow. The Soviet debate led to changes at the margin; the American debate established a new foreign policy consensus in which detente had no part.

Notes

1. P.D. Stewart, 'Gorbachev and Obstacles to Detente', *Political Science Quarterly*, vol. 10, no. 1 (1986).

2. P. Volten, *Brezhnev's Peace Programme* (Boulder, Col.: Westview, 1982); and H. Gelman, *The Brezhnev Politburo and the Decline of Detente* (Ithaca, NY: Cornell University Press, 1984).

3. Members included Kirilenko, Shcherbitsky, Grechko and Tikhonov.

4. *The Times*, 17 March 1966. See also *Pravda*, 30 Jan. 1966, for the argument that de-Stalinisation had gone too far.

5. Gelman, op. cit., pp. 98–102.

6. *Pravda*, 19 June 1968.

7. See Volten, op. cit., pp. 72–5.

8. V. Zorza, *Guardian*, 19 March 1971.

9. *Pravda*, 3 April 1971.

10. Ibid., 30 March 1968.

11. Zorza, op. cit.

12. 'USSR–Party', *Radio Free Europe Research Bulletin*, 5 April 1971.

13. R. Garthoff, *Detente and Confrontation* (Washington, DC: The Brookings Institution, 1985), p. 346.

14. See *International Affairs* (Moscow), no. 30 (Sept. 1973), p. 1.

15. *Soviet News*, 5 Feb. 1974, p. 40.

16. *International Herald Tribune*, 24 April 1975.

17. See G. Arbatov, *Cold War or Detente?* (London: Zed Books, 1983), p. 195.

18. P. Stern, *Water's Edge* (London: Greenwood Press, 1979), especially p. 49, p. 138 and p. 209.

19. L. Horowitz, 'Watergate and Detente', *Studies in Comparative Communism*, vol. 9, no. 3 (Autumn 1976).

20. *Pravda*, 11 Aug. 1974.

21. Quoted in R. Medvedev, *Political Essays* (London: Spokesman Books, 1976), p. 48.

22. R. Nixon, *Memoirs* (New York: Arrow Books, 1979), p. 1026 and p. 1033.

23. Garthoff, op. cit., p. 463.

24. See L. Lederer in *Observer Foreign News Service*, 29 May 1975.

25. Gelman, op. cit., and Volten, op. cit.

26. Volten, op. cit., pp. 111–32.

27. *Documents and Resolutions, Twenty-Fifth Congress of the CPSU* (Moscow: Novosti Press, 1976), p. 21.

28. Ibid., p. 25.

29. Ibid., p. 16.

30. Ibid., p. 39.

31. R. Medvedev, *On Soviet Dissent* (New York: Columbia University Press, 1980), p. 68.

32. See G. Edwards, 'Helsinki and Human Rights', *International Affairs*, vol. 61, no. 4 (Autumn 1985), p. 634.

33. See Brzezinski, *Power and Principle* (New York: Farrar, Straus & Giroux, 1983), pp. 155–6.

34. Quoted in Garthoff, op. cit., p. 711.

35. G. Breslauer, *Khrushchev and Brezhnev as Leaders: Building Authority in Soviet Politics* (London: Allen & Unwin, 1982), p. 191.

9

Arms Control, the Strategic Balance and the Demise of Detente

The relationship between arms control and Soviet–American detente in the early 1970s was mutually reinforcing. The arms control agreements of 1972 symbolised and strengthened the more general improvement in political relations between the superpowers, while this improvement provided an environment conducive to further arms control negotiations. During the course of the 1970s, however, the deterioration of detente and the changing political climate in the United States made arms control a much more vulnerable enterprise. Yet arms control was not simply a victim of linkage. The symbiosis which had given momentum to detente also contributed to its decline: the dissatisfaction with the apparent inability of arms control to prevent what was widely perceived as an adverse shift in the strategic balance was an important factor in the general disillusionment with detente. So too were the allegations that the Soviet Union was violating the SALT One agreement.

The 1972 SALT One agreement – or more properly the five-year Interim Agreement on Offensive Arms – was heralded as a major step towards more permanent and far-reaching limitations on the strategic force deployments of the two superpowers. It was hoped that it would be rapidly followed by a SALT Two Treaty, but this proved elusive. SALT Two was not signed until June 1979 – and by then, American antipathies towards the Soviet Union were such that there were serious doubts that the Treaty would receive the approval of the two-thirds of the Senate necessary for ratification. When the Soviet Union invaded Afghanistan in December 1979, President Carter deferred further consideration of an accord which was no longer politically defensible against its critics. The contrast between the high hopes for arms control in the early 1970s and the hostility which existed towards it, at least in the United States, at the end of the decade could hardly have been more marked. During his last year in office, Carter emphasised the achievement of security through greater unilateral effort. Concerns over adverse shifts in the strategic balance had become paramount, and it was widely argued that attempting to alleviate them through negotiations with the Soviet Union had been not only futile but counter-productive: the only prudent course was rapid modernisation of American strategic nuclear capabilities.

This chapter examines this process of disaffection. It considers why the superpowers were unable to reach a SALT Two accord much sooner than they did, and why expectations were so disappointed by the agreement that was reached. Attention is also given to the European dimension of arms control as well as to claims that a decade which had begun with the Soviet attainment of parity ended with the Soviet Union in a position of strategic superiority.

The Negotiations

The SALT Two negotiations were protracted and difficult. This was partly a reflection of their inherent complexity. The negotiations leading to the 1972 agreements had been complicated: those which began in December of that year were even more complex and intractable. Part of the problem was that even the relatively modest achievements of SALT One had been possible only by postponing troublesome issues. As a result, it 'left important strategic concerns on both sides unassuaged'.[1] The United States remained anxious about the large land-based Soviet missiles which were seen as a potential threat to the Minutemen force – especially when they were given a MIRV capability. For its part, Moscow had allowed American nuclear systems deployed in Europe – the so-called 'Forward Based Systems' – to be omitted from SALT One, but remained unhappy about leaving unconstrained weapons which from a Soviet perspective were strategic.

Another important difference was that in SALT One the asymmetries in each side's posture had more or less been balanced out: the unequal ceilings on launchers in favour of the Soviet Union were acceptable to the United States because of Washington's advantages in warhead technology. Although MIRVs had facilitated the 1972 accord, however, they hindered further agreement. Moreover, Moscow was intent on reducing the American technological lead, while US policy-makers, responding to the Jackson Amendment, were anxious to establish equal ceilings on launchers. As a result, the ability of the two sides to trade off respective advantages was significantly reduced.

A third difference between SALT One and SALT Two was that the Interim Agreement of 1972 had simply ratified the existing force levels of the two sides. In SALT Two there was an attempt to go beyond this in ways which would impose greater constraints on the future military programmes of the two sides. Yet finding a formula that balanced American technological advantage against the size and numbers of Soviet missiles 'was a task that defied solution during the first two years of SALT Two negotiations'.[2] It was not helped by Nixon's political weakness, and his visit to Moscow in June 1974 for a third Summit meeting with Brezhnev yielded no agreement on SALT. An agreement was reached on a Threshold Test Ban (TTB), but as a result of domestic opposition in the United States this was not formally submitted to the Senate for ratification. Nevertheless, in the subsequent months Kissinger, through a visit to Moscow in October and through the 'back channel' with Dobrynin, was able to identify areas of convergence.[3] As an additional inducement to movement, the United States also offered to relinquish its nuclear submarine base at Rota in Spain in the mid-1980s.[4] Consequently, at the Vladivostok Summit in November 1974 a broad framework was agreed.

The Vladivostok Accord set an equal aggregate level of 2,400 launchers and heavy bombers for each side, and a sub-limit of 1,320 launchers with MIRV capabilities. This was a significant advance in the negotiations. By agreeing to equal aggregate levels on ICBM launchers, SLBM launchers and heavy bombers, the Soviet leaders had made substantial concessions.[5] Yet difficulties remained. The United States was still apprehensive over the heavy missiles, while the Soviet Union remained anxious over the Forward Based Systems (FBS) in Europe. This may well have provided the basis for a tacit trade-off in which Washington accepted Soviet deployment of heavy missiles in return for Soviet acceptance of the FBS. It also proved a source of weakness for the Ford administration in the domestic debate.

Although the Vladivostok Accord clearly met the injunction of the Jackson Amendment for numerical equality, it did not win the approval of Senator Jackson. Concerns that the ceilings were too high were accompanied by complaints that the Accord did not constrain the Soviet capability regarding throw-weight and MIRV. Although Kissinger apparently dismissed the throw-weight issue as phoney, some critics, including, very significantly, Paul Nitze, 'felt that the throw weight loophole in the Vladivostok accord was in fact a serious deficiency that promised to create future strategic instability'.[6] Ironically, as well as proving difficult for the Ford administration to sell domestically, Vladivostok was difficult to consolidate in further negotiations with the Soviet Union.

One reason for this was that these negotiations were taking place in the context of rapidly evolving technology and the development and deployment of new weapon systems. Inevitably, several of these systems became contentious. The limitation of armaments is especially difficult when there is no consensus about what should be included in the negotiations. In the 1970s, though, such problems were inevitable: weapons developments were being driven as much by technological push as by political pull. This was especially the case with the cruise missile developed by the United States, which resulted, in large part, from the convergence of separate technological innovations.[7] Although cruise missiles did not fit readily into existing roles and missions, and consequently aroused little enthusiasm from the military services, the Secretary of Defense and the Joint Chiefs of Staff were reluctant to impose limits on a weapon system in which the United States had a considerable advantage. For the same reason, the Soviet Union was anxious to impose constraints on the deployment of cruise missiles.

In the aftermath of Vladivostok, the issue of whether or not cruise missiles should be included in the agreed ceiling became controversial and held up agreement on an *aide-mémoire*. The Soviet Union demanded that when bombers were equipped with air-to-surface missiles with a range over 600 kilometres, each missile should count against the 2,400 limit.[8] Washington, in contrast, wanted the language of the *aide-mémoire* to apply only to ballistic missiles, and although it agreed to drop the word 'ballistic' the cruise missile issue was not fully resolved until 1977.

The Soviet Union wanted restrictions on cruise missiles included in SALT Two, and certain groups within the US government were equally anxious to include the Soviet Backfire Bomber, on the grounds that it was a strategic weapon. Kissinger, in fact, was prepared to accept that the Backfire was a theatre rather than an intercontinental system, but the Pentagon objected strenuously to its omission from the negotiations. Moscow, however, having obtained Kissinger's acquiescence, was equally adamant. As a result, the Backfire not only became a major obstacle to agreement but remained controversial throughout the 1979 debate over SALT Two.

The result of all this was that, although Kissinger was to claim in 1975 that a new SALT agreement was 90 per-cent complete, the last 10 per cent was to take several more years to work out in a way acceptable to both sides.[9] Disagreements over what to include in the negotiations combined with the sheer intractability of the issues to extend the SALT negotiations well beyond the period initially anticipated. Yet the inherent complexity of the negotiations does not provide the whole story. Political considerations, especially in Washington, were an additional complication.

The American approach to the negotiations was characterised by discontinuities, by political controversy and increasingly by a disruptive, if unavoidable, linkage between arms control and Soviet behaviour in the Third World. Part of the problem was simply that the negotiations became caught up in the American electoral cycle. Consequently, after Kissinger's visit to Moscow in January 1976 failed to produce an agreement, the negotiations were effectively if temporarily halted.

The change of administration resulting from Carter's victory added further delays. 'Still in the innocence of transition' the new President and his national security team devised a radically new proposal, which included deeper cuts than had hitherto been contemplated.[10] This was partly a response to the personal concerns of the President, partly an attempt to respond to the widespread criticism of Vladivostok, and partly an attempt to placate Henry Jackson, who was increasingly insisting on the need for deep cuts, especially in the Soviet deployment of large ICBMs. Having developed a proposal which departed from the substantive principles which had guided the SALT Two negotiations, the Carter administration also changed the procedures: whereas Kissinger had used the channel with Dobrynin to sound out likely Soviet reactions to any new American initiatives, the new administration only informed Dobrynin of the proposal at a very late stage. Furthermore, the President and his advisers ignored several communications from Brezhnev reaffirming the Soviet position that SALT Two 'should be essentially a reflection of the Vladivostok understanding'.[11] Compounding the difficulties was Carter's decision to outline his scheme for a comprehensive approach in a speech to the UN General Assembly on 17 March. The emphasis on human rights and President Carter's support for Soviet dissidents also soured the atmosphere.

Consequently, when Secretary of State Cyrus Vance took the deep cuts proposal to Moscow in March 1977, it was rejected with a 'vehemence and finality' that angered the American delegation.[12] Although the style of the Soviet reaction surprised the United States, the rejection itself was not entirely unforeseen by at least some members of the delegation. Although Vance had a fall-back position along more traditional lines, this too was rejected, and the Soviet Union refused to introduce any counter-proposals. Vance's press conference in Moscow announcing the impasse worsened the situation. Indeed, the deep cuts initiative and the Vance mission was a case of 'muddled planning and muddled execution' which displayed not only political naïvety but an acute insensitivity to the concerns and problems of the Soviet leadership.[13]

The Soviet leaders had been working on one set of assumptions stemming from Vladivostok, and without any advance warning had suddenly been offered proposals which differed very significantly from those they were anticipating. It is probable that Brezhnev had succeeded only with difficulty in establishing a consensus around the deal worked out in the months prior to the Vladivostok meeting. A well-placed Soviet official in fact suggested to one of his American counterparts that 'Brezhnev had to spill political blood to get the Vladivostok accords.'[14] Although this is impossible to verify, it is certainly not inconceivable that the Soviet consensus on arms control remained fragile. In these circumstances, the Carter proposal was a major political embarrassment to the Soviet leadership. Yet this was not the only problem: Soviet rejection was virtually guaranteed by the terms of the proposal. By demanding cuts in Soviet heavy missiles while leaving the American Forward Based Systems intact, the Carter initiative appeared to renege on the trade-off that had already been agreed.[15] American insistence on this and other terms which appeared to the Soviet leadership to demand asymmetrical sacrifices not only made Soviet acquiescence impossible but almost certainly raised disturbing questions in Moscow about the seriousness of the new administration as a partner in detente.

With the Carter administration accepting that it could not simply create a new agenda in arms control, the negotiations were back on track within a few months. Agreement was reached on a three-part package: a treaty to last until 1985, an interim accord on difficult issues such as cruise missiles and a commitment to negotiate deeper cuts in SALT Three. Nevertheless, the problems of translating this package, based primarily on the Vladivostok Accord, into a treaty acceptable to both governments remained formidable. Nor did the negotiations become easier as they drew to a close in 1978 and 1979. On the contrary, as Strobe Talbott has observed, they became rather like the end game in chess, in which 'each surviving piece becomes more valuable, its sacrifice more painful, stratagems to protect it more elaborate, and calculations about whether to trade ... become more complex, more fraught with risk'.[16] This was intensified by the technical nature of the issues. As the negotiators were edging towards compromise on an accord, extraneous factors also intruded. The American decision in December 1978 to normalise relations with China made the Vance visit to Moscow somewhat strained and almost certainly added further delays to the attempt to reach final agreement on SALT.[17] The remaining differences were gradually overcome and the Treaty was signed at the Vienna Summit in June 1979. By this time, however, SALT was a highly controversial issue.

The politicisation of SALT Two had begun well before Carter arrived in office. The new administration exacerbated the process, which became bound up with the broader debate over American foreign and security policy. Indeed, the polarisation of this debate was reflected within the strategic community itself where there was a growing split between those concerned primarily about the 'action–reaction' process which fuelled the arms race, and those who saw the problem much more directly in terms of the Soviet build-up. The former group saw arms control as part of the solution; the latter saw it as part of the problem, and believed that it inhibited force planning and made it more difficult for the United States to take the measures necessary to counter the Soviet strategic threat.[18]

In the first three months of 1977 there were two developments which highlighted this polarisation and revealed that the politicisation

of arms control had become irreversible. The first was the controversy
over the nomination of Paul Warnke as head of the Arms Control and
Disarmament Agency (ACDA) and the chief American negotiator on
SALT Two. The main thrust of the attack on Warnke was that his
views on US foreign and defence policy, on the Soviet Union and on
arms control were sufficiently soft to suggest that he would make too
many concessions to Moscow in the search for a final SALT agreement.
In hearings before the Senate Foreign Relations Committee on the
Warnke nomination, Senator McClure of Idaho was brutally explicit on
this point: 'Instead of toughening the bargaining position of the United
States with the Soviet Union, as President Carter promised in his
campaign, I believe that the addition of Mr Warnke to the negotiating
team can only undermine any credible American posture.'[19]

If anything, Paul Nitze was even more outspoken in his testimony
before the Committee, casting serious doubt on Warnke's credentials
for negotiating with the Soviet Union, by claiming that he lacked
competence, 'clarity or consistency of logic'.[20] Although Warnke's
appointment was nevertheless confirmed by the Senate on 10
March, the vote was only 58 to 40 which, in itself, weakened
his position as chief negotiator. It was also a pointed reminder
to President Carter that he could not afford to have a treaty
with defects if he was to obtain the two-thirds majority in the
Senate necessary for its approval.

The second development which revealed the politicisation of
arms control was the proposal for deep cuts of March 1977. Partly
an attempt to deflect some of the domestic pressure, this proposal
succeeded only in making the final SALT Two agreement more
vulnerable. As Cyrus Vance noted,

> Perhaps the most serious cost of the Moscow discussions was to be felt
> later in the domestic battle over SALT ratification. The comprehensive
> proposal gave a weapon to anti-SALT and anti-detente hard-liners, who
> held up the deep cuts proposal as the only standard against which to
> measure the success of the ultimate agreement. A SALT Treaty that
> contained limitations less stringent than the comprehensive proposal would
> be attacked as falling short of real arms control.[21]

Doubts about the composition of the new administration's arms
control team, and the administration's abrupt climb-down in face of the
Soviet rejection of its proposal for deep cuts were soon accompanied
by growing concern over the reliability of the President himself on
national security issues. In this climate, it was inevitable that SALT
would become entangled with arguments over linkage.[22] Yet, even
without Soviet activism in Africa, SALT Two would have encountered
considerable opposition – as had been evident since 1974.

It is clear though that the opposition was all the more intense because of Soviet interventionism in the Third World. Moscow's actions were interpreted by the critics as the direct result of the change in the strategic balance. With American strategic superiority nullified, it was argued, the Soviet Union was able to embark upon courses of action which had hitherto been too risky. And if confrontation did occur, then it was American policy-makers, aware of the increasing vulnerability of their strategic forces, who were more likely to succumb to coercion. This argument was politically powerful, and helped the critics in the Committee on the Present Danger and elsewhere to transform the debate from one about arms control to one about the strategic balance.

The Strategic Balance in the 1970s

Concerns over the strategic balance and developments in Soviet weaponry have periodically come to the fore in the American national security debate. They were particularly intense in the 1970s for several reasons.

The first was that the Soviet missile programme in the late 1960s and early 1970s carried on well beyond the point where it was expected to stop. The general assumption was that when the Soviet Union matched the United States in the number of missiles, it would be satisfied. When this point was passed and the deployments did not cease, there was considerable concern over the nature and purpose of the build-up. 'It seemed a disturbingly open-ended process, without an obvious full stop' – an effect which was accentuated by Soviet reluctance to phase out older ICBMs.[23] Paradoxically, American anxieties were accentuated by the SALT One agreement: 'under an arms control regime, "threats" are more tightly defined than under a regime of unregulated mutual deterrence. The adversary is now expected to conform to far stricter standards than before – complying with both the letter and the spirit of the agreements.'[24] If this does not occur the sense of threat is intensified. This is precisely what happened in the period after SALT One. When set against the Interim Agreement, continued Soviet modernisation of its strategic forces (and in particular the controversy over whether the SS-19 which replaced the SS-11, even though it was 40 per cent larger, was permissible) added to the impression that Moscow was not only building remorselessly but was violating the arms control accords in order to obtain a decisive advantage in counter-force capability. Although the pace of Soviet ICBM deployments had eased in 1971, by 1973 it was evident that Moscow had four new ICBMs under development as well as a major Submarine Launched Ballistic Missile Programme.

It was not only the pace and scope of the Soviet strategic modernisation programme which were disturbing. The characteristics of the Soviet force structure, especially the fact that 'investment was concentrated in ICBMs, more numerous and, on average, individually larger than anything in the American arsenal', also excited American anxieties.[25] Even though the Soviet emphasis on size may have reflected a technological lag in areas such as miniaturisation and computer guidance, it made Soviet capabilities look particularly imposing. They became even more formidable when the Soviet MIRVing programme began, as the large land-based ICBMs offered considerable advantages in the number and type of warheads which could be carried. When this was allied with the general trend towards greater accuracy, it appeared that the Soviet Union had deliberately designed a force structure with a substantial capability for hard target kill. In so far as SALT had been seen as a way of protecting the US Minuteman force, therefore, it was argued that it had failed abysmally.[26]

These Soviet measures were particularly disconcerting to those who believed that they stemmed from a distinctive Soviet strategic culture and military doctrine which deviated very considerably from Western conceptions of strategic stability. Soviet notions of deterrence differed from those prevalent in the United States, at least at the declaratory level, in their continuing emphasis on the need to be prepared to fight, survive and even win a nuclear war. Almost inevitably such sentiments were seen by hard-line critics as a rationale for Soviet attempts to attain strategic superiority. The contention that the ABM Treaty had signified Soviet acceptance of Mutual Assured Destruction appeared unconvincing when set against some of the writings of Soviet military officers claiming that victory was possible in a nuclear war. There was a tendency by conservative critics of detente to treat these statements, which were clearly contentious and only one side of a doctrinal debate, as authoritative statements of the approach accepted by the political leadership.

An additional and closely related consideration intensifying American concerns was the growing preoccupation with perceptions of the strategic balance. Part of the argument was that if Moscow believed it had a meaningful strategic advantage over the United States then it would behave less prudently. It was also suggested that perceptions of strategic advantage – and perceptions by the United States that it was inferior – would give Moscow an edge in a superpower confrontation. This concern was extended to incorporate the argument that American status and credibility in the eyes of others depended upon the maintenance of strategic equality with the Soviet Union. This reflected a growing sensitivity over American power and prestige, which had as much to do with Vietnam as it did with Soviet strategic forces. Yet it also meant that the strategic balance was not simply considered as a whole but was increasingly scrutinised for discrete areas where one side or the other was 'ahead'. This was evident when Secretary of Defense Schlesinger announced that US doctrine and targeting was being modified to provide alternatives other than assured destruction. The Schlesinger Doctrine emphasised the need for the United States to maintain 'essential equivalence' with the Soviet Union in terms of both options and capabilities. Anything that Moscow could do Washington had to be able to match. Specifically, this required that the United States augment its capability for hard target kill. In a sense, this can be understood as the operational equivalent of the Jackson Amendment to SALT One, and was intended not only to prevent the Soviet attainment of nuclear superiority, but to make clear to all who were watching that the United States remained powerful.

Underlying such concerns was a major psychological difficulty for the United States in adjusting to nuclear parity. This was compounded by uncertainty over both the exact meaning of parity and the relative importance of asymmetries within it. The clearest exposition of parity has been offered by Richard Betts, who has not only distinguished between different meanings of the term but argued very convincingly that the looseness of the concept encouraged both the Nixon administration's premature acknowledgement that parity had been reached and allegations by critics that parity was giving way to Soviet superiority:

> If it meant mutual vulnerability to unacceptable damage, parity came in the mid-1950s; if it meant nearly equal levels of civil damage, it arrived by the early 1970s; if equality in missiles or delivery vehicles, by the mid-1970s; if the measure is the balance of forces as a whole or of counterforce capacity, by the late 1970s.[27]

Part of the problem was that the Nixon administration relied primarily on the indicator of mutual urban–industrial vulnerability, and did not make clear that in the overall balance of forces the United States in the early 1970s still retained an edge. The result was that the momentum of Soviet programmes was seen as engineering a transition from parity to superiority rather than a move from one kind of parity to another. The problem was intensified by the fact that parity (of any kind) was – and is – characterised by asymmetries in force structure. Within an overall equilibrium there may well be certain inequalities. This was the case in the 1970s when the United States had advantages in warhead numbers and technological sophistication while the Soviet Union could claim superiority in throw-weight and equivalent megatonnage. During the period of detente there was some movement in favour of the Soviet Union within this balance of imbalances, but it is far from clear that this had any strategic significance. The dominant American perception, though, was that Soviet developments were immensely significant and highly threatening.

This was not the position taken by the CIA, which was relatively sanguine in its assessments of the strategic balance and Soviet military programmes. These assessments were challenged in 1976 by the report of a group of renowned hard-liners, known as Team B, who were given access to CIA data and arrived at much more alarming conclusions. A key figure in Team B was Paul Nitze, who also helped to set the tone of the debate through several influential articles in *Foreign Affairs* and *Foreign Policy*.[28] Nitze was concerned about what he regarded as a growing and dangerous congruence between the precepts of Soviet military doctrine and the development of Soviet strategic capabilities. Pointing to Soviet military writings, and especially the emphasis on war as a continuation of policy, Nitze argued that the Soviet Union was developing a nuclear war fighting capability. His concern was that the Soviet Union was deploying not only substantial counter-force capabilities, but also a survivable reserve force capable of holding American population and industry at risk. When combined with active and passive civil defence measures and a Soviet willingness to pre-empt if necessary, these deployments placed the Soviet Union in an advantageous position.[29] The advantages would become even more marked after an initial counter-force exchange, when the Soviet Union would 'hold superiority in all indices of capability except numbers of warheads'.[30] In Nitze's view this could prove decisive. Unless there was a reversal of strategic trends, the United States 'would be conceding to the Soviet Union the potential for a military and political victory if deterrence failed'.[31] The Vladivostok Accord, in his view, did nothing to prevent this situation from arising. The solution, therefore, lay in unilateral American actions – especially improvements in hard-target kill capability and survivability of the land-based missile force.

Although Nitze's concerns appeared esoteric, they rested upon a scepticism about detente that was consistent with the long-term thinking of the man who had been the primary author of NSC-68 in 1950. Indeed, it was his anxiety about Soviet intentions that made Nitze so sensitive to adverse trends in the strategic balance. As a result he not only created a worst-case analysis but disseminated it with skill and vigour. In many circumstances the military planner's nightmare which Nitze had identified would have been dismissed as remote and outlandish; in a psychological climate in which parity appeared to be giving way to inferiority, it proved more compelling.

The picture that Nitze and other analysts such as Albert Wohlstetter presented was one of a relentless Soviet build-up for which there was no justification apart from the desire for superiority. Yet, from the Soviet perspective the strategic balance may have looked less favourable than was widely assumed in Washington. Although at the end of the 1960s the United States had levelled off its deployment of launchers, it had embarked on a MIRV programme that enabled it to retain a considerable, albeit declining, advantage in terms of warheads throughout the 1970s. Furthermore, the development of cruise missiles and the Trident submarine were evidence once again of the American technological lead that Moscow was striving hard to reduce. Although the Soviet Union had deployed cruise missiles on its ships for some years, these were far less sophisticated than their American counterparts that were being developed through the supposed decade of neglect.

In spite of these developments, the Soviet Union was more restrained than was claimed. Harold Brown summed up the dominant American assessment in the comment 'when we build they build; when we stop, they build'.[32] In retrospect, the Soviet build-up, while formidable, does not appear quite as alarming as was suggested in the mid and late 1970s. Nor did it have the inexorable momentum that is often attributed to it. In fact, during the latter half of the 1970s, there was a distinct slowdown both in the annual rate of increase in military spending and in the deployment of new systems. CIA estimates reveal that, whereas defence spending in the Soviet Union had increased at around 4 per cent per annum in the decade before 1976, it went up by only 2 per cent per year thereafter.[33] Furthermore, after 1976, Soviet strategic forces were being produced and deployed at 'relatively relaxed rates'.[34] In addition, there was far less emphasis in Soviet military pronouncements on the idea of nuclear superiority.

These changes should not be exaggerated. The Soviet military was not going from a period of plenty to one of famine. Yet the slowdown in the pace of the build-up suggests that the arms control process may have helped to constrain Soviet programmes. If so, this could well have been controversial. It is possible that there was a divergence in Moscow, paralleling that in Washington, between proponents of negotiated agreement and those who saw Soviet security as dependent upon unilateral military effort and the attainment of strategic superiority.[35] Yet, if there was open opposition to SALT, Brezhnev's continued endorsement of detente at the Twenty-fifth Party Congress in 1976 seems to have succeeded in containing it. The death of Minister of Defence Marshal Grechko in 1976 and his replacement by Dmitry Ustinov could have provided an additional opportunity for the Soviet leadership to reaffirm its commitment to the SALT process.

Although Grechko did not come out publicly against arms control, his death may have made it easier to reassess Soviet military priorities. His most obvious successors for the post of Defence Minister – all with impeccable military credentials – were overlooked in favour of

Ustinov, who aligned himself closely with Brezhnev, regarded 'his position in the party as more important than his role as an exponent of the professional viewpoint', and became more involved than his predecessor in discussions over arms control.[36]

Other changes seemed to reinforce the trend towards a greater emphasis on arms control. Kulikov, who had reputedly been close to Grechko, was replaced as Chief of the General Staff by Ogarkov, who had been a leading member of the Soviet SALT delegation and one of the few military men to write favourably about the arms control process. In addition, both Brezhnev and Ustinov were made Marshals of the Soviet Army. The result of all this was that Brezhnev not only became much more closely identified with defence policy but appeared to establish greater control over it. In a speech at Tula in early 1977, Brezhnev not only acknowledged Soviet acceptance of parity but also dismissed Western allegations that the Soviet Union was striving for strategic superiority.[37] Soviet military writings increasingly echoed the same theme. Although it is conceivable that this was a sustained exercise in disingenuity, the pattern of defence spending and the slowing down of the missile deployments make this unlikely.

This is not to claim that Soviet strategic restraint resulted from altruism. On the contrary, there were sound practical reasons for exhibiting such restraint and for the continued pursuit of a SALT Two agreement. The first was that by the mid-1970s the Soviet Union was relatively satisfied with the strategic and military balance with the West, and thought that restraint and regulation would best serve its interests.[38] There were fears that Washington was on the verge of new developments and deployments. In such circumstances, arms control could have been seen as the best way of preventing the United States from exploiting its technological advantage to surge ahead once again. Furthermore, the SALT process continued to ratify Soviet equality in the strategic realm, something that was all the more important because of the difficulty Moscow had found in translating strategic parity into political equality. An additional Soviet interest in restraint was economic: by the mid-1970s the economy was beginning to stagnate once again. Smaller increases in defence spending, therefore, had certain attractions.

Nothing in this analysis is intended to deny the formidable nature of Soviet military programmes in the 1970s. Yet it does suggest that the Soviet Union was not embarked upon an inexorable quest for superiority in the way claimed by Nitze and other American critics of the SALT process. It is perhaps one of the ironies of the superpower relationship in the 1970s that as the Soviet military build-up was slowing down and the commitment to arms control reaffirmed, domestic pressures for the United States to forgo arms control in favour of redressing the strategic balance were being intensified. Indeed, at this stage the anti-SALT coalition in the United States seized upon another issue – the damaging impact of arms control on the security of the European allies – to use against SALT.

The European Dimension

Although the dangers of East–West confrontation had diminished in Europe, the Soviet military threat to Western Europe had not disappeared. Throughout much of the 1970s the European allies increased their defence spending in a steady if unspectacular manner thereby confirming their adherence to the Harmel Report with its emphasis on both deterrence and detente. Furthermore, there was a certain ambivalence in Western Europe towards superpower detente: although the NATO allies were clearly in favour of East–West accommodation, they were concerned about possible collusion between Washington and Moscow. Similarly, although they were later to claim that they had been unequivocal in their support for arms control, this was something of an over-simplification. Their general sympathy for arms control was qualified by anxieties that the superpowers might conclude a deal inimical to European interests.

This concern became more salient during the Carter years and was related to the issue of Forward Based Systems. Although there had been strong support in NATO for American efforts to ensure the omission of FBS from SALT, this appeared less advantageous when the Soviet Union began to deploy SS-20s, which were also unconstrained by agreement. Difficulties arose in NATO because this new missile augmented the Soviet capacity to strike Western Europe, but did not impinge directly on the superpower relationship.

There are two broad views about Soviet deployment of the SS-20. The first is that it was a conscious attempt by Moscow to exploit strategic parity. By imposing a degree of regional military superiority, it might be possible to decouple the allies from the United States and move towards the Finlandization of Western Europe.[39] The second, suggested primarily by Garthoff, is that the programme was a necessary modernisation designed to fill a gap in the spectrum of Soviet military capabilities: the deployment of the SS-20 was not something which was prohibited by SALT One or Vladivostok, there was a production line available after the decision not to proceed with SS-16 deployment, and there was a continuing problem for Moscow resulting from deployment of US Forward Based Systems and French and British strategic forces in the west and Chinese military programmes in the east.[40]

Underlying these divergent interpretations are contrasting assessments of Soviet objectives. If it is accepted that the long-term Soviet aim is to split Western Europe and the United States, the SS-20 appears as essentially a political weapon – a view reinforced by the fact that it was so much more capable than the SS-4s and SS-5s it was replacing. Garthoff, in contrast, regards the increased Soviet capability as the natural result of technological progress and tends to view the SS-20 more in military than political terms. Whichever interpretation is accepted, however, Soviet policy seems to have had unintended and adverse consequences for Moscow. If the objective of SS-20 deployment was to decouple Western Europe from the United States, it was not only wildly optimistic but in fact counter-productive; if the deployment was based simply on the military rationale, it was short-sighted, failing as it did to consider possible Western reactions.

This is not to imply that the NATO decision of December 1979 to modernise its long-range theatre nuclear forces was dictated exclusively by the need to counter the SS-20 deployment.[41] In one sense, NATO was simply ensuring that it had the capabilities available to fulfil the military roles and missions associated with its strategy of flexible response. An additional incentive was almost certainly the neutron bomb fiasco. In the aftermath of this episode, as Secretary of State Vance has acknowledged, it was necessary for the alliance to demonstrate a capacity to make and implement difficult decisions.[42]

The SS-20 deployment, however, almost certainly provided an additional impetus for the modernisation decision. Concerns over the 'Eurostrategic balance' in an era of strategic parity – or, as some American commentators suggested, Soviet superiority – were discernible in an address given to the International Institute for Strategic Studies in October 1977 by the West German Chancellor, Helmut Schmidt.[43] Both the intent and the importance of the Schmidt speech subsequently became the focus of considerable controversy. It does seem, though, that Schmidt was becoming anxious over the likelihood that Soviet systems targeted against Western Europe would be left unconstrained while American deployments of ground- and sea-launched cruise missiles with a range of over 600 kilometres would be prohibited. In the event, the prohibition, contained in a protocol to the SALT Two Treaty, was only temporary. Nevertheless, even this was not entirely welcome: European defence ministries had been sold on the virtues of cruise missiles by briefing teams from the Pentagon and the defence industries. In the aftermath of the Carter administration's decision to deploy air-launched cruise missiles on B-52s, there were other consultations in which it was impressed upon the Europeans that they did not require cruise missiles. These briefings aroused considerable scepticism, and the allies came to regard any impediment to deployment with some suspicion.

The anti-SALT forces used this issue to cast themselves as the defenders of the Atlantic alliance. The result was somewhat paradoxical. NATO in 1979 was moving towards the decision to deploy cruise and Pershing missiles on the assumption that this would be accompanied by negotiations on long-range theatre systems in SALT Three. Accordingly, NATO governments generally supported SALT Two. Yet the American critics of arms control, who were most vociferous about alliance needs and most unhappy about the constraints on cruise missile deployment enshrined in SALT Two, were intent on derailing the arms control process altogether and ensuring that SALT Three did not take place. Although the allies formally and genuinely supported the Carter administration in the SALT Two debate in 1979, the anxieties that had previously been expressed were used by the opponents of arms control as additional ammunition against the Treaty. The European role in the political demise of SALT Two, if inadvertent, was not insignificant.

The SALT Two package itself was signed by Carter and Brezhnev in Vienna in June 1979.[44] The outlines of the accord had been known for some time, combining as it did the Vladivostok guidelines with the three-tier approach that had been suggested by the Carter administration in 1977. The agreement consisted of the Treaty, which was to last until 1985, an interim protocol to run until 1981 and a statement of principles for SALT Three. The Treaty established a ceiling of 2,400 missile launchers and heavy bombers (to be reduced to 2,250 after 1982) and sub-ceilings of 1,320 MIRVs and Air Launched Cruise Missiles, 1,200 MIRVs and 820 MIRVed ICBMs. The number of Soviet heavy missiles – the SS-9s and the SS-18s – was limited to the 308 already existing. In addition, the number of warheads that could be placed on existing missiles was limited, while each superpower, during the life of the Treaty, was permitted to deploy one new ICBM with a maximum of ten warheads. New SLBMs were permitted to carry fourteen warheads. The main item in the protocol was a limit on the deployment of air- and ground-launched cruise missiles with a range over 600 kilometres. The Backfire problem was dealt with in a written statement from Brezhnev at the Summit that the Soviet Union would not provide the Backfire with the capability to operate at intercontinental distances, and that the production rates of the plane would not be increased beyond the current rate – which the Americans were assured would be thirty a year. The final component was a commitment by the two sides to seek deeper cuts in their strategic forces in SALT Three.[45]

After seven years of negotiations, the major problems had been resolved. On several key issues, however, the outcome remained untidy. Furthermore, there was considerable doubt about President

Carter's ability to obtain Senate approval. Such doubts were well founded, and the second half of 1979 saw the debate over SALT Two enter its final and most intense phase.[46]

The Senate Debate

The Senate debate over SALT Two was the final battleground for the competing approaches to American policy that had been evident throughout the Carter years. Not only did it provide a test of whether detente retained any appeal in the American political system of the late 1970s, but it also highlighted the credibility problems facing the Carter administration. Furthermore, the course of events in the months after the signing of SALT Two revealed once again the political importance of linkage between Soviet policies in the Third World and arms control. The final outcome was effectively a rejection by the American body politic of the policies that had initially been designed by the Nixon administration and that had been pursued with a few variations by its successors.

If the debate over SALT Two was the Carter administration's most important defeat, it was also, in some respects at least, a self-inflicted wound. The administration's ineptness in mobilising support for the Treaty, as well as its clumsiness in dealing with the 'discovery' of the Soviet brigade in Cuba, contributed to the demise of what was by 1979 the only substantial element of Soviet–American detente which remained. Nevertheless, the difficulties inherent in selling SALT Two to a sceptical Senate should not be overlooked.

These difficulties stemmed partly from the shift in attitudes resulting both from changes in American domestic politics and what was perceived as the Soviet lack of restraint in the Third World. They were intensified by internal changes in the Senate which made it a less malleable and more conservative institution. During the 1970s the Senate had become increasingly fragmented as power passed from committee chairmen to sub-committees. This made coalition-building a demanding task. It was all the more formidable because changes in the distribution of power within the Senate had been accompanied by an important shift in attitudes. The struggle against the Imperial Presidency had left a legacy of resentment against the executive branch, coupled with an assumption that the President did not necessarily know best on national security issues. The days of congressional deference were over.

The institutional pride of the Senate encouraged a highly critical approach to SALT Two, and political considerations worked in the same direction. The Carter administration had spent much political capital in 1978 in obtaining Senate approval of the Panama

Canal Treaty in the face of enormous counter-pressure from right-wing groups such as the Conservative Caucus and the American Conservative Union. Although these groups had been defeated, they had realised the power of direct-mail campaigns and were active once again on SALT. The conservative lobbying campaign on Panama also left a number of senators feeling politically vulnerable. This had important implications for SALT, and as early as February 1978 the connection between Panama and SALT was made explicit, with several senators warning that they felt compelled to take a more critical approach towards the arms control treaty. In some cases – including that of Howard Baker, the Republican Minority Leader in the Senate – opposing SALT was a way of securing redemption from the Right for voting in favour of giving away the American Canal at Panama. Senator Henry Jackson was correct, therefore, when he commented that the close vote on the Panama Canal Treaty showed that SALT was in real trouble.[47]

The terms of SALT Two were also a source of discord. Critics contended that there was nothing in the Treaty to alleviate the concerns about throw-weight and the Soviet heavy missile advantage that had been evident since the early 1970s. Indeed, because of the Soviet superiority in these areas, it was argued by Jackson and his supporters that SALT Two had failed completely to meet the injunction of the Jackson Amendment for equal ceilings. To concerns such as these, which had long been articulated, were added a whole new set of anxieties about the 'precedential effect' of the protocol which, it was argued, might be used by the Soviet Union in SALT Three in an attempt to prevent NATO from deploying cruise missiles in Europe. The device of relying on a written guarantee about the Backfire, rather than incorporating it into the Treaty, was also criticised, even though the Soviet Union made clear that it regarded Brezhnev's note as a binding commitment. As well as criticising the form of the guarantee, critics also contended that the Backfire had an intercontinental range and therefore should be subject to far more stringent restrictions. The other important issue was verification. Although this never became as prominent in the debate as was expected, underlying worries about compliance were evident throughout the discussions, and were heightened by the loss of American monitoring stations in Iran after the fall of the Shah.[48]

These difficulties were, for the most part, unavoidable. Yet some of the Carter administration's problems were self-inflicted. Different commentators have different views about the timing of the administration's efforts to mobilise support for the Treaty. Some point to the fact that the Carter administration in June 1977 established an Advisory Group of thirty senators who were invited to visit the negotiators in Geneva and review the draft text of the Treaty.[49] One analyst has suggested that the 'extensive congressional involvement with the SALT Two process during the Carter administration was a marked departure from the earlier SALT period and is unprecedented in the history of Treaty negotiations', while another study concluded that SALT Two illustrated 'the remarkable revival of a senatorial role in advising on the substance and tactics of treaty negotiations'.[50] More critical assessments, however, suggest either that the Carter administration did too little too late or that its efforts were clumsy.[51] This divergence can be reconciled to some extent by distinguishing between formal consultation and effective mobilisation of support. The Carter administration succeeded at the first level but not at the second. Indeed, the administration was slow in responding to demands from sympathetic members of the arms control community that it develop a persuasive rationale and embark upon a major campaign to sell SALT Two. The 'national security case' for SALT Two had its roots not in the administration but with Senators and their staffs who supported the Treaty but who were concerned by the administration's apparent reluctance to take a lead.

The essence of this approach was that the United States would be far better off with the Treaty than without it. In the circumstances of the late 1970s such a sales pitch was likely to have more appeal than one which extolled the virtues of arms control as such. The problem, however, was that the administration transformed this into what has been termed a 'marginalist approach', which stressed that SALT Two was primarily important as a step towards more meaningful arms control arrangements.[52] Although this emphasis on the Treaty as 'modest but useful' was something which had the support of the Joint Chiefs of Staff, it was 'an important political miscalculation' which succeeded in highlighting the limitations of the Treaty rather than its accomplishments.[53] Whereas the Nixon administration was guilty of oversell, the Carter administration's efforts to mobilise support suffered, at least in the initial stages, from undersell.

The problems were compounded by the reluctance of the White House to commit itself to the mobilisation of support for SALT. Partly this reflected the failure of Jimmy Carter to use the resources of his office, and partly it was a matter of timing. By waiting until the Treaty was signed before the leading members of the administration became fully involved in the effort to secure Senate approval, the White House allowed critics and opponents of SALT to establish the terms of reference for the debate. 'The absence of a White House-directed SALT political coordinating group perceptibly hurt the Administration's lobbying in the period prior to June 1979.'[54] The difficulties were worsened by political misjudgments, the most important of which concerned Senate Minority Leader Howard Baker. Despite being under considerable pressure to take a hard line on SALT, Baker was prepared to play the role of 'honest broker'.[55] A more solicitous approach by the White House, therefore, might have gone at least some way to defusing his opposition.

Although the Carter administration made its share of mistakes, it did have some successes and worked closely with the Cranston group of about twenty senators who were not specialists on national security but who wanted briefings on SALT from the negotiators and other administration spokesmen. Many members of this group became strong supporters of the Treaty, and their efforts were coordinated by Larry Smith, a leading Senate staffer, and by Alan Cranston, one of the few remaining liberal Democrats in what had increasingly in the 1970s become a conservative-dominated institution. One estimate has suggested that at least twenty of these conservatives were irreconcilable in their hostility to SALT Two, while another fifteen would be satisfied only with an arms control agreement which had stringent verification procedures and clearly inhibited the Soviet Union. Although the numbers supporting SALT were larger, if the administration was to win Senate approval it had to gain the support of about twenty moderate senators who might swing either way and make inroads into the group which opposed SALT but was not totally beyond compromise.[56]

Somewhat surprisingly, in view of its earlier shortcomings, the administration proved skilful in its belated attempt to mobilise support for the Treaty. Officials testifying in favour of SALT Two adopted a hard-headed and practical approach, but one that emphasised the strengths of the Treaty. The tone was set by Vance early in the hearings before the Committee on Foreign Relations, with his claim that SALT Two would 'serve as a brake on Soviet military expansion and on the Soviet improvement we could otherwise expect', while it would permit the United States to move ahead with the improvement of its own strategic forces.[57] In particular, SALT would stop the Soviet Union from putting more than ten warheads on missiles which would otherwise be able to carry two or three times that number. A similar approach was adopted by Secretary of Defense Harold Brown, who argued that he would 'not recommend this treaty if it required us to trust the Soviets'.[58]

This attempt to mobilise support for SALT Two through combining it with a hard-line approach was strengthened by Carter's decision – announced prior to the Vienna Summit – to go ahead with deployment of the new mobile missile, the M-X, and the subsequent announcement in September that a mobile basing mode for the M-X had been agreed. The M-X decision, which the President personally found abhorrent, was intended as a concession to critics like Nitze who had been focusing attention on Soviet strategic advantages.[59] By this time, however, the issue had become as much a matter of symbols as substance – and Carter's increased emphasis on American strength was dismissed by SALT opponents as too little too late. Indeed, the critics, led by Jesse Helms and Howard Baker on the Foreign Relations Committee and by Henry Jackson and Jake Garn outside it, exploited this symbolism to the full. Baker, for example, suggested that the United States was becoming the Number Two nation in the world, and that on certain key indices of strategic capability, such as overall megatonnage, it was lagging far behind the Soviet Union. Treaty proponents like Secretary of Defense Harold Brown were able to refute these charges in detail, but still failed to alter the widespread perception that the Carter administration had damaged American security.

There were also one or two self-inflicted wounds even at this stage. In a letter to the Foreign Relations Committee, the Director of the CIA, Stansfield Turner, acknowledged that there were some provisions of the Treaty which could not be fully monitored, and accepted that the loss of the monitoring bases in Iran had made verification more difficult.[60] The Senate Intelligence Committee which had conducted a two-year study of the verification issue came to much the same conclusions.[61] Although the issue did not play the decisive role in the debate that many commentators had expected, Turner's frankness posed an additional question mark against SALT Two. Perhaps even more important was the testimony of several former officials, some of whom might have been expected to support SALT Two but who were critical or ambivalent at best. General Edward Rowny had been a member of the SALT delegation but had resigned when the Treaty was signed in order to campaign against it. Rowny claimed that the Treaty was 'unequal and unverifiable'.[62] General Alexander Haig, who had been Supreme Allied Commander Europe, not only suggested that Treaty ratification be held in abeyance until its flaws had been removed but also cast doubt upon the degree of support which existed in Europe.[63]

Even more important was the testimony of Henry Kissinger. As both the initial architect of detente, and a figure deemed to have influence with moderate Republicans, Kissinger's endorsement of SALT Two was something which the administration badly wanted. In the event, they obtained very qualified support. Kissinger's testimony portrayed a grave security threat to the United States arising from an adverse shift in the strategic balance and 'an unprecedented Soviet assault on the international equilibrium'.[64] The linkage between arms control and Soviet geopolitical behaviour which he had rejected in 1975 was something he now wanted formalised. He proposed not only that the administration be required to provide an annual report to the Senate about Soviet behaviour in the Third World, but that every two years the Senate should vote on whether the Soviet Union had behaved with restraint – with a negative result being followed automatically by a vote on the continuation of whatever arms control negotiations were in train at that time.[65] This was something which Kissinger, in office, would have dismissed as preposterous. Although Kissinger did support SALT Two on condition that it was accompanied by measures to redress the strategic balance and restore geopolitical equilibrium, it was evident that his support was half-hearted at best.

In spite of these setbacks, the administration, over the summer of 1979, was able to develop what was described as a 'bandwagon effect' in favour of SALT.[66] The growing consensus was that it was winning the arguments against the critics. The administration also began to work for the creation of a 'centrist coalition' that would accept SALT Two if it was coupled with increases in the American defence budget.[67] This idea originated with the testimony of the Joint Chiefs of Staff, who supported SALT Two but were worried that it might lead to complacency about US security. Senator Sam Nunn, one of the Senate's most respected and influential figures on defence issues, took up the theme of avoiding the tranquilliser effect of SALT, and along with Henry Kissinger, began to negotiate with the administration about the size of the defence budget. This was particularly welcomed by Brzezinski, who later claimed that SALT, 'rather than being the vehicle for acquiescent accommodation with the Soviet Union, was becoming the catalyst for a more assertive posture'.[68] Some senators embraced this package of SALT Two plus increased defence spending less for reasons of conviction than of political survival. As one commentator observed: 'They could approve SALT and earn the plaudits of the liberals and they could commit themselves to a bigger military budget and be ignored by the electoral shock troops of the conservatives.'[69] Some of the more committed liberals, however, were not entirely happy with this formulation, dissatisfied as they already were with what they saw as an arms escalation treaty. It is not certain, therefore, that the attempt to build a centrist coalition would have secured the passage of SALT Two. As it was, the effort was undermined by the intrusion of external events. The 'discovery' of a Soviet combat brigade in Cuba was essentially a fabricated issue, which was manipulated by both liberals and conservatives for domestic political reasons, but it effectively doomed SALT Two and Soviet–American detente.

The Soviet brigade episode has appropriately been described as an exercise in 'crisis mangling' as opposed to crisis management.[70] The mangling stemmed from several sources: the lack of institutional memory in the American government, the 'siege mentality' of the Carter administration in the summer of 1979 combined with the absence of several key officials from Washington, the polarisation of the national security debate, the preoccupation with Soviet behaviour in the Third World, continued neuralgia over Cuba, and electoral politics in the state of Idaho.[71]

The issue arose initially because of Brzezinski's concerns about Soviet and Cuban military activities in Central America. In March 1979 Brzezinski initiated a review of Soviet military activities in Cuba. Almost inevitably, this increased attention resulted in increased indicators of Soviet activity.[72] New information was combined with existing files in ways which suggested that the Soviet Union had introduced a 'combat brigade' into Cuba. In fact, all that was new was the designation: the Soviet troop presence in Cuba went back to 1962, and in 1963 'the Kennedy administration had agreed to a Soviet brigade remaining in the location where the combat brigade was discovered in 1979'.[73]

In late June or early July rumours about the presence of a Soviet combat brigade in Cuba began to circulate in Washington. These were picked up initially by Senator Stone of Florida, a Democrat who had voted for the Panama Canal Treaties but was taking a more critical approach to SALT Two. Either as a result of a deliberate or inadvertent leak, Stone became aware of the intelligence reports and began to pursue the issue in the Foreign Relations Committee. Reassured by official testimony, Senator Frank Church, the Committee chairman, issued a statement that there were only Soviet advisers in Cuba. Nevertheless, the administration increased its surveillance, and discovered in August that the brigade was engaged in field exercises. This was seen within the intelligence community as a new and important development, although, as Stansfield Turner later acknowledged, 'such exercises might have been going on unnoticed ... we detected the one in August only because we had begun paying special attention to the brigade and because the intelligence community's collection effort had been particularly well coordinated'.[74]

For the administration, such a discovery was extremely inopportune. The attempt to play down the issue and handle it through private diplomacy was undermined by a leak to *Aviation Week*. News of the leak prior to publication forced the administration to accept the need to go public. Before doing this, however, it was deemed prudent to contact key congressional leaders with the news. It was at this point that the issue was taken over by Senator Frank Church, the Chairman of the Foreign Relations Committee, a committed liberal and a strong supporter of SALT. Church was particularly sensitive over his earlier denial that there was a significant Soviet presence in Cuba, not least because prior to the Cuban Missile Crisis in 1962 he had refuted allegations that the Soviet Union had installed missiles in Cuba, and had then found himself in a very exposed position.[75] Facing a tough battle for re-election in Idaho, Church also attempted to use the issue to demonstrate that he too could be tough on the Russians. After consultations with Vance, Church convened a press conference at his home in Idaho at which he revealed the presence of the brigade. A few days later he stated that the Senate would not approve SALT Two while Soviet combat troops remained in Cuba.

The Carter administration felt compelled to adopt a similar position. Both Vance and President Carter announced that they were not satisfied with the status quo in Cuba. A series of diplomatic exchanges were initiated by the United States: between 10 September and 27 September Vance met Dobrynin six times and Gromyko twice, while there was also an exchange of messages between Carter and Brezhnev.[76] Pressure on the Soviet Union to withdraw the brigade, or at the very least to reduce its combat capability, did not succeed. This was hardly surprising. Moscow was almost certainly bemused by the whole episode, especially as Carter at the Vienna Summit had warned Brezhnev of the dangers of a further military build-up in Cuba, but had seemed willing to accept the status quo. Furthermore,

> the notion that Soviet leaders in 1979 would agree to compromise on an issue where no hard evidence could be presented to show a change in their behaviour from that which had been tolerated for 17 years by the US, on which concession could have serious ramifications for the image of reliability of Soviet commitment to military allies, which reawakened historically painful and humiliating memories, and where compromise could yield little of benefit to the USSR was simply preposterous.[77]

Ultimately the administration recognised this and, after deeming the presence unacceptable, was compelled to accept it. The Soviet Union agreed not to challenge a series of American statements about the status of the brigade, and on 1 October, President Carter made a television address announcing a series of unilateral measures such as increased surveillance of Cuba and expanded military manoeuvres. This effectively brought what had been a manufactured crisis to an end.

If the brigade issue was artificial, its impact was very real. It helped to delay SALT Two, and showed once again the political force of linkage even when the links were very tenuous. Senator Long of Louisiana, for example, used the issue to come out against the Treaty, citing Soviet 'bad faith' as the reason.[78] Furthermore, the Carter administration's initial overreaction combined with its subsequent retreat seemed to confirm the view that it was an administration in disarray and one which could not be relied upon to protect American security. Consequently, the attempt to build a winning coalition on SALT became even more formidable.

The difficulties were intensified by critics who contended that the Treaty required substantial amendment before they could even begin to consider its approval. The attempts to alter the provisions of the Treaty at the committee stage, however, did not succeed. The Foreign Relations Committee, while making clear that the Brezhnev letter on the Backfire should have the same status as the Treaty itself, resisted the addition of 'killer amendments' which would require renegotiation. The most important of these was Howard Baker's proposal to incorporate into the Treaty American rights to the same number of heavy missiles – 308 – as possessed by the Soviet Union. This was defeated by only one vote in an 8 to 7 split. If this was uncomfortably close, the final vote by the Committee to send the Treaty to the floor was almost equally disturbing to SALT proponents, with six of the fifteen members voting against such action. The continued dissent of a substantial minority was all the more significant because the Foreign Relations Committee was supposedly the most sympathetic group towards SALT in the Senate.

In December, the Committee on Armed Services published its own report which clearly reflected the hand of Jackson and his aide, Richard Perle, and was highly critical of the agreement partly on the grounds that it violated the Jackson Amendment to SALT One which had mandated equal ceilings.[79] The report, which identified twelve fundamental shortcomings of SALT Two and was easily assimilated, was a highly effective political document. Its conclusion, that major changes to the Treaty were essential if American national security was not to be jeopardised, revealed very clearly that the floor fight over SALT Two would have been bitter and protracted. It seems unlikely that the Treaty would have emerged without substantial amendment imposing conditions unacceptable to the Soviet Union.

In the event this did not occur. The seizure of the American diplomats in Iran complicated matters, as it appeared to be yet further evidence of America's declining power and prestige. Senator Nunn suggested that Senate consideration of the Treaty be deferred until the American hostages were released, thereby highlighting the vulnerability of the Treaty to derailment by extraneous issues. In this climate, the Soviet intervention in Afghanistan provided the final indictment against SALT Two and led Carter to ask the Senate to defer its further consideration. Whether or not the Treaty would have obtained the consent of the Senate in the absence of Afghanistan is uncertain. On balance, though, it seems unlikely. The prevailing mood in 1979 was strongly anti-Soviet and anti-arms control, and the draft Treaty had a number of demonstrable shortcomings. Afghanistan may have provided the final nail in the coffin of detente, but the debate over SALT Two in the American Senate suggests not only that the politicisation of arms control had become enormously destructive but also that superpower detente was dead well before the Soviet action.

Notes

1. T. Wolfe, *The SALT Experience* (Cambridge, Mass.: Ballinger, 1979), p. 14.
2. Ibid., p. 98.
3. R. Garthoff, *Detente and Confrontation* (Washington, DC: The Brookings Institution, 1985), p. 444.
4. W.G. Hyland, *Mortal Rivals* (New York: Random House, 1987), p. 86.
5. Garthoff, op. cit., p. 446.
6. Wolfe, op. cit., p. 191.
7. For a useful analysis of the impact of technological innovation, see M. Thee, *Military Technology, Military Strategy and the Arms Race* (London: Croom Helm, 1986).
8. For a fuller account, see Garthoff, op. cit., pp. 446–7.
9. Garthoff, op. cit., p. 451.
10. R.E. Neustadt and E.R. May, *Thinking in Time* (New York: Free Press, 1986), p. 119.
11. See D.S. McLellan, *Cyrus Vance* (Totowa, NJ: Rowman & Allanheld, 1985), p. 40.
12. C. Vance, *Hard Choices* (New York: Simon & Schuster, 1983), p. 54.
13. Neustadt and May, op. cit., p. 119.
14. S. Talbott, *Endgame* (New York: Harper & Row, 1979), p. 73.
15. See Garthoff, op. cit., p. 806.
16. Talbott, op. cit., p. 17.
17. McLellan, op. cit., pp. 120–4.
18. For a full and stimulating analysis along these lines, see M. Krepon, *Strategic Stalemate* (New York: St. Martin's Press, 1984).
19. See *Warnke Nomination: Hearings Before the Committee on Foreign Relations, United States Senate, Ninety-Fifth Congress,* 8–9 Feb. 1977 (Washington, DC: Government Printing Office, 1977), p. 116.
20. Ibid. p. 136.
21. Vance, op. cit., p. 55.
22. See Z. Brzezinski, *Power and Principle* (New York: Farrar, Straus & Giroux, 1983), pp. 178–90.
23. L. Freedman, *The Evolution of Nuclear Strategy* (London: Macmillan, 1981), p. 346.
24. L. Freedman, *US Intelligence and the Soviet Strategic Threat* (2nd edn) (London: Macmillan, 1986), p. 194.
25. Freedman, *The Evolution of Nuclear Strategy*, p. 346.
26. Freedman, *US Intelligence and the Soviet Strategic Threat*, p. 153.
27. R. Betts, *Nuclear Blackmail and Nuclear Balance* (Washington, DC: The Brookings Institution, 1987), p. 188.
28. P. Nitze, 'Assuring Strategic Stability in an Era of Detente' in *Foreign Affairs*, vol. 54, no. 2 (Jan. 1976), pp 207–32, and P. Nitze, 'Deterring Our Deterrent' in *Foreign Policy*, no. 25 (Winter 1976–7), pp. 195–210.
29. Ibid., pp. 197–8.
30. Ibid., p. 201.
31. P. Nitze, 'Assuring Strategic Stability in an Era of Detente', op. cit., p. 227.
32. See Garthoff, op. cit., pp. 794–5.

33. For a fuller analysis, see R. Kaufman, 'Causes of the Slowdown in Soviet Defence', *Soviet Economy*, vol. 1, no. 1 (Jan.–March 1985), pp. 9–41.

34. See Ibid.

35. For a fuller analysis, see S. Payne, *The Soviet Union and SALT* (Cambridge, Mass.: MIT Press, 1980).

36. M. Mackintosh, 'The Military Role in Soviet Decision-making' in C. Keeble (ed.), *The Soviet State* (London: Gower for RIIA, 1985), pp. 173–90 at p. 178.

37. See Garthoff, op. cit., pp. 771–4.

38. On this point we are grateful to Michael MccGwire of the Brookings Institution.

39. That this has long been the aim of Soviet policy is argued in J. Van Oudenaren, 'Containment: Obsolete and Enduring Features' in A.L. Horelick (ed.), *U.S.–Soviet Relations: The Next Phase* (London: Cornell University Press, 1986), pp. 27–54.

40. Garthoff, op. cit., pp. 870–86.

41. For a fuller analysis of the background to the December 1979 decision, see P. Williams (ed.), *The Nuclear Debate* (London: Routledge & Kegan Paul for RIIA, 1984).

42. Vance, op cit., p. 96.

43. H. Schmidt, 'The 1977 Alastair Buchan Memorial Lecture', reprinted in *Survival*, vol. 20, no. 1 (Jan.–Feb. 1978).

44. For a full discussion of the Vienna Summit, see Garthoff, op. cit., pp. 728–40.

45. A good summary of SALT Two and other arms control negotiations and agreements can be found in the Appendices to L. Freedman, *Arms Control: Management or Reform?* Chatham House Paper 31 (London: Routledge & Kegan Paul, 1986).

46. For a fuller analysis of the Senate debate, see P. Williams, 'The President, the Senate and SALT Two', *Journal of Arms Control*, vol. 1, no. 1 (May 1980), pp. 76–98.

47. See ibid., p. 87.

48. S. Flanagan, 'The Domestic Politics of SALT Two: Implications for the Foreign Policy Process' in J. Spanier and J. Nogee (eds), *Congress, the Presidency and American Foreign Policy* (New York: Pergamon, 1981), pp. 44–76, especially p. 63.

49. Ibid., p. 53.

50. Ibid., p. 53; and T.M. Franck and E. Weisband, *Foreign Policy by Congress* (New York: Oxford University Press, 1979), p. 291.

51. A. Platt, 'The Politics of Arms Control and the Strategic Balance' in B. Blechman (ed.), *Rethinking the US Strategic Posture* (Cambridge, Mass.: Ballinger, 1982), pp. 155–78.

52. Ibid., p. 162.

53. Ibid., p.163.

54. Ibid., p. 168.

55. See ibid., p. 169.

56. Flanagan, op. cit., p. 50.

57. C. Vance, Testimony before the Foreign Relations Committee, 9 July 1979. See *The SALT II Treaty: Hearings before the Committee on Foreign Relations, United States Senate, Ninety-Sixth Congress on EX Y, 96-1* – hereafter cited as *SALT Hearings* – (Washington, DC: Government Printing Office, 1979), Part 1, p. 91.

58. H. Brown in ibid., p. 97.

59. For Carter's position on the M-X, see J. Carter, *Keeping Faith* (London: Bantam, 1982), p. 241.

60. This was acknowledged in a letter to Senator Church. See *SALT Hearings*, Part 3, pp. 276–7.

61. See Flanagan, op. cit., p. 64.

62. *SALT Hearings*, Part 5, p. 306.

63. Ibid., Part 3, p. 279.

64. Ibid., p. 171.

65. Ibid., p. 175.

66. See *Congressional Quarterly Weekly Report*, 13 Oct. 1979 (Washington, DC: Congressional Quarterly Inc., 1979), p. 2279.

67. See ibid.

68. Brzezinski, op. cit., p. 345.

69. See Leslie Gelb, *New York Times*, 19 Aug. 1979.

70. G. Duffy, 'Crisis Mangling and the Cuban Brigade', *International Security*, vol. 8 (Summer 1983), pp. 67–87.

71. For the 'siege mentality' point, see ibid., p. 69.

72. On the general point here we have benefited from discussion with Arnold Horelick of the RAND Corporation.

73. See S. Turner, 'The Stupidity of Intelligence', *The Washington Monthly* (Feb. 1986), p. 32.

74. Ibid., p. 32.

75. Duffy, op. cit., pp. 77–8.

76. Garthoff, op. cit., p. 838.

77. Duffy, op. cit., p. 81.

78. Ibid., p. 83.

79. *Military Implications of the Proposed SALT II Treaty Relating to the National Defense Committee on Armed Services United States Senate* (Washington, DC: Government Printing Office, 1980).

10
Afghanistan and the Return to Cold War

On the night of 25 December 1979 large numbers of Soviet troops crossed the border into Afghanistan and occupied Kabul. According to *Pravda* the Soviet Union had responded to an 'insistent request from the Afghan government and sent a limited contingent which would be withdrawn as soon as the factors precipitating this action were no longer present'.[1] The interpretation of events by the Carter administration was very different. Soviet intervention was regarded as an act of adventurism which compelled a reassessment of superpower relations. President Carter denounced the invasion, imposed sanctions on the Soviet Union and effectively abandoned superpower detente by deferring further Senate consideration of SALT Two. Afghanistan provided the occasion for the Carter administration to embrace the cold war orthodoxy that had come back to the forefront of American thinking but which the President and Secretary of State Vance had hitherto resisted. After the invasion, the Carter administration, in effect, accepted that the arguments of the Committee on the Present Danger had offered a more compelling basis for US foreign policy than the 'world order' approach. Within the administration, Brzezinski emerged triumphant as both Carter and Vance acknowledged the need for a firm response. Indeed, one of the most striking results of the Soviet invasion was that it produced a degree of consensus within the Carter administration that had hitherto been unattainable.

Whereas there was little divergence of opinion in the administration over the threat posed, directly and indirectly, by the Soviet military intervention, the key figures differed in the way in which they reached their conclusions. For Brzezinski, the invasion vindicated his earlier assessments of Soviet behaviour in the Third World and demonstrated that US reluctance to adopt a hard-headed geopolitical approach had encouraged increased Soviet risk-taking. In his view Afghanistan was the result of the failures of recent American policies in regions such as the Horn: 'Had we been tougher sooner, had we drawn the line more clearly ... the Soviets would not have engaged in this act of miscalculation.'[2]

Vance and Carter agreed with Brzezinski's overall conclusions – that the United States had to adopt a tougher stance towards Moscow to prevent further adventurism – but they emphasised that Afghanistan represented an essentially *new* and more virulent strain of Soviet activism than anything previously discernible. As Carter noted, the Soviets had intervened directly, for the first time since February 1948, in a sovereign country outside its acknowledged sphere of influence.[3] Furthermore, it was a move which had serious implications for Western security. According to the President, 'a successful take-over of Afghanistan would give the Soviets a deep penetration between Iran and Pakistan and pose a threat to the rich oil fields of the Persian Gulf area and to the crucial waterways through which so much of the world's energy supplies had to pass'.[4] Such fears were compounded by the instability and loss of American influence in Iran, which meant that 'if the Soviets could consolidate their hold on Afghanistan, the balance of power in the entire region would be dramatically modified in their favour and they might be tempted toward further aggression'.[5]

In his State of the Union Address on 23 January 1980, Carter emphasised the global implications of the Soviet incursion: 'Let our position be absolutely clear: any attempt by any outside force to gain control of the Persian Gulf region will be regarded as an assault on the vital interests of the United States of America, and such an assault will be repelled by any means necessary.'[6] This statement, inevitably dubbed 'the Carter Doctrine', provided an epitaph for detente, highlighting as it did the American reversion to traditional notions of containment. Although there was still a gap between commitments and capabilities, the increasing prominence given to the Rapid Deployment Force was designed to ensure that American interests in critical areas of the Third World could and would be upheld.

Afghanistan was widely seen in the United States as the culmination of the geopolitical offensive which had been initiated under the cover of detente. Soviet objectives were viewed in global rather than regional terms, and it was generally accepted that the invasion of Afghanistan not only reflected a qualitative change in Soviet willingness to use force outside its accepted sphere of influence in Eastern Europe, but that it was directed towards the Gulf and would give the Soviet Union a hand on the West's jugular vein. A more persuasive analysis is that the intervention resulted essentially from local factors, but that any incentives Moscow had to refrain from the action for the sake of detente had been taken away by the Senate debate over SALT Two. The Soviet leaders faced what they deemed to be a threat to Soviet security interests. Even had superpower relations been less strained, it is unlikely that Moscow would have eschewed action necessary to rescue the deteriorating situation in Afghanistan. In the aftermath of the furore over the Soviet combat brigade in Cuba, and with the benefits of detente appearing increasingly problematic amidst the hostile Senate debate over SALT Two, the incentives for Soviet restraint were minimal. The irony is that the Carter administration was still attempting to maintain detente despite the emerging consensus in the United States on its inadequacies and dangers, but was galvanised by Afghanistan into precisely the kind of stance that the hard-line critics had long been demanding.

Soviet–Afghanistan Relations

Afghanistan's importance to Moscow is nothing new. During the nineteenth century it was the focus of intense competition between the Russian and British empires, while the common border ensured that the country remained salient in Soviet security calculations after the British had departed. One analyst of Soviet–Afghan relations has even suggested that 'the 1979 military move was only another, long-delayed, step forward in a lurching Russian advance' into the territories on its periphery which had been evident well before the 1917 Revolution.[7] This move was in some respects more disconcerting – and in some respects less – because it did not come against a background of continued great power competition in the country. In the late 1940s and early 1950s, Afghan requests for American economic and military assistance were given a low priority in Washington, where relations with Pakistan took precedence. The result was that Afghanistan increasingly looked to Moscow for support. This suited Soviet objectives very well, and Afghan–Soviet relations were frequently cited in Moscow as an example of the mutual cooperation that could occur between states with different social systems.

Prince Daoud, the Afghan Prime Minister from 1953 to 1963, was a key figure in drawing the two countries closer together, and when he seized power from the monarchy in 1973 this was greatly welcomed by the Kremlin. His autocratic and extremely conservative rule, however, was a considerable disappointment to Moscow, especially when he began to shift away from Moscow and towards closer links with Egypt, Pakistan and Iran. Consequently, when Daoud was killed in a coup in April 1978, there were allegations of Soviet complicity. The 1978 coup, like that of 1973, 'pulled Afghanistan back from pragmatic or rightist policies disliked by local communists and the Soviet Union'.[8] If Moscow was not averse to a change of government in either 1973 or 1978, however, there is little evidence that it played a major role in either Daoud's seizure of power or his overthrow. The regime's demise came when the military turned against Daoud. After a confused sequence of events the functions of government were transferred to the leaders of the communist movement.

The movement was totally unprepared for the power that unexpectedly, even accidentally, fell into its hands. Its misuse of that power with a combination of idealistic reformism and brutal authoritarianism started the country on a downward spiral into civil war and foreign occupation.[9]

The Communist Party, the People's Democratic Party of Afghanistan (PDPA), was made up of a loose and highly fractious coalition of two main groups – the Khalq and the Parcham – lacking in organisation, governmental experience and a coherent policy programme. In the power vacuum that emerged in the immediate aftermath of Daoud's ouster, however, the PDPA was the one group willing to take on the burden of government. This burden was considerable. The internal situation in Afghanistan was so desperate that successful government would have taxed the ingenuity of the most skilled and experienced political leaders – which the new leaders most certainly were not.

Afghanistan needed a strong, united government and a broad base of support for its policies. The PDPA could provide neither: it was riven by personal and factional rivalries which resulted in large-scale purges and rapid turnover of leading personnel. The Khalq–Parcham alliance broke down and Babrak Karmal, the leader of the Parcham faction, was exiled. Within the Khalq, Hafizullah Amin, the Foreign Minister, and Nur Muhammad Taraki, who had become President emerged as the dominant figures. At the outset, institutional and mass support for the new government was slight – and it declined thereafter. A reforming government was bound to meet opposition, but the PDPA made what a leading Soviet commentator described as 'serious mistakes', which weakened its position.[10] Its attacks on the Islamic religion and Muslim clergy proved particularly damaging, not only alienating the mullahs but encouraging the disaffection of the great mass of Afghans, who remained deeply religious. Indeed, the attempt to centralise control over the Afghanistan tribes and to introduce a new social order 'violated practically every Afghan cultural norm and strayed far beyond the allowable bounds of deviance in the social, economic and political institutions'.[11] By introducing ambitious proposals for land reform the new leadership alienated the landowners, who helped to transform opposition into open revolt.[12]

The Soviets were not opposed to the general aims of the PDPA government: constraints existed in Soviet Central Asia on the traditions and culture of Islam, while some kind of land reform was clearly necessary to alleviate the worst of rural poverty and loosen the political grip of the 'obscurantist feudal lords'. Nevertheless, Moscow was concerned over the hasty way in which these policies were implemented.[13] In spite of their reservations, however, the Soviet leaders clearly saw benefits in supporting the PDPA government and attempting to save it from its own ineptness. Consequently, the Soviet commitment was steadily deepened. The number of Soviet military advisers in Afghanistan increased from 350 before the April revolution to 1,000 in May 1979. Just before the invasion in December there were around 4,000 Soviet advisers in Afghanistan.[14]

The growing Soviet involvement was formalised in the Treaty of Friendship and Cooperation, which was signed in December 1978, and would later be used as justification for the Soviet military intervention. Even more significant was the uprising in the town of Herat in March 1979 in which a number of Soviet advisers and their families were killed.[15] One analyst has suggested that this was 'a major turning point in the Afghan situation. Moscow's reaction to it led on inexorably, even inevitably, to the Soviet invasion nine months later.'[16] Military aid to the regime was significantly increased and, in April, General Yepishev – who had gone on a similar fact-finding mission to Czechoslovakia in the spring of 1968 – was sent to Kabul to assess the situation. Equally important was the fact that within the government Amin consolidated his power at the expense of Taraki, and became even more repressive. A Soviet official, Vasily Safronchuk, was sent to Kabul to act as adviser to the Amin government but succeeded only in encouraging cosmetic changes. Despite Soviet pressures for moderation Amin continued his excesses and the country drifted towards anarchy.

Increasingly Amin was seen in Moscow as 'an obstruction to the Soviet effort to save the regime from its own mistakes'.[17] As early as May 1979 American intelligence reports suggested that the Soviet Union was profoundly dissatisfied with the leadership, and had plans to change it. Within a few months the search for an alternative had become more insistent. Although Soviet advisers were taking a hard line against the insurgents, it was obvious that without a change of government this would not be sufficient.

Other signs of Soviet unease were also evident during the middle of 1979. In late June military preparations in the southern part of the Soviet Union were monitored by Western intelligence, although their precise purpose – and whether they were related to Afghanistan or the unrest in Iran – was not clear. In July a small but elite military unit was stationed at Bagram air base, the key communications and logistical centre for the Kabul region.[18] The following month a further military delegation under General Pavlovsky, who had been commander-in-chief of the invading forces in Czechoslovakia in 1968, was sent to assess the situation.

In September, Taraki met with the Soviet leadership on his way back from a meeting of the non-aligned countries in Cuba. By this time Moscow had decided that stability in Afghanistan was impossible with Amin at the helm, and Soviet interests required his speedy removal.[19] As well as impressing upon Taraki the need for changes in government policy, therefore, the Soviet leadership almost certainly encouraged him to remove Amin, if necessary by assassination. In the event, it was Taraki who was captured and executed. The Soviet plan had misfired: 'Like a later bungled attempt to remove Amin that led to the overt Soviet invasion instead of a smoother introduction of Soviet troops by internationally acceptable invitation, the September attempt created the worst possible result for the Soviet Union.'[20] Amin's power was increased and his hostility towards Moscow was intensified. It seems to have been in the aftermath of Taraki's failure that General Pavlovsky, who was still in Afghanistan, was directed to evaluate the requirements for a direct military intervention.

In the following months Amin's distrust of the Soviet Union expressed itself in efforts to improve relations with the West. Not only did he seek a *rapprochement* with General Zia of Pakistan, but he also began to adopt a more conciliatory approach towards the United States.[21] For its part, Washington remained aloof. Since the abduction and death of Dubs, the American Ambassador, in February 1979, relations between Kabul and Washington had been strained. Moreover, the White House was preoccupied by the developing crisis in Iran and paid scant attention to these soundings from Amin.[22] The result was that the United States was 'virtually oblivious to the frantic signals Amin was sending in November and December'.[23]

By then crucial decisions had been taken in Moscow. When General Pavlovsky returned from Kabul in October, the situation in Afghanistan was regarded as desperate, and there appeared to be only two alternatives – both involving some risks. The first was to abandon Amin in the hope of reviving Afghan–Soviet relations with his successor. This option would have left Moscow with no influence over events and could have resulted in the emergence of an Islamic regime which was just as unstable as its predecessor, but more anti-Soviet – the model of Iran was not very comforting. In comparison, the second option of a military intervention looked relatively attractive. The aim appeared to be to replace Amin with a more popularly based government including both Parcham and Khalq factions. In the short term, Soviet troops would be needed to ensure Amin's fall and establish a new leadership. It was hoped, however, that the population would be won over eventually – as it had been in Soviet Central Asia – by moderate but progressive policies implemented by firm government. There were dangers with this option. It was almost certain to arouse national emotions and, at least in the short term, could exacerbate rather than ease internal tensions. Possibly in an attempt to forestall this, the Soviet Union invited Amin to visit

Moscow in November. The Afghan leader declined, and Soviet preparations for intervention were intensified.

The Soviet Intervention

The Soviet decision to intervene was both a continuation of existing policy towards Afghanistan and a result of the inability to achieve Soviet objectives through limited involvement. The failure to get rid of Amin by indirect means left Moscow with little alternative if it was to uphold its influence in Afghanistan. Indeed, despite claims about the broader strategic intent of the Soviet invasion, it resulted primarily from the peculiar dynamics of the relationship between Moscow and the Amin regime. Having established the commitment to the PDPA, Soviet policy was subsequently based on an incremental approach. Furthermore, the presence of a significant number of Soviet troops in Afghanistan probably encouraged this incrementalism by magnifying Soviet assessments of what was at stake. The limited presence was not proving viable, yet could not be easily withdrawn. In these circumstances dramatic reinforcement seemed to be the most compelling option. In other words, the December invasion can be explained in part in terms of a military involvement which took on a dynamic or momentum of its own. Important as this is, however, it should not obscure the broader considerations which influenced the unfolding decision-making process in Moscow. Several anxieties seemed to weigh particularly heavily on the Soviet leadership.

The first of these was concern over the increasing instability on its southern border as a result not only of developments in Afghanistan but also events in Iran. In these circumstances, a limited but decisive military intervention in Afghanistan probably seemed to be the best way to retrieve a deteriorating situation. After all, Amin was increasingly a liability who might not only become a 'counter-revolutionary' traitor but also a loser.[24] Reports from Soviet officials in Afghanistan assessing the prospects of Amin re-establishing control became increasingly pessimistic. Furthermore, the Soviet military was unhappy about the course of events. 'It is probable that Pavlovsky, Yepishev and other Soviet generals, mainly those in charge of the military districts adjacent to Afghanistan, urged a massive intervention to assist pro-Soviet elements to stabilise the restive southern borders and put an end as quickly as possible to the killing of Soviet advisors.'[25] After the invasion, the commander of the Turkestan military district, Colonel-General Y. Maksimov, and other Soviet generals of military districts in Central Asia, suggested that there had been a real threat of war on the USSR's southern border.[26] Now that the Soviet Union had attained full superpower status this was something that it was simply unwilling to tolerate. Ironically, traditional insecurities may have combined with a new sense of power and assertiveness to encourage Moscow to resort to military force.

An additional Soviet concern may have been over what is sometimes called 'spillover' or 'contagion', and its impact on the 'nationality' question. Events in Iran and Afghanistan almost certainly made the Soviet leadership more sensitive about the loyalty of its own Muslim population in the Caucasus and Central Asia. If Islamic fundamentalism found favour in the southern Soviet republics, then the danger to the national security of the Soviet Union would be considerable. The level of support for Islam in the USSR, however, is a matter of contention.[27] On the one hand the Muslims represent a significant and rising proportion of the Soviet population, which has not been integrated fully into the Soviet way of life. In view of the Slavic dominance of Soviet society this leads almost inevitably to tension. Although for the most part this tension seems to be contained, there are some reports of overt unrest. Indeed, in 1978 there seems to have been a nationalist riot in Danshanbe in the republic of Tadzhikistan.[28] This event may have had some relevance to the subsequent intervention in Afghanistan. Some concern over the possible contagious properties of Islam was revealed by the launching of a so-called 'vigilance campaign' by the KGB and MVD in the southern republics immediately after the invasion.[29]

On the other hand, the fear of 'contagion' from across the border was far less than in the case of the Ukraine and Czechoslovakia in 1968. During this crisis, Ukrainian party chiefs – most notably Shelest – repeatedly demanded military intervention to prevent the spread of 'reformist' ideas to the Soviet Union. There is no evidence of similar pressure on Moscow in 1979 from party chiefs in Muslim areas.[30] The fact that Muslims made up a large part of the original invading force was probably a sign of Soviet sensitivity to the Islamic issue and part of an attempt to minimise the alienation of the Afghan population. Yet it also casts further doubt on any great Muscovite fear of Islamic contagion.[31]

This complacency may have resulted partly from the split within the Islamic movement. Whereas the Muslims in Iran and Afghanistan were Shi'ites, those in Soviet Central Asia and the Caucasus were Sunnis. Moreover, the Soviet Muslims had higher living standards and better educational opportunities than their co-religionists across the border. Consequently, the Islamic revival may have seemed relatively unattractive to citizens living inside the Soviet Union. In view of all this it seems unlikely that concerns over contagion were critical in the decision to invade Afghanistan.

Nevertheless, it would be wrong to dismiss it entirely. The sensitivity of the Kremlin was starkly revealed when the deputy prime minister of Kirgizia was prematurely retired after admitting that the spread of Islamic fundamentalism was of some concern.[32] Furthermore, on occasion local party chiefs have hinted that concerns over the spillover of instability did have a bearing on the final decision to intervene. Although not decisive, therefore, worries over contagion could well have been an additional factor propelling Moscow towards invasion.

If security considerations demanded decisive action by Moscow, the international situation was relatively permissive for such action. This permissiveness had several dimensions, all of which were related in one way or another to the United States. In the first place, Soviet military intervention carried no risk of direct military confrontation with Washington. Critics of the Carter administration – and indeed some members of it – suggested that this was because of the failure of the United States to take a firmer line in previous regional crises such as the Horn of Africa. This argument is spurious. It overestimates the ability of the United States to exert influence in circumstances where it has only marginal interests at stake. The reputation of the Carter administration was relatively unimportant: even if Carter had adopted a tougher approach towards Moscow in the past it would have been extremely difficult to deter Soviet military action in Afghanistan. Not only were American interests in Afghanistan negligible, but they seemed to be declining.[33] Throughout 1979 the Carter administration was scaling down what was already a modest American presence by withdrawing most of its diplomats and aid workers. In contrast to the Middle East in 1973, therefore, there was a clear asymmetry of interests which gave Moscow considerable discretion in deciding how to deal with the deteriorating situation.

During 1979 Brzezinski was pressing for stronger US reactions to what he described as 'the Soviets' creeping intervention in Afghanistan'.[34] Largely as a result of his urgings the United States, between March and August, gave Moscow several public and private warnings about Soviet military intervention in Afghanistan. The way in which these were disregarded, however, confirms rather than challenges the argument that the asymmetry of interests was decisive. American warnings were not heeded in Moscow because Afghanistan was peripheral to American security interests. Such an assessment may have been reinforced by the lack of congruence between warnings and actions: American words were designed to inhibit Soviet behaviour; yet Washington's continuing disengagement from Afghanistan probably reinforced the view that Moscow need not feel inhibited.

The tendency to disregard American pronouncements on Afghanistan was probably reinforced by the Soviet combat brigade fiasco, which both perplexed the Kremlin and helped to devalue American warnings. As Marshall Shulman, special adviser on Soviet affairs to Cyrus Vance, put it, 'The weight of our views was diminished by the frayed state of United States–Soviet relations and the fact that we had already invoked the prospect of damage to United States–Soviet relations on several other issues.'[35] If the indiscriminate nature of American warnings diluted their impact, they appeared particularly inappropriate when they were directed at Soviet behaviour towards a country where the United States had nothing at stake.

Nor was there much incentive for the Soviet Union to refrain from what was deemed a necessary action in order to maintain detente and avoid the derailment of SALT Two. Detente had not prevented the Carter administration from normalising relations with China; SALT Two had not prevented the decision to deploy the M-X missile nor had it stopped NATO from agreeing to deploy in Western Europe 572 cruise and Pershing missiles capable of hitting the Soviet homeland. By December 1979, even if SALT Two was ratified, it was beginning to look far less attractive than it had appeared at the Vienna Summit. This in no way provoked the Soviet Union into taking the action it did in Afghanistan, but it removed a possible, if always limited, constraint. SALT Two had become dispensable and, as a result, Washington had little leverage over Soviet actions. It is possible that the Soviet decision to use force in Afghanistan was taken in full awareness that this could mean the postponement or even the demise of the Arms Limitation Treaty.

In other words, the Soviet Union had both the motive and the opportunity. The leadership may have also believed that large-scale military action would be decisive. Although in retrospect such optimism seems totally unwarranted, it was understandable. The American failure in Vietnam, if it was considered as a possible warning, was probably dismissed as irrelevant: direct rather than vicarious experience generally proves decisive in shaping expectations about likely outcomes. If the Soviet Union had a model for the intervention in Afghanistan it was probably the move into Czechoslovakia in 1968. The temptation to adopt the same framework of assumptions and expectations was strengthened by the fact that the crucial military assessments in the months prior to the invasion decision were made by General Yepishev and General Pavlovsky, both of whom had played a crucial role in 1968. The optimism may have been strengthened by the successes that had been obtained through a mix of proxies and advisers in Angola and the Horn of Africa. The precedents seemed auspicious, while the fact that the Army had never had to engage in a large-scale counter-insurgency campaign may have made the military leadership less sensitive to the difficulties involved.

The Czechoslovakia model may have been relevant in another way. In 1968 the Soviet military had rounded up the Czech leaders and sent them to Moscow. It is certainly not inconceivable that the Soviet leaders thought they could deal with Amin in much the same way. Arranging this may have been the task of Lieutenant-General Paputin, a First Deputy Minister of the Interior, who was sent to Kabul in late November, possibly with the intention of initiating a coup against Amin. Whether the purpose was simply to topple Amin or to assassinate him is not clear. An assassination attempt on 17 December failed, and in its aftermath Amin took refuge in the Tajbeg Palace on the outskirts of Kabul. By this time, 'it must have been clear to Soviet leaders that their efforts to control the situation in Afghanistan had failed yet again ... they had failed to rein Amin in during the autumn, and now they had failed to destroy him in a quiet, plausible way'.[36] In these circumstances, a decision to use force was inescapable, and was made in a climate which, Marshall Shulman has suggested, was characterised by intense emotionalism, anger and frustration.[37]

Even at this stage Amin continued to frustrate the Soviet leadership. Unlike Dubcek and his colleagues in 1968, the Afghanistan leader was prepared to resist. On 27 December a special unit of Soviet forces, probably led by Paputin, stormed the palace, and in the ensuing fighting Amin was killed. Speculation that the manner if not the fact of Amin's demise meant that the Paputin mission was a failure is reinforced by Paputin's own death and possible suicide a few days later. It seems, therefore, that in their dealings with Amin, the Soviet leaders lurched from one fiasco to another. They had planned a much smoother removal of Amin which might have made the invasion unnecessary and at the very least would have given it greater legitimacy.

This gives some credence to Brezhnev's claim in *Pravda* that the decision to intervene was not an easy one.[38] The delay in taking action after the failure of the September coup may be another indication of hesitancy, indecision and possible division within the Politburo. Speculation to this effect has been intensified by rumours that some Soviet leaders were unhappy at the decision. At a high-level meeting between President Carter and his chief foreign policy advisers in February 1980, it was revealed that both Soviet Party Secretary Ponomarev, and the Foreign Trade Minister, Patolichev, had claimed to Western diplomats that they were opposed to the intervention.[39] A close reading of the election speeches to the Supreme Soviet in February 1980 also hinted at some shades of opinion among Politburo leaders. For example, Andropov and Chernenko sounded less enthusiastic than others about the Soviet intervention. Significantly, though, there was no change in the substance of Soviet policy when they later assumed the General Secretaryship.[40]

In so far as there was a debate, however, it was probably a very narrow one, revolving about means rather than ends, and not challenging the principle of consensus on which Brezhnev apparently operated. The increasingly overt nature of the threat to Soviet security concerns, and the fact that the costs of inaction were seen as outweighing the costs of invasion, suggest that there was little room for controversy and debate about the need for a decisive move to retrieve the situation. Any discord is likely to have centred on the timing and scale of the invasion, rather than on whether or not it should take place.

An additional item of debate might well have been about the likely reaction both inside Afghanistan and elsewhere. If so, there appears to have been a systematic underestimation of the difficulties. In attempting to gauge the American reaction, the Politburo was hampered not only by the unpredictability of the Carter administration but also by the absence of some of the more experienced Soviet figures more attuned to American attitudes. Arbatov and his deputy at the US Institute were both ill and played a less prominent role than might have been expected. It seems unlikely, however, that this affected the final decision. The absence of the academicians was hardly decisive, especially as the Politburo still had available much expert advice on the United States. Brezhnev's assistant, Aleksandrov-Agentov, was a specialist on the United States, while Dobrynin, who had been the Soviet Ambassador to Washington since 1962, was flown back to Moscow for consultations.

The fact that Brezhnev and Kosygin were also ill might have had more impact on the decision. Yet there was a sense in which much of the discussion about the United States would have been irrelevant. As suggested above, Washington's ability to influence Soviet behaviour towards Afghanistan was, for a variety of reasons, extremely limited in late 1979 – and so long as the Carter administration would not respond in ways likely to provoke a military confrontation, then the Soviet Union did not have to be too concerned.

Without more direct information about the Politburo's deliberations this is speculation. There is circumstantial evidence about division within the Politburo, but no more. Furthermore, in view of the apparent failure to predict the kind of difficulties that a large-scale invasion would encounter, it seems equally legitimate to contend that the Soviet leadership suffered not from too little consensus but from too much. What Western analysts sometimes call 'group-think' – a tendency for individuals to conform to the dominant attitudes within the group and suppress doubts about the proposed action for the sake of consensus and group cohesion – could well have been present in the Soviet decision to invade Afghanistan.[41]

If there were problems in the formulation of policy, even greater difficulties arose in its execution, which seems to have been bungled very badly. Evidence of Soviet sensitivity towards Afghan nationalism and world opinion can be found in the attempts by Moscow to suggest that Amin was overthrown by locals and not by the invading Soviet Army.[42] Because of the circumstances of his death this claim lacked credibility. Soviet military intervention was widely seen as a violation of the sovereignty of a non-aligned state and an attempt to install a puppet regime. The UN General Assembly reflected this view when only 18 states voted in support of the Soviet action while 104 were opposed. In Afghanistan itself, the invasion and subsequent fighting precipitated a massive exodus to Iran and Pakistan. In addition, the Afghan Army was decimated by desertions. After the invasion, the size of the Army fell by two-thirds to around 30,000, and would have been lower had it not been for press-gangs, a reduction in the age of conscription, and the high material incentives offered to officers and conscripts who remained.[43] As a result, the Soviet Union had to commit its forces to a longer struggle than anticipated at the outset.

The justification for the initial intervention and the subsequent Soviet presence was cast largely in terms of dealing with external forces. This was evident in Brezhnev's first statement on the intervention, which claimed that 'a well developed conspiracy by external reactionary forces' had 'created a real threat that Afghanistan would lose its independence and be transformed into a military staging ground for the imperialists on our country's southern border'.[44] Other Soviet statements also emphasised the external nature of the counter-revolutionary forces. Reports appeared in the Soviet press that American trained mercenaries in Pakistan were attempting to undermine the 'gains of the April revolution'. It was claimed that the Afghan government, under threat from outside, had invited Soviet military forces into the country to defend the revolution, and that the Soviet response was fully in accord with Article 4 of the Soviet–Afghan Treaty of Friendship and Cooperation and Article 51 of the UN Charter.[45] This assessment of events portrayed the West as the aggressor and the Soviet Union as the defender of Afghan sovereignty.

Even excluding the wilder claims that Amin was a CIA agent, the Soviet interpretation was disingenuous and contrived. The problem of stability in Afghanistan was internal rather than external. If the concerns about foreign assistance to the rebel forces were exaggerated, however, they were not completely groundless. There seems to have been some limited aid to the rebel forces from China, Pakistan, Iran, Saudi Arabia and Egypt.[46] Furthermore, the instability in Iran, and the possibility that the United States would respond to the seizure of the hostages with military force, added an additional element of unpredictability. As a result of the overthrow of the Shah, the United States increased its naval presence in the Indian Ocean quite significantly during 1979, while the decision in June to create a quick reaction force – which was later to become known as the Rapid Deployment Force – may have added to Soviet neuralgia. This is not to suggest that these activities either provoked or justified the Soviet invasion. Underlying the Soviet rhetoric, however, there may have been an element of genuine, if largely unwarranted, concern – and the activities of the United States and its allies may have inadvertently intensified security concerns which stemmed primarily from internal developments in Afghanistan.

The other element in Soviet justifications was what appeared to be an extension of the Brezhnev Doctrine. Brezhnev, in January 1980, declared that the Soviet Union could not allow another Chile on its southern borders. This reference to a country whose socialist government had been overthrown by a combination of internal and external forces was hardly surprising.[47] Whereas it was necessary for Moscow to accept the loss of socialist countries which were far from its borders, a reversal of the revolution was intolerable in a neighbouring country, where ideology, prestige and national security were inextricably intertwined.[48] In other words, the application of the Brezhnev Doctrine was simply an acknowledgment of the depth of Soviet security interests in Afghanistan and an attempt to legitimise Soviet actions in response to what was deemed an intolerable situation.

Soviet spokesmen also emphasised that the intervention in Afghanistan did not presage a broader Soviet assault on Western interests. From the outset officials and commentators denied any intent to further aggression.[49] Arbatov dismissed Western fears about the Soviet drive towards the Persian Gulf on the grounds that the Soviet Union recognised that such a move 'would invite world war three' – and this was something that the Politburo dared not contemplate.[50] Such reassurances had little impact in Washington, and did little to temper the American reaction.

The American Reaction and the Return to Cold War

The American response to the Soviet intervention in Afghanistan revealed the continued relevance of the same kind of security dilemmas which had played a major part in the development of the cold war in the late 1940s. Although the Soviet invasion was a clear-cut case of aggression, it seems to have been provoked more by security considerations than by ambition. 'The Soviet leaders did not see their decision to intervene militarily as an opportune option but as a security imperative; not as an opportunity for expansion but as a reluctant necessity to hold on.... It was a decision forced by events not an opportunity created by them.'[51] In Washington, however, the debate revolved far more around the consequences of the invasion than the motivation. Soviet aggressive intent was taken for granted. As a result, several aspects of the Soviet action caused acute anxiety.

First, the direct military intervention of Soviet troops into a country which, ostensibly at least, was non-aligned represented a significant departure from previous Soviet policy. It appeared, at a minimum, to cast doubt on the views of those who had argued that Soviet behaviour under Brezhnev was cautiously opportunistic rather than openly adventurist and expansionist. Furthermore, Western discussion about the extension of the Brezhnev Doctrine reflected the belief that Moscow was willing to take higher risks than ever before and had embarked upon a course of action which was qualitatively different from previous interventions in Hungary and Czechoslovakia. The Brezhnev Doctrine was unpalatable, even in the well-established Soviet sphere of influence in Eastern Europe; it was doubly so when extended to new areas. The Soviet perspective, in contrast, was that the 1978 coup had changed the situation in Afghanistan, and that the December 1979 invasion was simply an attempt to maintain the status quo within Afghanistan.

This was unconvincing to the Carter administration partly because the intervention came against a background of concern over what appeared to be a major Soviet geopolitical offensive. Furthermore, the invasion appeared to presage a new and ambitious policy of expansion aimed at Western interests in the Persian Gulf. Moscow's action was seen not only as part of a pattern but as a new and dangerous element in that pattern. In fact, Afghanistan, with its geographic position and its inhospitable terrain, was not the most obvious route to take if Moscow had serious designs on the Gulf. This is not the way it was seen in the United States. The dominant view in Moscow was that Afghanistan was a local issue; the dominant view in Washington was that it was a fundamental geo-strategic issue.

The other two elements which shaped the American reaction were personal and political. Jimmy Carter almost certainly felt betrayed by the Soviet invasion. After all, he had been campaigning vigorously, if not always effectively, for SALT Two and had been attempting to resist pressure for a much tougher stance against Moscow. In these circumstances, the Soviet action was an acute political and personal embarrassment. This sense of personal betrayal – similar to that of John Kennedy in 1962 when he discovered that the Soviet Union had installed missiles in Cuba – was intensified by an exchange of messages over the hot line. Carter's message, which he described as the sharpest of his Presidency, evoked a reply from Brezhnev justifying the invasion as a Soviet response to a request for help from a government attempting to deal with external interference.[52] Because Carter knew that the United States had not been interfering, Brezhnev's message was regarded as insulting as well as devious.[53] The President's subsequent comment that Afghanistan had taught him more about Soviet goals than anything Moscow had previously done, reflected both his sense of betrayal and his anger at Brezhnev. Yet it also compounded the political embarrassment, and was widely regarded as a display of Presidential naïvety. By admitting that he had failed to appreciate the nature of the Soviet threat, Carter was virtually accepting the critique of his foreign policy made by the Committee on the Present Danger. The victors in January 1980 included not only Zbigniew Brzezinski, but Paul Nitze, Henry Jackson and Richard Perle. Once the President had acknowledged, if only tacitly, that they had been right, it was inevitable that there would be a hard-line American response. This is not to claim that Carter's volte-face resulted simply from political expediency. While the President was facing a very tough re-election fight in a climate in which a hard-line response could have political benefits, the sense of conviction and outrage in Carter's pronouncements had a degree of conviction which would have been hard to fabricate. It appears that strategic calculation, political expediency and personal commitment were mutually reinforcing elements in determining the American reaction.

This response was designed to deter further aggression. In order to achieve this the United States had to demonstrate that military intervention was not a cost-free option for Moscow and that business as usual between the two superpowers was impossible. Even so there was an element of over-reaction in American policy. The President himself used highly exaggerated rhetoric, and on 8 January characterised the Soviet invasion as the 'greatest threat to world peace since World War Two'.[54] With all the zealousness of the convert, Carter also took a tough line on sanctions. His advisers drew up a list of possible measures for consideration, but instead of choosing certain options from the list, the President – with a minimum of consultation with his NATO allies – adopted virtually all the proposals. This surprised even Brzezinski, who felt that restrictions on grain sales and technology transfer would suffice to show the strength of American disapproval.[55] As well as placing restrictions on high-technology exports, and initiating a grain embargo on anything beyond the 8 million tons of grain that had been guaranteed by the five-year agreement signed in 1976, the President curtailed Soviet fishing privileges in American waters, delayed an opening of new consulates, deferred cultural and economic exchanges, and warned that the United States might withdraw from the Olympic Games to be held in Moscow in the summer of 1980 – a warning which was later carried out. All this was in addition to the request to the Senate to defer further consideration of SALT Two.

Another strand in the administration's response was to move towards the restoration of the traditional strategy of containment. This was done by the consolidation of US–Pakistan relations, by a shift in emphasis in the fiscal year 1981 defence budget away from European defence and towards global contingencies, by moves towards the creation of a Sino–American military relationship, and by the enunciation of the Carter Doctrine. Perhaps more than any other development, the Carter Doctrine and the increased emphasis placed on the Rapid Deployment Force marked the abandonment of the US detente policy. In so far as Kissinger's policy of detente had been intended to contain the Soviet Union, it had clearly been a failure. Consequently, the Carter administration felt compelled to revert to the more traditional forms of containment dominant before 1968. The restoration of cold war policies and rhetoric was not accomplished by the Reagan administration in 1981, but by the Carter administration in 1980. President Carter embraced these policies with reluctance rather than enthusiasm, however, and even after his conversion to a hard-line approach was still criticised for doing too little too late. The Reagan administration, in contrast, brought a new sense of dynamism and assertiveness to the Soviet–American relationship. Its major changes, however, were in rhetoric rather than substance, and for the most part it did little more than carry out the policies which had been formulated by Carter in the early months of 1980. In some respects, such as the cancellation of the grain embargo, Reagan even weakened the position adopted by his predecessor.

In considering the American response to Afghanistan, however, it is necessary to look not only at politics but also at psychology. The policies of January 1980 can be understood as a major landmark in the drive to regenerate American power and prestige, which was to become a major motif of the Reagan administration's approach to international politics. The Carter administration had already taken steps in this direction, increasing the defence budget, for example, well before December 1979. In January 1980, this process was crystallised, but was then undermined by the continuing problem of the American hostages in Iran. The apparent impotence of the United States, together with the ill-fated rescue attempt, confirmed critics in the view that in spite of the conversion of January 1980, President Carter was not the man to reverse the decline of American power and remove the sense of malaise which had become increasingly pervasive as reverse followed reverse in the 1970s. Although the Reagan administration would later characterise the 1970s as a decade of neglect, the problem was not so much lack of power but lack of the will to use it in the face of domestic constraints. By 1980, the dominant impulse in American politics had changed and these constraints had diminished. The emphasis was no longer on the arrogance of American power – as it had been in the early 1970s when Vietnam was the issue – but on the need to acquire and exercise that power. The Soviet Union had exploited the weaknesses of the United States, but would be allowed to do so no longer. In the aftermath of Afghanistan the views expressed by the Committee on the Present Danger became the new orthodoxy.

These trends in American attitudes and policies inevitably received a hostile reception in Moscow. They also caused consternation in Western Europe and ushered in a period of considerable tension in Atlantic relations. Helmut Schmidt, the West German Chancellor, opposed President Carter's hard-line response to Afghanistan. He attempted to protect the achievements of the Ostpolitik by insulating detente in Europe from events elsewhere. In France, Giscard d'Estaing was more sympathetic to the Carter administration, but he too insisted on the need to persist with the policy of detente in Europe. It was in 1980, therefore, that superpower detente and European detente seriously diverged. West Europeans were reluctant to follow the lead of the Carter administration in imposing sanctions on the Soviet Union; moreover, in a number of cases European firms were able to benefit by obtaining contracts which, in the absence of the sanctions, would almost certainly have gone to American companies. If there was an element of expediency in the European approach, the fundamental issue revolved around the results of detente. Europeans argued that detente had worked in Europe and should not be sacrificed simply because developments elsewhere had led to renewed tensions between Moscow and Washington.

This divergence between the United States and Western Europe was the result of several considerations. It reflected the different perspectives and priorities between a superpower with global responsibilities on the one side and a group of regional powers on the other. For Europeans detente had always been focused primarily on normalisation in Europe. This is not to argue that the allies were oblivious to other dimensions of detente. Their interest in arms control – as something which clearly impinged on them – was sustained and enduring. Soviet activism in the Third World, in contrast, did not evoke anything like the depth of anxiety in Western Europe that it did in the United States. There was an element of European parochialism in this. Apart from occasional French military excursions in Africa, most Western European governments focused their activities much closer to home. Although they criticised Soviet military involvement in Africa, they tended to dismiss this as part of the superpower competition, and not as something which really impinged on East–West relations in Europe. Their response to the Soviet invasion of Afghanistan was similar. Although they were unequivocal in their public condemnation of Soviet actions, underlying this was a sense that the invasion resulted from regional Soviet security concerns and did not necessarily presage a new militancy in Soviet policy towards Western Europe. Consequently, the European allies resisted the appreciation of the Soviet threat that President Carter arrived at in January 1980. Since they were not convinced that detente should be abandoned in favour of a reversion to cold war policies, they found the hard-line policies of Carter – and subsequently of Reagan – disconcerting.

West European reluctance to fall in line with the new hard-line policies of the United States, however, cannot simply be dismissed as parochial or naïve. In part, it reflected a realism about detente that had not always been evident in Washington: never as euphoric about detente as the United States, the Europeans were not as disappointed by its results. Furthermore, there was concern in Europe that the United States was engaging in another of the extreme pendulum swings that periodically characterised its foreign policy. Rather than slavishly follow this, the Europeans felt that it was more appropriate to continue with the judicious and balanced approach towards the Soviet Union which had been pursued through the 1970s. This was particularly the case in the Federal Republic, which had based its foreign policy 'on the premise that its security would best be ensured by a combination of defence capability within the Western alliance and willingness to negotiate with the Soviet Union and the other states of the Warsaw Pact'.[56] Furthermore, the benefits of such an approach were very real – and did not appear to be worth sacrificing because of Soviet intervention in a region that was remote from European concerns and interests. East–West trade was one element in this, but perhaps even more important were the gains that had been made in terms of human contacts, especially between the two parts of Germany.

West European reluctance to fall in line with Washington's preferences also marked a new independence and self-confidence on the part of the allies, especially the Federal Republic. The Europeans had become sceptical about Carter's conduct of foreign policy, and saw no reason why the latest in a series of abrupt decisions and reversals should determine their agenda. Yet for Bonn, the difficulties resulting from the American abandonment of detente were intense. The latent conflict of priorities between security – which depended on the United States – and Ostpolitik – which depended on the Soviet Union and its East European clients – had been brought to the fore by Afghanistan and the Carter administration's reaction. The result was a two-track policy.

Despite its different assessment of the crisis, Bonn attempted by finely measured acts of alliance solidarity (Olympic boycott, increases in defence expenditures, support for Turkey) not to do any irreparable damage to US–German relations. It also took pains not to sever its ties with Moscow and rather to repair the broken channels of communication between East and West.[57]

In the event, it proved impossible for the Europeans to insulate themselves from the deterioration in Soviet–American relations. The unrest in Poland led in late 1980 to intimations of a possible Soviet invasion of Poland, and in late 1981 to the imposition of martial law by the Polish Army. Whereas the United States under President Reagan reacted strongly to the action of General Jaruzelski, the Europeans regarded it as preferable to a direct Soviet invasion. These differences of attitude manifested themselves in arguments over sanctions, and it was clear in the early 1980s that the Soviet invasion of Afghanistan had ushered in not only a period of more tense and competitive relations between Moscow and Washington but also a more difficult and often acrimonious relationship between the United States and its West European allies. The crisis of detente also became a crisis of alliance. The reasons for this lay largely in differing appreciations of the detente experience of the 1970s. With this in mind, the concluding chapter offers some reflections on this experience and considers what lessons it may hold for Soviet–American relations in the future.

Notes

1. *Pravda*, 31 Dec. 1979.
2. Z. Brzezinski, *Power and Principle* (New York: Farrar, Straus & Giroux, 1983), p. 432.
3. J. Carter, *Keeping Faith* (London: Collins, 1983), p. 471.
4. Ibid., pp. 471–2.
5. Ibid., p. 473.
6. Quoted in ibid., p. 483.
7. H.S. Bradsher, *Afghanistan and the Soviet Union* (Durham, NC: Duke University Press, 1983), p. 3.
8. Ibid., p. 5.
9. Ibid., p. 74.
10. G. Arbatov, *Cold War or Detente?* (London: Zed Books, 1983), p. 191.
11. L. Dupree, *Red Flag Over the Hindu Kush* quoted in R. Garthoff, *Detente and Confrontation* (Washington, DC: The Brookings Institution, 1985), pp. 899–900.
12. Arbatov, op. cit., p. 191.
13. Ibid., p. 191.
14. See S.T. Hosmer and T.W. Wolfe, *Soviet Policy and Practice Towards Third World Conflicts* (Lexington, Mass.: D.C. Heath, 1983), p. 114 and p. 156.

15. Garthoff, op. cit., p. 900–1.
16. Bradsher, op. cit., p. 101.
17. Ibid., p. 104.
18. Ibid.,. p. 107.
19. Garthoff, op. cit., pp. 906–8.
20. Bradsher, op. cit., p. 113.
21. Garthoff, op. cit., p. 910.
22. Ibid., p. 944.
23. Ibid.,
24. J. Valenta, 'Soviet Decision-making on Afghanistan, 1979' in J. Valenta
and W. Potter (eds), *Soviet Decision-making for National Security* (London: Allen
& Unwin, 1984), pp. 219–20.
25. Ibid., p. 225.
26. Ibid.
27. For two very different views, sce the chapter by A. McAuley in C. Keeble (ed.),
The Soviet State (London: Gower, 1985), and the contribution by A. Bennigsen in J.
Azrael (ed.), *Soviet Nationality Policies and Practices* (New York: Praeger, 1978).
28. Bradsher, op. cit., p. 156. For further examples, see F. Halliday, *Threat from
the East* (London, Penguin, 1982), p. 50.
29. This information from dissidents was reported in *Daily Telegraph*, 21 Jan.
1980.
30. J. Valenta, 'From Prague to Kabul', *International Security*, vol. 5, no. 2
(Fall 1980), p. 124.
31. Nevertheless, Muslim troops were withdrawn when their 90-day term ended and
were increasingly replaced by Slav forces.
32. Bradsher, op. cit., p. 157.
33. For the importance of interests in establishing credibility, see A.L. George
and R. Smoke, *Deterrence in American Foreign Policy* (New York: Columbia
University Press, 1974), especially p. 559.
34. Brzezinski, op. cit., p. 426.
35. Quoted in Bradsher, op. cit., p. 152.
36. Ibid., p. 179.
37. Quoted in ibid., p. 179.
38. *Pravda*, 13 Jan. 1980.
39. Brzezinski, op. cit., p. 435.
40. See J. Hough, 'Soviet Succession' in *Hearing Before the Select Committee
on Intelligence, United States Senate, 97th Congress, Second Session*, 29 Sept. 1982
(Washington, DC: Government Printing Office, 1982), p. 6.
41. The notion of 'group-think' is developed in I. Janis, *Victims of Groupthink*
(Boston: Houghton Mifflin, 1972).
42. See Bradsher, op. cit., pp. 184–5.
43. A. Hyman, *Afghan Resistance*, Conflict Studies, No. 161 (London: Institute for
the Study of Conflict).
44. *Pravda*, 13 Jan. 1980.
45. Ibid., 31 Dec. 1979, and 13 Jan. 1980.
46. See Garthoff, op. cit., p. 922.
47. For Brezhnev's reference to Chile, see *Pravda*, 13 Jan. 1980.
48. See A. Bovin, *Soviet News*, 22 April 1980.
49. *Pravda*, 31 Dec. 1979.
50. Arbatov, op. cit., p. 192.

51. Garthoff, op. cit., p. 931.
52. See ibid., p. 949 and Carter, op. cit., p. 472.
53. Ibid., p. 472.
54. Garthoff, op. cit., p. 957.
55. Brzezinski, op. cit., p. 957.
56. H. Haftendorn, *Security and Detente* (New York: Praeger, 1985), p. 145.
57. Ibid.

11

Conclusion

The story of Soviet–American detente in the 1970s is a story of aspiration giving way to recrimination, of conciliation being replaced by confrontation. By the end of the 1970s detente was dead. The decisive events in its demise were not those surrounding the election of Ronald Reagan, but the American debate over SALT Two and the Soviet invasion of Afghanistan. During 1980 President Carter reverted to the policy of containment which, initially, he had attempted to transcend. The increase in tension and the restoration of a domestic consensus on the need for a tougher stance towards the Soviet Union heralded what was to be the 'new orthodoxy' of the Reagan administration.

Although the Reagan administration's policy did not differ greatly from that of it predecessor, Reagan's hard-line stance towards Moscow displayed a clarity of purpose, a commitment of will and a degree of enthusiasm which was absent under Carter. This was not surprising: Reagan himself had been an outspoken critic of detente, and key figures in his administration were drawn from the ranks of the Committee on the Present Danger. Their view was that detente had been an abject failure, for which the Soviet Union bore full responsibility. The analysis in the preceding chapters, however, suggests that such an interpretation is fundamentally flawed: it not only begs several questions about the achievements of detente, but also distorts the events of the 1970s. It is not self-evident that detente was as complete a failure as is often alleged: steps were taken to restrain the arms race, the superpowers avoided direct military confrontation in the Third World, and 'normalisation' was achieved in Europe. Nor is it adequate to blame the decline of detente on Soviet ambition and perfidy; the increase of tension and the reversion to cold war had several distinct causes, most of which concerned the dynamics of the superpower relationship rather than the inherent expansionism of the Soviet state. The implication is that the lessons of the 1970s may differ from those drawn by the Reagan administration in the early 1980s. Before considering what these lessons are, however, it is necessary to return to the questions that were asked at the outset of the study concerning the rise and fall of detente.

The Rise and Fall of Detente

The rise of detente can be understood as a process of adaptation in the international system and on the part of its leading members.[1]

The cold war system was based upon a stark bipolarity which was a temporary consequence of World War II, on cohesive blocs clustered around each superpower, on the primacy of the military instruments of foreign policy and on strict ideological divisions. Changes in each of these conditions inevitably prompted change in, and indeed the decline of, the cold war international system.[2] Strict bipolarity began to give way to a more complex order, with other power centres developing to challenge the superpowers, at least on some issues. The ideological supremacy of the Soviet Union in the communist bloc, for example, was increasingly threatened by China. Similarly, the economic preponderance of the United States was reduced as a result of the resurgence of Western Europe and Japan. Furthermore, the development and deployment of large numbers of nuclear weapons by both sides made it imperative that the superpowers managed their competition in a way which prevented it from degenerating into hostilities. As a result of all these changes the cold war system was gradually, if at times very subtly, transformed. Detente represented a new stage in the process of adapting to these changes in the distribution of power and the instruments of influence. New modalities of behaviour were worked out as part of an attempt to establish what Gordon Craig and Alexander George describe as 'a less dangerous and more viable international system'.[3]

Such an analysis is persuasive. It suggests that there is a logic of detente that impels the superpowers towards a moderation of their relationship. It is a particularly good explanation for the moves towards a minimalist detente in the 1960s, which came after the Cuban Missile Crisis had underlined more starkly than ever before the dangers of cold war. Yet it does not adequately explain the efforts to establish a more far-reaching *modus vivendi* in the early 1970s. Furthermore, by focusing upon a common theme of adaptation it ignores important differences in the Soviet and American approach to detente. While both superpowers were engaged in a process of adjustment, they were adjusting to different vulnerabilities and responding to different concerns. This led to divergent conceptions of what detente was, as well as to competing, and ultimately incompatible, interpretations of what was permissible or legitimate behaviour within the detente framework. It also meant that the two superpowers, while acknowledging that there were common interests and mutual benefits in detente, continued to pursue unilateral gain. 'Each partner in the relationship sought to skew the definitions of restraint and reciprocity in ways that would play to its own strengths, insulate its weaknesses, and maximise its comparative advantage.'[4]

If this gave detente a fragility that became more apparent as the 1970s wore on, it was inherent in the circumstances that led Moscow and Washington to embrace detente. Each side was not only responding to problems of its own but to opportunities resulting from the difficulties faced by the adversary. What the Soviet leaders saw as vulnerabilities to be minimised and constraints to be loosened were seen by American decision-makers as potential opportunities to be exploited. Conversely, the pressures which pushed Washington towards detente were seen by Moscow as offering significant opportunities for advancement.

The damaging impact of this was compounded by the changes in each superpower's conception of its status and role. The United States was anxious to establish a set of norms for the international system which would ensure that Moscow did not take advantage of two major developments – the emergence of strategic parity and the loss (because of the domestic constraints associated with Vietnam) of American willingness and ability to compete effectively for influence in the Third World. For Moscow, however, its new-found status as a superpower was something which it wanted to translate into increased influence. The only model it had for superpower behaviour was the United States – and part of America's expression of its status was its global reach. The USSR's emergence as a superpower brought with it similar 'rights' and opportunities in the Third World as had long been available to the United States. And if Washington, for reasons of its own, was no longer able to exercise these rights and take advantage of the opportunities, that was its problem. It was at this point that the considerations which propelled the superpowers to move towards detente merged with their conceptions of the new relationship and what they expected to get out of it.

The American conception of detente was most fully articulated by Kissinger. He emphasised the idea of a legitimate international order in which there were rules or norms of behaviour accepted by both superpowers. Soviet–American competition would continue but would be regulated and controlled. Ultimately, it was hoped, the superpowers would move from competition to cooperation. To do this, however, required that they both observe the principle of restraint. In emphasising this, Kissinger was attempting to encourage Moscow to engage in a self-denying ordinance. Not only was this desirable in terms of global stability, but, moreover, it was essential because the United States no longer possessed the military superiority deemed necessary to hold the Soviet Union in check. Although Kissinger emphasised the positive aspects of detente, in fact he was making the best of a situation that, from the American perspective, was something less than ideal. When critics contend that detente led to the neglect of America's security needs and allowed the Soviet Union to behave unchecked in the Third World, they are, for the most part, confusing cause and effect. Detente was not the cause of America's apparent weakness in the 1970s; rather, it was a means of coping with and compensating for the loss of American will at a time when there were few other options available. As such, it was based on a hard-headed calculation of the constraints on American foreign policy. Kissinger clearly hoped that detente with the Soviet Union, reinforced by American inducements and penalties, would inhibit Moscow from taking advantage of these constraints. The problem with this, however, was that it conflicted with the Soviet conception of detente.

Although Moscow wanted a more relaxed relationship with the United States because of fears about China, concerns over an unregulated arms race and a desire to obtain access to Western technology and credits, it also saw detente as a means of securing American acknowledgment of the Soviet status as an equal super-power. Although the Soviet and American conceptions of detente overlapped, therefore, at a fundamental level they were incompatible. The American conception demanded a reduction of Soviet activism in the Third World, while the Soviet conception of detente accepted no such commitment. Superpower status was meaningless if it did not allow the Soviet Union to intervene, directly or indirectly, in areas of instability and attempt to influence outcomes in its favour. While such support had an ideological flavour – and was cast in terms of supporting wars of national liberation – it also symbolised a Soviet desire to enjoy the political benefits of strategic parity. After years of strategic inferiority, the attainment of parity must have been regarded as a considerable achievement in Moscow, and one which carried with it significant advantages in terms of Soviet ability to act decisively in the Third World. In short, Moscow saw detente as offering new opportunities for the exercise of power, whereas the United States saw it as a way of disciplining Soviet power.

These differences in conception exacerbated the difficulties that were an inevitable consequence of the differing motives and interests lying behind the detente policies of the two superpowers. George Breslauer has suggested that 'for detente to maintain its momentum as a process, given the numerous differences between the superpowers, it had to be buttressed by norms of restraint in the competitive relationship and norms of reciprocity in the collaborative'.[5] The problem, though, was that there was no real agreement on the norms of restraint. Furthermore, reciprocity in collaboration was not easy to define or to achieve, particularly in a relationship in which linkages between various areas of activity were both a strategy and a fact of political life. Inevitably, this led to allegations that the adversary was getting most of the benefits from detente – allegations that were made in both Washington and Moscow.

The implication of this is that the seeds of decay were inherent both in the origins of detente and in the differing conceptions prevailing in Moscow and Washington. During the period of high detente, which lasted from about May 1971 to the outbreak of the Yom Kippur war in October 1973, these differences were obscured by the progress that was made on issues such as East–West trade, arms control, normalisation in Europe and the development of a code of conduct. Yet it was inevitable that as soon as Soviet–American relations were subjected to strain they would come to the fore. Furthermore, because the differences had been obscured or overlooked – probably through a mixture of calculation and inadvertence – the sense of disappointment and betrayal was all the more intense. This became apparent in the Middle East war of October 1973 which began a deterioration of Soviet–American relations that was to continue through the 1970s.

The problems stemming from conceptual incompatibility were heightened by difficulties in the management of detente in the mid-1970s. Such difficulties may have been inherent in the interaction of two very different political systems, but were worsened by developments in American domestic politics. The decline of the Presidency and the rise of the Right eroded the domestic base for detente and added to the problems of managing a difficult relationship. In addition, detente was undermined by the fact that it was bound up with what was perceived to be a major change in the relative power and status of the United States and the Soviet Union. Finally, detente proved vulnerable to extraneous events: the idiosyncratic, the fortuitous and the unforeseen all took their toll.

The problems of implementing detente were greatest on the American side where the congressional resurgence made it difficult for Kissinger to apply the strategy of linkage with any consistency. The difficulties were exacerbated in the latter half of the 1970s by the fact that the Carter administration was divided about the circumstances in which linkage – which by then had become punitive rather than positive – should be imposed. Indeed, with Kissinger's departure, any pretence at managing superpower relations within a coherent conceptual framework disappeared, and American detente policy was implemented in a manner that can only be described as haphazard and fragmented. The problems were compounded by the fact that even when linkage was not used as a strategy there were still important political linkages between issues. Arms control, in particular, suffered from this.

These problems did not exist to anything like the same extent in Moscow, where policy-making was marked by a high degree of continuity and stability. Nevertheless, Brezhnev was not wholly unconstrained, and had to maintain the support of his colleagues. The result of this was to reinforce the incompatibility between Soviet and

American conceptions of detente. One of the persuasive arguments in favour of detente in Moscow was that it facilitated Soviet revolutionary activities in the Third World. Without this, Brezhnev might have had a more difficult time in maintaining a consensus in favour of his detente policy. The problem, however, was that the very elements of the Soviet conception of detente which were necessary to keep the Soviet sceptics on board made it more difficult for the architects and supporters of detente in the United States to mobilise and maintain the domestic consensus necessary to the success of their policy.

A closely related consideration which further diminished the viability of detente was that both superpowers were adjusting to alterations in their relative power and status. Such a process can hardly fail to be traumatic, especially in an international system which, in military terms at least, remains bipolar. Thucydides, for example, attributes conflict between Athens and Sparta in ancient Greece primarily to the fear that the growth of Athenian power provoked in Sparta. The decline of detente and the reversion to a more overtly hostile and competitive relationship between the superpowers in the late 1970s reflected similar concerns in the United States about the growth of Soviet power. Partly this resulted from the premature acknowledgment of strategic parity in SALT One. Since the Interim Agreement on Offensive Arms was presented as the formalisation of parity, the continued momentum of Soviet military programmes in the next few years inevitably aroused fears in Washington that the Soviet Union was not content to accept strategic parity and was embarked on a systematic effort to achieve strategic superiority. Although these concerns were exaggerated – parity is a relatively elastic concept which can embrace considerable asymmetries – they were exacerbated by Moscow's apparent unwillingness to discipline the exercise of its power in the Third World.

The United States was all the more sensitive towards these manifestations of Soviet power because of difficulties it encountered in exploiting its own capabilities. The 1970s was a difficult decade for the United States in which humiliation followed humiliation. Not only had Washington, for the first time in history, lost a war, but there was also a loss of faith in the institution of the Presidency, which for most of the postwar period had been seen as the key to competing effectively against the Soviet Union. The energy crisis of the early 1970s also highlighted American economic vulnerability. In terms of dependence on overseas oil, the United States was far less exposed than Western Europe or Japan. Nevertheless, psychologically the impact of both the 1973–4 energy crisis and the problems of 1978–9 was probably greater in the United States than elsewhere. Vulnerability has more impact when it is novel and unexpected.

The concerns over American malaise and decline were intensified in the Carter years and were brought to a head by events in Iran. If the American inability or unwillingness to take steps to save the Shah, who after all had been America's regional gendarme in the Gulf, underlined once more the limits of American power, the hostage crisis revealed a degree of impotence that was not only unprecedented but totally humiliating. Events in a region of considerable strategic significance to Washington had a neuralgic impact on the American psyche. The failure of the hostage rescue attempt seemed symptomatic of a decade in which American power had declined.

Although the Soviet Union was not directly involved in most of this, the impact was heightened by the contrast between the fortunes of the United States and those of the Soviet Union. By the late 1970s Moscow seemed to be riding high. Despite concerns over the declining rate of economic growth, Soviet military strength was still increasing, while Moscow had a record of foreign policy successes that made the American performance look even more dismal. In these circumstances, it was almost inevitable that the United States would have problems adjusting to Soviet status as an equal superpower. Although the difficulties faced by Washington were for the most part unrelated to detente, American decline and detente somehow became synonymous. Conversely, the rejection of detente and the regeneration of the United States went hand in hand.

The decline of detente also went hand in hand with the restoration of American self-righteousness and the replacement of Kissinger's pragmatic stance by a more ideological approach. Although Kissinger had not been immune to cold war thinking – often disguised in the language of geopolitical competition – his concern with the Soviet Union's international conduct rather than Soviet internal politics facilitated detente. This focus was challenged by Henry Jackson (and subsequently by Jimmy Carter) who contributed enormously to the re-emergence of an ideological foreign policy. Along with Paul Nitze, Jackson was also the key figure in the restoration of the 'inherent bad faith model' of the Soviet Union – a task which was facilitated by Soviet behaviour in the Third World.

The impact of Soviet activism was sharpened because it came against a back-drop of wishful thinking in the United States about the extent to which Moscow was prepared to accept American conceptions of restraint. Yet there was also a major Soviet failure to assess the effect of its actions on the United States. If the United States was over-sensitive to Soviet actions, Moscow was grossly insensitive to American concerns. Because its involvement in Angola and the Horn of Africa did not trespass directly on American interests, Moscow may well have believed that it was refraining from attempts to obtain unilateral advantage. Short-sighted opportunism and, in the case of Afghanistan, fearful blundering resulted in geopolitical gains which were relatively modest. In achieving these, Moscow alienated supporters of detente in the United States and strengthened the position of those who had never liked Kissinger's policy. Yet Soviet leaders persisted in the belief that they could pursue good relations with the United States while simultaneously pursuing an activist policy in Africa and elsewhere. Deliberately or unwittingly, they not only eroded the American conception of detente, but also challenged American power and prestige. A challenge of this kind was inherent in the divergence between Soviet and American conceptions of detente, but it was made inevitable by the fact that the United States, for all its emphasis on restraint, was itself behaving competitively in both the Middle East and Angola. Even so, there seems to have been a failure by Soviet leaders to appreciate that their actions would provoke attempts to reassert American power and contribute significantly to the rejection of detente by Washington.

The decline of detente also resulted from unanticipated events. The widespread unrest and instability in the Third World which occurred in the mid and late 1970s was not something which had been planned or foreseen in either Moscow or Washington. Furthermore, some of the clients and allies of the two superpowers not only resented detente but actually pursued policies which were inimical to its maintenance. This was most obvious in the Middle East war of 1973 which placed detente under considerable strain and highlighted the difficulties of keeping clients on a tight rein. The problem for both superpowers was that they could not repudiate the actions of their clients without undermining their credibility as patrons and thereby their influence in the Third World.

Turbulence and instability in the international system were accompanied by considerable domestic turbulence in the United States. Although its impact should not be overestimated (and many of the domestic problems would have arisen in any event), Watergate clearly helped to derail detente. It not only created a vacuum at the centre of American politics, but removed the one figure who could effectively neutralise the Right. With Nixon's departure the way was open for the major domestic assault on detente, which began with Henry Jackson, continued with the activities of Paul Nitze and the Committee on the Present Danger and culminated in the attack on SALT Two. This assault on detente was critical and was perhaps the most important single factor in its decline. Change in American internal politics made detente possible, then did much to destroy it. Soviet activities in the Third World encouraged these pressures, but with a different domestic climate in the United States these activities might have been accepted rather more readily as part of the continuing competition. After all, US involvement in Vietnam had not prevented the moves towards detente in the early 1970s. Kissinger in practice saw competition as a natural accompaniment to detente rather than inconsistent with it. What he found difficult to tolerate, though, was the fact that in Angola the United States came out second best from this competition. The situation seemed to deteriorate further under Carter, with the result that the Soviet invasion of Afghanistan was seen not as a response to regional instability in a sensitive area but as part of a coherent geopolitical offensive that had been initiated by Moscow under the cover of detente. The result was that by January 1980 the disintegration of Soviet–American detente was more or less complete. What are the lessons of this for the future?

Lessons for the Future

Any attempt to distil lessons for the future from the experience of the 1970s has to be treated with considerable caution, as in many ways the circumstances of the 1970s were unique. Nevertheless, it is possible to identify several considerations which have continued relevance to Soviet–American relations.

The first is that the superpowers operate within fairly narrow limits of 'adversary partnership'.[6] The United States and the Soviet Union are adversaries partly because of the logic of bipolarity in an anarchic international system and partly because of ideological antipathy. As Kenneth Waltz has pointed out, 'in the great power politics of a bipolar world, who is a danger to whom is never in doubt'.[7] The implication is that superpower rivalry results from structural factors: the competition between the United States and the Soviet Union has distinct parallels with that between Athens and Sparta and would exist even if there were no ideological differences between the two states. Although this is persuasive, ideological factors should not be discounted as they increase Soviet and American concerns over security, add to the difficulties of cooperation, and give superpower competition an intensity that goes beyond power politics.

At the same time, the dangers of this relationship make it essential that there are attempts to manage it: far from precluding cooperation, cold war requires it. Some minimal restraints or 'codes of conduct' are vital to ensure that cold war does not degenerate into hot war. Detente in the 1970s can be understood, in part, as an attempt to extend these cooperative elements. At the same time, more extended cooperation does not prevent continued competition. The forms of cooperation and conflict may become less direct and more subtle, but they do not cease to exist as both superpowers pursue what might be termed a 'hidden agenda of detente'. The result is a curious and at times almost schizophrenic relationship in which cooperation and conflict coexist uneasily and in which 'first steps towards agreement do not lead to second and third steps. Instead they mingle with other acts and events that keep the level of tension quite high' and make it virtually impossible to translate detente into entente.[8] If Soviet and American 'concern for peace and stability draws them together ... their fears and ambitions drive them apart'.[9] Rather than detente leading to entente, it is much more likely to lead back to cold war. Such fluctuations are inherent in superpower relations, and from this perspective the decline of detente should not be a surprise.

The second lesson follows from this. It concerns the dangers of glossing over differences of approach and expectation. This happened at the Moscow Summit in 1972, and brought short-term gains at the expense of long-term acceptability. Superficial or ostensible agreement leads inexorably to charges of bad faith which not only sour the relationship but undermine the very legitimacy of detente policies. Closely related is the problem of oversell. This is a particular danger in the United States, where the political structure encourages an oscillation between overselling threats and overselling remedies. If detente is oversold as a remedy it can only lead to disappointment, frustration and resentment – and subsequent exaggeration of the threat.

Another lesson is that if detente is to endure it has to be broadly based. Single areas of cooperation cannot stand alone in the event of conflict and tensions elsewhere. This is particularly true of arms control which simply cannot bear the whole burden of superpower detente. Although it can contribute to a less acrimonious political climate, it also depends for its continued legitimacy on the maintenance of a favourable atmosphere between the superpowers. There is a sense, therefore, in which Brzezinski was right: detente has to be seen to be comprehensive and reciprocal. Linkage is a basic fact of life in the American political system. The implication of this for Moscow is that opportunism in the Third World can only be based on myopic self-interest which is counter-productive in the longer term. Restraint has its benefits. There may well be greater realisation of this in Moscow now that the gains of the 1970s have become the drains of the 1980s. Angola, Ethiopia, Yemen, Vietnam and Afghanistan have imposed considerable demands on limited Soviet resources.

At the same time there has to be a greater acknowledgment in Washington that it is possible to be over-sensitive to Soviet involvement in Third World conflicts. The imposition of global perspectives on regional issues may be both unnecessary and unwarranted. Although this was recognised by Cyrus Vance, his appraisal was shared by few other American policy-makers during the 1970s. Yet subsequent events have almost certainly vindicated his position: nationalist forces have been as resistant to domination by Moscow as they were to Western colonialism during the postwar period. This suggests that the superpowers can afford to be more relaxed about each other than they were during the 1970s. Geopolitical gains by either side are rarely permanent, and even if they are lasting they do not easily threaten the overall stability of the superpower relationship.

The other major lesson is the need for greater self-awareness and less self-righteousness. The problem with a moralistic approach to foreign policy, whether it stems from Marxist-Leninist ideology, liberal internationalism or conservative fundamentalism is that it inhibits awareness of the possible gap between self-image and the image held by others. As a result it makes policy-makers less sensitive to the security dilemmas which confront the adversary, and more likely to construe defensive actions as offensive in character. The most obvious example of this was Afghanistan, but even in Angola the US government did not fully appreciate the extent to which the Soviet Union was responding to American actions. If the superpowers accept that their rivalry is determined as much by the basic structure of the international system as by their differing internal structures they might be more tolerant of each other's actions. Recognising the security dilemma is the first step towards mitigating it. The detente of the 1970s, for all its imperfections, offered a way of easing this dilemma and relieving the dangers of superpower competition. It was conceptually flawed, badly managed and vulnerable to domestic critics and unanticipated events. Nevertheless, the attempt to extend the areas of cooperation in Soviet–American relations was an experiment which bears repeating. The experience of the 1970s revealed the problems that can occur when the superpowers approach detente with different conceptions, objectives and interests. It also highlighted the fact that asymmetries, whether in domestic politics or in perceptions of power and status, can significantly erode the legitimacy of detente policies. Awareness of these difficulties might make future attempts at detente somewhat easier to sustain. If greater sensitivity to potential problems is a necessary condition for success, however, it is not a sufficient condition. The possibility of failure is inherent in a relationship which remains predominantly competitive in character.

Notes

1. On this point we have benefited from several helpful discussions with Brian White of North Staffordshire Polytechnic.

2. This notion of a cold war international system has been developed very thoroughly by Michael Cox; see, for example, his 'Western Capitalism and the Cold War System' in M. Shaw (ed.), *War, State and Society* (London: Macmillan, 1984), pp. 136–94.

3. G. Craig and A. George, *Force and Statecraft* (New York: Oxford University Press, 1983), pp. 126–7.

4. G. Breslauer 'Why Detente Failed: An Interpretation' in A. George, *Managing US–Soviet Rivalry* (Boulder, Col.: Westview Press, 1983), p. 321.

5. Ibid., p. 336.

6. Coral Bell uses the term 'adverse partnership'. See *The Conventions of Crisis* (London: Oxford University Press, 1971), p. 50.

7. K. Waltz, *Theory of International Politics* (Reading, Mass.: Addison-Wesley, 1979), p. 170.

8. Ibid., p. 175.

9. Ibid., p. 175.

Index